Late Style in Film

Cover image *A King in New York* © Roy Export S.A.S.

Late Style in Film

Collin Brinkmann

Foreword by Joseph McBride

Sticking Place Books
New York

Contents

Foreword by Joseph McBride

It might seem paradoxical that there has been an urgent need for a good book on late style in cinema. For decades now in the U.S. and to some extent internationally, theatrical films have been made mostly for the youth market. As a result, even the most celebrated directors for too long tended to be shunted aside when they aged out of "bankability." And still today, with the population rapidly aging, relatively few theatrical films are aimed at the older audience. But since the global pandemic that began in 2020 brought about a major upheaval in filmgoing habits throughout the world, the survival of the theatrical market has been in jeopardy or at least changing in ways no one can predict. Most filmgoers, younger as well as older, are content to stay home watching cable or streaming channels, and so audiences willing to pay for home entertainment have more opportunity to see films made with mature viewers in mind, more classical in style and concentrating more on characters than mindless explosions.

And fortunately now, for a variety of reasons, it is no longer unheard of for elderly directors to be given chances to prolong their careers, as seen in the remarkably durable cases of Clint Eastwood (whose latest film was made when he was 94), the late Portuguese director Manoel de Oliveira (who began working in 1927 and kept making films until shortly before dying at the age of 106 in 2015), Woody Allen (who continues to defy blacklisting by American film companies and made his most recent film when he was 87), and the late documentary master Frederick Wiseman (who made his last film at the age of 93 in 2023). When I came to Hollywood in 1973 and would ask producers and executives why certain old directors were no longer being given the opportunity to make films, the answer was that it was impossible to get insurance on them. That was mostly a cop-out, but eventually a way around that problem was found, with "backup directors" sitting on sets as possible replacements in case of a health issue with the original director. That meant, for example, that Karel Reisz was ready to take over from John Huston when he directed his magnificent final film, *The Dead,* based on the classic story by James Joyce, from a wheelchair while hooked up to an oxygen tank due to his emphysema. Huston died before that film was released in 1987, a classic example of late style in every way, a valedictory suffused with reflections on mortality, as well as a testament film with Huston's worldview turning its focus to a subject he had not explored before but knew in depth, a cross-section of Dublin society in 1904, during a moribund period with the nation on the cusp of revolution.

The late style of writers, composers, and artists has been the subject of much critical attention, especially in recent years, and in his Introduction to this lively study, Collin Brinkmann explores that terrain thoroughly and vigorously. In the field of film studies, some critics, biographers, and other film historians since the 1950s have been engaging with the issues surrounding late style in the work of major directors. As one of those writers who has been studying the late work of John Ford, Orson Welles, Howard Hawks, Billy Wilder, George Cukor, and other veteran directors since my youthful beginnings as a critic in the late 1960s, I vividly recall the mostly uninformed, ageist arguments about how elderly masters were going "senile" by making films out of step with contemporary trends. Those sneering dismissals of such splendidly mature, richly humane, impeccably crafted masterpieces as Ford's *7 Women,* Hawks's *El Dorado,* Wilder's *The Private Life of Sherlock Holmes,* and Welles's *Chimes at Midnight,* to name some late films I defiantly defended, unfortunately were predictable when the old studio system was collapsing and younger directors were given greater opportunities amidst the fertile chaos of the briefly flourishing New Hollywood.

During those years of transition when veteran filmmakers were making their final films, colleagues in the field of film history and criticism such as André Bazin, Lotte H. Eisner, François Truffaut, Andrew Sarris, Robin Wood, Peter

Bogdanovich, Donald Richie, Molly Haskell, and David Bordwell eloquently defended and analyzed the late works of such directors as Ford, Hawks, Alfred Hitchcock, Fritz Lang, Yasujirô Ozu, Max Ophüls, Jean Renoir, Douglas Sirk, and Carl Dreyer in the face of hooting by short-sighted reviewers and career-damaging neglect by youthful audiences. We valued those films with tender affection and deep respect because of what Cukor interjected when I said, "Older directors seem to have a kind of…"—"Wisdom?," he completed the thought by making it a hopeful question. (When I wrote a 1981 article in *Daily Variety* pointing out that Cukor, at age 81 when he made *Rich and Famous,* was the oldest director yet to work in Hollywood, he told me that distinction "thrilled" him, a healthy attitude not always shared by his peers in the business.)

The rare virtue of wisdom, which often takes a lifetime to acquire, was exemplified in those transitional years by such films as Cukor's *Love Among the Ruins,* his tenderly comical look at an old couple in Edwardian London who reconstitute their long-ago romance; Wilder's Lubitschean romantic comedy *Avanti!,* about a modern couple in the age of "free love" re-enacting their parents' clandestine love affair; Hawks's raucously funny yet elegiac and autumnal Western, *El Dorado;* Don Siegel's somber, largely unsentimental, but deeply moving eulogy for John Wayne's archetypal gunfighter in *The Shootist;* and Ford's *7 Women,* his apocalyptic final feature about the defiant survival of humanistic values in a time of barbarism and social collapse. All those films, insufficiently embraced by their contemporary audiences, explore mortality and the question of how to live well in a society that is on its way out.

Sometimes filmmakers in their youth, such as Welles, already revered and empathized with old people (bearing out Lillian Gish's remark, "I was never young, and if you were never young, how can you ever feel old?"), and when I was a young critic I tended to identify more with aging directors than members of my supposed peer group. The veterans tended to uphold classical artistic virtues while dealing with more thoughtful, serious, and enduring matters than, say, the aimless motorcycle riders who start off *Easy Rider* by making a coke deal to fund their nihilistic, pseudo-revolutionary road journey across America, supposedly in search of something they don't believe in and don't expect to find before they are gratuitously gunned down by rednecks.

Today the youthful prodigies of that period when the New Hollywood came to prominence with better, groundbreaking films—such as Francis Ford Coppola, Steven Spielberg, Martin Scorsese, and George Lucas—have reached old age themselves. They have been making their own testament films reflecting on their lives, bodies of work, and views of the world, or, in Lucas's case, regrettably squandering his former creative ambitions by building an "empire" while continually revising his artistically shallow *Star Wars* cycle before unloading his company to add more billions to his coffers. Spielberg and Scorsese, on the other hand, have kept taking on new artistic challenges as they age while refining and questioning their themes, as David Lynch did with continual daring before he died, and Coppola has been fulfilling his promise of making offbeat, avant-garde films with his own money (Lucas failed in his own promise to meet that challenge).

Although late style in cinema tends to manifest itself in minimalism or its close equivalent, an effortlessly disciplined sense of economy, some of these great filmmakers have shown that *Rules Don't Apply* (to quote the title of a trenchant, darkly comical, and neglected late work about Howard Hughes and Hollywood starring, directed, and co-written with Bo Goldman by 79-year-old Warren Beatty in 2016, a box office flop that is his last film to date). Welles's *The Other Side of the Wind*, his testament film about filmmaking and the self-destruction of an old filmmaker trying to survive in the New Hollywood, took more than five years to shoot and decades to finish (1970-2018). Filmed in two styles, neither of which is recognizably Welles's own—a highly fragmented framing story and a film-within-the-film with languidly beautiful Antonioniesque compositions—it is as adventurous and kaleidoscopic and avant-garde as any young filmmaker's experimental film. And Coppola's 2024 futuristic vision, *Megalopolis*, is another daring cinematic experiment, heedlessly opulent and fantastical, all the more so coming from an 85-year-old master gambling $120 million he had earned not from the film business but by owning wineries.

The task of coming to terms with filmmakers' late work, as with that of other now-deceased international masters who kept making great, if sometimes misunderstood or undervalued films alongside the younger generation before passing from the scene, such as Ingmar Bergman, Akira Kurosawa, Luis Buñuel, Jean-Luc Godard, Agnès Varda, and Stanley Kubrick, has demanded more serious attention to the vexing questions of just what constitutes "late style" in cinema and why it is to be valued rather than dismissed in knee-jerk contemptuous fashion. Truffaut, Godard's contemporary in the *Nouvelle Vague* that revolutionized modern cinema, was deprived of a late period by his untimely death, but his colleagues Godard and Varda kept experimenting with the film and video media until their deaths after long and adventurous lives and careers.

The need for a comprehensive study of the nature and ramifications of late style has become increasingly urgent in the twenty-first century as the cinematic medium itself has been aging, well past its centenary now and often even viewed as in the process of dying, while shooting on film has mostly given way to digital cinema, a process fraught with its own fragility. Brinkmann cites James Morrison's point that digital cinema is one of the three major turning points in the historical development of motion pictures. And as previously happened with the coming of sound and the breakup of the old studio system (combined with the coming of television), when much of the earlier work was discarded or lost, this latest period of technological change runs the danger of the loss of many modern "films," since the hardware of digital cinema keeps rapidly changing in ways that tend to make preservation of "films" forbiddingly expensive and difficult or unstable (that's why Spielberg insisted on the restoration of his megahit *Jaws* being protected by transferring it to the ironically more stable medium of celluloid). But cinema is an inherently transient medium, and as Alfred Hitchcock once said, "In a hundred years, it'll all be cornflakes in a can." Meanwhile, the new forms of cinema keep morphing into something unfamiliar, proving William Goldman's famous declaration that in the movie business "NOBODY KNOWS ANYTHING," while the medium undergoes a series of developments that most generously can be regarded as a process of rebirth.

So the medium of cinema from its beginnings in the 1890s up to this point in 2026—when films survive—can be seen broadly as an example of late style. But unlike in the criticism of other art forms, general studies of late style in cinema have been slow and relatively few in coming. Although such scholars as Karina Longworth, Joe McElhaney, and Laura Mulvey have stepped into the fray to help define the nature of late style and the evolution of cinema history and technology, those of us who cherish the works of older directors nevertheless have mostly had to be content with examinations of individual filmmakers in biographies and critical studies—at least in the ones that take sufficient space to deal with their subjects' late periods—rather than book-length critical overviews of the general and specific issues involved in late work. So I am delighted that the bright young American film critic and historian Collin Brinkmann has tackled the subject of cinematic late style in this wide-ranging, thoughtful, and important book.

Brinkmann makes a passionate, well-researched case for discarding the prejudice too many film scholars, reviewers, and fans display toward the late works of major (and minor) directors. The book makes many cogent and insightful points about late style while it argues for a broader, more generous, more open-minded and attentive appreciation of how film artists develop in their often eccentric but challenging and wise late films. For his lengthy Introduction, Brinkmann did extensive research in the literature about late style in other art forms, drawing cogently on those studies to help illuminate issues about cinema.

While showing a becoming modesty and sense in pointing out "the futility of making generalized statements about late-life creativity," Brinkmann does not shy from the task of observing distinctive qualities that tend to show up in late style in cinema. Along with a devil-may-care sense of freedom and bold willingness to reveal one's self more openly than ever before, a filmmaker making a late work tends to defy expectations by operating in what appears to be a "different temporal context," as Brinkmann puts it. That unfashionable tendency manifests itself in unorthodox stylistic approaches that can seem odd, awkward, or flawed to unsympathetic observers. With the "desire for simplicity" Eric Rohmer discerned in late work, directors are often in a self-reflexive mood dealing bluntly with the themes and obsessions that have preoccupied them throughout life and as they examine or attack the conventions of their medium. Often a director's late film challenges and shatters cinematic norms, showing its defiant individuality in a philosophical, meditative manner that is most striking because it is expressed in such transgressive ways and with a sense of urgency in conveying its essence, even if the work can seem difficult and disdainful of general understanding and acceptance. We can recognize many of these qualities—though not the same ones each time—in most of the late works by directors mentioned here and discussed in Brinkmann's study.

After his in-depth, impressively scholarly and elegant Introduction, Brinkmann applies his theories and those of other scholars in digging with gusto into the careers of three important filmmakers (Hawks, Chaplin, and Hitchcock). He offers acute, fresh, and insightful analyses and spirited defenses of their late work, boldly biting the critical bullet to demonstrate how his observations help us understand and appreciate such often unfairly scorned and misunderstood films as Hawks's *Hatari!*, *Red Line 7000*, and *El Dorado;* Chaplin's *Monsieur Verdoux, Limelight, A King in New York*, and *A Countess from Hong Kong;* and Hitchcock's *Torn Curtain, Topaz*, and *Family Plot,* while putting these films into the full context of their directors' lengthy and influential careers. Brinkmann's critical analyses of these three masters whose careers lasted defiantly and admirably into their old age while they were being written off as irrelevant to the youth era are provocative and often eloquent.

Stravinsky once observed that in old age, an artist finds the freedom to be truly himself and no longer cares what other people think of him. Brinkmann quotes Roberto Rossellini's moving tribute to *A King in New York* (1957), Chaplin's defiant thumb in the face of the United States from his political exile in Europe, as "the film of a free man." And a comment that has always meant a lot to me as a film critic is my friend Richard Thompson's observation in his eloquent 1967 review of Ford's artistic finale, "*7 Women* is Ford's most pessimistic film to date, culminating a progressive reappraisal of the myths he once celebrated and created. The dark vein of *Two Rode Together, The Man Who Shot Liberty Valance* and *Cheyenne Autumn* is now fully realized. Ford, of course, is The Old Order. Like Duke Ellington, Ford goes his own way, following his vision regardless of stylistic change around him." Liberated from most of the worries about ephemeral success that beset artists in their so-called prime years, elderly artists tend to disregard contemporary fashion and pursue their own obsessions, often in ways that seem too eccentric or abstract or minimalist to people who don't show them the grace of letting them be themselves. As Ford said when I asked if he was surprised that the American audience didn't like *7 Women,* "I didn't give a God damn whether they liked it or not…. It was over their heads." For that freedom, directors are often thoughtlessly rebuked.

As Brinkmann observes, it was the auteurist critics, of whom I was one before expanding my focus to the concept of collective authorship, who primarily fostered respect for the late works of the aging masters as they gave way to the *Nouvelle Vague,* the New Hollywood, and the other modern schools that were transforming the medium. The influential French film theorist André Bazin, in his 1957 *Cahiers du Cinéma* article "De la politique des auteurs"/"On the policy of authors," offered his seminal comment on the subject of late work in the cinema: "What kind of absurd discrimination has decided that filmmakers alone are victims of a senility that other artists are protected from? There do remain the exceptional cases of dotage, but they are much rarer than is sometimes supposed.... A great talent matures but does not grow old.... The drama does not reside in the growing old of men but in that of the cinema: Those who do not know how to grow old *with* it will be overtaken by its evolution."

Brinkmann's admirable work in this book shows us how to appreciate the evolution of cinema by embracing rather than dismissing the masters who broke the ground and rode their own paths through the rubble of an aging medium. While we go about discovering whatever uncharted paths the present uncertain evolution will pursue, for better and for worse, we would be wise to understand that "who we are *is* who we were," as former President John Quincy Adams (Anthony Hopkins) declares in *Amistad,* one of Spielberg's most misunderstood and underappreciated works. Without that understanding, which Adams says it took him a lifetime to reach and accept, our appreciation of the evolving medium of cinema would be impoverished and would squander the treasures that the masters of the medium, those from the past and those still working, have bequeathed to us.

Late Style in Film:
An Introduction

1

The 2024 Cannes premiere and subsequent fall release of 85-year-old Francis Ford Coppola's *Megalopolis* may well go down as one of the most illustrative moments in the history of 21st-century film reception. The decades-in-the-making self-funded passion project combined high-profile (and highly polarizing) names in front of and behind the camera with an experimental, anything-goes filmmaking ethos on a blockbuster-sized canvas to create what everyone—whether they ultimately found it fascinating or repellent or boring or inspiring or whatever else—could agree was simply one of the *strangest* movies ever released into mainstream theaters. In the attempt to define what the movie even was, let alone what one personally made of it all, much of the resultant discourse seemed to quickly and unavoidably dredge up deeper questions about the nature of movies themselves, the unspoken rules governing our reactions to them, and even the criteria for measuring artistic achievement in general. It made sense: it would be dishonest to grapple with a film as boldly unorthodox as *Megalopolis* without also interrogating the usefulness of the conventions that make it so. Coppola had long established himself as one of Hollywood's most (in)famous risk-takers, first making his name in the 1970s on the back of multiple films that, though seemingly doomed to fail in more ways than one, are now some of the most highly-regarded films of all time; but what truly set Coppola apart as an adventurous film artist was his refusal to rest on his well-earned laurels thereafter, even to the tune of critical drubbings, commercial failure, and personal bankruptcy. But to quote the English novelist Thomas Hardy, "When a man not contented with the grounds of his success goes on and on, and tries to achieve the impossible, then he gets profoundly interesting to me." The later Coppola is profoundly interesting to me. And as Hardy could announce in 1906 that he preferred the music of late Wagner and the paintings of late Turner to their earlier work, "the idiosyncrasies of each master being more strongly shown in these strains," so I can say in 2026 that I hold the Coppola of the 1980s, 1990s, 2000s, 2010s, and 2020s to be just as interesting, meaningful, and profound—if not even more so—than the famed Coppola of the 1970s. *Megalopolis* is the very late epitome of this supremely idiosyncratic body of post-"success" work, and as such is an extrapolation (albeit on a much bigger, wine empire- and luxury resort-financed playing field) of the series of films Coppola made upon returning to filmmaking after a decade's absence in the late 2000s, projects he explicitly approached as "student films" in which he sought to discover his own style in the trenches of an independent, post-Hollywood context. Mike Figgis's behind-the-scenes documentary *Megadoc* (2025) shows not a Coppola fretting over the realization of some grand set-in-stone vision, but rather a director content to approach his dream project with the playfulness of a child and to let loose his cast in a series of theater games; the octogenarian Coppola appears as an artist who embodies "Youth Without Youth," to borrow the title of his 2007 comeback film. The resultant film wears its playful audacity on its sleeve, in ways alternately silly and profound, awkward and dazzling, bizarre and moving—often at one and the same time. At every turn, *Megalopolis* was a surprising film (to its admirers and detractors alike), and the intensity of its specific, never-before-witnessed offerings seemed to magnify the subjectivity of each individual viewer's response to it.

But *Megalopolis,* as well as the wild range of reactions it garnered, above all seemed to exemplify a certain category of films that have come to be known as *late films.* Attached to every other remark about it, positive or negative, was the fact that Francis Ford Coppola made the film in his eighties, and along with it the suggestion that this fact in some significant way contributed to why the film was the way it was, why the film meant what it did, or why the film was "good" or "bad" in the specific way it was deemed to be those things. The discourse surrounding the film was implicitly—often explicitly—also a discourse about the wider subject of late films in general. Does the mere fact of "getting old" have any generalizable effect on the work of filmmakers the world over, and if so is it a positive or negative one? Should our knowledge of a filmmaker's past triumphs influence our reception of their latest works? Is the inherent lateness embodied in the works fascinating in a largely productive or unproductive way? Do we have a responsibility to approach late works with a different set of critical parameters? That these and other questions like them weren't inspired by *Megalopolis* specifically, but simply further crystallized by it, was obvious to anyone who'd spent significant time engaged in the discussions common to contemporary film culture. Coppola was just one of many long-revered film directors who had in recent times released substantial new work in their seventies, eighties, or even nineties that warranted the adjective *late*: Martin Scorsese, Steven Spielberg, Michael Mann, Terrence Malick, Clint Eastwood, David Cronenberg, Claire Denis, Mike Leigh, Paul Schrader, Brian De Palma, Ridley Scott, and Woody Allen are just a dozen of the names that fit the bill, to say nothing of recently deceased masters like David Lynch, Jean-Luc Godard, Terence Davies, William Friedkin, Monte Hellman, or Peter Bogdanovich. Indeed, the amount of filmmakers continuing to work into what is commonly denoted as one's "old age" is enough to fill a long and ever-expanding list, and the work they keep churning out gives us the privilege of seeing a couple dozen new late films every calendar year. If it's true that George Cukor became the oldest person to ever direct a Hollywood film when he completed his last movie *Rich and Famous* (1981) at the age of 81, it's a record that seems positively quaint today, having been broken repeatedly and impressively by numerous contemporary filmmakers, including the potential new record-holder in Clint Eastwood, who recently released his latest film *Juror #2* (2024) at the age of 94. (And that's just Hollywood; the ultimate recent example is of course Portuguese filmmaker Manoel de Oliveira, who was making films right up to his death in 2015 at the age of 106.) It's enough to make one declare that we're in a golden age for late films—and that's exactly what I'm going to do. But there's a highly relevant precedent here demonstrating the beautiful circularity of film history, for the very same filmmakers who today constitute a golden age for the late film entered the film industry in the 1950s, 1960s, and 1970s and were therefore around for a previous golden age, when an earlier generation of filmmakers who inaugurated their careers in the silent film era—think John Ford, Fritz Lang, Alfred Hitchcock, Howard Hawks, Raoul Walsh, Jean Renoir, Yasujirô Ozu, Carl Theodor Dreyer, or Charlie Chaplin—were making their last films and living out their final years amidst the tides of a radically shifting industry. The young mavericks of what has come to be termed the New Hollywood or the various international New Waves of the 1960s are now (or, for a time, were), in the 21st century, in the same position as their filmmaking forefathers were then, making undeniably *late* films amidst an industry that is once again, if for different reasons, in acknowledged turmoil.

Late films of both generations, and of others besides, share a curious place in the annals of film history, and the simplest way of beginning to explain why is to note the *lateness* that all these films partake in to a greater or lesser degree: the sense of a film being simultaneously discordant with, yet still necessarily a product of, the time in which it was made, wherein a palpable dissonance is felt that can be traced back to the simple yet all-pervading fact that the artist behind the work comes from a different temporal context—socially, culturally, artistically, etc.—than the one in which the film was produced. Thus the razor's edge on which late films are often perceived to live or die is their ability to come across as "out of time" (i.e., timeless) rather than merely "out of touch." Unfortunately, the overwhelming consensus of contemporaneous reviews, retrospective appraisals, biographical estimations, and encyclopedic judgments claim that the latter is more often the case than the former. The generally poor status accorded to the late work of a director relative to their early or "mature" work is so prevalent that, among the great land of myths that is film culture, there is perhaps none greater than the unquestioned insistence that filmmakers "peak" in their middle age and then more or less peter out afterwards in terms of the quality of their work. "It is impossible to think of an important director in world cinema whose late work is his or her best," wrote prolific cinema documentarian Mark Cousins in 2001. Paralleling our societal obsession with youth and its achievements, cinema—given its apparently taxing physical and logistical nature—has often been viewed as more of a young man's game. Historically, the director who continues working into old age is greeted with, if not outright critical disparagement, then the slightly condescending considerations that come from being viewed as past one's prime; warm thanks for your glorious contributions to the medium past, but we'd sooner remember you by those than whatever it is you're making, or trying to make, now. Thus we encounter situations like that of Orson Welles, who received honorary Oscars and Lifetime Achievement awards while struggling to finance *The Other Side of the Wind* (shot 1970-1976; posthumously finished for release in 2018), left uncompleted along with a host of other projects at his death in 1985;[1] or the case of John Ford, who after the poor response to *7 Women* (1966) never saw another fiction feature to completion despite John Wayne's insistence that, "Up until the very last years of his life... [Ford] could have directed another picture, and a damned good one. But they said Pappy was too old. Hell, he was never too old. In Hollywood these days, they don't stand behind a fella. They'd rather make a goddamned legend out of him and be done with him."[2] The narrative of

---

[1] Joseph McBride's *What Ever Happened to Orson Welles?: A Portrait of an Independent Career* (2006) is the rare exemplary book to sympathetically explore the later work and career of a filmmaker considered to have "fallen off" after his most famous achievements.

[2] That *7 Women* remained out of circulation besides a difficult-to-see, decidedly low-quality version until the Warner Archive released a Blu-ray version, sourced from a 4K scan of the original camera negative, in 2025 is indicative also of the generally poor status of late work not just figuratively but literally: many late films remain essentially unavailable outside the deep corners of the internet, or otherwise in noticeably degraded quality, sporting the wrong aspect ratio, or weathering other such defects that come from cultural neglect. (In the case of *7 Women*, the battle still isn't entirely won; while the high-definition home video offering of the film's theatrical release version is a great first step, Ford scholars Joseph McBride and Julie Kirgo remain campaigning to have the film fully restored to its intended 93-minute length.)

end-of-career decline circulates also, and perhaps most damagingly, in the faux-authoritative tone of most biographies and critical studies of filmmakers where the sections covering the final films are comparatively dwarfed by those covering films from the early or middle years. The short shrift given to the late life and the late works discourages study and appreciation of them, leaving them stranded as the disappointments they are perceived to be, which discourages study, which leaves them stranded, ad infinitum—a circular feedback loop that perpetuates the myth of diminishing late-career returns which permeates film cultural groupthink.[3]

Yet to a certain subset of filmgoers, late films can exert a kind of mystic pull over the cinephilic imagination that broader consensus narratives fail to capture. These bizarre,

---

[3] My generous take on the disregard for late work in biographies is that some writers, nearing the end of their projects and experiencing burnout, display a (humanly understandable) slackening quality of effort and thought in their reaching for the finish line that leads to merely perfunctory engagement with their subject's later work. But that still doesn't excuse it. Michael Millgate, writing of the literary careers of Browning, Tennyson, James, and Hardy, suggests that "in modern biography it is the post-romantic and especially post-Freudian fascination with origins and early development which has most encouraged the tendency to move rapidly over the later and apparently uncreative stages of a literary career," and Thomas Dormandy burrows into a similarly insightful point in his book about the old age of great painters: "Monographs which lovingly explore parents, grandparents, aunts, uncles and second cousins often wrap up their hero's sunset years in a paragraph or two. This is odd—or perhaps not. 'We arrive as novices at every age of our life', Sébastian Chamfort observed. It is a profound truth. Novitiate implies ignorance. No twenty-year-old has ever fully understood a forty-year-old and no forty-year-old has ever properly understood a seventy-year-old. Every self-respecting writer likes to write about things he understands—or thinks he understands. Art historians are no exception. Hence there are hundreds of books—some excellent—about the childhood and youth of famous artists and virtually none about their old age. There is also often a disturbing air about the last creations, an element of mystery about their appeal and even more about their faults. Neither the appeal or the faults are easy to categorise or explain. Perhaps they are best left alone."

dissonant, anachronistic, strange, unorthodox films often bring us to them and keep us coming back to them in ways that more traditionally satisfying films don't; and in their disregard for conventional cinematic methods, they can suggest new definitions of what a film can even be. Thus late films have often been the site of discursive battles over the very things one values in the art of cinema. Writing on the occasion of a 1988 series called "Testaments: Final Films of Great Directors" programmed by Richard Peña for Chicago's Film Center, Jonathan Rosenbaum noted that "almost invariably," the movies included in the series "were dying at the box office and at the hands of most mainstream reviewers, while a team of passionate and informed enthusiasts were singing their praises. Bloody religious wars were waged over these movies; in most cases, they're still being waged." It's difficult to put a finger on the exact *je ne sais quoi* that makes late films a thrilling prospect for the cinephile attuned to them. J. Kim Murphy locates a "vital, existential intrigue to directors who may seem over the hill, or encased in amber, and who can be easily dismissed as unfashionable," and Karina Longworth speaks forthrightly of the "subset of cinephiles that treasure these oddities, if nothing else for the don't-give-a-fuck sense of freedom bleeding from the frame." Part of the interest, too, is undeniably polemical: faced with a film industry and movie culture that views older artists as expendable and their late work as dismissible, what more radical, table-turning gesture is there than to proclaim these artists and their work some of the most vital of all? Cinephiles passionate about re-writing film history find in late films a field day of reclamatory work. Skeptical about the ability of box-office statistics, anecdotal evidence, and whatever the judgment of the film critic-in-residence for the *New York Times* was at the time to form the whole truth of a reception narrative, they look for outlier voices and burrow into the substance of the work itself for a better view of what the film—often buried under years of repetitive, knee-jerk misinterpretation—actually *is*.[4] The ways in which reception narratives are publicly formed and crystallized often rest on complex anecdotal evidence that's used as simplistic ammunition against the film: comments from collaborators and crew (especially those not 100 percent artistically aligned with the director) misconstrued or taken out of context, stories from people close to the director purporting to show the film-maker being lazy or uninterested, or even quotes from the director themselves speaking regretfully about or flat-out denouncing films they've made (statements that may arise more from tangled contextual situations beyond the film than the film itself). Perhaps the lesson here—to keep us in check with any generalizations going forward—is simply that the reception of any given film is almost always, to some degree, less overwhelmingly positive or negative than the common narrative supposes it to be.

My own initiation into cinephilia quickly coincided with a fascination, still never quelled, with the films that directors made late in their careers. As I fell under cinema's spell in the mid-2010s, two of the most formative filmmakers in my personal education were in their seventies and eighties respectively: Terrence Malick and Clint Eastwood. Eastwood, argu-ably already two decades into his "late period" by then (and already familiar to me as a cinematic figure, although less so as a director), was churning out ostensibly modest works of clas-sical Hollywood craftsmanship that nevertheless without fail snuck up on me to profound emotional effect. His informal trilogy of everyday heroism in *Sully* (2016), *The 15:17 to Paris* (2018), and *Richard Jewell* (2019) had the outward markings of the banal Inspired-by-a-True-Story realism that Hollywood lives on, yet their structural experimentation, risky casting coups, and melodramatic tenderness outed them to me as

---

[4] When fed up with the public narrative surrounding a film, I person-ally like to imagine the hypothetical viewers dotting the world whose voices are left out of the discussion: that one woman who was moved by the film but never told anyone, that one guy too timid to defend the film to his colleagues but who kept thinking about it for weeks afterwards, etc. etc.

among the most radical and interesting films then being made in a mainstream context. I didn't understand why so many critics didn't share that viewpoint. Having also been lucky enough to begin my cinephilic journey at the same time that Terrence Malick picked up his notoriously slow filmmaking pace, my experience of falling in love with his late work quickly became a demonstration of how out-of-step late films can be with prevailing critical attitudes. *Knight of Cups* (2015) and *Song to Song* (2017), derided by the majority of critics as self-parodic imitations of his earlier masterpieces, hypnotized and enthralled me on first watch, and then drew me back again and again for rewatch after rewatch where my admiration became more tangible and concrete and overwhelming; *A Hidden Life* (2019) sealed the deal if it ever needed sealing. The late films of Eastwood, Malick, and other directors convinced me, before I had ever theorized anything about late films or the "late style" that supposedly connected them, that filmmakers late in their career not only continued to make interesting work, but even made work that was arguably more interesting than anything they'd made before. Such works rubbed up against current movie culture and the critical standards that maintained it in ways that I found endlessly rich. The streak of youthful polemicism in me fed off this friction, first finding satisfaction in the process of praising a director's early work only to turn around and say the late work was even better, and then joy in the process of actually defending the thought. Early on, what I liked about my favorite critics was that they seemed completely agnostic as to where the best films of a given year came from: it didn't matter whether they came from young independents radically pushing the form, established artists in their middle age making career-best work, or old masters finding new languages to express their pet themes with more urgency than ever. Part of what I also loved about late films is, I suppose, true of all films, but it seemed especially significant to me that the reception of new late films was completely *democratized*—since all of the books, articles, etc. about a filmmaker instantly became out of date with the introduction of new work, absolutely everybody could play a part in writing this new history.[5]

I eventually learned that my interest in late work in cinema could be subsumed under a broader concept of inquiry known in English as *late style,* one that had been inspiring intermittent writing by scholars across the other artistic disciplines going back at least a century. Although one can point to art historical writings from the European Renaissance as the first attempts to locate a generalizable late style in the work of older artists, modern conceptualizations of late style have their roots in the early 19th-century Romantic period, were discussed in earnest beginning in early 20th-century Germany, and have seen an international boom in interest here at the beginning of the 21st century. Beethoven's musical achievements in the last decade of his life (he died in 1827) are perhaps the locus classicus for late style discussions—"Some may disagree about the precise dates of the inception of the late style, differ over the extent to which it emerged from immanent or external sources, and struggle to describe its characteristics in a coherent and meaningful way," writes Maynard Solomon, "but few have disagreed about the existence of the phase itself, let alone its seismic character or its chief examples..."—although arguments could be made for Titian or Michelangelo in art or Shakespeare or Goethe in literature as similarly prevalent case studies. But undoubtedly, even a quarter of the way through the 21st century, it is under the banners of art, music, and literature that the vast majority of late style theorization has occurred. As the latest of the acknowledged major art forms, it's perhaps understandable that cinema has been late to the late style conversation. Even if the German theorists of the 1920s, 1930s, and 1940s had felt like adopting cinema into their studies, there would have been few apparent examples to choose from given that the medium itself was not yet 50 years old. But well over a century on from cinema's conception, with books touching on late style

---

[5] The existence of the internet, social media, and film-specific sites like Letterboxd makes this even truer in current incarnations of film culture.

in painting, the plastic arts, poetry, fiction, classical music, and even architecture becoming commonplace, the absence of cinema in such works has become increasingly glaring. Only popular music remains as plainly on the outs when it comes to serious consideration for late style analyses, which is perhaps a clue that cinema is still, despite ostensible advances, fighting the battle of being taken seriously as an art form on par with its older brethren. Gordon McMullan brings up a salient point:

> The materials of late-style theory tend, by definition, to be those of high art. And while it is all very well, it might be said, for literary critics, art historians and musicologists to focus solely for their understanding of late-life creativity on the complexities and inaccessibilities of the work of a handful of unquestioned geniuses, what of popular culture, what of art forms that stand ostensibly closer to the majority experience of creativity, modes that in some way feel a little more within the grasp of someone who is not, has not been, a creative professional? How might we move away from high art to address the conjunction of old age and creativity in forms considered, broadly speaking, to be culturally ephemeral?

As *the* art form of modernity, the most popular, far-reaching art form of the last century, cinema should be able to claim a privileged position within contemporary discussions of art. Yet only bits and bobs of work specifically dedicated to the concept of late style in film are scattered throughout the history of the relevant literature; a sustained, in-depth meditation remains to be written. While time has turned the tables a bit in the other arts, making the last paintings, compositions, or writings of certain artists newly central to their artistry (think Beethoven again, or J. M. W. Turner), it's difficult to think of many film artists whose last works are commonly considered among their best or most important.

But just because it often takes the passing of time—sometimes a great deal of it—in order for late work scoffed at incredulously in its time to become appreciated and treasured, that doesn't mean relying on that fact isn't a lame excuse to not just get the work done *right now*. Leaving it to the next generation of critics and audiences is a dereliction of duty. "People love to love late work when our appreciation of the work itself is late," writes Isiah Medina, "but to love the late now is when it gets exciting." Living in an age in which so many legendary film artists are winding down their careers, there's a particular urgency, too, in finding the critical tools to properly grapple with their latest works as they give them to us—if they're even able to, that is. While a small handful of filmmakers might have big enough names to ensure financing for almost anything they'd like to do, many struggle to get backing for their projects in a changed commercial landscape that prioritizes high-budget works based on marketable properties in lieu of the return-on-investment risk presented by the kind of original mid-budget projects that many older filmmakers once thrived on. Poor responses from critics and audiences stemming from philosophies of viewing resistant to the oddities of late work, on the back end, certainly don't help inspire confidence from financiers and distributors. Sadly, any history of late style in film is also in some ways a history of what directors *haven't* been able to make. But given the increased awareness of how many artists, especially those from minority backgrounds, have fallen through the cracks of appreciation to the detriment of their ability to continue making films, people who care about cinema are more disposed than ever to wanting to recognize great filmmakers in their time, rather than after they've been forcefully retired or, worse, have died. Adding to the urgent relevance here is the fear in contemporary film culture that—unlike the first golden period of aging directors, who in retrospect most would acknowledge had a largely talented, historically-aware generation of youngsters in line to replace them—this current generation of late artists doesn't, at least from the present vantage point, seem to have a similarly visionary group of young people that will one day make up a third golden age of the late film; nor, perhaps more pressingly, does it seem a sure thing that there will even be a functioning film industry to support such a hypothetical bunch. "In this light," writes Cobi Chiodo Powell, "the preoccupation with late style feels different from the prior half-century of auteur worship: almost anticipatorily mournful, a proleptic elegy for a world soon to be without strong perspectives." But such pessimistic prognostications are familiar to anyone who's lived through any era of film history; cinema has always been "dying," and every generation of film artists and viewers has their own "deaths" (real or perceived) to react against. Part of what makes late style thinking constantly relevant is the way it deals with now vs. then dichotomies and continuities, acknowledging changes for what they are and the complex ways in which they add or subtract from what an artist is able to do in current artistic contexts. A nuanced understanding of how the medium has shifted over the years can, when looking at an ostensible harbinger of the death of cinema (say, the switch from analog film to the digital dominance of the 21st century), simultaneously recognize how that change has taken tools away from filmmakers *and* help appreciate how such an evolution has, in other ways, offered older filmmakers more freedom and opportunity than ever before. "It appears that film scholarship still has a long way to go in evaluating the contributions of filmmakers at the end of their creative life," says Amir Cohen-Shalev. "While old age is not a guarantee of quality art, the difference and ambiguity of *lateness* can make it unpopular. Both film scholarship and gerontological research should benefit from the attempt to decipher late style in cinema." That was written in 2009. With not just the population of film directors aging, but with a higher percentage of the whole world's population made up of older people than ever before, the relevance of this topic should be clear. Indeed, "lateness" in general is on the minds (or at least itching the subconsciouses) of many, given that we live in the latest time in a long era of self-aware lateness that's been around since the early 1800s—when humans began to take on a new relationship to the past, a burdensome sense of "coming after," a feeling of epochal lateness that views the present more as a palimpsest of the past. Contemporary concerns in political, cultural, economic, and ecological realms only magnify the sense of living near an—or *the*—"end." The perspective of late style can bring productive clarity to these anxieties.

But what even *is* "late style?" According to the Google Books Ngram Viewer (a program that charts the frequency of language usage in printed sources), the phrase has seen an exponential uptick in usage in the 21st century, and anecdotally I can confirm seeing the phrase bandied about with increasing frequency during my tenure as an internet user within online film communities. But its meaning varies, often wildly, depending on who's using it and in what context, such that it can often be difficult even to be sure that one is talking about the same thing. Indicative of this is the inconsistency in how the term is even written: I've seen both late style and late-style, as well as the common usage of capitalization or inverted commas to render it Late Style or "late style" (even Late Style™), often in what appears to be a self-conscious distancing from commitment to acknowledging it as a 100 percent *real thing*, i.e., something other than a critical construction. The ambiguity is valid, and just as I've seen the phrase used to discuss late films with an eye toward genuinely appreciating their oddness, so I've also seen people deploy it pejoratively as a kind of ironic pseudo-reclamation tactic to imply that, though one could theoretically make the critical maneuvers necessary to consider a certain late film "good," it would nevertheless be somehow dishonest to do so. Naturally, the confusion over late style's definition has prompted concern that its usage therefore becomes meaningless, a code word spoken as though its deployment alone constituted a coherent argument. Lawrence Garcia writes that, "In the cinema, as elsewhere, the notion of 'late style' has become a critical commonplace—shorthand for dealing with an artist's 'mature' work, particularly when said artists are dismissed or misunderstood after a period of acclaim. The problem with shorthand, of course, is that not everyone can read it, the result being that appeals to 'late style' can come across as abdications of critical responsibility, promissory notes that have yet to be fulfilled." Topics addressed by late style in film have also reached a wider circle of acknowledgment in recent years than ever before. The popular film history podcast *You Must Remember This*, produced by Karina Longworth, premiered a new season in 2025 called "The Old Man Is Still Alive," covering the later careers of 14 directors who lived through the golden age of classic Hollywood and its subsequent takeover by the "New" Hollywood.[6] Both print and online publications have dedicated pieces to roundups on recent late films, including Britain's *Sight and Sound* magazine, which named one 2024 year-end piece that touched on new films by Francis Ford Coppola, David Cronenberg, Paul Schrader, Víctor Erice, Mike Leigh, and Clint Eastwood "the year in late style." But it's been the public comments made by Quentin Tarantino that have stirred up the most conversation around late-career achievement in film of late, as Tarantino has been vocal about his desire to retire from filmmaking in order avoid late style altogether: "Who knows what I'll do? I just don't want to be an old-man filmmaker," he's said. "I want to stop at a certain point. Directors don't get better as they get older. Usually the worst films in their filmography are those last four at the end." Long having intended to give up making movies after completing his tenth film, Tarantino has become the star of an interesting will-he-or-won't-he drama in the news as he deliberates just what he wants his tenth and final film to be, or whether he'll even get around to making it—at 62-years-old, he's already as old as many of the classic Hollywood film-makers were when they made the late films that Tarantino has scoffed at. His dilemma brings up fundamental questions about the narrative of late-career decline so prevalent in film culture, while at the same time pointing up the pertinent fact that many filmmakers of his own generation—Wes Anderson, David Fincher, James Gray, Kelly Reichardt, and Tarantino himself to name just a few—seem to be encroaching upon their own late periods.

---

[6] In an interview with *Variety*, Longworth said she nearly titled the season "Late Style" before going with "The Old Man Is Still Alive," a phrase sourced from a quote by George Cukor.

One senses, floating in film cultural ether, a clear desire to engage with this idea of late style, but only so much can be done in cramped online spaces and with only a cursory understanding of the concept's history. The go-to critical maneuver in film writing when attempting to engage with the idea of late style historically is to cite a few lines from either Theodor Adorno or Edward Said and then call it a day. On the one hand, it's understandable—the history of late style thinking is complex, opaque, and scattered in ways not easily digestible without undertaking significant research—although on the other, the names of Adorno and Said have become little more than perfunctory citations that merely gesture at an effort to historize rather than offering substantive engagement with their thinking. Adorno's 1937 essay on Beethoven's late style and Said's posthumous 2006 book *On Late Style* have become the two lodestars for late style thinking in the 21st century. It's ironic, though, because neither of these works purports to offer a unified theory of late style, and both are in fact highly fragmentary: Adorno's merely a short, gnomic, four-page missive dedicated to Beethoven alone, Said's an unfinished work stitched together by an editor from several discontinuous writings. Their monopolization of late style discourse has been a concern for the others as well; Gordon McMullan and Sam Smiles have made the similar critique that "elucidating late style requires more than deploying a few sentences from Said, whose book, for all its flaws, seems to function all too often in current critical writing as the only required evidence of research into ideas of lateness." (McMullan's name, for one, deserves to be known as widely as either Adorno or Said's in the realm of late style discussion, even though he leans heavily skeptical of the idea in general; my frequent citation of him will surely prove why.) Adorno is often cited incorrectly as the inventor of late style, when in truth he merely popularized one (radically different) conceptualization of it, and Said's Adorno-influenced take on it is almost always invoked in a way that leaves out the implicit political thrust of his (and Adorno's) aesthetic arguments. Both writers assuredly have valuable insights that've made their words resonate as widely as they have, but the attention paid to them has been disproportionate to the extent of their contributions. Who's rethinking late style today? Said's 2006 book has in many ways revitalized the genre of late style research, which has resulted in a decent outpouring of books associated with the subject, although few present any strong unifying theorizations that might bring about the desired widespread clarity. In fact, it's an ironic truth that before any book offering a fully coherent conceptualization of late style made it into the world, there was published a book that fully and coherently attempted to debunk the very idea: Gordon McMullan's *Shakespeare and the Idea of Late Writing: Authorship in the Proximity of Death* (2007). McMullan's thoroughly researched and articulate book traces the history of late style thinking as it pertains to (oft convoluted) historical attempts to fashion a coherent version of late Shakespeare, and in the process deflates the universalizing methods that have tried to make late style a one-size-fits-all critical construction. Many of the works on late style published subsequently, such as the anthology volume McMullan co-edited with Sam Smiles called *Late Style and its Discontents* (2016), have followed McMullan's lead in problematizing late style as a critical category. I'm sympathetic to this trend—I too am convinced of the near-complete non-universality of late style, and of the need to poke holes in certain past theories—and yet my book aims to be a largely positive contribution to late style studies that goes beyond current and former conceptualizations: an attempt not to undo the work of others, but to move on from it in order to offer a constructive vision of late style for the future.

As one might expect, the journey late style has made from art, literary, and musical criticism in decades and centuries past to scholarly debate in academic contexts and to the wild world of the internet in the present has destabilized a concept that was already rather vague from the start. To try and take a panoramic view of the late style landscape is to encounter confusion and contradiction at every other turn. In a 2008 article reading late style in music together with disability, Joseph N. Straus compiled an inventory of the words and phrases most commonly used to describe late style and ended up with six main adjectival categories: "introspective," "austere," "difficult," "compressed," "fragmentary," and "retrospective." But it becomes obvious when combing through the compiled sub-descriptors assigned to each category that many seem to directly contradict each other; for example, the words "personal" and "impersonal" both appear. Many, if not all, of the words could also easily be used to describe work that one wouldn't consider "late" at all. How to reconcile, then, the clearly incredibly diverse amount of extant late work under comprehensive categories that aren't also so large as to render them basically pointless? Lydia Goehr has worried that "late style is… about to lose its meaning altogether, the more it is used to signify everything and anything… one does towards the end of one's life as a writer." Nevertheless, paradoxically, I've come to believe that that's exactly what needs to happen in order for late style to retain any coherent meaning at all. The very inclusion of "everything and anything" that falls within one particular, concise, inherent parameter—that of *lateness*—will liberate late style as a concept from any fallacious universalizing and push us toward case-by-case profundities. As it pertains to film, late style as an approach can hardly be said to be reinventing the wheel: in almost every way it is an extension of (the best of) that old approach called *auteurism,* and of your classic trace-a-filmmaker's-evolution criticism, but with a heightened attention to the evolutions visible at the tail end of a filmmaker's career (where neglect usually rules the day). Yet late style criticism welcomes any and all critical lenses that have something productive to offer in the task of grappling with late work; in this way, late style is less of a singular track on which to pursue insight and more of a general paradigm, a paradigm within which to focus oneself toward the goal of finding edification in late work, both *as* late work and also simply as work, as art, full stop. Rather than contributing to the reification of what Gordon McMullan calls "a *discourse of lateness*—that is, a construct, ideological, rhetorical and heuristic, a function not of life or art but of the practice of reading or appreciating certain texts within a set of predetermined parameters," this take on late style will show that it *is,* indeed, an inherent function of life and art, of living through time, and that it can be applied fruitfully to anything, including film, in ways that retain the individualized complexities of said life and said art.

In many ways, the definition of late style I'm proposing could be more intelligibly, if prosaically, reworded simply as *later* style. Late style isn't a category for which any given work of art either does or does not qualify, but rather an orienting descriptor that operates by degrees of relative lateness: for example, Luchino Visconti's *Senso* (1954)—made in Visconti's late forties and well within the first half of his career—is late relative to *La terra trema* (1948), and *The Leopard* (1963) is late relative to it and *Senso,* and *Ludwig* (1973) is late relative to them all. One can trace this lateness both within a director's individual career as well as within the wider contexts of, say, a national industry or film history overall. Although "late style" as construed historically by certain theorists may not exist (the reality of art-making is just too complicated to withstand their sweeping claims), late style construed as *later style* undeniably does, merely based on the principle of inherent change, which is constantly acting on individuals, culture, society, etc. Thus each and every film participates in lateness to a greater or lesser degree; if we can still speak of a filmmaker's late style, or of a distinct "late period" in their work, it's in an attempt to recognize a productive point at which to mark the invasion of that "greater," or greatest, degree of lateness in their work. (The three example chapters to come will demonstrate this in action.) Working from this sliding scale allows us to be as scientific as we can in doing something that's admittedly thoroughly unscientific. If one wanted to determine the *latest* of the late work, for example, or figure out a film's lateness "quotient" (I'm speaking playfully here now), it would simply be a matter of calculating—creatively, critically—how stylistically and/or thematically estranged the film is from the contemporaneous cinematic landscape, how clearly it's the product of a filmmaker who cut their teeth in a previous era, and so on and so forth (beyond simply how old a filmmaker literally is).[7] But this redefinition of late style as, essentially, later style—the later style of one's later works—clears up some of the awkwardness of picking and choosing what to admit into the category, while it also democratizes the concept to be more inclusive: the field of late style opened wide to include everyone, not just the elite, canonized "geniuses" of the arts. (This move may remove some of the romanticism of late style as historically utilized and make it into a more banal, quotidian sort of concept, but the benefits far outweigh the losses because of the way they reshape our engagement.) As nice as it would be to come up with a new term that encompasses all of this, "late style" is here to stay, and it would be arrogant to assume that I could change it; it should be obvious to anyone that "later style" just doesn't have the same pop, and more antiquated terms like "the late manner" just don't have the same level of current cultural cachet. But thankfully neither the connotation nor the denotation of "late style" has ever been static. The term's entrance into English largely fused what in the original German were two distinct concepts: *Spätstil* (late style) and *Altersstil* (old-age style). While *Altersstil* referred to the style of aged artists, *Spätstil* could be used to refer to either the style of artists near the end of their life (whether young or old) or, in a larger historical sense, the style of an epoch nearing its end. Just as it would be difficult to undo the conflation of the two terms, so too is it easier to just roll with "late style" as is and sprinkle in as much definitional nuance as possible as we go. Yet to round out this definitional work, the words of Bailey Trela—that "to fruitfully define late style, we'd have to possess a solid working definition of style itself"—should be briefly heeded. Although the word "style" seems to imply concerns of form above all, it will become obvious that in the term "late style" it incorporates more than just that. Reluctant as I am, anyway, to fully separate or indeed separate at all the ideas of form and content, or style

---

[7] Colloquially, you'll often see people online attempt to get at the lateness of particularly late late films by playfully coining terms like "latest style," "last style," "style so late it's posthumous," etc.

and substance, my definition of style includes them both: both the how and the what of a work—in short, the work's *is-ness*.

The suitability of this particular definition should become clear when it's realized that the goal of late style criticism isn't, above all, to pronounce judgment on a late work's quality, but to get down to the task of appreciating, in all of its uniqueness, what the work actually *is*. This brings me to an important and fundamental point that must necessarily underpin our investigation of late style in film: we will never, ever get to the bottom of what's truly interesting about late works, or fully appreciate them, if we abide by the common conventions of judging motion pictures. These conventions are so ingrained in our methods of cultural engagement that we rarely think twice about them, and they are so widely prevalent that, even though casual filmgoers and hardcore cinephiles might have vastly different sets of criteria from which they judge films, almost all of them uphold the same entrenched methods: of declaring given films to be varying degrees of "good" or "bad" and judging them based on their ability to fulfil communal or individual expectations of what "good" films *should* do; that is, to base our judgment on a film's ability to be or do what we want it to rather than, simply, what it *is* or *does*. These words ("good," "bad," "better," etc.) have their place—in everyday conversation they're often unavoidably useful signals that gesture at harder-to-articulate analyses—yet as concepts within the realm of art, their usage more often than not ossifies the conventional set of implied meanings behind these words, rather than challenging and/or expanding them. That's why I prefer to use sliding scales like "more or less interesting" or "more or less edifying" as ways of conferring value on given works of art; even though one could argue the words fulfil the same function as "good" or "bad," I think there's a strong connotational difference that allows one to avoid rigid adherence to predetermined rules and conventions of art-making and art appreciation.[8] As it pertains to appreciating late films

---

[8] Of course, merely to bring up questions of what words like "good" and "bad" even mean is to go to the core of critical thought and reach

especially, if we jump into this endeavour thinking we can use the conventional measures of quality, then we're just going to be repeating the same mistakes that led to the lack of appreciation for late films in the first place. And if questions over the value of the late style label have tended to circle around varying opinions on the "greatness" or lack thereof of a filmmaker's late works, then with a little humility we can approach the subject differently—and achieve richer results—from a stance less concerned with artistic merit per se than with impassioned attunement to each individual film's unique "is-ness." "An important precondition for exploring the land of old age," writes Amir Cohen-Shalev, "is that we suspend the issue of artistic *merit*. The late works are not necessarily better than, nor are they a-priori inferior, aesthetically, to works produced in earlier phases of artistic careers. Old age is a collative notion…. It implies the potentiality of change and regards this change as creative." In an age when so much pressure is placed on the artistic "masterpiece," and the unhelpful dichotomy of "major" and "minor" works dogs the reception of each new addition to a filmography, and the vogue for snap-judgment social media pronouncements in the form of 280-character hot takes is as high as ever, the need for critical thinking and writing that burrows into what's *different*[9]—rather than "better" or "worse"—about filmmakers' new films is increasingly crucial.

Art is not a competition to make masterpieces, so neither should our appreciation of it be one. Where late style thinking thrives is in experiencing the careers of filmmakers not as a series of artistic peaks and valleys to be charted on a graph, but as a reflection of the give-and-take complexities of a film-maker expressing themselves in a constantly changing world with a constantly changing set of tools: films not as "major"

---

fundamental questions about artistic value and our criteria for evaluating it—a subject too impossibly vast and far-reaching to get into here. But the subject is undoubtedly important; it might be less so if our lifespans were infinite, but, lacking that, prioritization becomes necessary and artistic judgment doubly meaningful.

[9] …and also somehow always the same…

or "minor" individual works, but the specific result of specific human and artistic struggles, the sketches and scribbles of an artist working against their contextual limitations, the moans and groans of a person expressing themself via their chosen medium—a meandering journey that the viewer intimately follows and participates in instead of sitting back and savoring only the most unimpeachably well-wrought productions. This perspective renders irrelevant, or at least decidedly less important, the conventional expectations of a "good" movie; it's much closer to the redefinition suggested by Orson Welles, as quoted in the epigraph to François Truffaut's *The Films in My Life,* that "a work is good to the degree that it expresses the man who made it." Late style thinking confronts "faults," "flaws," "failures" or what-have-you—ostensible pockmarks on the work as largely determined by convention—with a fundamentally different attitude, one open to embracing them as features rather than bugs. Especially when it's dealing with the late work of filmmakers who've repeatedly proven themselves to be masters of the medium. In an essay on Chaplin's *Limelight* (1952), André Bazin writes that

> Undoubtedly everyone has the right to have reservations about masterpieces—to criticize Racine for Théramène's speech, Molière for his dénouements, Corneille for his awkward handling of the rules. Nor do I suggest there is anything false or barren about such criticism. But given a level of artistic creativity, and certainly when faced with evidence of genius, a contrary attitude is necessarily more rewarding. Instead of thinking of removing so-called faults from a work it is wiser, rather, to be favorably predisposed to them, and to treat them as qualities, whose secret we have not so far been able to fathom.

Bazin's compatriot at *Cahiers du cinéma,* Éric Rohmer, went even further in a 1952 piece defending Jean Renoir's American films, which is worth quoting at length:

In any case, as a token of my admiration for Renoir's last films, I would like to show the extent of their greatness by reminding us of the most esteemed masterpieces of certain great musicians, writers, or painters. To admit a possible decadence on the part of their creators—all extenuating circumstances aside—would be to recognize that their evolution follows the laws of those with ordinary talents; for as far as I know, the history of art offers us no example of an authentic genius who, at the end of his career, had a period of real decline. Rather, beneath the seemingly unrefined or meager appearance of the aforementioned films, we are prompted to seek evidence of the desire for simplicity that characterized the final works of a Titian, a Rembrandt, a Beethoven or, closer to us, a Bonnard, a Matisse, or a Stravinsky. Having mentioned these great names, I would now like to propose a critical approach that will focus neither on "beauties" nor on "faults" but that has its roots in the internal reasoning of an evolution whose path evaded us. This critical approach will help us discover the virtues beneath these pseudofaults, which the poorly trained eye has been unable to appreciate. Such an idea reverses certain commonly admitted values, but I believe our times are better prepared to recognize that the nature of a masterpiece is to suggest a new definition of beauty. Given the reputation that today's intellectuals have for being nonconformists, I am always surprised when they are quick to copy the canons of their own aesthetic from that of a work declared sacrosanct by the very fact that it was, in its time, revolutionary. To invite them one day to adore what they burned is enough to make those most practiced in the subtleties of dialectical reasoning jump with indignation. I am tempted by this prospect. However, the works I am speaking of deserve better than the ever-so-tempting response that their good parts are those that are considered *bad*…. It is important to note that the director whose career is already one of the longest, has, by a secret instinct, or simply because of destiny, found his "personal philosophy" constantly adapted to the trends of his art....

Rohmer sees in the ostensible blemishes on the latest, less-beloved works of Renoir hidden virtues that require a different perspective to see aright. "The type of criticism Rohmer is proposing," notes William Routt, "rejects *a priori* standards and attempts instead to find the source of a film's art in the experience one has watching it. This suggests subordination of one's self—or at least of certain of the presuppositions one tends to bring to bear upon aesthetic experience—to a field of vision, a world, present in the film. We are not to look at the screen, but through the camera eye." An exemplary case of a late film that benefits from subordination to the artist's vision, and the assimilation of its "failures" as features, is Carl Theodor Dreyer's final completed film, *Gertrud* (1964). Although now in certain cinephile circles firmly ensconced as the crowning achievement of a great career, *Gertrud* was greeted upon its Paris premiere as a humiliating failure for the revered 75-year-old filmmaker and inspired mass walkouts at its New York Film Festival appearance the next year. But others saw through its old-fashioned surface for the modernist work it was, such as Jean-Luc Godard, who wrote that it was "like Beethoven's last quartets." James Schamus, in his 2008 monograph on the film, suggests that *Gertrud* "is a perfect case study for turning artistic 'failure' into—or, rather, for accepting a kind of artistic failure *as*—the precondition for another kind of aesthetic achievement." Citing groundwork laid by Immanuel Kant for this kind of "achievement-through-failure," of the sublime as "a shock to the system," Schamus goes on to write, "In the experience of the sublime, our initial failure and displeasure... is followed by the exhilarating feeling of having experienced something that, by definition, is greater than anything our faculties could ever allow us take in.... Better by far for the artwork to stage a kind of unpleasant failure, thus generating in the beholder the struggle to grasp the greatness of the concept the artwork enables." By emphasizing what a film is rather than what it isn't, the late style approach works through ostensible defects toward constructing holistic ways in which to productively encounter the film in all of its specific—and sometimes paradoxical or contradictory—complexity. Writing of Adorno's interpretation of late style in relation to the poetry of Friedrich Hölderlin, Robert Savage notes the importance to Adorno of making "the recognition that the late work is contrasensical, *widersinning,* the spur to further interpretation rather than its defeat. The critic's task is to embrace this resistance to meaning without trying to circumvent or surmount it." In sum, the critic's task always remains: "late style" isn't just a magic phrase to bandy about that automatically makes the late work praiseworthy, but a kind of lens through which to become ultra-sensitive to the particularities of the work, and thus to think and write about it in a way that shares or clarifies as much of the work's *sui generis* value as possible.[10]

Talking about her recent podcast series "The Old Man Is Still Alive" in *The Guardian,* Karina Longworth makes a casual, if telling, admission: "I'm not trying to change the paradigm," she says of the late-career subjects of her show. "I'm

---

[10] Lest it appear that I find no place at all for what, for lack of a better term, I'd call negative criticism—i.e., criticism of a given film that despite all attempts finds the work more unedifying than not—I'd like to share something from Adorno's essay on Beethoven's *Missa Solemnis,* where he criticizes the effort "of 'debunking,' of tearing down recognized greatness for the sake of tearing something down," and speaks of how criticism "can only be a means of penetrating the work. It is the fulfilment of a duty vis-à-vis the work and not a means of gaining malicious satisfaction from knowing that once again there is one less great work in the world." I've papered over some of the context of Adorno's words here for simplicity's sake (his ambiguous take on the Beethoven work is highly complex), thus making their meaning as much mine as his, but toward the goal of simply recognizing that even negative criticism has a responsibility to the work as the work. Thus negative criticism, too, works from solid ground if it respects the integrity of the kind of approach late style thinking embodies. (It's just that human nature, being the way it is, makes this a rare achievement.)

just reacting to movies the way I react to them." Well—to put all of my cards on the table up front—I *am* trying to change the paradigm. One implicit (if not simply explicit) purpose of this book is to suggest a reformulation to our approach not just to late films, but to all films, and to all art in general. But it's the late art that arguably demands our attention the most. Some goals, then, as we get into this book about late style in film: 1) to dispel the decline myth and attendant ageist stereotypes in the art of film. The idea that filmmakers have a "prime"— as though they were professional athletes with a ticking clock on their careers—remains a prevalent notion, although one arguably antithetical to the very idea of artmaking. Yet to flip the script and declare a universal rise in quality in the work of aging artists is ageist in its own condescendingly one-size-fits-all way. Respect for the complex contingencies of each individual career is therefore needed in order to humbly and truthfully navigate each artist's later work. 2) To de-romanticize late style as a concept while nonetheless imbuing it with profundity. Late style studies up to this point have usually failed on one side of the issue or the other: either making late style too co-dependent on the Romantic trope of the "genius," or deconstructing it so far as to drain it of whatever worth it actually might have. By taking a middle track here, appreciation of late works becomes independent of dated critical categories and offers a wider playing field on which to deploy late style thinking toward productive ends. 3) To suggest a simple unifying theory/definition of late style that makes it more meaningful and intelligible. It's clear that in order to make the idea of late style something we can work with unproblematically, it will have to be redefined and relegitimized away from the ways it has been historically used and abused—to make it mean something other, and fuller, than what it has historically meant. When accomplished, late style can simultaneously be something more encompassing and more specific than it has been; and not as an academic theory, but as a tent under which serious emotional-intellectual-spiritual grappling between art and audience can occur. And lastly, 4) To become "late stylists" as viewers/critical thinkers and expand our ability to appreciate non-normative films and art in general.[11] I coin this term as a kind of nomenclature for the person who takes the principles behind the concept of late style thinking and uses them as a prompt to shift their perspective to a new level of openness and appreciativeness. Principles like looking at a film for what it *is*, rather than for what we might like it to be according to our own subjective proclivities or apprehension of conventional cinematic rules. The question of late style is, as Gordon McMullan and Sam Smiles point out, "paradigmatic (perhaps synecdochic would be better) of the larger issues that confront us all the time when considering the nature of creativity." Some works go down easily; others—often late ones—challenge our expectations. How do we respond? I'm partial to Hans Robert Jauss's literary concept of the horizon change, wherein encounters with works that subvert, frustrate, or in some way leave our expectations unfulfilled furnish us with an expanded sense of aesthetic possibility. For it's exactly such possibility-expanding encounters that late stylists relish the most.

---

[11] If it wasn't already clear, most everything I say about film in this book can be extrapolated to the other arts (and vice versa).

2

The history of late style is difficult to synthesize, let alone quantify. One could reasonably include not only the history of writers theorizing "late style" as a specific concept (scattered everywhere from critical writings to artist biographies and beyond), but also precursors to its theorization, the criticism written about late works throughout history, all the late works themselves, and any and all thinking, published and preserved or otherwise, re: art and artists later in their careers/lives. And if we factor in that understanding the specific lateness of any given late work involves familiarity with its creator's earlier work—not to mention familiarity with contemporaneous work from other artists—our circle of investigation has suddenly ballooned to nothing less than the entire history of art. The absurdity of the situation necessitates an admission that any history of late style, no matter how thorough, will always remain incomplete. As I attempt to provide a scaled-down synthesis of this history, I do so with knowledge of my own limitations[12] and gratefulness toward the scholars whose work in this area I lean on. Although a book on late style in *film*—and it will be useful, as we come upon the turn of the 20th century in the narrative ahead, to keep in the back of our minds where cinema stands while all this is going on—I hope also to have this book be an original contribution to late style studies; and if nothing else, to create a kind of written timeline of significant late style benchmarks through the ages that can be easily referred to by people wishing to orient themselves to these debates.

Late art and critical commentary about it have existed in some form for as long as art and criticism themselves have existed, to be sure. But each era and culture sees its own domi-

---

[12] For one, this would arguably be a better-researched book if I had kept up with my German after my four years of high school study, as most of the early-20th-century texts that begin to explicitly theorize late and/or old-age style come from Germany and remain largely untranslated.

nant attitudes about old age reflected in the view taken toward whatever those of old age produce, and thus one can assume that, long before it was ever given the name, late style thinking was shifting according to whatever a given society's general views about old age were. Perhaps the first work commonly identified and praised as the creation of an elderly artist is Homer's *The Odyssey,* which as evidently posterior to *The Iliad* was early on taken as the work of an old man, regardless of our modern inability to accurately determine the date of the works or whether in fact an individual named Homer even wrote them. But as Hermann Broch wrote in the 1940s, "Whether Homer existed or not, he is described as a very old man, blind as Milton, blind as Bach, blind as Fate; the style of old age in all its greatness, coolness, and abstract transparency is so obvious in his work that people had necessarily to conceive him in this form." Ancient Greece was also witness to the late life achievements of its tragedians Aeschylus, Euripides (both of whom lived and wrote up to an estimated age near 70), and Sophocles, whose trilogy-capping *Oedipus at Colonus* is dated to the very end of his life at age 90. Yet, as Gordon McMullan has written, "The Greeks had little regard for old age and would have considered a resurgence of creative energy at the end of life highly improbable.… [and], for the most part, old age appeared to the Greeks a marginal and often grotesque parody of life, offering at best a tangibly diminished role to the old." A select few positive spins on old age from the ancient world can be found in writers like Plato, Cicero, and Plutarch (the latter thought it a duty for older people to be involved in politics), and arguably the first late style theorization comes from the hand of Pliny the Elder, who locates some of the inherent pathos in last or unfinished works when he suggests that "sorrow for the hand that perished at its work beguiles us into the bestowal of praise." But little else has been identified from this world to suggest any particular ancient appreciation for the later phases of an artist's life. Of additional note only is the early classification of lives and artistic careers into discrete phases, such as those of the poets Virgil or Ovid, whose paths were thought to somehow model the progression or regression suitable (or not) to the artistic life. McMullan also identifies the life of St. Augustine as a potential model for later constructions of the artistic life into early and late phases, citing "the shift he makes away from the political and poetical to the spiritual" after his conversion to Christianity as "arguably the earliest model of the life to posit an upturn at the very end...."

Of course there was that long period of art history when art was less concerned with the idea of individual expression and achievement than with the submission of one's (often anonymous) craftsmanship to a wider tradition or a greater glory—usually God's. (Here's where I insert A. E. Brinckmann's to-me beautiful and profound claim, as paraphrased by Ben Hutchinson, "that even God himself can be understood as always already late... and that humanity may thus be said to represent his late work.") But the birth of the Renaissance period changed that. Indeed, one of its earliest artists—the Italian sculptor Donatello, born in the late 14th century—is cited by multiple accounts as the first artist to whose work the word *Altersstil* (old-age style) was later applied. Then, with the arrival of artists like Leonardo da Vinci, Michelangelo, and Raphael onto the scene in the later 15th century, "the emancipation of artists was more or less complete," according to Carel Blotkamp:

> They had evolved from humble craftsmen to divinely inspired geniuses whose artistry could compete with God's creation of nature. The anonymity of earlier centuries no longer suited such an exalted status, and the name of the artist was now proudly added to their work, as a mark of quality and an expression of their individuality. This change was also reflected in the way artists were written about. They became personalities with interesting or peculiar traits, and what may have been an ordinary life was made extraordinary by their unusual abilities.

The introduction of the individual artist into the public consciousness meant that evolutions of style occurred not just on an epochal scale but on an individual one, too. And while the belief that artists' achievements waned as they got older remained the standard narrative, the description of that decline could now be particularized for each artist, opening up the possibility for insight dedicated specifically to their late work and its creation; old-age style, or an artist's "late manner," became a proverbial concept. Giorgio Vasari's *The Lives of the Most Eminent Painters, Sculptors, and Architects*, published in 1550 with an expanded edition in 1568, offered biographies of the age's prominent artists in unprecedented detail. Vasari, himself a painter and an acquaintance of many of the still-living artists covered, used his access to describe in some cases the ailing physical and psychological states of the artists whose most famed creations were behind them. Among these were Michelangelo and Titian, Vasari's older contemporaries, and the subject of what Amir Cohen-Shalev calls the first artic-ulations "in art history [of] the distinction between early and late style." Titian's method of working on his final paintings is described as "very different from the one he employed as a young man," and the old age of Vasari's friend Michelan-gelo is viewed benevolently as befitting his transcendent and divine art. Vasari nevertheless subscribed to the commonly held opinion that the powers of an artist gradually left him as he grew older, and the general indifference with which Titian and Michelangelo's last works were greeted—even while they themselves were publicly revered—was par for the course. Nor did that pattern change, even as "old artists became a subject of analysis, instruction, and moralizing" at the tail end of the 16th century, according to Philip Sohm, in tandem with the spreading belief of "modern cultural degradation." Sohm credits the invention of a *universal* late style to the Frenchman Roger de Piles a century later, whose 1699 work *The Art of Painting and the Lives of the Painters* mapped out "three stages that applied to all artists: the first style of youth, where artists follow their masters; the second style of maturity, where they become truly themselves; and the third style of old age, when they become mannered or caricatures of themselves." The basic three-pronged understanding of the artistic life span became typical. Bryan Gilliam cites Johann Joachim Winckelmann's later *History of Ancient Art* (1764) as a work that laid the groundwork for this paradigm in Germany, Winckelmann conceptualizing phases of ancient Greek art as parallel to the phases of human existence, the "structural backbone" of the concept being "the triad of development, achievement, and decline." It's not difficult to see how these theorizations (and their attendant antipathy toward late-life creativity) map onto the basic division of artistic careers into early, mature, and late work that remains prevalent today. But even while inklings of late style began to gradually creep into understandings of artistic careers, the idea that said style might be a largely positive development was still a ways off; indeed, as Karen Painter makes clear, "Before the romantic period, when the concept of late style gained a foothold in aesthetics, the greatest praise one could bestow on an older artist's output was to report no change—which is to say, no *decline*—in quality from earlier works."

It wasn't until the early 19th century that late style as we know it today really began to take shape. What once seemed the domain of art history was rebirthed out of the field of musicology and, later, literary theory, especially via attempts to understand the late works of Beethoven, Goethe, and Mozart—this last name (dead at 35) suggesting for the first time that late style perhaps meant something other than just old-age style. Moreover, thanks to Romanticism and its cult of genius, the individual artist became more than ever a subject of far-reaching fascination; the practice of reading the artist's life and work together became commonplace and produced a steady stream of monographs and biographies on the worthiest subjects. Gordon McMullan specifically cites "the Romanticism of Fichte, Schelling and Goethe as expressed in the development of the idea of organic growth and the subsequent application of that idea to the particular growth seen in the mind and art of the individual artist. This understanding of creativity refused to differentiate the art from the artist; artistic development was understood to derive not from epoch, context or imitation of others but from the interior genius of the creative individual." Individual artworks were now stepping stones on the path of the artist's life, to be understood linearly as a markers of an evolving genius; the chronology of their works became important. "When genius became a synonym for the creative person or for human creativity," writes Goethe biographer Rüdiger Safranski, "it was inevitable that not only the work of art but, through and beyond the work, the person who created it would become interesting. The cult of the star author began with Goethe. The author outshone his work, and the life of the artist was now considered a kind of artwork." Mozart and Beethoven were two of the most famous beneficiaries of this new stance toward the great artists of the age, and per McMullan "the idea of the 'late work' began to emerge as a way to make sense of" their final compositions after their deaths. Early biographers utilized the idea of artistic phases in order to organize the composers' works into meaningful groupings. Following the example set by Giuseppe Baini's 1828 biography of Renaissance composer Palestrina, where the life and career is separated into ten phases with the last reaching "the highest level of perfection," Alexander Ulïbïshev's 1843 biography of Mozart cut the number of phases down to two but included what he saw as a late, post-decline resurgence of transcendent creativity before his death: a kind of artistic coda that foreshadows later understandings of Beethoven and others who seem to produce a set of final works that don't easily betray a sense of continuity with earlier ones. There's a reason that Beethoven remains the one name all discussions of late style in classical music revolve around; the works of his final period are strikingly unorthodox, and their coincidence with his profound deafness continually suggests an artist composing to his own inner voice, estranged from the outside world. Almost immediately after his death in 1827, there were proposals to apply a three-period structure (early, middle, and late) to Beethoven's life. But the strongest synthesis of these suggestions came in 1855 with the publication of Wilhelm von Lenz's *Beethoven and His Three Styles*, where his analysis of Beethoven's "third style" became representative of the biographical attempt to confer and describe a distinct late period for great artists.

During the second half of the 19th century, many commentators began to view Beethoven's late work as the "climax of his lifework," according to Margaret Notley, and late style as something "more likely than before to be taken as signifying culmination rather than deterioration." The last works of not just Beethoven and Mozart but many others, even a composer as young as Schubert (dead at 31), took on a special aura as late missives from the artist about to be touched by death. The standard narrative of development and decline now had an opposing force to contend with in the new narrative of late-life redemption and transcendence. The re-evaluation of Beethoven's late works along these lines was joined by the late literary achievements of Johann Wolfgang von Goethe, whose late period overlapped with Beethoven's and gave literary history its own exemplary late style to come to terms with. Goethe had been the star author of the German *Sturm und Drang* movement, but after his early achievement with the 1774 epistolary novel *The Sorrows of Young Werther* he led a life in the shadow of his own youthful brilliance; Rüdiger Safranski writes that "from the time of its publication to the end of his long life, the general public thought of him only as the author of *Werther*.... Goethe could never get rid of his early stroke of genius." His late offerings, worked on sporadically in the final decades of his life in the early 1800s, largely involved the continuation and/or finishing of earlier works: the novel *Wilhelm Meister's Journeyman Years* of the 1820s followed the *Wilhelm Meister's Apprenticeship* of the 1790s and *Faust, Part Two* was the culmination of his life-long work on the play, the first part having appeared decades earlier. Both showed signs of what later became trademarks of late style. Safranski describes the second *Wilhelm Meister* novel as "typical of Goethe's style in old age: he simply claims the freedom to leave the heterogeneity of a work without feeling the need to justify it"; the second *Faust* is described by Anthony Barone as "subject to extensive analysis as [an icon] of late style"; and Goethe's late poetry too has been described as incredibly personal and incomparable to other examples of contemporary verse. Goethe himself offered in his *Maxims and Reflections* this aphoristic definition of old age: "gradually receding from appearance." The rise in the reputation of Goethe's late works as the 19th century approached the 20th was indicative of the shifting winds of the time, seen in both the loss of authority accorded to academic views on art and in the developing idea that the late works of artists like Beethoven and Goethe "constituted a distinctive body of work requiring a different standard of judgement," per McMullan and Smiles. In 1855 Jacob Burckhardt could suggest that "several of the greatest artists [of the Italian Renaissance] produced most of their works and their best at a late period in life," Jacob Grimm argued in an 1860 lecture on old age that the creativity particular to it should be much more esteemed, and in 1878 William Kingsley drew on the new reputation of Beethoven's late work to suggest that the late paintings of J. M. W. Turner were just as worthy of re-evaluation. Shakespeare, too, had become a central figure in literary discussions about lateness, and the attempts to establish a chronology for the plays that began a century earlier became the basis for conceptualizations of a Shakespearean late style (usually under the sign of *The Tempest*), exemplified by Edward Dowden's 1875 book on the subject—a work which later becomes a central text in Gordon McMullan's 21st-century unraveling of the problematic nature of such theorizations.

As a kind of bridge between Romanticism and Modernism, the late 19th century has been seen as a decadent period in which many felt a sense of greater cultural lateness, an epigonal, end-of-an-epoch feeling that suffused attempts to both make original art and talk about it. The modern era would be late from its very beginning: what's to be done in music after Wagner? What's to be done in painting after the Impressionists? Amidst this epochal awareness of lateness, as well as a new attentiveness to the specifics of form, previous epochs disparaged as lesser stylistic periods were rehabilitated in ways that bled over into considerations of individual styles.

"These new formal enquiries," according to Sam Smiles, "thus proposed that epochal 'lateness' need no longer be associated with an inevitable decline…. [and] the late work of individual artists was re-examined and its formal integrity asserted." These and other paths of inquiry swirling around fin de siècle culture contributed to the coining of the word *Altersstil* and a miniature explosion of works (largely in German[13]) attempting to deal with it in ways born from several historically conditioned approaches. For as Ben Hutchinson points out, "the discourse of individual lateness emerges from a broader epochal consciousness, whether that of ageing subjectivity (the romantic model), belated decadence (the late nineteenth-century model), or fractured disenchantment (the modernist model)." Georg Simmel approached the topic at the end of his own life in writings about da Vinci (1905), Michelangelo (1911), Goethe (1913), and Rembrandt (1916), the second-to-last of these offering "what may be the earliest extended and systematically argued theory of late style" according to Anthony Barone. Art historian Georg Gronau wrote works on Michelangelo (1906), Rembrandt (1923), and Bellini (1928), further contributions to the growing body of studies that partook in the recognition of individual late work's specific qualities. The year 1923 saw a chapter devoted to *Altersstil* in Richard Hamann's *Impressionism in Life and Art* as well as the publication of Heinrich Wölfflin's *The Principles of Art History*, wherein he theorized epochal late style as "a 'baroque' elaboration of a preceding 'classic' phase of style," and then suggested "that the formal changes which he ascribed to period late style were paralleled and reflected in the development of personal style," per Stephen Katz. Following these was A. E. Brinckmann's *Late Works of the Great Masters* (1925), the first full-fledged study of late style, where an attempt was made

---

[13] The prevalence of German contributions to the history of late style is notable, and has itself been theorized according to factors such as its late emergence as a nation in 1871, German idealism's influence in the compulsion to viewing artists in phases, and the post-WWII necessity of retrieving Germany's artistic heritage from the taint of Nazism, among other things.

to describe and define common attributes of late works from a variety of artists across the centuries as well as analyze the inner transformations they underwent to produce them. At this point, though, late style was largely seen as the reflection of a kind of harmonious spiritual state reached by artists whose increased introversion and indifference toward material matters showed up in the formal properties of their work.

Then came Adorno. Written in 1934 and published in 1937, Theodor W. Adorno's "Spätstil Beethovens" ("Late Style in Beethoven") put forward a vision of late style that emphasized instead the thorny, dissonant, fractured, rebellious, and unreconciled nature of late work. "The maturity of the late works of significant artists does not resemble the kind one finds in fruit," writes Adorno. "They are, for the most part, not round, but furrowed, even ravaged. Devoid of sweetness, bitter and spiny, they do not surrender themselves to mere delectation. They lack all the harmony that the classicist aesthetic is in the habit of demanding from works of art, and they show more traces of history than of growth." Adorno concludes his short essay with aphoristic flair: "In the history of art late works are the catastrophes." His view of late style as the productive friction resulting from the rejection of classical harmony found its apotheosis in late Beethoven, whose last works he saw as exemplary of the alienated, exilic relationship that exists between the late artist and their social and artistic milieu. Adorno's stance on late style was in many ways born from his historically situated position within the modernist landscape, as a classically trained musician who'd studied under modernist composer Alban Berg, as a German-born Jew living through the inter-war years, and as a core contributor to the nascent school of critical theory; Ben Hutchinson writes that "over the course of [Adorno's] subsequent work, late style emerges both as a consequence of, and a response to, the perceived lateness of modernity."[14] Part of what thrilled

---

[14] Yet Hutchinson also points out that one of the terms used in Adorno's essay—*Zerrissenheit*, or "torn-ness"—was also a prominent term in discussions of lateness of the 1820s and 1830s, and therefore "it

Adorno about late Beethoven was the way in which it foreshadowed, a century earlier, the musical modernism of Arnold Schoenberg, whose work he admired for its resistance to easy assimilation within bourgeois musical consumption.[15] For Adorno, then, lateness was an implicitly political concept: to say that Beethoven's final works were *late* is to signal the way their musical form both articulates the moribundity of the prevailing bourgeois order and embodies an authentic resistance to it. The anachronistic adoption of Beethoven into modernist discourses demonstrated Adorno's belief that his late music not only critiqued the society of Beethoven's time but offered a reverberating critique to the late capitalist one of Adorno's own.[16] Lateness amounts to a category of artistic resistance for Adorno, not just politically but in a way fundamentally resistant to neutralization, appropriation, standardization, or domestication—a resistance, it should be noted, that Adorno's own work simulates. Adorno's notoriously difficult prose style "is peculiarly resistant to paraphrase for the very reason that it enacts the resistance that it diagnoses,"

---

is worth noting… the overlap between conceptions of lateness and late style from the 1830s and the 1930s. *Zerrissenheit…* strikingly remains a salient aspect of modern lateness from post-romanticism to modernism, however much the contextual inflections and epochal emphases may change."

[15] Schoenberg is one of the other, non-Beethoven artists that Adorno will on occasion write about in relation to ideas of lateness or late style more generally across his work, along with other composers like Wagner, Schubert, or Mahler, artists like Michelangelo or Rembrandt, and writers like Goethe, Hölderlin, Kafka, Beckett, and Mann. But Beethoven undoubtedly remained the center of his conception.

[16] Although it never came to fruition until fragments of it were gathered after his death in 1969, Adorno had been planning and working on a book about Beethoven throughout his lifetime. Significantly, he began writing the book in 1933, the year the Nazis came to power in Germany. Richard Leppert writes of Stephen Hinton's suggestion "that Adorno's Beethoven project is likely a response to the fact that in 1933 the National Socialists claimed Beethoven as one of their own. The connection Adorno draws between Beethoven's music and emancipation directly counters the composer's colonization by the fascists."

per Hutchinson, and the struggle to comprehend his meaning amidst the rigorous intricacies of his form betrays him as less a pure critic than a kind of critic-as-artist. "To be an essayist in Adorno's sense," Edward Said would later write, "meant to be permanently on strike from, and at odds with, everything fashionable, à la mode, in, intellectually speaking." At times cryptic, at times contradictory, that Adorno's writing is nonetheless captivating and rewarding when given the effort to engage with it marks it out as *late* despite the fact that, to take one example, the essay on late Beethoven was written in Adorno's late twenties or early thirties. But lateness for Adorno is somewhat radically defined not so much biographically or chronologically as it is formally or philosophically; for the musicologist Adorno, it's the objective formal qualities of Beethoven's late music that mark it as late rather than any subjective psychological interpretation of Beethoven the aging composer. Thus why Adorno can appear inconsistent in his determination of just which, exactly, of Beethoven's compositions actually *are* late. The Ninth symphony is in places discounted as a late work completely and the *Missa Solemnis*, to which a 1959 essay is dedicated, is given the ambiguous designation of a "late work without late style"; and the line for where Beethoven's lateness begins is located in different places at different times. "In his influential writings on Beethoven," writes Karen Painter, "[Adorno] seems to insist that the key to late works lay not in any psychological or organic life trajectory of the artist or composer but in the relation of art to the age itself." Indeed, it was this slant on late style that appeared in Thomas Mann's chronological narrative of fictional composer Adrian Leverkühn, the late novel *Doctor Faustas* (1947), which Adorno assisted him with while the two lived in exile in California—both specifically in the form of a short lecture on late Beethoven given by Leverkühn's composition teacher and more generally in the way Leverkühn's music is presented as an untimely reckoning with the age of Germany's crisis across the first half of the 20th century. It was *Doctor Faustus*'s publication that inspired the reprinting of Adorno's Beethoven essay from a decade earlier and led to its repopularization; and despite its brevity, the essay—from an author who Edward Said could later call "a sort of high priest of late-style gloom"—remains the single most well-known work on late style today.

Other German writers in the 1940s and 1950s, such as Hermann Broch, Gottfried Benn, and Erich Neumann, made further contributions to the conceptualization of late style that followed Adorno's sense of late works as out-of-time missives from outside of society, while also reverting to more traditional notions of the transcendence of old age. As Broch writes, "The artist thus graced and cursed with the 'style of old age' is not content with the conventional vocabulary provided him by his epoch. For to render the epoch, the whole epoch, he cannot remain within it; he must find a point beyond it." But the genealogy of formative German contributions to the idea of late style had, by the mid-20th century, basically come full circle: "Thus if German Romanticism was responsible for the invention of late style," writes Gordon McMullan, "then German modernism was in a sense responsible for its reinvention." The lateness inherent to the modernist epoch turned late style into an urgent and arguably everyday affair, and if late style has survived as a subject worth talking about into our own century it's likely linked to ever-renewed feelings that articulating our late predicament takes more than traditional, conventional art is able to specifically offer. Amir Cohen-Shalev writes of Kenneth Clark, who in his 1970 lecture "The Artist Grows Old" partially "attributes the rekindled interest" in late style in the 20th century "to the pervasiveness of abstract art, which allows for a fair treatment of abstraction in the late works of famous artists from pre-abstract eras." The sculptures of Rodin opening up appreciation for the late sculptures of Donatello and Michelangelo, for example, or the paintings of Monet shedding light on the proto-impressionism of late Turner—these and other connections, whether valid or not, leading to the common suggestion that late work often has a prophetic quality, of anticipating future trends in art before their time. If, on the one hand, the assertion that there's some kind of "transhistorical line of modernist art that runs right back to Sophocles" seems silly if not blindingly ahistorical, as McMullan's phrasing of it attests, on the other hand there's been genuine insight into history's late works gleaned via the anachronistic reappraisals common to modernism, which—given the anachronistic nature of much late work itself—feels supremely fitting. Meanwhile, the attention given late works and late style branched into more global debates, and books about artists more often approached their subject's late offerings in tandem with glancing comments about the field of late works in general. In 1943 Aldous Huxley wrote in the foreword to a book about the etchings of Francisco Goya "there are anthologies of almost everything... but there is one anthology, potentially the most interesting of them all, which, to the best of my knowledge, has never yet been compiled; I mean, the Anthology of Later Works." But as the category of late works became a more generalized topic of consideration in the second half of the 20th century, the field was still left without a unifying theory and instead largely consisted of two competing (positive) narratives of late style, the choice of which often depended upon the temperament of the critic writing about it. For some, following writers like Simmel and Brinckmann, the more classical view of late style as the spiritualized culmination of the master working in old age, in a reflective and redemptive mode, was what best characterized the majority of history's late works. But for others, notably Adorno and his acolytes, late style was the result of a radical break with the comforts of bourgeois art, discordant and dissonant, formally modernist and beyond subjectivity, and exemplified by works resistant to merely casual appreciation.

The latter of these two narratives received a big boost at the beginning of the 21st century thanks to Palestinian-American writer Edward Said, whose work toward the end of his life repopularized the topic of late style via Adorno-influenced investigations into an aesthetics of resistance. Said's discovery and exploration of Adorno in the late 1970s began to coalesce into a specific interest in lateness and late style at the tail end of the 1980s, and in the 1990s Said began to articulate his own slant on the subject in a series of classes and lectures at both Columbia and elsewhere. A book on late style was in the works when Said died in 2003 from the leukemia that he'd been diagnosed with in 1991; indeed, his time with the disease had paralleled his interests in late style and had inevitably deepened the urgency of his engagement with the subject, although to suggest that his interest was solely determined by subjective concerns is to miss the way in which lateness comingled with his political engagements and his interest in beginnings, middles, and endings more generally. "Said's interest in late style or anything else was never merely autobiographical," according to his editor Michael Wood. "Thoughts of his own death deepened his attachment to the question of late style; they didn't instigate it." Indeed, as early as his first book, *Beginnings* (1975), Said articulates an interest in the shape of artistic careers, a thread continually pulled at across his writing life; a 1990s essay finds him writing that "beginnings are usually associated with youth, not with age, although literature, music and art are full of examples of renewal, beginning-again, that are found in the work of older artists." It's fitting, then, that Said ended his publishing career with a book on lateness, published in 2006 as *On Late Style: Music and Literature Against the Grain.* Even though the book is unfinished, consisting of partial drafts as well as other writings and lectures on a diverse array of creative figures not originally intended for inclusion, a coherent throughline remains of late style as an aesthetic and political category wherein artists working "against the grain" of contemporary convention participate in "artistic lateness not as harmony and resolution, but as intransigence, difficulty and contradiction"—a type of lateness that "is a sort of deliberately unproductive productiveness, a going against." Said is most interested in creatives like Beethoven and Sigmund Freud (to whom a relevant lecture published in 2002 as *Freud and the Non-Europeans* was dedicated), in whose cases "the intellectual trajectory conveyed by the late work is intransigence and a sort of irascible transgressiveness, as if the author was expected to settle down into a harmonious composure, as befits a person at the end of his life, but preferred instead to be difficult, and to bristle with all sorts of new ideas and provocations." Like Adorno, Said found valuable the "notion of tension, of highlighting and dramatizing what I call irreconcilabilities," which when left unreconciled allowed for the articulation of difficult and contradictory elements of existence via formally defiant styles "uncooptable into one or another of the accredited schools of the day." The political implications of this shared view of late style were for Said, as a politically engaged Palestinian familiar with exilic life, urgently central to his conception. For Said, "far from being a purely aesthetic concern," write Moustafa Bayoumi and Andrew Rubin, "late style had been shaped by forces of political failure and loss." The signing of the 1993 Oslo Accords was seen by Said as a betrayal of the Palestinian people by their leadership and turned Palestinian liberation into an even more untimely cause; this, and the continued elusiveness of Palestinian peace, caused Said to live the "last decade of his life, according to his son, Wadie, in a permanent state of rage and hurt." That he spent that time immersed in ideas of lateness and aesthetic intransigence was no coincidence, and connecting political implications to formal analysis came intuitively to him. In the late book on Freud, Said draws on the way Freud's late work *Moses and Monotheism* (1939) "seems to be composed by Freud for himself, with scant attention to frequent and often ungainly repetition, or regard for elegant economy of prose and exposition" for the purposes of contrapuntally arguing, as Bayoumi and Rubin put it, that Freud's book "provided the foundations for a binational state in which both Israel and Palestine are parts and not adversaries of each other's history." Ultimately, although thoroughly indebted to Adorno, Said intentionally builds a more constructive version of late style than Adorno's pessimism, which "bothered" Said, allowed; the alienated, estranged status of late style providing not just an aesthetic critique against (politically inert) artistic convention, but through its untimeliness suggesting an alternative path forward.

Said's work undoubtedly sparked a revival of interest in late style studies. In the 21st century so far, the list of artists to whom book-length studies of their late styles have been dedicated include Edgar Degas, Beethoven, Igor Stravinsky, Shakespeare, Johannes Brahms, Robert Schumann, Claude Debussy, Giacomo Puccini, Turner, Anthony Trollope, D. H. Lawrence, Franz Schubert, and Bob Dylan.[17] Works about or tangential to the idea of late style more generally in both English and other languages—Sandro Zanetti's *Avant-gardism of the Aged?: Late Works and Their Poetics* (2012) furthers the German tradition—continue to proliferate both inside and outside of academic contexts. Yet unified understandings and usages of the term "late style" remain elusive, both within contemporary publications and relative to the centuries-long history we've just rehearsed. As Sam Smiles writes about the authors who've contributed to the defining of late style over the years, "Their approaches are therefore better understood not as sure guides to a widespread aesthetic phenomenon but as historically conditioned attempts to reconcile the 'problematic' last works of selected artists with what they considered to be the relevant progressive developments of their own time." Just as modernism reacted to romanticism's understanding of late style and redefined it to its own ends, so too has today's postmodernism reacted to both—not just redefining it, but asking whether it's even worth keeping the concept around at all. "Since the 1970s," writes Karen Painter, "theorists have decisively turned away from *Spätstil*, a change occurring in tandem with the shift from biography toward contextual interpretation." Even so, any particular invocation of late style in recent decades is likely to be a palimpsest of shifting historical understandings: as McMullan and Smiles note, "The late-style trope takes from romanticism its emphasis on biography, subjectivism, the relationship between creativity and selfhood; from modernism it derives its interest in tradition, the avant-garde, abstraction, the subordination of self to epoch, the loss

---

[17] Notably, for our purposes, books I'm aware of dedicated specifically to the late films of specific individual directors published in this time include works on Jean-Luc Godard, Claude Chabrol, and Robert Bresson. However, this list neglects biographies, the best of which can contain some of the most illuminating studies of artists' late works available.

of linearity." To which we might add that from postmodernism it, or rather those that write about it, get their self-aware suspiciousness toward the very idea of late style's earnest invocation. Thus, even while it's difficult to put the late style debates of recent decades under a single philosophical banner, an air of scholarly skepticism toward the concept largely holds sway in the 21st century. The work of Gordon McMullan has spearheaded this trend, and his own words demonstrate his stance when he argues in *Shakespeare and the Idea of Late Writing* that

> late style is less a demonstrable phenomenon than a redemptive fantasy of rejuvenation, a form of wish-fulfilment shared by artists and critics which may at times approximate biographical truth but which is far more often the product either of the imposition of an understanding of the creative process inimical to the actual conditions in which the art works in question were produced or of complicity on the part of the artist, who consciously produces work that fulfils the criteria for the attribution of a late style.

Those interested in late style are then in the position of responding, if this is true (and I believe it is, if only partially), to what this means for their approach and whether or not late style can be rescued as a paradigm from which to view late work—for it is the work that is ultimately the focus here. As McMullan and Smiles admit, "To offer a critique of the concept late style, we wish to underline, is absolutely not to belittle the late works themselves; on the contrary, much of the pleasure of working on the subject of lateness is the opportunity it provides to discover and closely assess a range of culturally significant works of art created by artists, writers, composers, and film-makers late in life." The question, then—which I hope to answer—is this: does late style as a concept hinder, or can it help, that assessment?

3

If late style remains a culturally relevant lens through which to view the creative life of artists in old age, I would argue it's partially because as humans we recognize that, despite the obvious reduction in certain capabilities physical or otherwise that come with aging, there nonetheless exists some unquantifiable asset that is gained by, and only by, growing older. Call it wisdom, call it experience, call it whatever you want, there's the undeniable sense that there are virtues to old age that, when infused with the creative instinct in artists, have the potential to result in work that gains in overall expressiveness what it may lose in formal polish. However, the rulers by which we conventionally measure artistic achievement aren't inherently sensitive to these nuances, and therefore late works often suffer for it—condemned to the realm of curiosities. It's a demonstrable fact that the majority of what are considered canonically "great" works of art are made by artists in middle age or younger. Indeed, one interesting sub-field relevant or at least tangential to late style studies has been the attempt to scientifically determine the age or age range at which artists in a given medium reach their creative "peak." This is usually done by surveying a number of, say, art history books, and then collating mentions of artworks to formulate what the most significant ones are considered to be: the more mentions across these texts, the more significant the artwork. The age at which the artists produced these works are then tallied, and a range is generated. Such research has determined that, across the arts, most artists peak creatively somewhere in the 30-45 years range. In Harvey Lehman's 1953 study *Age and Achievement* he uses similar methods to briefly determine the creative peaks of movie directors, where the 35-40 years range wins out; a more recent book by David Galenson, *Old Masters and Young Geniuses: The Two Life Cycles of Artistic Creativity* (2006), theorizes the same question but groups artists into one of two categories—as either "conceptual" or "experimental"—and offers examples across various mediums in an attempt to show that conceptual artists tend to peak earlier and experimental artists later. Touching on filmmakers, Galenson writes that

> the evidence… clearly supports the prediction that conceptual directors [his examples are Eisenstein, Fellini, Godard, and Welles] make their best movies earlier in their careers than their experimental counterparts [Ford, Hawks, Hitchcock, and Renoir].… [and] the difference is clearly understandable as a consequence of the differing styles and contributions of the two types of director, with the visual and storytelling skills of the experimental directors developing over long years of experience, in contrast to the radical new technical devices the conceptual directors invented in the enthusiasm and energy of their youthful iconoclasm.

Yet the problem with trying to discern "peaks" of artistic creativity via mathematically-determined consensus should be obvious: not only is that consensus based on ideologically-determined ideas of what constitutes "good" and/or "significant" (and/or "major") art that are inherently disposed against non-normative expression, but the singling out of certain "masterworks" as representative achievements also considerably flattens the moment-to-moment complexity of the arc of any given artistic life. Ever-skeptical of consensus to begin with, the late stylist is much less concerned with conventional age-based narratives than they are with meeting the artist where they're at and squeezing every last drop of interest—no matter how unconventionally embodied—from whatever artwork, early or late, is at hand.

This becomes especially relevant when dealing with the artistic expressions of those in old age, as the uniqueness of the artist's life situation and accumulated experience has the potential to result in works of hard-won wisdom and economical expression. Elderly artists are themselves already a special phenomenon: unlike most other occupations, artists tend to forgo traditional retirement and often work until they die; the creative impulse stays with them. This impulse also evolves in ways responsive to the artist's prolonged accrual of insight into their craft or into life in general, and no shortage of quotes exist to demonstrate the fact that many artists near the end of their careers still consider themselves students of one sort or another. "'Still I'm learning' was the aged Michelangelo's favorite maxim," writes Thomas Dormandy, and Aldous Huxley tells of us of how centuries later Goya similarly "drew a picture of an ancient man tottering along under the burden of years, but with the accompanying caption, 'I'm still learning.'" Perhaps the most famous statement of artistic humility in old age comes from the Japanese artist Hokusai, who at the age of 75 could write this:

> From the age of six I had a penchant for copying the form of things, and from about fifty, my pictures were frequently published; but until the age of seventy, nothing I drew was worthy of notice. At seventy-three years, I was somewhat able to fathom the growth of plants and trees, and the structure of birds, animals, insects and fish. Thus when I reach eighty years, I hope to have made increasing progress, and at ninety to see further into the underlying principles of things, so that at one hundred years I will have achieved a divine state in my art, and at one hundred and ten, every dot and every stroke will be as though alive. Those of you who live long enough, bear witness that these words of mine are not false.

In the realm of cinema, Akira Kurosawa wrote in a letter to fellow filmmaker Ingmar Bergman of another late-blooming Japanese artist, Tessai Tomioka, and of how "every time I see his paintings, I fully realize that a human is not really capable of creating really good works until he reaches eighty…. I am now seventy-seven years old and am convinced that my real work is just beginning." Bergman himself, in turn, admitted to a neighbor that "I rather like being old…. It's a bit like climbing a mountain. You climb from one plateau to the next. The higher you get, the more tired and breathless you become, but the view gets better and better." This view of artistic expression as akin to a good wine which gets richer with age certainly emphasizes the way late art is born out of a lifetime of patient refinement, and as a product of that lifetime is buoyed by the entirety of all a given artist has learned and lived through. An artist's late period is therefore dense with meaning and significance. Bookended by an entire life and career on one end and by the sheer matter-of-factness of an inevitable death on the other, late works become the inherently intensified site of an artist's metaphorical (or literal) "last words," and late style the means through which they are spoken. "O, but they say the tongues of dying men/Enforce attention, like deep harmony," as Shakespeare writes in *Richard II*. "Where words are scarce they are seldom spent in vain,/For they breathe truth that breathe their words in pain." The awareness of both artist and audience that limited time remains produces, therefore, a highly charged encounter between the two via the medium of their art; and any obstacles faced by the former should ideally also be surmounted by the latter. As Linda and Michael Hutcheon write of Verdi, Strauss, Messaien, and Britten, the "various challenges of aging turned out to be first threats and then stimulants to the creativity of these composers." To repurpose the sentence, I'd hope that any challenges or threats presented to audiences by their late works would in turn become stimulants to curiosity and receptivity toward them.

Yet we should be careful lest we repeat the mistake of claiming a generalized artistic decline by simply replacing it with a generalized theory of gerontic exceptionalism. Yes, older artists have had all this time to absorb experiences, culture, life lessons, etc. as a human being—so how could they not have at least *something* of interest to express?—but to uncomplicatedly assume old age equates with the possession of wisdom is also to flatten and de-individualize the experience of late-life creativity, merely in the opposite direction. Looking at the positive and negative views of aging, Stephen Katz finds that "both narratives tend to isolate artistic creativity from its material and often contradictory conditions of production and the historically situated lives of the heroic artists themselves." Every artist from every place and every era ages at their own specific rate as biology, environment, lifestyle, and a host of other factors determine; any generalizing concept is bound to give short shrift to the complexities and contingencies of a given artist's life. There's little difference then between talking about an artist "overcoming" age to produce great work and in talking about an artist "letting age get the best of them" when they produce less-than-great work, as both reactions give the implication of age as a monolithic obstacle to be either surmounted or succumbed to. The reality is far less clear-cut, and reactions to the various challenges of aging, like the human beings they are presented to, can often be contradictory—genuine human shortcomings, say, combined with the creation of complex and perceptive art.[18] Regardless of the individual scenarios of old age one may be dealing with, though, the late stylist begins from a stance of empathy and attempted understanding: not romanticizing late-life creativity, but openly respecting it. Which partly comes from the admission that we don't and probably cannot fully understand it; thus why the whole field of gerontology is relevant to late style issues, and why strides have been made to bring the two areas into meaningful conversation. A recent volume titled *Creativity in Later Life: Beyond Late Style* (2019), co-edited by Gordon McMullan and David Amigoni, attempts to do just that, and to fulfil what is "arguably an ethical obligation," as McMullan and Sam Smiles phrase it in an earlier work,

---

[18] The nuanced portrait of old age that late style appreciation works from, then, is attentive to the ways that humans can be both progressive and regressive creatures simultaneously, and therefore the unfortunate situation wherein an older artist is revealed to have significant moral shortcomings, either as an individual or as someone with creative authority and social power, can be approached (and reproached) for what it is without feeling the need to be unduly dismissive of the art—often incisive and insightful in ways running counter to the person's personal actions—that that particular person has produced.

to find a more appropriate, a less (or even an un-) mythologized means of validating the productions of old age or of proximity to death than this repetitive attempt to negotiate a one-size-fits-all adaptation of… whatever [past or] current schema offers a shape for the long and varied creative life. It is arguably incumbent on us—as medical science has ensured that more of us will live for so much longer, and will therefore be old for so much longer than previous generations—to find new, more reflective, more critically and theoretically nuanced and rigorous ways to account for the creative possibilities associated with the end of the artistic life.

The futility of making generalized statements about late-life creativity is underscored when confronted with the commonly-suggested theory that an artist's late phase may in fact be the period in which the most intense individualization occurs—i.e., in which each artist becomes most themselves, and the least like anyone else. Decades of experience in their chosen craft, and refinement of their artistic preferences, makes second nature many otherwise complex decisions and processes; long-distilled instinct and intuition take over, often resulting in structural or stylistic choices that are palpably specific to an artist's vision, as though beamed straight from their head onto the canvas, page, or screen. Influences and inspirations that may have loomed large over their early work have at this point been so fully assimilated that their presence, if felt at all, is felt only through the unmistakable filter of the artist's own style. The thing about late style is that there's nowhere else to go; you can't transcend lateness—you can only go deeper into it. This, however, is exactly the fact that most thrills those with an "affinity for particular artists," as Richard Brody writes, which "involves a craving for the fullness of their character, for its self-revelation in a display of its widest and wildest range of powers and possibilities." It's this wide and wild display achieved by the most singular of late artists that often leads to difficult and dissonant works that eschew, like Adorno's late Beethoven, the "harmonious synthesis" expected of them. Such works are rarely concerned with placating the audience's expectations or desire for closure, and thus are disinclined to "splendidness and tonal monumentality" (Adorno) in ways that foreground contradiction or unorthodox creative juxtapositions. Formal or structural innovation in late work, for example, often sits side by side with the use of naked convention—a trait almost all Beethoven scholars, not just Adorno, find essential to the particular lateness of the composer's late works. This willingness to play around with the "rules" of storytelling or style, to use them or not use them to the artist's own specific ends, lends credence to Erin J. Campbell's "definition of old-age style as practices that are resistant to theory"[19] while also allowing the late work of art to be a site of sundry and diverse pleasures—and productive displeasures—for an engaged public not looking to be spoon-fed. "This is the prerogative of late style," writes Edward Said: "it has the power to render disenchantment and pleasure without resolving the contradiction between them." Or as Amir Cohen-Shalev frames it via "Robert Frost's famous metaphor of the two roads in a yellow wood," "instead of taking the road not traveled by, [late artists] took them both, at once. There is a paradoxical integrity in aging, having devoted a lifetime to weighing conflicting impulses through creative endeavor, and to embrace no-resolution completely and with no fear." The highly individual, enigmatic, and seemingly incongruous nature of much late work, however, often leaves such accomplishments in a state of what Carl Dahlhaus calls "chronological 'homelessness'"—"the form their influence takes is not so much that they lay a foundation for later work, as that they are validated by later developments which they have done little or nothing directly to generate. Their after-history is discontinuous." Unlike youthful or middle-age achievements that may be similarly radical in form or content, late work rarely establishes any artistic movements or lines of easily traceable influ-

---

[19] Borrowing from Paul de Man's "definition of literary practice as the resistance to theory."

ence; their un-zeitgeisty, anachronistic leanings[20] tend instead to leave them stranded as solitary expressions lacking direct descendants, what Robert Kastenbaum terms "shadows" that surface only long after their original dismissal or what Kurt Badt more loftily calls works that "tower above the flow of history as solitudes inaccessible to the context of time."

That out-of-time quality is one of the most appreciable aspects of much late work, as surface rhythms often betray the inescapable fact that its creator is working in a vastly different context from the one in which they first came of age. Experiencing such work amidst a diet of other contemporaneous offerings inevitably highlights this discrepancy; as Carl Dahlhaus writes, it's "characteristic of a late work" that "it is inwardly alien to the age to which it outwardly belongs." This aspect of lateness echoes Adorno and Said's idea of late art as untimely and the late artist as a "catastrophic commentator" on the present. The distance provided by lateness, however, can be utilized in two different (and, of course, potentially overlapping) ways: as a position from which to comment upon the present obliquely—via a retreat into the past or an anachronistic handling of contemporary material—or as a vantage point from which to attack the present head-on as, simultaneously, a visitor to the present and an inhabitant of it. For the late artist is both a part of, and apart from, the times in which they operate. The title of Nicholas Ray's late film *We Can't Go Home Again,* an experimental work made in collaboration with his students at Binghamton University in the 1970s, could usefully double as a meta-thematic label for much late work: as it's impossible to go "home" to the land of one's early or middle years, one must instead work in the strange land of the present. The frequently-slung criticism of much late work as being "out of touch" often misses the way in which that alienating feeling is in productive tension, formally and

---

[20] The fact that anachronisms tend to become exponentially less bothersome the more time passes from the context in which the work was originally produced raises the question of why we don't simply accept anachronisms as unbothersome—indeed, even interesting— right from the get-go...

thematically, with the social mores and stylistic conventions of one's own era.[21] And so what if a work is "out of touch," or "dated," anyways? Why is it a requirement for artists to update themselves to the times when we know full well that the times will just change again? Better to just remain themselves, free to use or not use elements of contemporary life regardless of fashion. Indeed, where some artists forge ahead unconcerned with matters of cultural relevancy, others find themselves invigorated by engagement with up-to-the-minute moods. Take Robert Bresson's *The Devil, Probably* (1977) and Paul Schrader's *First Reformed* (2017), for example: two films made by men in their seventies that parallel each other in their socially urgent grappling with environmental concerns and the despair of contemporary young people. Yet late style can embrace the zeitgeist just as readily as it can reject it, and there is pathos to be found in both choices. However, as is usually the case, what might look like an either/or proposition is really a more complex phenomenon; the layering of history and memory with the omnipresence of present-day concerns leaves the late artist with a unique, multifaceted perspective. Said talks about lateness as "being at the end, fully conscious, full of memory, and also very (even preternaturally) aware of the present." Or, reaching back further to a 19th century perspective, Ben Hutchinson writes of how "late style, for [the French littérateur] Chateaubriand, can be understood as a 'timequake' (*tremblement du temps*)—[Giovanni] Berchet remarks that the celebrated phrase represents 'a way of characterizing the *tremor* that the superposition of epochs and places introduces into the old artist's memory'—and this

---

[21] Lest we forget that this out-of-touchness isn't just a matter of outdated content or of ostensible thematic "progressiveness" or lack thereof, Said reminds us: "There is first of all the artist's connection to his or her own time, or historical period, society and antecedents, how the aesthetic work, for all its irreducible individuality, is nevertheless part of—or, paradoxically, not a part—of the era in which it was produced. This is not simply a matter of sociological or political synchrony but [emphasis mine] *more interestingly has to do with rhetorical or formal style.*"

metaphysical timequake has metaphysical consequences." In short, regardless of its particular work-by-work expression, late style has a unique and productively charged relationship with time.

And with time comes change or, if "change" seems in some cases too dramatic a word, then repetition with a difference. It often seems as if artists, late ones especially, find themselves in a no-win situation: either they continue to make and refine the same type of work over and over again, which is pegged as "boring," or they change and evolve into making new kinds of work, which makes critics uncomfortable and leaves them nostalgic for an artist's earlier efforts. Woody Allen confronts the latter situation in *Stardust Memories* (1980), where his director character, having made a dramatic film for the first time, is bombarded with a chorus of preference—even from a visiting flock of aliens—for his "early, funny ones." The repeated joke takes aim at the inability of the public to let an artist evolve, instead demanding that he remain who they want him to be (i.e., who he was when the public first fell in love with him).[22] The problem isn't a new one, particularly in

---

[22] It's ironic, then, that Woody Allen later also became a main target for the criticism that he "makes the same movie over and over again." In the grand scheme of things, this critical tic seems supremely silly. As Matthew Wilder remarked in 2016, "when I see people on social media rolling their eyes about 'the same old Woody Allen movie again,' I think—did people used to complain about 'the same old Anthony Trollope novel again'? 'That same old tired Titian painting'? Woody has achieved a level of reflex mastery…. [and] as his heroes feel about their fickle, evanescent beloveds: you're going to miss them when they're gone." While we're on the subject, in 2010 Richard Brody identified a difference amidst the ostensible sameness of Allen's late work: "Allen's films move more swiftly now; they don't linger on anecdotal pleasures but go, sketch-like, right to the idea. It's entirely normal for a person, when aging, to get out less than before and to partake less of the social whirl, and one no longer goes to a Woody Allen movie to get a report from any particular milieu (and he was, in his younger days, a stellar urban folklorist); rather, he offers a report from the rueful height of experience, offered as if, in a way, he had already halfway passed out of this world (despite happily being, to all appearances, active and in the pink of health)."

cinema. "Crocodile tears over the alleged decline of Alfred Hitchcock," wrote James Agee in 1944, "have for years been a favorite cocktail among those who take moving pictures seriously. That has always seemed to me an impatient and cheap attitude to take toward any kind of change, or disturbance, in the work of a good artist." Difference is so often equated with decline that to deny or subvert audience expectations (whether re: genre conventions or relative to one's past work or whatever it may be) is almost always to risk their displeasure, yet from the artist's perspective such a reception must seem a profound failure of imagination and sympathy—to the truly engaged and searching artist, how boring, on the contrary, must resting on one's laurels be? "Art demands of us that we shall not stand still," said Beethoven upon completing some of his last string quartets. Novelist J. M. Coetzee has casually theorized a view of "a life in art, schematically, in two or perhaps three stages. In the first you find, or pose for yourself, a great question. In the second you labor away at answering it. And then, if you live long enough, you come to the third stage, when the aforesaid great question begins to bore you, and you need to look elsewhere." Yet even those artists whose careers seem to follow a largely linear trajectory, or whose late work seems to represent a return to their artistic roots, are inherently experiencing changes that worm their way into the fabric of their later work. Repetition or recapitulation are never simple matters; even if, say, a filmmaker were to make the same exact movie with the same exact script, cast, crew, etc. one after another, they wouldn't be the same because of the way time, environment, mood, or a whole host of other intangible factors affect the way artistic decisions are made. (Do the same experiment, but 10 or 20 years apart, and the impossibility of true repetition becomes even more obvious.) More fascinatingly, for the principles behind late style, is the way artists change and stay the same simultaneously—or to invoke Willem de Kooning's koan, the way "You have to change to stay the same." Complex and mysterious though the idea of continuity of self may be, it's the perspective of someone who both is and is not the person they were when they made their earlier work that lends late art its captivating relationship to both itself and its place within an overall body of work. For sometimes hiding behind the veneer of an ostensible late decline may really be a renewal, in new and unfamiliar terms, of the very ideas that animated that artist's beloved earlier work.

One of the most prevalent beliefs about late style, as it is casually discussed on a work-by-work basis as well as in its historical theorization, is that late work somehow represents the "essence" of an artist's work—a profound distillation of their career-long concerns into its simplest or most primal form, often communicated via a "stripped-down" version of their stylistic palette. Meditative and minimalistic, these works are thought to transcend the poverty of their surfaces to offer a kind of summative synthesis of their creator's body of work. Technique is looser; presentation is economical; realism becomes insignificant; detail is traded for overall effect; and the soul of the artist finds its plainest, least ornamented expression. Rodin, faced with the late works of Rembrandt, talked about "the kind of simplification in which there is true grandeur." For a cinematic example, Richard Brody categorizes Michael Mann's *Ferrari* (2023) as "the kind of purified, rarified film that major filmmakers make late in their careers, in which they get to the heart of the matter plainly and present their subjects unadorned and unamplified." As both a summing-up and a distillation of essence, some have characterized late style as a kind of combination or synthesis of an artist's early and mature styles. "If… youth is built on rebellion (antithesis) while adultness constructs a mature thesis," writes Amir Cohen-Shalev, "then 'old age style' may be the synthesis of both, or perhaps even more than a synthesis, a juxtaposition of two antithetical polarities that do not combine or blend, but rather keep their indispensable essences intact. This is what makes works of old age style so wondrously difficult to define with existing disciplinary and critical tools." No doubt this emphasis on late works as representative of "essence," or other such metaphysical catch-words, stems from late style's association with death. Proximity to the end, whether known or merely suspected, is thought to pressurize an artist's creativity into the inspired expression of what has mattered, what does matter, the most to them. "To the young *Memento Mori* is never more than a boring cliché," says Thomas Dormandy. "To the old the approach of death can add new urgency to thought, action and prayer. In many ways, some obvious and some less so, changed perceptions are reflected in their creations." Yet as Adorno and Said suggest, because art cannot die, death can only be refracted by it rather than reflected in it; this psychological interpretation of late style cannot, therefore, fully explain the discordant elements one finds in it. I would argue that though the increased awareness of death plays an indisputable role in catalyzing late style, nothing so simple or shallow as "Oh, the artist is getting older and must be thinking about death" can explain the complex resonances of late art. It's an idea in play, to at least some degree, but perhaps it's more a result of older patterns of thought butting up against a changed world—wherein the friction created conjures a metaphor, both abstract and tangible, for the more consequential and concrete life-death binary.

Whatever the case may be, the expectation for late art to meaningfully wrestle with, or at least obliquely comment upon, the cold hard facts of death is almost certainly born partly from audiences' pressing desire to make sense of their *own*, or another's, mortality. Unfortunately, this expectation is often responsible for what you might call the *narrativizing* of late style—the intentional or unintentional rewriting, simplifying, or overinterpretation of late art/careers in order to make them mean more, or other, than they actually do. This could mean reading a work as the Artist's Final Vision™ when it was never intended as such (rarely do artists know for certain what their last work is going to be), or it could mean the deliberate obfuscation of historical chronology to either lend credence to a specific interpretation—that *The Tempest* was Shakespeare's last play and an implicit farewell to playwriting, for example (in truth he subsequently co-authored multiple plays with John Fletcher before his death)—or to navigate around seemingly awkward incongruities—an early biographer of Henrik Ibsen, for instance, "had such a hard time digesting the master's apparent inconsistencies of plot structure and style in his last play [1899's *When We Dead Awaken*] that he 'adjusted' the playwright's biography so that his stroke occurred prior to the writing of the play, and not, as the case was, a year after," as Amir Cohen-Shalev relays. The problem is that the messy contingencies of life and artistic expression are constantly complicating what we might prefer to remain simple overarching narratives. Rather than embracing them in all their complexity, it's easier by far to pick and choose particular works and events as representative and ignore or be dismissive of whatever doesn't "fit." At times it's a serious case of critical wish fulfilment deployed to paper over dissonances, at others it's a deliberate move made for the sake of neatness and thematic maximalization—take, for example, Harold Bloom's *Till I End My Song: A Gathering of Last Poems* (2010), where he confesses to be collecting not "last" poems technically speaking but rather later poems from authors that more fittingly resonate with the *idea* of personal or universal lastness. The use of late style as a narrativizing tool has also faced criticism when it comes to marketing, especially in the art world where the conferral of the "late style" tag can add significant value, critically or financially, to a work of art. The praise bestowed upon a Rembrandt self-portrait considered exemplary of his late style in one gallery, for example, wasn't shared by another self-portrait held in a different gallery—until, that is, a "cleaning showed that it too was painted in the last year of his life." Also questioned has been the trend of selling off paintings found in an artist's studio after their death; what might be unfinished works, or mere sketches, become marketable via the application of the late style label— a situation in which "the predication of lateness enhances the aesthetic significance of all work so described simply by association with that same pantheon," per McMullan and Smiles. No doubt knowledge of the lateness of a late work primes us to feel or notice things about it that we might not if deprived of that particular context. That's often an unavoidable necessity—art isn't experienced in a vacuum, and context always helps in understanding a work relative to its author and era—yet we should be careful not to flatten the complexities of an artist's late period for the purposes of drawing a neat line through it, nor to let the connotations and associations of the late style label stand in for the actual task of grappling with a given late work or late period in all its individual is-ness. The fact is that "perfect" career arcs just aren't common (if they exist at all), and late works are rarely the summative statements one might like them to be. But this doesn't stop either the arcs or the works from being interesting; in fact, it arguably makes them more so, and all the unique ways a career or an individual work zigs and zags are great ins for reckoning with what's specifically fascinating about them. McMullan and Smiles again:

> In depending on a certain transcendent understanding of lateness, critics tend to sideline or exclude the contingencies involved in the production of late work. Yet it can be argued that it is contingency, not transcendence, that is a, if not the, defining factor of late style, and if we ignore it we may well end up denying to artists in old age the actual nature of their achievement; perhaps, in fact, we should redefine old-age style as something which is directly or indirectly the product of the adjustments and collaborations necessary for creative artists in old age, not something that exists despite such contingencies.[23]

---

[23] McMullan elsewhere voices concern over the self-conscious narrativizing of late style by artists themselves and the way work on late style can result in "critical complicity with authorial self-fashioning." If I merely gloss over this in a footnote it's because I don't find McMullan's point here particular compelling—that is, that "there has not, in other words, been an innocent, uncomplicit late phase for two centuries." I think he overestimates the number of artists who deliberately shape their late careers in this way, or who even have the luxury to do so, and even if what he says is true I don't buy that it matters in a way damaging to late style as a concept (at least as I've redefined it). That one artist thinks about and intentionally self-fashions their late style, and another artist doesn't care to think about it

Emphasizing contingency over transcendence is what keeps individual artists from floating up into a great undifferentiable blob of "lateness and greatness," just as it keeps us productively earth-bound in the way we engage with lateness in art in our own day-to-day lives. "Late style may be the visual expression of what it feels like to face the end," writes Max Norman, "—or it may be nothing more than a critic's fantasy, a by-product of our hunger for hidden meanings, narrative closure, and valedictory statements. More likely, it is both at once: the subjective expression of an artist, viewed subjectively. That's why lateness means something, if it means anything at all, only in our time-bound experience of late works."

By redefining late style as, essentially, whatever comes from lateness—instead of a host of vague, generalizing descriptors—the products of lateness can thrive in their individuality, without needing to *be* or *do* anything in particular in order to qualify. Historically, an artist isn't granted a "late style" unless their work displays a distinct shift involving the introduction of new stylistic or thematic features, clearly demarcated by what scholars call a "caesura" (in poetry, a pause or break). Said talks about "the way in which the work of some great artists and writers acquires a new idiom towards the end of their lives." This new idiom marks the late work as separate from the early or mature, as either a new phase or as a kind of coda to the artistic career. Thus artists who lack any distinctive turn in their art in the back half of their careers, though they may have late works, are traditionally denied a late *style*—a denial often correlated with a failure to be considered as belonging to the highest tier of artists. However, a certain distinctiveness could be argued to be inherent in the late work of all artists as, again, each new work is inherently different because of the constantly changing world in which it is created by the artist who in turn is constantly changing in relation to that world. It *is* enough to simply get older and make more things, to simply age and continue expressing

---

at all, isn't relevant other than as it pertains to individual accounts of each individual artist's late period.

yourself, dramatic shifts or not; whatever the style of those works is, that's the late style—by virtue of the shifting context of their creation, no matter if defined more by continuity or caesura, they are different. If late style is typically linked with biographical criticism, then I defend that association by the simple fact that, to the degree that a human being's life is the layering of all their previous thoughts and experiences through time, one's late style is the result of a lifetime of pruning and adding and shifting and transforming and connecting and etc. Late style cannot just be one's style, as is, like a youthful style is closer to being, but must necessarily be a style that has been *evolved into*. We can perhaps most easily see the way lateness asserts itself via the mere temporal slippage of context, and the way artists consciously remold themselves (and/or unconsciously become remolded) as a reaction to that, by looking at late works that partake in the same basic content or "world" of works created by the same artist years earlier. In film and television, two of the most instructive examples are George Lucas's *Star Wars* prequels (1999-2005) and David Lynch's *Twin Peaks: The Return* (2017)—Lucas's trilogy for its recontextualization two decades later of the original films in the new playground of digital cinema, and Lynch's series for its drawn-out subversion and expansion of the '90s show's televisual sandbox into even darker and more absurd directions, also rendered via the new textures of digital moving-image surfaces.[24] The existence of prior works from which these later efforts blossomed makes especially obvious their status as late objects, yet their profound idiosyncrasies make it nigh impossible to generalize about late style beyond that.

––––––––––

[24] There's so much more to be said about these two works—so much more—but suffice it to say their pride of place in wider cultural discussions (the *Star Wars* prequels especially), combined with their obvious lateness as remarked on above, make them my go-to examples when trying to explain late style in film to the uninitiated. *Twin Peaks: The Return* also brings up questions about the role television and streaming have played in the history of late style as additional or alternative avenues, with different degrees of prestige, for film artists expressing themselves outside of a strictly theatrical context.

The unavoidably problematic nature of a universalized late style should, by this point, be clear. Not only are the descriptions commonly attributed to late work potentially contradictory, the words and phrases associated with them are often so vague and abstract as to lose almost all meaning without concrete referents; those who use them run the risk of descending into jargon or quasi-mysticism, yielding little in the way of substantive insight. And then, of course, there are always counterexamples: if one were to posit as a universal late style trait for film, say, the tendency to "strip-down" formally, for every example of radical formal spareness like Eastwood's *Juror #2* or William Friedkin's *The Caine Mutiny Court-Martial* (2023), there's a counterexample like the liquid digital maximalism of Steven Spielberg's *Ready Player One* (2018)[25] or James Cameron's dedication to ever-bigger and more incursive tunnelings into his original 3D fantasy worlds in his 2020s *Avatar* sequels. For Linda and Michael Hutcheon, "no generalized late-style discourse can encompass all the variety of individual careers, creative work, and reception. These could be unified only by a critical agenda that ignores diversity and complexity in the name of ideology or aesthetics." So when we talk about late style, then—redefined under the umbrella of lateness, all individual diversity maintained—we are in fact always talking about late styles, plural. In truth there are as many late styles as there are late artists; indeed, there are even as many late styles as there are late *works*, as no two late works by the same artist are exactly the same. "Any counter-measure to" universalizations, writes Gordon McMullan, "must therefore dwell on the specifics of a given late manner. What is needed are accounts of late styles that do not resolve into easy generalisations." Late styles come in all shapes and sizes; the only thing they necessarily have in common is, simply, lateness itself (to differing degrees). If we can keep the category of late

---

[25] I credit a fair amount of my original realization that late style couldn't have universal traits to something tweeted casually by Neil Bahadur on March 29, 2020: "I love how everyone else late style is 'minimalism!' and Spielberg's is like 'but what if the camera... could fly.'"

style at all, it's largely as a signal to be open and attentive to the way time and context act on the artist and how the artist reacts back—how lateness engenders difference, not necessarily decline—and to use that awareness to be maximally alert to the specificity of the particular late art at hand as, then or now, a present-tense expression of that particular artist. This isn't to say that all work done on late style previously has to be thrown out the window. The truth is that many of the descriptors frequently applied to late style *do*, in fact, often appear in late works. *Often*, not always—and if we keep that distinction there are certainly relevant groupings of late works one could make that possess certain traits, just as there are certainly relevant groupings of late works one could make that possess opposite ones. Part of what may be interesting about one artist's late style is the lack of a trait that often appears in other late work, or the appearance of a trait that other late work often lacks. It may be useful to reference the series of binaries that some scholars have compiled in pointing out the contradictions of different late style discourses, such as those of McMullan—personal/impersonal, involuntary/knowing, serene/irascible, childlike/difficult, archaic/proleptic, completion/supplement—or of Sandro Zanetti: caesura/continuity, senescence/rejuvenation, madness/lucidity, revision/innovation, fragmentation/unification, completion/supplement. Joseph N. Straus has suggested from his own categories (shared earlier) that, given these contradictions, it

> might be useful to understand late style as descriptive of a group of works that share at least some of these characteristics, but not necessarily all of them. We might wish to speak of late styles (in the plural), with variation depending on the composer and the work and, to a significant degree, on the temperament and interests of the critic. It would be unlikely for any single work to exhibit all these characteristics, but a late-style work would necessarily have most of them. Or we might simply assume that late-style works may involve internal contradictions, so that inherent

tensions among these different characteristics are themselves a marker of stylistic lateness.

Adapting this idea to our own definition of late style, there are clearly still valuable paths to be taken in comparing and contrasting different late works under existing categories and against existing binaries, or in sussing out interesting internal or external frictions individual works may have relative to such taxonomies. Conceptions of late style proposed by previous thinkers can be applied wherever and whenever to artists who seem to benefit by the application of such classifications; on a case-by-case basis, it might indeed be fruitful to talk about a more specific taxonomy of lateness—"Adornian" lateness, perhaps, or "Saidian." The point is to stay away from false generalizations on a large scale while otherwise attacking individual late works with absolute freedom: whatever weapon pries the most interest and edification from a work, use it.

The final point to be emphasized in our redefinition of late style follows on from this message of freedom to proclaim that we are also free to consider through the lens of late style any and all artists—not just an elite group who meet some criteria of canonical excellence. The historical tendency to crown only the creative elect with the supposed glory of the late style label has not only prevented the thorough study of less canonical late artists, but it's also gone hand-in-hand with the problematic assumption that the acquired taste of some kind of cultural elite is needed to recognize the profundity of such late style achievements. "An air of connoisseurship and good taste invariably clings to the idea of late style," writes Robert Spencer, and thus, he goes on to say, "Critics preoccupied by the manner of important artists in the last period of their life frequently substitute a really attentive engagement with aesthetic form and an equally sensitive scrutiny to form's manifold indebtedness to context for encomia to the artist's singularity, airy generalizations about the work, and predictable references to the composer or poet or whoever raging against the dying of the light, in Dylan Thomas's by now wearingly familiar phrase." Late style has always been uncomfortably intertwined with the myth of genius—of Great Men transcending material contingencies to express lofty sentiments with superhuman ability (and, per late style, defying age to do so)—and the association hasn't done late style any favors when "brought before the jury of theoretical or posttheoretical scepticism," as McMullan terms it. Yet rather than perpetuate this myth, and instead restore creativity to its rightful place among the muck and mud of (beautifully) contingent human expression, our new understanding of late style opens it up to everyone in order to create a field of inquiry with room, again, for as many late styles as there are late artists.[26] Under our understanding of lateness, it should be clear that to allow a late style to every single artist doesn't water down the concept of late style to pointlessness any more than allowing artistic achievement to any artist waters down the concept of art. The opposite, elitist conceptualization has choked off unexplored paths of late style appreciation for too long; in fact, that cinema has been denied a place in most late style studies to date has itself likely been a consequence of the condescension toward film as too unserious, too popular, or too commercial an art form. Yet even within film-specific communities where the idea of late style (named as such or not) has been in play, a hierarchical elitism of their own has centered respected art-house filmmakers in these discussions while leaving neglected vast swathes of the medium's artists: Hollywood-centric directors, non-canonical international filmmakers, genre craftsmen, underground, avant-garde, or non-narrative artists, as well as women, other minority filmmakers, and generally just about everyone not traditionally considered an "auteur."[27] Even

---

[26] It should be said that the term "genius" needn't become totally useless—for example, to casually use it to mean an artist with a particularly profound ability to express themselves in interesting and edifying ways isn't cause for alarm—as long as we stay away from the unrealistic mythologizing of past usages.

[27] A recent *Screen Slate* article demonstrates the kind of late oddities that remain totally off-the-map of distribution and discourse, centering German actor and director Ulli Lommel's final film *America Land of the FreeKS* (2018) and asking a question few if any have thought to ask:

"bad" filmmakers, as so considered by any given person or by consensus, can have a late style—and to admit as much isn't to upend any sacred hierarchies: just as the work of some artists is more interesting than the work of other artists, so too are some late styles more interesting than others. Naturally the more interesting ones are going to receive the bulk of attention, for obvious and understandable reasons,[28] but that doesn't prohibit the less interesting ones from existing; a study of an example of the latter could even shed light on just why an example of the former is as interesting as it is. It's all relative: some films are more "late" than others, some filmmakers are more interesting than others, and some late films are more interesting than other late films. What's thrilling about late style as an approach, then, is the chance to articulate the nuances of all this on a case-by-case basis, via sustained engagement with individual films and artists, and in the process to discover the too-long-hidden riches of late cinema.

"With 'late style' discourse escalating in recent years, virtually everyone knows what 'late Eastwood' or 'late Malick' means aesthetically, but what about 'late Lommel'? It's impossible to say, as a majority of his final works remain completely unavailable and shrouded in mystery."

[28] Including the fact that many of the less interesting filmmakers lack a strong personal style in the way that the more interesting ones do, making it difficult to trace any significant evolutions in their work—or if there are evolutions, whether they can even be reasonably credited to them. Thus a less idiosyncratic or engaged artist, though in a later phase of their career, surprises no one in producing art less demonstrably "late" than a sui generis master does, "late" though it may technically be.

4

"Official" late style history's relationship with cinema has not been a very intimate one. As a relatively young art, it had neither the prestige nor the history to be a major player in the late style discussions of the first half of the 20th century. Having then spent the century's second half simply fighting the battle to be even considered a serious art on par with the others—cinema's eventual adoption into academia in the late 1960s seeming to signal significant progress in that direction—subsidiary concerns like the role cinema might be able to play in late style studies (itself hardly a robust or organized area of research) weren't exactly at the top of anyone's mind. Besides, the physical and logistical demands of filmmaking perhaps seemed to eliminate cinema's older artists from late style considerations ahead of time, the concept being more obviously suited to the private, stationary acts of writing, composing, or painting. Yet the tides of an auteurist cinephilia, catalyzed in France and later sweeping the English world and beyond, put cinematic debates over authorship in implicit conversation with late style concerns from the very beginning; that the first golden age of late style in film—cinema's old guard making their final films as new blood in the form of Hollywood's youth invasion and various international new waves flooded in—coincided with these debates, and made the expression of filmmakers amidst shifting contexts and old age a core cinephilic concern, certainly amplified the late style angle of it all. Although no one—at least that I know of—put any of it in those specific terms. Thus why attempting to study or trace late style through film history, as an idea, is an extremely daunting task—because it largely wasn't one. Unnamed, however, it still finds itself (if only in spirit) scattered throughout the history of film literature wherever specific late films are discussed, and on occasion a writer may gesture toward a generalization about late films as a broader category. In a *New York Post* review of Alfred Hitchcock's *Family Plot* (1976), for example, critic Frank Rich makes the suggestion that, "Like many modern painters (such as Klee and Kandinsky), great movie directors often become more intrigued by the abstract possibilities of style as they get older—and Hitchcock's other '70s films, *Topaz* and *Frenzy* (like the late films of such other one-time storytellers as Ford, Hawks, Renoir, Buñuel, and Chaplin), showed open disdain for many of the narrative conventions that had served his movies in the past." Lacking the time and resources to scour everything written about every late film, however, I make no claim to have discovered every time such an aside may have been made, and a more exhaustive history of late style film criticism certainly remains to be written. What I do know is that, from my experience, extant writing about late films is representative more often than not of the kind of attitudes that late style thinking, as I've outlined it, aims strictly to avoid. Yet there also exists plenty of film literature (and programming) that, merely by taking honest aim at understanding and appreciating the late film at hand, has been doing the things that late style criticism should do without ever needing to reference "late style" as a specific term or concept, and such work is a worthy foundation for our own. And as late style has been repopularized in the 21st century, more lines are being drawn between the two subjects in both academic research and the wider culture. Amir Cohen-Shalev, a prominent name in contemporary late style studies, has for one consistently made it a point to include cinema in his field of examples, and writes appealingly of how "the applicability of the notion of old age style to cinema provides, I believe, an unanswered, innovative, and challenging exploration that is of interest to students and scholars of cinema, humanistic gerontology, psychology of art, sociology of old age and popular culture, and the public at large." In film studies, Joe McElhaney's book *The Death of Classical Cinema: Hitchcock, Lang, Minnelli* (2006) has centered ideas of lateness—specifically re: the conversation auteurist classical cinema was having with new modernist trends in the 1960s—and the way cinephilic approaches can spark productive reappraisals: "While the cinephilia that informs this book has always been fixated on narrative cinema above all others, the category of the 'old man's film' has always been a central aspect to it: works dismissed at the time of their initial release because they were thought to be indications that greatness was now eluding the once-great, works that the cinephile transforms through the process of reading." Even Edward Said, although it's not central to his writings on late style, touches on cinema in ways largely unavailable to Adorno[29] via his discussion of Luchino Visconti's 1963 adaptation of Giuseppe Tomasi di Lampedusa's novel *The Leopard.* The film "inaugurated the final phase of its director's career," Said writes, marking a "puzzling break in aesthetic continuity" that retreats "back into a more sophisticated and refined version of an older form, the grand historical epic associated with Hollywood films of the 1940s and 1950s, using as his subject matter a sort of nostalgia for an old class that is threatened by the depredations of both popular revolution and the new bourgeois order." But *The Leopard* "is not in the end a Hollywood film at all but the work of a late-style artist indebted to aspects of Wagner, Proust, and of course Lampedusa himself."

As a technologically-forward medium, however, cinema has faced transformational shifts at an expedited rate relative to the other arts, and despite currently having a history no longer than the average lifespan of two men laid back-to-back, the medium has undergone so many evolutions that the idea of cinema having essentially speed-run the traditional classi-

---

[29] Although movies were part of Adorno's critique of the culture industry, and an oft-quoted snippet from his book of autobiographical fragments *Minima Moralia* seems to suggest a deep antagonism toward the medium ("Every visit to the cinema leaves me, against all my vigilance, stupider and worse"), Adorno's negative stance towards cinema has been overplayed. Good friends with Fritz Lang, Adorno saw potential and possibility in the medium relative to, say, television, and didn't speak from a place of unfamiliarity. "The current belief that Adorno's elitist preference for high culture implied a contempt for the film as an art form is contradicted not only by the value he placed on Chaplin but also by the esteem in which he held Lang," writes his biographer Detlev Claussen. "Film had been a prominent feature in the Adorno household from the 1920s on. He went regularly to the cinema with his aunt Agathe and was able to discuss films on equal terms with the much older Siegfried Kracauer."

cism-to-modernism path of the other arts is a common sugges-tion.[30] This constant shifting of film's industrial context makes particularly relevant the vision offered by late style, as film artists of earlier contexts enter and adapt (or don't) to later ones; indeed, the two golden ages of late style I'm proposing both come at two of the most significant transitional points in the medium's history. "The question of late style is especially fraught in art forms like cinema," wrote James Morrison in 2015,

> that are industry-based and typically governed by organized institutions that tightly regulate accepted norms, the Hollywood cinema remaining the paragon. Certainly three turning points in Hollywood history, the coming of sound, the collapse of the studio system, and the transition to digital technologies, at a stroke (or strokes of varying duration, the last one still pain-fully underway) rendered any previous style that managed to survive such shifts 'late' in some literal sense. One need only revisit Griffith's sound films to encounter the fascinating spectacle of a master out of his element, producing work of a stunning discor-dancy.

The introduction of sound in the late 1920s, like no other turning point in film history, irrevocably stamped almost the entirety of cinema as "late"—and this not even 15 years after the standardization of the feature-length film. As the first blow to the very foundations of how motion pictures were made, it foreshadowed the way cinema was always going to be changing in ways that simultaneously retracted the avail-ability of some tools while offering the use of new, different ones. Many filmmakers adapted themselves to the new sound regime—even if belatedly, in Charlie Chaplin's case—but for

---

[30] Mind you, to emphasize too strongly some neat classical-modern division in film history is to make things, well, too neat; for one thing, it ignores the way that silent cinema was very much attuned to the modernist currents of its era.

some, like D. W. Griffith, Buster Keaton, or Erich von Stroheim, the paradigm shift contributed to career lane-switches and/or forced early retirements. In the case of F. W. Murnau, killed in an automobile accident in 1931 before ever making the switch to sound, no connections can be made other than tragically metaphorical ones. We can perhaps point to 1948 as a year of symbolic significance, marking both the end of the early sound era and the beginning of cinema's first late golden era (when the oldest of the silent-era directors began to stare down the final decade or so of their careers, just as stirrings of a new kind of cinema started making waves in postwar Europe); it's the year that both D. W. Griffith and Sergei Eisenstein died, two founding masters of silent cinema and, along with Murnau, the acknowledged progenitors of so much of extant film grammar. Their deaths signaled an end-of-an-era of sorts (Ernst Lubitsch had died in late 1947, too), and the difficulties they'd had in making films after the coming of sound, albeit in different cultural and industrial contexts, anticipated the challenges to be faced by older directors at the end of the classical era in the 1950s and '60s. André Bazin had written in 1947 of Eisenstein's *Ivan the Terrible* (1944) in the context of his contemporary Carl Theodor Dreyer's *Day of Wrath* (1946) as films that weren't "with it," and the latter as "a film simultaneously anachronistic and an ageless masterpiece. Unlike literature, a more evolved art, for example, where the writer can remain faithful to his style and technique throughout his life, the filmmaker does not enjoy the same freedom."

Older filmmakers' responses to that lack of freedom make up the fascinating history of the first golden age of late style as it played out during the end of film's classical era over the next two or three decades. The changes affecting mid-century cinema, particularly in Hollywood, in many cases revoked old freedoms while granting new ones at the same time. A non-exhaustive list of factors involved: the Supreme Court's Paramount Decree in 1948 that stripped studios of their exclusive exhibition practices; increased unionization; new independences gained by stars; the rise of television; the introduction of new approaches to screen acting; an increasingly relevant teen culture; the popularization of color film; the adoption of stereo sound; experiments with 3D; and the introduction of widescreen formats, often tied to large productions or shot-on-location epics, designed to lure back audiences lost to TV. The discordancy of studio craftsmen who'd worked decades in the system doing black-and-white pictures in Academy ratio since the silent days now assigned to pictures almost twice as wide and in beaming color was obvious, and filmmakers like Henry King, Raoul Walsh, William Wellman, Michael Curtiz, King Vidor, and Frank Borzage found themselves as old dogs learning new tricks. Their films of the 1950s and early 1960s possess the inherent fascination of that discordancy, but careful attention also reveals how they nonetheless continued to find avenues to put their personal stamp on works despite perhaps less-than-artistically-ideal circumstances. By the 1960s studio contracting had largely given way to independent producing, and filmmakers accustomed to the solidity of studio operations were forced to navigate the new world of developing and packaging ideas, finding financing, and procuring stars that hadn't previously been within the scope of their work. Film production became a more global enterprise, too, given the influx of foreign-language films into domestic markets post-WWII and the subsequent rebuilding of international film industries no longer as reliant on U.S. productions. Hollywood products were increasingly being filmed in Rome, and American directors were taking work in British studios as part of the diversification of cinematic production from the late 1950s onwards.[31] Peter Bogdanovich has written of a "golden age of movies" which by his calculations began in 1912 and, having lasted a perfect 50 years, ended in 1962; for him this era's final film was John Ford's *The Man Who Shot Liberty Valance* (1962), a kind of requiem for cinema, and—no surprise—a late film that allegorizes an America of

---

[31] Eric Marsh has compiled a fascinating list of films Hollywood directors made in Britain stretching from 1957 to 1979, many of which lend themselves to readings through the late style lens, on Letterboxd: https://letterboxd.com/marshlandz/list/classic-hollywood-directors-making-boring/.

false legends and lost ideals and which, initially, "was generally dismissed by critics and public as a weak, minor Ford Western." We could perhaps pair it with Vincente Minnelli's *Two Weeks in Another Town,* another 1962 film that, per Joe McElhaney's centering of it in his book on the subject, allegorizes the death of classical cinema via the story of an international film shoot. The studio system's decline also seemed to coincide with a period of experimentation and subversion from many of Hollywood's best filmmakers, perhaps spurred on by the general feeling of collapse within the industry. As Laura Mulvey writes,

> Some directors who had aged alongside of cinema itself, who knew that their own days and those of their industry were numbered, made genre films that were darker than before, emotionally contorted, with haunted characters, challenging narrative convention, overthrowing or ironizing the happy end. An early example would be Fritz Lang's *Rancho Notorious* (1952) but would also include Raoul Walsh's *The Revolt of Mamie Stover* (1956), Douglas Sirk's *Written on the Wind* (1956), Anthony Mann's *Man of the West* (1958), John Ford's *The Man Who Shot Liberty Valance* (1962), and Alfred Hitchcock's *Vertigo* (1958). These directors, having spent most of their lives negotiating with an iron production system dedicated to standardization, achieved a transcendence of genre while still working within it, verging, in some cases, into self-reflexivity.

Perhaps Hollywood (or even the medium itself) had entered a kind of industry-wide late style, having been around long enough to begin reflecting on itself from a perspective that was knowingly near the end; this does parallel Karina Longworth's demarcation point for individual filmmakers in her series "The Old Man Is Still Alive," where the age of 60 is posited as the point "where things start to fall off and get weird."

Things generally got even weirder as the 1970s dawned. Slackening censorship across the 1960s had finally been formalized in 1968 with the end of the Production Code; directors that had made one or more films almost every year for decades slowed their pace to only one every two or three years. Quentin Tarantino marks 1970 as the year in which the "New Hollywood *was* Hollywood," and (late) leftovers from a previous era's sensibilities like Alfred Hitchcock's *Topaz* (1969), Billy Wilder's *The Private Life of Sherlock Holmes*, Vincente Minnelli's *On a Clear Day You Can See Forever*, George Stevens' *The Only Game in Town*, William Wyler's *The Liberation of L.B. Jones*, and Howard Hawks' *Rio Lobo* (all 1970) landed with a thud upon release in the contemporary film landscape. James Morrison notes that "hindsight reveals that the rise of New Hollywood in the late sixties, virtually overnight, cast an enervating dusk on every facet of the industry." While some filmmakers tried to find a place in the new state of things (or desperately tried to hold on to their place in the old one), others contented themselves with a place far outside of the Hollywood halls they once haunted. Andy Rector writes of a time in the early 1980s when *Cahiers du cinéma* assigned Bill Krohn to find the most interesting filmmaking happening on the margins of American cinema and, dissatisfied with "an institutionalized avant-garde," focused in on former Hollywood directors still working in old age: "The filmmakers on the margins who were found not to be stagnant, or 'D.O.A.', were the aged masters of this young art, who in their late films of the 70s and 80s were using images and sounds, biography and reality—narratively, formally, politically—in more complex ways, and also proving themselves more radical masters of their own lives, their own production, and old age." Late experiments with the essay and interview film by King Vidor, Nicholas Ray's *We Can't Go Home Again*, Orson Welles' *The Other Side of the Wind*, and Budd Boetticher's totally independent mid-'80s work with video are all highlighted as examples; we could potentially add the short films Douglas Sirk was making with German students at the end of the 1970s. But even the work of older filmmakers who remained in Hollywood had a fruitful strangeness and off-beat sensibility that sprang at least partly from the kind of in-house exile such directors were working from, and looking back we can see how such films productively challenge common narratives of late style. "In simpler times," writes James Morrison, late style

> meant ripened wisdom, consummate mastery, an apotheosis of serene self-consciousness so fully assured that it rose unfettered from the anxious morbidity of the more youthful forms of introspection. But if we turn our gaze from such a bastion of the Late Style as, say, the Renaissance—new in concept, old in fashion—to, say, the more dubious precincts of Hollywood cinema, we are likely to find that it means something else. Anyone who has studied the careers of Ford, Cukor, Hawks, or Minnelli—or even of Elia Kazan or Robert Aldrich—knows that they had their full-fledged apprenticeships, intern work as technicians, for instance, or early periods as assistant directors. And anyone who's seen their major films of the studio era will likely grant that these films constitute, at least, yeoman work of some distinction. But how can one witness [Ford's] *Seven Women* [1966] or *Cheyenne Autumn* [1964], [Cukor's] *Justine* [1969] or *The Blue Bird* [1976], [Hawks'] *Man's Favorite Sport?* [1964] or *Rio Lobo,* [Minnelli's] *Goodbye Charlie* [1964] or *A Matter of Time* [1976], [Kazan's] *The Arrangement* [1969] or [Aldrich's] *Twilight's Last Gleaming* [1977], to name only a few, without feeling that one is being confronted by a *late* style, to be sure—but one marked, not so much by grace or supple maturation, as by a sort of elegiac clumsiness, a fully wrought sensibility daunted by a theoretical modishness, a dirgelike, ungainly straining for newfangled effects that remain in view but beyond reach, a near hysterical effort to appear *current,* or at least remotely timely. Yet the feeling that these films conjure, of

being both authoritative and weirdly inept, cannot be put down to questions of mere fashion. In its way, each of these movies combine[s] a sort of backward mastery with a timorous self-reflexivity. Even in the worst of them, a residual technical skill—as in the uses of color in *Man's Favorite Sport?* or of widescreen composition in *A Matter of Time*—emboldens their retrogressive leanings, and the final effect is of a kind of doddering grace, a euphuistic refinement. Obviously, what's on view in these films is the spectacle of studio-trained directors working in an era just past studio dominion; and, if for first-generation American filmmakers, a definitive "late style" emerged in the clunky relics of the early years of sound, like Griffith's feeble, archaic *Abraham Lincoln* [1930], then for the second or third or fourth generations, it coalesced in the utterly distinctive ambience, at once ripened and stunted, of these films by the aging Hollywood *auteurs* of the 1960s or 1970s—poststudio, preindie, after a mythical past and before a dreaded future, stranded, grounded, upon the same irreconcilable present we all inhabit.

In other words, many late films of the era seemed to walk a line between unfashionable awkwardness and self-reflexive refinement but which, when taken as a whole, couldn't be reduced to either—or, as Morrison later puts it in the same piece, "how a perceived decrepitude or out-of-touchness could skirt autumnal ripeness or mastery." By the late 1960s thoroughly moved on from whatever paradigm had sustained these filmmakers previously, Hollywood wasn't exactly providing the freedom or resources needed to nourish a period of late mastery for them; in fact the industry's stubborn desire to fit the square pegs of older directors into the round holes of contemporary expectations merely accentuated whatever dissonances were causing the poor reception of most of their late films. But Orson Welles, long-aware on an intimate level with the way Hollywood stifled creative freedom, spoke adamantly in 1969 of how all the great directors' best work was still ahead of them. He and Peter Bogdanovich had gotten "on the subject of older directors," remembered the latter.

> I gave him a bleak rundown on their position in Hollywood. Orson was deeply affected, and the next day he said: "You told me about all these old directors whom people in Hollywood say are 'over the hill,' and it made me so sick, I couldn't sleep. I started thinking about all those conductors—Klemperer, Beecham, Toscanini—I can name almost a hundred in the last century—who were at the height of their powers after seventy-five. And were conducting at eighty. I think it's just terrible what happens to old people," Orson went on. "But the public isn't interested in that—never has been. That's why *Lear* has always been a play people hate.... And a king or a conductor or a director *can* go on—as long as there's no physical breakdown. It's only the *idea* in people's minds that will stop them.... And there are these *great* directors, all ready with their *best* work ahead of them—really their best. I believe that Jack Ford today given a script a little better than anything he's ever done—demanding more of him—would give us better pictures than he has ever made. Because it's only in your twenties and in your seventies and eighties that you do the greatest work.... The enemy of life is middle age. Youth and old age are great times—and we must treasure old age and give genius the capacity to function in old age—and not send them away...."[32]

But "age must pass as youth enters," to quote Chaplin's *Limelight* (1952), and what made the late work of older directors so apparently late was the massive influx of work by younger filmmakers being distributed at the same time.

---

[32] Welles would become increasingly aware of the nature of Lear's plight, and a project of *King Lear* was one of the last he attempted to get made before his death in 1985.

"Whereas many of the Great Masters continued to make films during the 1960s," writes Joe McElhaney, "the nature of the investigations of the New Wave and other art cinema practices are such that this recent work by the canonical 'first generation' of filmmakers was felt to suffer from historical dislocation by comparison." In the moment, while the hankering for newness and cinematic revolution was at its strongest, it's not difficult to imagine why most looked at the late films of the older generation and merely saw yesterday's news. But many of the new generation—especially the filmmakers of the French New Wave—didn't set out to erase the work done by the greats that came before them, but were instead explicitly inspired by it and riffed on it in appreciative homage. While, say, Roberto Rossellini was beginning to make pedagogic historical films for television for the final decade of his career, Jean-Luc Godard and Éric Rohmer were reaching back to the realist melodramas he'd made with Ingrid Bergman as inspiration for their own films; while Alfred Hitchcock tried to navigate executive and commercial pressures while making his last handful of films, François Truffaut and Claude Chabrol were explicitly drawing on his earlier moral thrillers for their own genre experiments. Many of the established French filmmakers Truffaut had singled out for praise in his explosive 1954 article "A Certain Tendency in French Cinema"—and which he and his friends were partly modeling their own careers on—were also still making films as the French New Wave began making and releasing their own: two Jean Renoir films accompanied Truffaut's *The 400 Blows* in the country's 1959's offerings, for example, and 1967 saw not only three Godard films but also, alongside them, Jacques Tati's late passion project *Playtime*. Part of what lends additional fascination to the late films of the 1950s, '60s, and '70s, then, is the way they exist in conversation—whether intentionally or inadvertently—with the films being made by those replacing them in the film-historical continuum. An e-mail conversation between film scholars and curators Miguel Marías and Peter von Bagh called "The Wondrous 60s" gives a glimpse of the extraordinary generational layering taking place at the time that made contemporary cinephilic filmgoing such a diverse and invigorating activity. They speak of five distinct generations of film-makers all making work at the same time, and how they "could impatiently and eagerly expect, and run to the premieres, or first showings, on one hand… of the late (and sometimes last) works" of John Ford, Yasujirô Ozu, Carl Theodor Dreyer, Jean Renoir, Fritz Lang, Leo McCarey, Frank Capra, Alfred Hitchcock, Howard Hawks, Raoul Walsh, Mikio Naruse, Henry King, Luis Buñuel, and Abel Gance; to "the works of maturity of the 'middle-aged'" like those of Otto Preminger, Robert Bresson, Akira Kurosawa, Michelangelo Antonioni, Federico Fellini, Robert Aldrich, Joseph Losey, Samuel Fuller, and Jean-Pierre Melville; and to "the revelation" of new film-makers like Jacques Rivette, Alain Resnais, Bernardo Berto-lucci, John Cassavetes, Jerry Lewis, Sam Peckinpah, Roman Polanski, Maurice Pialat, Andrei Tarkovsky, Stanley Kubrick, and Jean-Marie Straub and Danièle Huillet—to list only a few of the dozens upon dozens of names mentioned, from all over the world. While reactions to this diverse bunch of filmmakers from different points on the age spectrum naturally depended on one's personal proclivities, to those of a certain cinephile persuasion it was a treat to be able to hop from early films to late films to ones somewhere in the middle. Marías, contrary to the common retrospective view of the era as one of anxiety and change, talks about living through it "without any sort of anguish, tension, fear, uneasiness, discomfort or negative feel-ings. Rather than a rupture, the end of cinema or the start of some vague sort of revolution, we saw cinema well alive and plentiful and marching on…. I did not have the slightest diffi-culty in passing from *Gertrud* (Carl Theodor Dreyer, 1964) to *Bande à part* (Jean-Luc Godard, 1964)…. I recall it as a joyful triumphant moment of cinema throughout the world, the old filmmakers daring and wise, the young daring and confident and strong."

The ability to approach cinema this way—to face each work with present-tense interest merely as the new film from so-and-so, whether it was their first or 50th—was spawned in large part by the auteurist perspectives introduced in 1950s France via the *politique des auteurs*, later transplanted to the

English-speaking world as the "auteur theory." In an age in which the word "auteur" has been diluted of much of its original meaning (whether through co-option by branding and marketing departments or by sheer indiscriminate and ubiquitous usage, among other reasons), it can be difficult to recapture the way in which the idea, as first articulated by the young critics at *Cahiers du cinéma* and later in British and American publications, fundamentally altered how movies were viewed. Common textbook definitions of auteurism often define it as the assertion that the director is the primary author of a film akin to the way writers authored books or painters authored paintings; yet the idea that the director was the primary creative intelligence behind a film wasn't anything new in the 1950s, having long been the going assumption not only in previous French criticism but even in the advertising practices of silent-era Hollywood. What the early auteurists newly emphasized, rather, was a *way of looking*. "Auteurism said that film criticism as it was currently practiced was wrong," according to William Routt. "It said that film critics and reviewers had been deluded and were incapable of seeing what was most worth seeing." That directors working in collaborative industrial contexts could be artists on par with poets or composers was one thing, but what the younger French critics like Godard, Truffaut, Rohmer, Rivette, and Chabrol were really advocating for was a passionate intuitive relationship to films as the expressions of an artist's vision of the world. An auteur, to them, wasn't just a filmmaker whose personal signature could be found in each of their films, but one whose moral vision (articulated via mise-en-scène) resonated with the particular philosophical and aesthetic premises that nourished them. Yet the *politique des auteurs* was never a systematically theorized proposition, and was largely articulated via the critical encomiums they wrote about the films that moved them rather than by any logical statement of principles. Thus why auteurism's adoption by English-language critics likewise lacked totalizing coherence and also why, despite the translation of *politique des auteurs* into the more prosaic and ostensibly concrete term "auteur theory," the revolution offered by it nevertheless remained not a "systematic doctrine," per Routt, but primarily "a point of view or a critical *regard*." What may have seemed like near mysticism to the uninitiated—Hollywood genre filmmakers the equals of Dostoevsky or Picasso?—was to those primed by this way of looking the most obvious thing in the world, the evidence on the screen all the proof one needed. Yet this wasn't the result of brash contrarianism or undiscriminating youthful pretension; as Routt says, "this cannot be other than an act of intuition, resulting from [emphasis mine] *an application of intense and meticulous critical attention.*"

Coming as it did right alongside the first golden age of late style, auteurism became intimately connected with efforts to view the late works of aging directors in a positive light. Auteurism's intuition that an individual film could be seen as a synecdoche for a director's entire filmography made such works not discrete offerings in the flow of industrial entertainment but vital present-tense expressions of a specific cinematic world, arriving with the force of history and chronology behind it. And if filmmakers were artists, and films works of art, then late-career films derided as disposable, laughable, and out-of-touch commercial duds were actually objects worthy of serious consideration and appreciation. Early-career blindspots from such newly-minted auteurs as Alfred Hitchcock and Howard Hawks could now be filled in at college film societies, revival theaters, film museum retrospectives, or even at home as old movies began to circulate regularly on television, providing contextual grounding for their late counterparts. Writers associated with *Cahiers du cinéma* in particular became champions of old age; Rohmer paralleled the late work of Titian, Rembrandt, and Beethoven with the work of older directors like Jean Renoir in an attempt to "discover the virtues beneath [...] pseudofaults" in the "internal reasoning" of an artist's evolution (quoted in full earlier), and even the youngest critics like Serge Daney and Louis Skorecki, who traveled to California barely past their 20th birthdays to talk with many of Hollywood's aging figures, were self-professed "gerontophiles." "We were thrilled," Daney later wrote, with the late works of the great masters like Titian's last drawings, the solitude purged of style, the boldness in the midst of a certain obsolescence, a certain way of approaching a pure logic of cinema—and only cinema. *The 1,000 Eyes of Dr. Mabuse* [1960], *Gertrud, Seven Women*, like *Anatahan* [1953] or *A King in New York* [1957], are the films of old-timers, exposed to the condescendence of official criticism, running to their aid ready to fight for them. And the fact that even if today—given my age—I admit that there is often something essential in the first works of an auteur, I am still moved by the films of the old-timers: Kurosawa, Oliveira, Buñuel. At both ends of the chain, between the carelessness of a spoiled energy and the economy of a time that one can't afford to waste, there is the beauty of cinema, this art where the physical state of those who make it is so clear.

As the loves of the French auteurists trickled down to the filmmakers on the receiving end of it, either directly through interview contact or indirectly through word of mouth, it's interesting to note that many filmmakers were now making their late films with the knowledge of their new reputations amongst auteurists; although the effect on the actual late films was arguably minimal, reactions ranged from cool bemusement to sincere gratefulness, and a fascinating study could certainly be made of the intergenerational and largely cross-cultural dynamic of (sometimes mutual) appreciation going on in the era. Something happened when auteurist eyes fixed themselves on these autumnal creations, for "although the movement was youthful, impetuous, and romantic," writes James Naremore,

it was often dedicated to antique virtues and to praising the work of directors who were entering their twilight years. Josef von Sternberg's *Jet Pilot* (1957), Fritz Lang's *The Thousand Eyes of Dr. Mabuse* (1960), and Howard Hawks's *Red Line 7000* (1965) were all made during roughly the same period as the early films of the New Wave; but they occupied a world apart from both the current Hollywood hits and the new European art cinema, as if they were still clinging to dated formulas or dead modes of production. Few mainstream critics in the Anglo-Saxon world took them seriously, but the auteurists passionately embraced them, sometimes ranking them above the same directors' more celebrated films of the 1930s and '40s. One of the most sweetly charming features of auteurism lay in its love for old pros or cinematic father figures who were still alive, making unpretentious genre movies or quiet, meditative films such as Ford's *The Sun Shines Bright* (1953). Truffaut, who could be devastatingly sarcastic in some contexts, was quite touching when he spoke of such films, or when he used them to rebuke current fashions.

Even when auteurism faced a crisis in the late 1960s and 1970s as more political-analytical modes of reading films came into fashion, late films remained a site of interest and advocacy on the part of magazines like the newly Marxist-oriented *Cahiers*, often discussed, according to Daniel Fairfax, "for the way they shed light on the struggles experienced by these filmmakers to orient themselves to a situation in which many of the pre-established codes of Hollywood classicism—the 'rules of the game' that had governed the institution for five decades—were no longer operative."

Even if the word "auteur" has grown less useful in recent years, watered down by overuse and lacking its original distinctions, it nevertheless remains a foundational idea relevant to the way we view films. In truth, fealty to the exact way auteurism was understood by the *Cahiers* critics or by their English translators needn't be a sticking point; as long as we stay connected to the idea of auteurism as a way of looking, a way of seeing *more*, re: films as the expressions of individual artists, then there's no need to be pedantic about it nor to discard the whole concept as somehow outdated and regressive. Nuanced perspectives about the complexities of film production which incorporate the contributions of collaborators and crew, the role of genre, studio politics or aesthetics, industrial standards, cultural and economic factors, and more can sit side-by-side an understanding of films as, in the main, the expression of their directors. My personal policy with auteurism, as it is with late style as articulated earlier, is to simply extend it to absolutely everyone. But it's a matter of degree, relative to the specific situation of each individual production: everyone—from the writer, cinematographer, editor, and production designer to gaffers, grips, and greensmen—can claim authorship of a film to a greater or lesser degree; it just so happens that, usually, the director's slice of authorship is of a greater degree, and, say, the prop man's is of a lesser one. Which isn't to deny that a scenario may exist where a writer or a producer or a cinematographer or an actor, for example, is responsible for a greater portion of authorship than the director. But, again, it's all relative, and despite the collaborative nature of filmmaking it is usually the director—like a chef overseeing a fully-staffed kitchen to make his recipes, or a conductor guiding a whole symphony orchestra to express his vision of a score—whose personal stamp is most visible in the finished product—a personal stamp present or visible to a greater or lesser degree depending on the force of their artistic personality, the freedom they're given to exercise it, and so on. Auteurism latches onto these personalities through the films, creating a real relationship between the individual artist and individual viewer that is "suffused by love," as Routt puts it. The proof of auteurism's effectiveness, then, is in the simple fact that the viewer who experiences this relation, the viewer more vulnerable and open and engaged with a specific filmmaker's work, will inevitably extract more interest and edification from it than someone lacking that relation. The act of watching their films turns from passive consumption to an active and productive mutual exchange. The late style perspective performs a similar reorientation subordinate to this auteurist relation: it prompts the viewer to notice more and feel more toward a work vis-à-vis the artist who made it. In a piece titled "Last Film, Best Film?,"

Richard Brody ponders the question of whether truly liking a director necessitates liking their later work:

> Packed in the chatty trope of "really liking" an artist is a dynamic principle that I think is at the very heart of criticism and, for that matter, at the very heart of art: imaginative sympathy. The essential human relationship on which movie-going depends is the one in which one's own inner world vibrates to the tones of someone else's and gets significantly retuned, enduringly changed, in the process. The "really liking" that's at stake isn't flag-waving or claim-staking but an active vulnerability, a readiness to expand, to see how far one can wander into inner realms that someone else has charted—at the risk of losing oneself there.

The failure to appreciate—or at least put in the work toward appreciating—a late film from a director whose earlier work one admires, then, is often the result of a shortsighted dismissiveness that's a betrayal of the imaginative sympathy that both auteurism and late style depend on. It's like looking at a person and saying, "Even though you're still alive, I'm not interested in who you are right now; I only have time for a past version of you." Accusations that efforts to find greatness in or valorize the late films of great filmmakers are just a fallacy of some kind of über-auteurism miss the point: it's not the intention to place the artist in the role of a god who can do no wrong, but rather simply to reach for, and settle for nothing less than, the absolute maximum a film can offer. This is what that active relationship looks like in which the subjectivities of artist and viewer mix at the point of contact which is the film; a mixture with room for honesty about moral shortcomings, but no room for the kind of faux-objectivity that latches onto "flaws" as demerits against the film as though it were a homework assignment and not the no-rules expression of an artist. The auteurist and late stylist may even adopt a kind of innocent naivete, one unconcerned with hierarchies that get in the way of the pleasures of reckoning with the most recent cinematic offering from a significant artist; like the kind exemplified by Éric Rohmer, for instance, when faced with the release of Orson Welles's *Mr. Arkadin* (1955): "We cannot say the critics were harsh. Yet, I would have hoped for less measured praise. What, the best Orson Welles film? Why not? It is just as great as *Citizen Kane* [1941] or the *Ambersons* [1942], and before time imposes a more objective judgement, it is normal for my current choice to be for the most recent." The passion of Rohmer and the other auteurists demonstrates the fruitfulness of a deeply subjective engagement with filmmakers as one ages alongside them throughout life. In the end it does come down to just one word, in its deepest and most profound sense, which characterizes the viewpoints of auteurism and late style as practiced by those most truly in tune with them, a word which Richard Brody leads up to when he says that "the recognition of the supreme merits of artists' later works is a crucial sign of critical engagement, because it reveals where criticism, far from objective analysis or sociology, descriptive nuance or consumer guidance, is most like love."

This love, particular as it related to late films, continued to suffuse some of the most essential work being done in cinema (both in filmmaking and the literature that tried to understand it) as film history marched into the 1960s, '70s, '80s and beyond. The explosion of cinephilia resulting from the concurrence of international New Wave filmmaking, auteurist criticism, and the changes attendant to the generational takeover by the New Hollywood meant that for many younger cinephiles, their entry points to work of the great filmmakers came in the form of late films—seen in first run by those on the older end of the spectrum, or by those on the younger via VHS, laserdisc, or other early home-video formats that granted accessible afterlives to contemporary releases ahead of earlier, more canonical works by the same directors. Matthew Wilder talks of how, "as a kid who became aware of cinema in the late seventies, then moved into adolescence in the eighties, I had an experience of the Old Masters of Classical Cinema that I suspect is shared by many Gen-X people.... We got the 'late style' first; then the heyday second, then the juvenilia last of all…. We encountered the Grandmasters in Benjamin Button fashion. How exciting to see George Cukor mature from *Love Among the Ruins* [1975] and *The Blue Bird* [1976] into *The Women* [1939] and *Holiday* [1938]! Imagine that the guy who made *Seven Women* [1966] would go on to do *The Searchers* [1956]!" Having one's first taste of a director's world be the late expressions of it can have a kind of "thrown in the deep end" quality that is paradoxically capable of forming a deep bond between viewer and artist that a strictly chronological approach might be unable to replicate. I know that my own relationships with certain modern filmmakers have benefited from this backwards approach; I can't imagine, for example, having a better relationship with the films of Brian De Palma than I do as a result of his latest film, *Domino* (2019), being one of my first introductions to his work. Adrian Martin, for one, has wondered "whether the 'wrong end of the telescope' entry into cinephilia is not an almost universal experience? One that has a particularly 'ritual' intensity, too, in that one often encounters these strange, charged last works already 'primed' on whatever auteurist writing one has read—and so you get— and partly no doubt hallucinate!—in one almighty hit, the vision/sensibility of that director in its compacted, 'testament' form." But critics, directors, and film historians of the 1960s and 1970s were also approaching late films in a more hands-on way, via direct contact with the elder statesmen of cinema that were making them. The critics-turned-filmmakers of *Cahiers*, sure, but American filmmakers too, like Martin Scorsese, Clint Eastwood, and Peter Bogdanovich, also became friends or mentees of Hollywood's golden age icons—indeed, perhaps two of the greatest "late" films of the era were actually the young Bogdanovich's first and second signed films, *Targets* (1968) and *The Last Picture Show* (1971), for the way they thematized lateness, youth vs. age, and the despairing drift of culture over time. Just as essential, however, were the relationships Bogdanovich formed with filmmakers like Orson Welles, John Ford, and Howard Hawks, interviewing them, learning from them, and campaigning on their behalf as others began to see them as "over the hill." Other critics and historians like

Kevin Brownlow, Joseph McBride, and Bill Krohn similarly performed essential work gathering the stories of Old Hollywood before it disappeared from memory and supporting, critically or materially, the current artistic ventures of whatever aging legends they became acquainted with. Such intergenerational camaraderie has been and continues to be a hallmark of those who care about cinema, and it's rare to find a true-blue auteurist who isn't deeply invested in the plight of the oldest filmmakers. Joe McElhaney in 2010 writes of how his "relationship to contemporary cinema can be dominated by a passion for aging filmmakers, the older the better: Rohmer (deceased, but just barely), Resnais, Rivette. And who older (and perhaps better) than Oliveira?" Thus, even though "late style" hasn't been a much-theorized term in cinema, its spirit has permeated the cinephilia of the last 70-odd years as much as if not more so than the literary, musical, or visual art equivalents in the same period.

But the differences between late style in film and late style in those other arts are striking. To the degree that cinema is an industrial and commercial medium—where huge amounts of money get thrown around to make films that, as part of the deal, are expected to make it all back—the challenges and pressures faced by a filmmaker are comparatively outsized. In a hypothetical late-career scenario, the writer, composer, or painter can whenever so compelled merely pick up the needed tools for cheap and embark in solitude on their art; the filmmaker has to wrangle the capital, the cast, the crew and everything else that goes into making movies at the level they're accustomed to.[33] Part of what may separate more successful cinematic late periods from less successful ones (at least in terms of getting films made, and not uncomfortably when

---

[33] Of course, taking a digital camera into the backyard for a no-budget production with free labor from family and friends—or some other variation on non-professional methods—is always more or less available as an option. And some late filmmakers have certainly done that! But it's understandable for a filmmaker who's spent decades making movies at a certain budgetary level to be dissatisfied with such a downgrade when their ambitions remain at their previous scale.

doing so) is a filmmaker's ability to be their own producer. In conversation with Jean-Luc Godard in 2000, Richard Brody later relayed Godard's "formula for the directorial fountain of youth…. He said that what distinguished the filmmakers who were able to keep going [after the collapse of the studio system] was that they were also producers with their own production companies." Though not necessarily putting up the actual capital for their films themselves, "they managed financiers' or studios' investments, and had a hands-on relationship to the film's finances." In talking of Visconti and Lampedusa re: *The Leopard,* Edward Said has also contrasted the "mass-consumer forms" of cinema and the novel with the "far more specialized and basically resistant media" of late artists like Adorno and Richard Strauss, "the philosophical essay and classical music." Facing shifting cultural, sociological, and political landscapes, oscillating budgetary resources, and rapidly changing technologies, on top of it all filmmakers have to contend with a sandwich of expectations from executives on one side and audiences on the other; just getting one's own directorial vision across despite it all can be a massive challenge in ways perhaps only comparable to architecture in the other arts.[34] But other

---

[34] Given the large logistical challenges involved in getting a film made, it would seem that cinema is also the medium in which it is most possible for the end product to slip away from the director's vision through interference or compromise or sheer creative fatigue (especially if there's a script or cast or something else involved that the director doesn't find ideal). Many films, late and otherwise, have been disowned by their directors for less. Yet I think it's somewhat silly to suppose, just because a filmmaker is working with people or material or under circumstances they don't particularly like, that they're going to "phone it in." Given the enormity and all-encompassing nature of film production, where a filmmaker can spend multiple years on a single project, I think it more likely the case that a filmmaker will do their utmost to redeem the project in whatever ways possible (as I like to say: there's always mise-en-scène) from the obstacles preventing unfettered creative expression; it just isn't human nature, especially artistic nature, to simply write off something that's taking up so much of one's time (no matter what one might say afterwards). Thus why in the realm of late films you can never take anyone's word for the poor quality of a work, even the director's!

aspects of filmmaking suggest ways in which it might uniquely enhance the physical or creative longevity of its practitioners. Paradoxically, the physically demanding nature of film work might be seen as healthy and therapeutic for the aging artist's body and with a rejuvenating visual and spatial component to go along with it. Kenneth Clark doesn't mention film in his 1970 lecture on old age artistry, but it's easy to see the parallels with film in his remarks on painting:

> No writer enjoys the movement of his pen, still less the click of his typewriter. But in the actual laying on of a touch of colour, or in the stroke of a mallet on a chisel, there is a moment of self-forgetfulness. Harassed public servants—presidents, statesmen and generals—take up painting; they do not (with the exception of Lord Wavell) write poetry. It may seem ridiculous to compare the therapeutic activities of these amateurs to the struggles of Titian or Rembrandt; but I think that they do indicate a fundamental difference between the two arts. A visual experience is vitalising. Although it may almost immediately become a spiritual experience (with all the pain which that involves), it provides a kind of nourishment.

Filmmaking keeps one in touch with the physical, mental, emotional, social, and spiritual all at once. Amir Cohen-Shalev cites Simone de Beauvoir's view of painters also "as privileged over writers and composers, since they receive constantly renewed sense-nourishment from the external world, while the latter have to rely on ever-dwindling inner resources." Filmmakers receive the same, if not more, via the actual three-dimensional ordering of people and environments (and at three separate stages—writing, shooting, and editing—to boot). The remarkable creative endurance of many filmmakers can perhaps be partly explained by the opportunity afforded them to constantly come into contact with the world—with actors and crew members, on locations and sets—which gives them immediate material pleasure and keeps them both rejuvenated while working on the job and motivated to get back to work again while off of it. The essentially collaborative nature of filmmaking, too, not only keeps one socially engaged but diversifies the completion of tasks in ways that allow older directors in particular to be a creative hub without wearing a hundred different hats. Thus why it's not unheard of for a director to make a film while, say, confined to a wheelchair; assistants and assistants to assistants and all the different collaborators on a film set can all ideally be extensions of the director themself. Yet the collaborative nature of filmmaking is not without precedent, even in the other arts we're comparing it to. The painter's studio in Renaissance times, for example, was in some ways analogous to a film set, the master the director and the apprentices doing bits of work here and some spots of painting there in the style and manner of their teacher, acting less as their own individual selves than as vessels for the master's vision; even Shakespeare, held up by many as the exemplary genius of individual art, dealt with the contingent pressures involved in commercial considerations for the theater, navigating repertory company politics, and working with collaborators—in some ways, he resembles nothing so much as the Hollywood studio filmmaker as auteur. "So it perhaps comes as a surprise," writes Gordon McMullan, "to realise that collaboration is in fact a consistent feature of lateness across the range of art-forms within which late styles have been established, causing significant problems for the definition of late style as a manifestation of individual genius beyond the reach of contingency." Collaboration is also one of the factors that David Galenson uses to explain his findings that certain movie directors were "at their best" during a later period in their life than most artists of other art forms:

> Making movies under the Hollywood studio system was obviously a more highly collaborative activity than the other kinds of artistic work considered in this study, and this may have allowed these great directors to use their skills to best advantage without being constrained as severely by their advancing age

as they might have been in more solitary activities.... A possible lesson for experimental artists and scholars from these great movie directors and architects may involve the benefits of collaboration, for working with younger colleagues or assistants may permit experimentalists to continue to use their valuable skills and expertise to best advantage later in their lives than would otherwise be the case.

The same differences apply to late style in film in the 21st century, although seismic shifts like the introduction of digital technology, the increased ability to make films independently outside the Hollywood studios, and online distribution networks have changed the material ways late artists operate in the contexts of cinematic production and exhibition. And just as the filmmakers of the first golden age of late style had a laundry list of new challenges to face, so too the filmmakers of the second: the digital revolution that's overhauled the entire industry, of course, from cameras to workflows to theatrical screening norms; the squeezing out of mid-budget movies for adults by the sure-bet financial juggernauts of popular film franchises, resurrected IP, and comic book movies; the competition from prestige television; the rise of streaming; the decline in theatrical attendance; the disappearance of print movie journalism; the emphasis on box-office diagnostics; the outsized role of social media in visual culture; the rewiring of brains by short-form videos; and the threat of artificial intelligence. (To name just a few.) Despite increased avenues for the making and sharing of work that subverts mainstream convention, the infrastructure that allowed classic Hollywood filmmakers to make films comfortably and consistently just isn't there anymore; thus most filmmakers have a harder time getting films made and take longer in doing so, producing in many cases what feel like bigger leaps in "lateness" between films than in years past. The lateness of many contemporary late films feels exaggerated, too, by the sheer difference that digital surfaces lend to the texture of movies made by filmmakers who knew nothing but analog film for the first two or three or four decades of their career. For some, the advent of digital has re-invigorated their art in the direction of the radically hand-made, like Jean-Luc Godard or Jean-Marie Straub (after the passing of Danièle Huillet in 2006) who, before their deaths, "further[ed] the microsystems of production they'd already solidified late last century," per Andy Rector. "They risked an embrace of the latest means of their age, for and against the age, shed all sentimentality about past formats without forgetting their craft, and made new works without compromise, in liberty, without capital, on video, in their homes, used like a set and workshop." Those of New Wave pedigree entered the 21st century and made their last films with the freedom of the 1960s mixed with the cinematic wisdom accrued over decades of life and work; those of the New Hollywood adapted to new contexts and often beat younger filmmakers at their own game while shaking up their art with the new tools of the time. Many of these filmmakers left us incisive, recontextualizing, and endlessly rich works before dying, and those who remain, joined in ongoing waves by the filmmakers who came slightly after them, continue to do so. Strides have been made in appreciating current late style filmmakers relative to those of earlier generations—the democratization of film criticism via the internet has helped—yet I worry that the shift is partially due to a nostalgia for familiar names and a fear that there'll be no one to fill their shoes when they're gone, leaving neglected the essential way in which the early auteurists put late films in conversation with early ones as part of the same cinematic vanguard. Such a comparison will always be fruitful, especially when it's realized, as James Morrison did in 2001 writing about later films of Stanley Kubrick and Roman Polanski, that "it is not, in any case, the surface features of contemporary film culture that their movies reject; indeed, they both *embrace* such features with apparent zeal. It is something deeper that they both refuse: the sensibility that underlies that surface, or the milieu that produces it." Morrison also emphasizes the way modern late styles in film draw from the diversification of the film landscape in terms of style, genre, quickly-changing fashions, or shifting audience tastes in speaking of how "the more distinctive late styles of some [European filmmakers] seem directly linked to a loosening, if not of rigor, then of a certain categorical rigidity—a greater receptiveness to possibilities, across cultural strata, from 'high' to 'low'.… In an era where high-art cineastes alternate between gleefully prophesying the end-of-cinema or piously calling for it, this general feeling of belatedness, however various the particular styles in which it might manifest itself, may well become a definitive feature of contemporary film culture." The importance of the idea of "belatedness" to post-1960 filmmakers has also been noted by David Bordwell (borrowed for his own purposes from Harold Bloom's similar literary theory): "With your career wholly in your own hands, facing the competition of past and present, how could you achieve something distinctive?… Belatedness is a pervasive feature of modern Hollywood, creating a new self-consciousness about the act of making a film." Contemporary late style, therefore, often faces a double lateness: one's own personal lateness plus one's status as a latecomer to cinema as a whole. A French New Wave great making films in the 2000s, for example, might have to be self-reflexive and allusive about the very self-reflexivity and allusiveness that defined the film-historical riffing of their earliest films. What's fascinating about many 21st-century late films is the way they approach this challenge almost unconsciously, as though the anxiety of influence that shaped their early films had been fully digested and as though the history of cinema, rather than breathing down their neck, had become a part of their very being.

There's a settling-in that's often a part of growing older as an artist, but not necessarily one to be equated with artistic contentment; more often, the most distinctive late artists "settle in" in a way perhaps better described as "burrowing in"—that is, burrowing deeper and deeper into one's own style and pet themes and artistic methods, hungry to outdo what one's already done. Especially in an era for film with less rigid genre boundaries, what often happens is that a director's work essentially becomes its own genre, easier to classify by reference to their name than by any traditional genre nomenclature. Ruth Nevo has talked about this phenomenon in relation to Shakespeare's later plays, arguing that he, "like late Yeats, like late Picasso, yields to his themes, loosens or even abandons the constraints of classical category and moves beyond genre towards an indeterminate mode akin to reverie." If late style is "beyond genre," it's a suggestion that harkens back to ideas explored earlier of how late artists become increasingly individualized. In film, this shift is sometimes prompted by a resounding artistic and commercial success, after which some mixture of industrial goodwill and artistic confidence prods a filmmaker into more distinctive, less classifiable territory: for example Howard Hawks' *Rio Bravo* (1959), both a box-office hit and a personally revitalizing experience, catalyzing a shift for Hawks into a sui generis cinema of laidback profundity in his final decade; or Martin Scorsese's *The Departed* (2006), a particularly vigorous incarnation of his crime saga template that was fêted by a handful of Oscar gold, leading to his 2010s run of diverse, original, genre-hopping late work. To borrow a phrase Joe McElhaney uses in talking about the Chaplin of *A King in New York,* late style could perhaps most easily be categorized as "that which cannot yet be categorised." No doubt that uncategorizability sometimes works against those filmmakers most steadfastly hanging onto the artistic methods which make their films tick in the richly specific way they do; as financiers become more skeptical of unconventional production processes, filmmakers like Mike Leigh, for example, who resolutely refuse to budge from their original (yet ostensibly risky from a financial standpoint) ways, find it more difficult to get backing for their work. The stylistic and dramatic austerity of Leigh's most recent film, *Hard Truths* (2024), certainly presents a surface—abrasive yet gentle—unfashionable to modern viewers resistant to the patient complexity of Leigh's dramaturgy. Such viewers do present a potential obstacle to reception for the kind of late films, of which there are more than a few, that "are marked by their formal asceticism," as Cobi Chiodo Powell puts it in one of the more engaging recent pieces on late style in film. Powell identifies three main strains of contemporary late style: minimalism (the aforementioned formally ascetic), autobiography, and return. (The second denoting an explicitly memoiristic or more obliquely self-reflexive mode, and the third filmmakers undergoing a kind of circular home-coming to earlier themes and subjects—a strain associated with the rise in franchise filmmaking and IP regurgitation, which Powell suggests might "grow in popularity over the years as auteurs increasingly resort to making the only sort of films they are allowed to anymore, this being the type of film with a baked-in audience and somewhat guaranteed box office success.") "While late style is not stable enough to be a genre," writes Powell, "indexing its tropic continuities demythologizes the auteur figure while simultaneously respecting the profundity of their work. Late style as a series of tendencies: not a wizened engagement with the Sublime." But there's more work to be done in articulating these tendencies, and in identifying the ways in which contemporary late style filmmakers follow them, subvert them, or do neither or both simultaneously; and in comparing or contrasting them to tendencies in previous eras of late work, not just in the other "golden age" I've indicated but in the (also rich) interstitial periods between the two, or even in smaller intervals within them like, say, late works pre- and post- the near-complete digital takeover of cinema circa the early-to-mid 2010s. In short, there's still so much more to be done, and I hope the paths and ideas I've explored here are proven to be just the tip of the iceberg.

The application of lateness as a paradigm through which to view cinema shouldn't be restricted to individual film-makers, either. Numerous angles exist from which to attack cinematic lateness in more oblique or unconventional ways. Work remains to be done on the lateness inherent to specific junctures in film history, for example, like the way film artists reacted and adapted to the shift from silent to sound pictures or from analog to digital in our own day—directors, of course, but also cinematographers, actors, editors, etc., who are subject to all the same temporal and contextual shifts that we've been talking about. Indeed, any filmmaking role can be examined for late styles in similar ways as we've been doing for directors. Some of the more authorial personalities in acting, for example, have begun to see their work approached in this way:

Tom Cruise's shift away from certain kinds of roles and toward others in the early 2010s has been examined, and similar work could be done on, say, John Wayne's late films (Don Siegel's *The Shootist* [1976] would be a gold mine for that exploration), or on any one of numerous former movie stars in our day who've shifted to doing genre-heavy direct-to-video work. Other avenues of lateness-adjacent interest include films that explicitly take old age as their subject matter; studies of "last things" related to cinematic figures and their deaths, as Stanley Schtinter has done in his book *Last Movies* (2023) via a webbed investigation into what certain famous people (both cinematic and otherwise) watched as the last movie they saw before dying; or a genre-focused approach which examines the depopularization of film genres like the Western or the musical through representative post-classical Hollywood examples. Interest could also be found in the later work of comedy groups like the Marx Brothers or The Three Stooges. I'm partial to the overarching category of late comedies in general, late films made in the genre which often butt up against the modern world in fascinating ways via anachronistic styles that bypass fashionable humor. Jean-Luc Godard's comment about Jerry Lewis upon the release of the latter's *Hardly Working* (1980; along with 1983's *Smorgasbord* the epitome of this category) that "even when it's not funny, it's more funny" often applies to such films; I also find that comedy provides a uniquely efficient way of discovering what's specific about a film's creator, to the degree that senses of humor can act like fingerprints of a personality. As the comedy angle demonstrates, individual late style studies can narrow in on specific outlier incarnations of lateness shared by some, few, or merely one filmmaker. Even though the kind of robust careers filled with many films across decades lend themselves more easily to late style analysis, that isn't to say that directors with as few as two or three films to their name can't receive a similar treatment, nor does it disqualify filmmakers who died or retired before stretching their filmography to a conventionally ample size. We could even make a case for filmmakers who essentially debut their careers with late films, like Eleanor Coppola, who released two fiction features in her eighties despite only having made a few documentary works previously, or Jerry Seinfeld, whose *Unfrosted* (2024) is not only an exemplary "late comedy" but marks a fascinating late medium shift from stand-up and television to cinema.[35]

"Last films," of course, have long been a category of interest for obvious reasons, with screening series programmed around the idea; the way they do or do not act as summative statements for the careers in question provides a real fascination born from the contingencies of individual and industrial histories. Late films that *do* seem to offer a profoundly testamentary vision, intentionally or unintentionally, make up a similar but different category, and the clarity with which they capture the retrospective messiness of a life or career lends them a certain elevated status among late cinema; an excellent recent example would be Víctor Erice's *Close Your Eyes* (2023), the filmmaker's first fictional feature in forty years and a sublime metacinematic poem on the mysterious trajectory of personal histories over time. Another avenue of interest particularly relevant to the age of home video is the phenomenon of older filmmakers revisiting, remastering, re-editing, or otherwise tweaking earlier films of theirs for some sort of re-release—to the chagrin of many fans in the case of a George Lucas or Wong Kar-wai, or mostly to their delight in the case of Francis Ford Coppola; either way, to the degree these re-releases embody artistic choices made by an artist later in their career, they are late style, and should be approached openly as such.[36] Some

---

[35] Kent Jones, who came late to directing fiction films after a career in film criticism, has talked about the potential advantages of this lateness: "I started late with narrative cinema…. But in retrospect, I'm glad that I skipped past the movies that I would have made in my twenties or my thirties, because they would have been like, you know, an homage to whoever. But I think that coming at it from the other angle, or when I did, I had that behind me and I understood that making movies is something different."

[36] Although more prevalent today, there are important precedents in the 20th century, such as Charlie Chaplin's revision of 1925's silent film *The Gold Rush* for a 1942 sound re-release, which is addressed in the context of Chaplin's career later in this book.

outliers defy explanation and any analyses of them should be approached above all with awe and appreciation: the great Portuguese filmmaker Manoel de Oliveira, who only began making feature films regularly past his 60th birthday and never let up until the astounding age of 106, is one such case.[37] Another thread to pull can concern both individual filmmakers and cinema more generally, and that is the matter of reboots, remakes, and sequels, which in their modern association with cash-grab Hollywood rapacity are not regarded highly but can nevertheless be fascinating experiments with lateness. Directors remaking their own earlier films late in their career—think Yasujirô Ozu's *Floating Weeds* (1959, remaking 1934's *A Story of Floating Weeds*) or Leo McCarey's *An Affair to Remember* (1957, remaking 1939's *Love Affair*)—is almost something of a tradition and therefore a great place to see lateness up close and personal, and sequels contain a similar opportunity to see lateness in action, whether the individual lateness of series directed by the same person or the more general cinematic lateness of a sequel or a reboot made by different people at a different time. There's a profundity re: time that can slip into even the most otherwise uninteresting works of this sort, and the best of them wrestle with the concept of change in earnest: *The Matrix Resurrections* (2021), directed by Lana Wachowski (one half of the original trilogy's director duo), is a recent example that does just this while also offering a metacritique of its own making as it relates to the very idea of Hollywood's obsession with IP reboots. Which brings us to the final idea about cinematic lateness I want to suggestingly touch on: the lateness of cinema itself. We've already noted its status as the latest of the acknowledged major art forms, and also the sense of cinema's death that creeps into the fears verbalized by every single generation of film culture. We could even get micro-

---

[37] Dennis Lim on the matter: "Mr. Oliveira, force of nature that he is, represents both kinds of lateness [the ones identified by Said as largely serene and largely intransigent], often in a single film. In this, as in so many other respects, he is his own special case. What are we to make of an artist who hit his stride in his 70s, and for whom 'late style' is in effect the primary style?" It's a good question.

scopically philosophical about it and quote Karen Leeder on how film scholar George Kouvaros has raised "the question of the conservative function of photography and film. They are always late, he points out, premised on the extinction of a moment, but uniquely among the arts, they also preserve and repeat this unrepeatable moment." But what I want to get at above all is the idea that cinema *is always the latest it's ever been*. Each batch of films the new year brings us is stuffed full of the lateness inherent within their very newness; and since every film was once new, so in that sense every film in the history of cinema has been a late film. I don't point this out to advocate for a shallow championing of the new for the sake of its newness (new equates with later, never necessarily with better), but to suggest that an appreciation for the textures and is-ness of this newness—for whatever virtues of its era-specific differences one can productively glean—can potentially transform one's relationship to contemporary cinema, turning what merely feels like the glut of new (and presumably worse) content into a potential cornucopia of uncharted riches.

5

The late style perspective is intended as a paradigm shifter. It looks at the way critics and audiences have approached late films in the past and, in dissatisfaction, shuns it for a new philosophy of viewing: one in which the odd and unorthodox are openly respected, in which "flaws" and "faults" are no longer part of the critical vocabulary, in which the films are appreciated for what they are in all their specific is-ness. Less an intellectual theory than a bone-deep reorientation of one's very way of looking, "late style" acts as a prompt to shift one's critical regard toward the empathetic observation of changes and evolutions in an artist's career through shifting temporal contexts; to meet the artist where they're at, rather than where we might like them to be. And by swapping out ideas of "better" or "worse" for the nuances of "different," the analysis that flows from late style prizes the search for understanding in regards to late work rather than the hasty judgment of it by conventional standards. What's great—and, in a world inundated by consumerist opinion-slinging, radical—about the investigation of late style is that, in the end, it always comes back to the work. "The importance of the late works and lives of older artists," writes Stephen Katz, "goes beyond the strategic uses to which they have been put in popular narratives of peak-and-decline and creativity across the life span precisely because they beckon us to look intensely into the stone and pigment of Titian, Michelangelo, and many others, and behold in their historical dilemmas a deepening of our own questions about the arts of life and the passage of time." Late style embraces no single critical ideology, but operates via the usage of any and every critical tool that helps pry the most interest and edification from any given film. Invaluable insight can come from the passionate filmmaker-viewer relationship inspired by auteurism and the context-heavy examination of relevant cultural and industrial contingencies both. Subjective fire and cool objectivity each have their place; C. S. Lewis reminds us that "the ancient Persians debated everything twice: once when they were drunk and once when they were sober." It's a simple fact that the uncurious dismissal of a late film will almost always show itself to be a shallow action by even the slightest of efforts in the opposite direction. A study of context, history, and a filmmaker's wider career undertaken with an open and curious mind will inevitably deepen understanding, increase at the very least one's *chance* of appreciating the film in question, and—on the whole—make the work and the artist(s) behind it much more interesting to think about, regardless of where one's personal value judgment ultimately falls. For the appreciation of late work also has a residual benefit, in that it productively recontextualizes an artist's earlier work. As Lawrence Garcia writes,

> It is a quirk of film history—and perhaps history more generally—that it is only after a detour in evolution that certain techniques or elements may be said to reveal possibilities that were there all along. The purpose of articulating an artist's "late style," then, is not to extend their mythos according to some criterion of consistency, but to uncover heretofore unappreciated aspects of their cinema, and indeed the medium itself. It is to show how the introduction of a new work changes how we see all the others—a fact we are apt to miss if we hold on to critical clichés.

Hence why the narrative about filmmakers "peaking" at the beginning or middle of their careers remains an unhelpful obstacle to appreciating the complexities of individual artists expressing themselves across disparate temporal contexts.

None of this is to lose sight of the fact, however, that sometimes appreciating late work is hard. The human impulse is to always expect the latest film from a filmmaker we admire to equal if not surpass the achievements of their past, and when the work is different it can be difficult to orient ourselves to elements that at first blush leave us questioning why the filmmaker didn't just repeat what worked so well before. I think disappointment, in small or large doses, is almost always an inevitable and unavoidable part of encountering new work by an artist one loves. But to make no effort to recontextualize the causes of that disappointment as new—and potentially uniquely productive—features of that artist's work is, to me, the literal definition of being a "fake fan." The perspective of late style pushes you not to be one. It offers you philosophical tools to reconfigure your relationship to the artist via the presence of the new work and to discover the most up-to-date expression of who, in all their complexity, they are; it may force you to redraw with new colors whatever mental image you had of them and their work, but it also supplies the perspective from which to find that new image as humanly beautiful as the one from before. This is what late style is about, though—the way neither life nor art stand still for us, and the adjustments we have to make to stay appreciatively abreast of it; or as Lecia Rosenthal suggests, "Perhaps this is the 'point' of late style, its refusal to come to a point, to end well, to withdraw easily, without resistance, before our efforts to pin it down." The resistant quality of much late work, though perhaps at first an obstacle to smooth enjoyment, can with the help of late style principles be reconceived as part of the pleasure of engaging with it. Margaret Notley writes that "late-style criticism invites an approach that tries to find meaning despite the contradictions rather than expecting to resolve them." And before you know it, the vulnerability to the irreducible specificity of late art fostered by all these philosophical angles leaves one fundamentally changed; the late works themselves start to act on you in ways previously unimagined. Thomas Dormandy, at the end of his book *Old Masters: Great Artists in Old Age* (2000), articulates this phenomenon too beautifully to not just quote him in full:

> After trying to survey the seemingly endless individual variations in the art of old age, only three generalisations appear to be justified. The first is the sense of liberation which came to many great artists in their last decades…. The second is a commitment to truth…. The third and last is not a characteristic of

the art of old age but of one's response to it. On first acquaintance there is hardly a work of an old master which does not demand—or at least invite—a plea in mitigation. Their technique was often clumsy. Their paintings may be packed with confusing and unnecessary detail. They may, on the other hand, be uncomfortably empty. In either case they may lack coherence. They may be unbalanced. The storyline may make no sense. The presentation may be muddled. They may appear unfinished. But since the master's past record commands respect, even admiration, one begins to search for extenuating circumstances. One points to the master's physical or mental frailty at the time the work was completed. A specific infirmity may be worth special emphasis. One recalls, when appropriate, the master's material difficulties. In a more positive vein, one praises his or her indomitable (if perhaps slightly misguided) spirit. Then suddenly the futility of the enterprise hits home. It is the works themselves which bring belated but blinding illumination. Whatever else they need, they do not need extenuation and apology. Their offences against conventions show up conventions for the vanities and artefacts they are. Their faults by ancient canons make ancient canons look foolish. Their disregard of the "cans" and "can'ts" of art reveal the "cans" and "can'ts" as the arid pedantries of hopelessly prosaic minds. To try and apologise for such "errors" is not only futile, it is inane. The realisation is humbling but inescapable. The master in his eighties may have been physically frail and mentally odd. He may have been three-quarters blind. His memory may have become like a sieve. His grasp of detail may have become non-existent. His sense of form, colour and balance may have become bizarre. His command of line may have gone by the board. One could go on. But in some way, in some miraculous way, none of these shortcomings suggest decline and decay. On the contrary, they bear witness to human creativity at its most indestructible and at its most sublime.

There's a pathos in late work that goes to the very heart of the human journey as we experience it vis-à-vis the artistic expressions of others along the way. Part of the reason late style became an interest of mine relatively early in my life is because it seemed to be able, through art, to teach me things about life that as a young person I didn't yet have access to through the traditional channel of personal experience; I yearned for the wisdom gained through time and age without having to wait for either one. Part of me knew this was impossible; there's no shortcut to this kind of wisdom, and there's no speed-running the experience of life.[38] But looking at how, for many people, the work made by artists later in their careers seems to become more resonant as one grows older—as we mature alongside them, or as we begin to catch up to the age at which they made a certain work—and how, with a little more life experience under our belts, that work seems to mean a little more than it once might have, I can't help but wonder: why we can't skip a step? Why do we have to deny ourselves the pleasure of that later work until we've caught up with it? Why can't we just start appreciating that later work *now,* at whatever age we're

---

[38] In full disclosure I began writing this book at age 26 and finished it at age 28 and, before embarking on the task, I did wonder whether it wouldn't be more prudent to wait to write this book until I was older; but the timeliness of the topic demanded it be written now, so I forged ahead. (Adorno had written his essay on late Beethoven at a similar age, anyway.) The ambitious watchlist of unseen-by-me late films I wanted to get to before writing received a much smaller dent than I would have liked, and I remain thoroughly aware of not just the blindspots in film and film literature that, had they been filled, might have made this a richer book, but also of the impossibility of truly understanding the life situation, intentions, or motivations of those older artists which make up its subject. Michelangelo once said that "he who does not know what old age is should wait with patience until it arrives, since before that he cannot know what it is." I do hope I've sufficiently humbled myself beneath that truth during the writing of this book.

at, and glean from it what we can? Yes, age will change us, and time will cause the work to change with us, too; but we lose nothing—and potentially gain everything—by just appreciating it, finding interest in it, and being edified by it right from the jump. It should be obvious by now that the principles of late style appreciation can be applied to all films, to all art, to early works or late works or any works in between. "Late style" could very well be reimagined as "early style," for example, and the wise refinement of lateness traded in for the I-don't-know-any-better freshness of youth. The same principles even apply to watching a film with no context of the filmmaker's age whatsoever, and simply appreciating it for what it is rather than what it's not.[39]

But the three in-depth essays that follow this introduction come loaded with as much context and appreciation as I could possibly combine, either to aid the novice in their introduction to the particular late work under discussion or to enrich the relationships with it held by those already familiar. Because it is, as stated above, and as I'll state again, *all about the work.* Late style is merely a tent, a paradigm, under which work directed toward that work is done. If after all this you still dislike the associations that dog the popular usage of "late style" as a term, then by all means don't use it; I barely use the term at all in the following essays, while still letting the prin-

---

[39] Which I think answers the question some have had of whether late style appreciation can exist without a familiarity with the artist and their work. On the one hand, to suggest that "you wouldn't like the film as much if you didn't know it was a late work from a specific director" is to play a game of meaningless hypotheticals; if you have context and knowledge you have context and knowledge, and there's no use pretending you don't if it's going to enhance your appreciation of the work. On the other hand, someone genuinely coming to a late film blind to that information can still appreciate the work for what it is, and will maybe jump to the other camp over time and have the context to appreciate it even more. I've experienced late films both ways in my life. But neither art nor your appreciation of it exists in a vacuum, and there's no use not using tools you know you have available to you out of some desire for a faux-objective "pure viewing" or what-have-you.

ciples behind late style appreciation flow through the writing and thinking. Easy psychological narratives blanketed over the complexities of these three late artists have been avoided, and the works have been laid bare in all their contingent historical interest; at least that has been my attempt. The goal is to demonstrate what a late style criticism might look like in action in the context of a sustained investigation of particular individual artists. I've chosen Howard Hawks, Charles Chaplin, and Alfred Hitchcock as my example subjects for a number of reasons. All three filmmakers are core figures not just in my own personal pantheon but in the annals of cinephilic history; their fame and acknowledged artistry has made their bodies of work among the most studied and scrutinized within the last 75 years of film culture. (Hawks and Hitchcock especially, as the twin pillars of auteurism immortalized by the "Hitchcocko-Hawksians" tag given to the early auteurists.) Yet despite the prominence of the three, none of their late periods possesses distinction in consensus appraisals of their filmographies, and their final works remain neglected within the majority of the relevant literature—dismissed as films made in the afterglow of their worthier achievements. Yes, all three were powerful white men with strong personalities and complicated (to say the least) relationships with women, but this actually provides ample opportunity to navigate the art-artist complexities that the history of late work is often wrapped up in. And I know they all worked in the context of 20th-century Hollywood; but 1) as an American myself, this is the industry I have the most contextual knowledge of, 2) it gives us the opportunity to do fine-grained studies within the first golden age of late style, and 3) it leaves open the world of international late style for future studies by those with more intimate knowledge of the relevant cultural and artistic contexts. The selection of three long-dead artists is also deliberate; not only do we have a full picture of their lives and careers in ways we obviously couldn't for living artists (hypothetical essays on which would immediately become out of date), but there's also been enough time for a significant body of literature to accrue from which to pull important contextual information. So that's that. I try to offer potential boundary points at which the three artists' late periods might be said to begin, but know that it's not a science—as Michael Spitzer reminds us, "exact stylistic beginnings are a figment of periodization, so it is absurd to designate the appearance of any single work as the official start date of the late period." Yet the playful suggestion of, let's say, temporal points of interest in the evolution of an artist's later career can be helpful in their own way, and just as I suggest my own so, too, can you suggest yours; let the late style discussions begin.

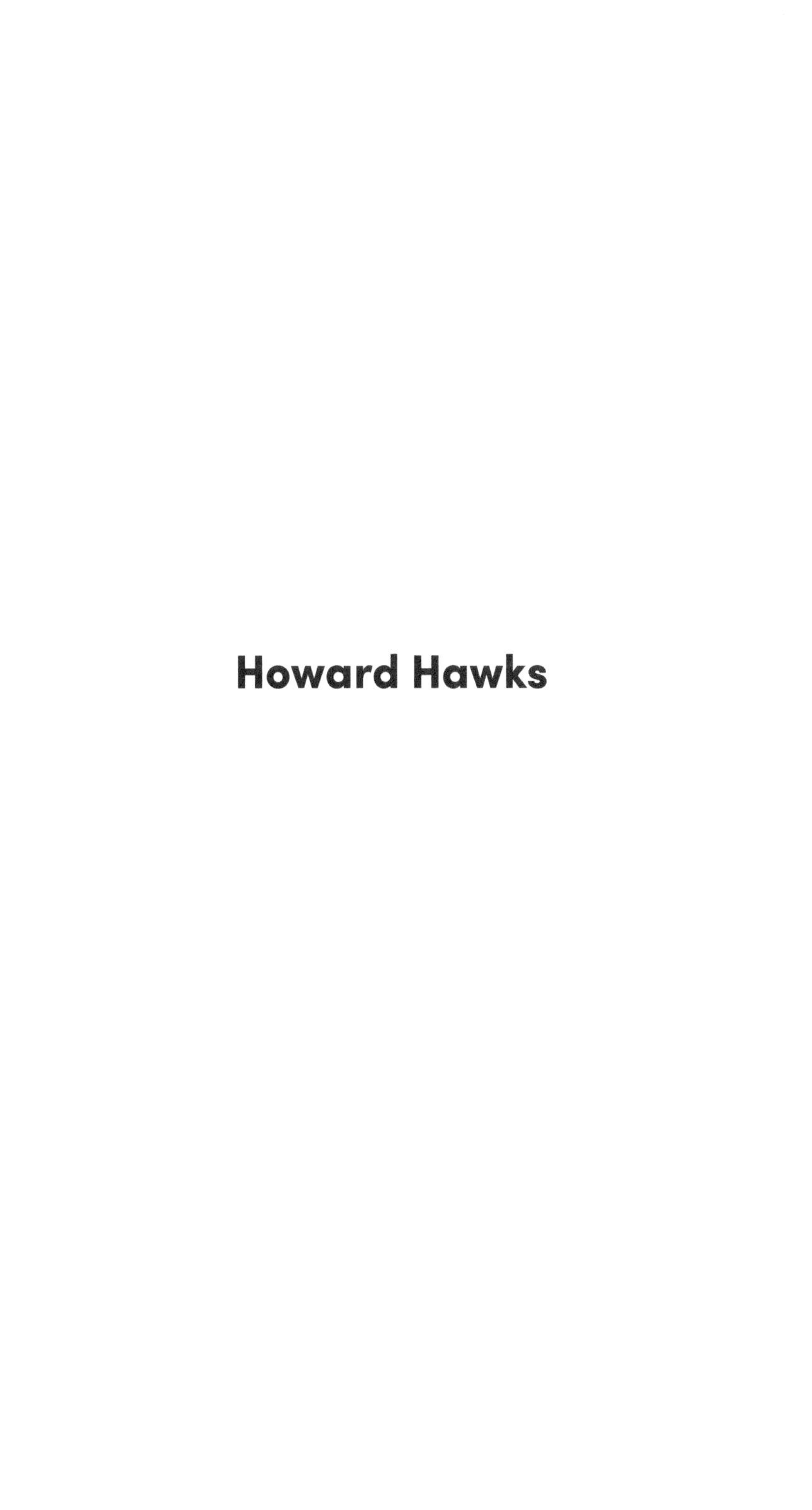

Howard Hawks

When the 56-year-old Howard Hawks landed in Europe for the first time in February 1953, he had just gotten married for the third time, had directed an almost unbroken string of hits going back a dozen years, and—unbeknownst to him—was being proclaimed, by a small yet passionately vocal group of young film lovers in his first destination of Paris, to be nothing less than a genius. It would be that May, in the pages of *Cahiers du cinéma,* that a 25-year-old Jacques Rivette would open his article "The Genius of Howard Hawks" with the polemical broadside that, "The evidence on the screen is the proof of Howard Hawks's genius: you only have to watch *Monkey Business* to know that it is a brilliant film. Some people refuse to admit this, however; they refuse to be satisfied by proof. There can't be any other reason why they don't recognize it." 1952's *Monkey Business,* one of the only blips in Hawks' recent commercial success, had been received in America as no more noteworthy than any other product being churned out by Hollywood; the boldness of Rivette's statement, therefore, could hardly have registered as particularly sane to anyone outside of the initiated, which mostly included friends that also wrote for *Cahiers* and gathered around their primary site of viewing, Henri Langlois's Cinémathèque française—friends such as Jean-Luc Godard, who had already declared Hawks "the greatest American artist" in the middle of a September 1952 *Cahiers* article, as well as Éric Rohmer, who would soon write a December 1953 piece that ended with a similarly bold proclamation, that "one cannot really love any film if one does not really love the ones by Howard Hawks."

Despite the radicality of such proclamations, this love for the films of Howard Hawks didn't entirely come out of the blue. Indeed, a film as early as *A Girl in Every Port* (1928) was a big hit in France and, according to Langlois, was seen as a completely modern film by a Parisian culture beginning to reject expressionism. But while there was precedent to Rivette & co.'s polemics, in the early 1950s loving Hawks was still a controversial position even within the *Cahiers* stable in a way that, for example, loving Hitchcock (the other masthead of the "Hitchcocko-Hawksian" auteurist policy) was not. Hawks himself took a mildly bemused attitude toward such adulation, content to play along even if unable to see himself in their specific ideas, and always game for a chance to talk about his films and the making of them; his first of several interviews with *Cahiers* came in late 1955 soon after the release of his Egyptian epic *Land of the Pharaohs*. Ironically, Hawks' reputation amongst his French admirers at this point rested mainly on his 1950s films—*The Big Sky* (1952), *Monkey Business, Gentlemen Prefer Blondes* (1953), and *Pharaohs*—none of which Hawks harbored a particularly great liking for. But such was the French ability to recognize art where Americans (even the films' own makers) saw only entertainment.

There was no parallel auteurist accounting of Howard Hawks happening in American criticism yet; contemporary reviews might mention his name alongside the films, but almost never with any greater awareness of his body of work in mind, let alone the idea that he might be a cinematic artist in the same way that, say, Hemingway was a literary one. Hawks was viewed by most as little more than a competent craftsman working mainly on assignment, rather than someone who organized his own projects with conspicuous artistic intent like a number of other prominent Hollywood directors. Critic James Agee was the exception that proved the rule when he began his review of *Red River* (1948) this way: "When people discuss the real artists in picture-making, they seldom get around to mentioning Howard Hawks. Yet Hawks is one of the most individual and independent directors in the business." Given that Hawks had, and wanted to have, nothing to do with projects of literary prestige, intellectualism, social causes, or really anything with the veneer of artistic importance, it's no wonder that he wasn't viewed as an artist—he himself would go on to repeatedly repudiate the idea that he was one. Hawks was in the entertainment business, and his job was to make movies, and make them good. He was a rugged individualist, an instinctive, straightforward American filmmaker who sculpted the stuff of life into the stuff of movies to the best of his ability, not for awards or accolades but for audiences. Hawks liked making comedies, or putting comedy into his dramas (increasingly so as he went on), because those were the kind of films whose success was easiest to measure: a laughing audience was an immediate and incontrovertible sign of quality work. Hawks was a storyteller first and foremost, the films somehow loose and taught at the same time, fast-moving but with a willingness to linger, good-humored but unsentimental. Hawks prized his independence above all else, refusing to work when a producer was on set and rarely ever offering his services to the same studio more than a few times in a row (*Scarface*, made in 1930 but released in 1932, always remained a favorite of Hawks' because it was made in defiance of the studio system with renegade producer Howard Hughes). He often went over-budget and over-schedule because his way of squeezing the best possible film out of his material meant taking the time to work out new and better ideas as they arose on set. Despite his fierce independence and need to put his personal stamp on whatever he was making, Hawks was also intensely collaborative, which ironically made his personal stamp even more evident. He was like the leader of a jazz band, his film sets jam sessions like the ones filmed so thrillingly in *A Song Is Born* (1948)—everyone, from actors and writers down to the lowliest crew members, was given free rein to suggest ideas, ideas which Hawks unpretentiously used if they bettered a scene, constantly riffing on the (ever-reworded) scripts toward something funnier, more dramatic, more honest, or more alive. The camera was mostly kept at eye level, simply the way you look at a thing, nothing ostentatious or "pretty." Orson Welles would say that where John Ford was great poetry, Howard Hawks was great prose— or in Rivette's words, "each shot has a functional beauty, like a neck or an ankle. The smooth, orderly succession of shots has a rhythm like the pulsing of blood, and the whole film is like a beautiful body, kept alive by deep, resilient breathing." It is this anatomical, biological metaphor that captures something of the mysterious pleasure of watching a Hawks film unfold, of witnessing all its parts working together to perform a seemingly simple but actually complex function; in other words, a Hawks film is beautiful in the same way that a human being is beautiful.

Maybe no Hawks film is as beautiful in just this way, then, as *Rio Bravo*, whose beauty can be allegorically summed up by John Wayne, languid yet poised, walking down the nocturnal street of the film's Western town. *Rio Bravo* is a significant pivot point in the career of Howard Hawks, and for our purposes an important film in that it previews and in some way launches Hawks' late period (as we shall soon see). But as explained earlier, such demarcations are only as rigid as they are useful, and any number of Hawks films participate in the idea of lateness, to a greater or lesser degree, before we ever reach his late period proper as we will define it: that is, the five films Hawks made after 1960. As I see it, Hawks' career can be reasonably partitioned into six loosely defined eras: the first, his silent films; then from his first sound film *The Dawn Patrol* (1930) through *Come and Get It* (1936); then from *Bringing Up Baby* (1938) to *To Have and Have Not* (1944); from *The Big Sleep* (1946) to *The Big Sky*; *Monkey Business* to *Rio Bravo*; and finally *Hatari!* (1962) to his last film, *Rio Lobo* (1970). I mark the full flowering of Hawks' lateness as beginning with *Hatari!*, but given Hawks' penchant for tackling similar subject matter throughout his career, even to the point of direct remakes, a film like *Ceiling Zero* (1936), for example, can be seen as late relative to a film like *The Dawn Patrol*, and a film like *Only Angels Have Wings* (1939) as even more late relative to both. (Even *The Dawn Patrol* could be seen as late relative to his lost silent film *The Air Circus* [1928], but there's no way to know for sure.) The same point could be made using Hawks' comedies. The remake, remix, variation—call it what you may—is one of the identifying elements of Hawks' cinema, and increasingly so as his career accumulated more and more films, to the point where the question of originality, at least in genre and subject, barely arises when looking at the five late films, so unconcerned are they with pretending to be anything other than variations on situations that Hawks was intimately familiar with from his previous work.

A smattering of earlier Hawks films precipitate many of the defining features of the late films. One important pivot point halfway through Hawks' career comes in the form of *The Big*

Sleep, where Hawks the storyteller starts to become less interested in plot and more interested in character, less interested in narrative logic and more interested in *scenes*—moments given over to reveling in the dynamics between actors and their characters, "to let them handle the plot, rather than let the plot move them," as Hawks would later say. The film had been finished for a 1945 release but war-related release scheduling led to it being pushed back—but not before producer Charles K. Feldman suggested reshoots and recuts to add more scenes between Lauren Bacall and Humphrey Bogart to capitalize on the chemistry that Hawks had first discovered in *To Have and Have Not* and which their marriage (between shoots) had solidified. Hawks' biographer Todd McCarthy notes that the film's "first cut represents the culmination of Hawks's dedication to narrative, to classical storytelling principles, to the kind of logic that depends upon the intricate interweaving of dramatic threads. The revised, less linear cut sees him abandoning these long-held virtues for the sake of 'scenes,' scenes of often electrifying individual effect, but scenes that were weighted heavily in favor of character over plot and dramatic complexity. When Hawks saw that he could get away with this, it emboldened him to proceed further down this path through the remainder of his career."

A Song Is Born saw Hawks remaking his own *Ball of Fire* (1941) with new actors, in color (a first for him), and with a musical twist on the encyclopedic concept. The only official remake of Hawks' career, its obviousness parallels with the earlier film makes its relative lateness easy to notice, and spotting this lateness helps one to see it not as the less interesting retread it has the reputation of being, but rather as a fascinating statement of where the Hawks of 1948 was, stylistically and otherwise, compared to the Hawks of 1941. The way the film gives itself over to the joy of simply experiencing the musical performances of its cast is an example of Hawks reveling in the non-narrative in a way that sets it apart from the earlier *Ball of Fire,* as one comes to expect from the post-*Big Sleep* Hawks. It may be pertinent to note that Hawks had recently passed the half-century mark in his life, and *A Song Is Born* marked the second film hence after *Red River*, itself a preview of the late Wayne-Hawks films in that the actor is made up to look as old as he'd actually be in those films years later. The Cary Grant reteam *I Was a Male War Bride* (1949) can't help but call back to *Bringing Up Baby* and *His Girl Friday* (1940), although Dan Sallitt remarks that "the confident fore-grounding of the Hawksian ethos in *Male War Bride* is in some ways closer to the ambient pleasures of late films like *Hatari!* and *Man's Favorite Sport?* [1964] than to Hawks' earlier comedies and action films." *The Big Sky* also continued to further Hawks' loose attitude toward narrative, often feeling less like a straight story and more like a compendium of scenes lined up end-to-end, letting the characters rule the day over strict plot—that nearly 20 minutes were cut from Hawks' preferred 140-minute version hints at the rambling, roaming nature of the kind of art Hawks was drifting toward.

Given the previously discussed relation between auteurism and late style in cinema, it's apt that *Monkey Business* was the subject of Rivette's tide-turning essay that helped lead to the consolidation of Howard Hawks' reputation as one of Hollywood's premier artists. The film represents Hawks' first direct, conscious engagement with the idea of lateness itself, a Cary Grant comedy (his fourth and last for Hawks) that by virtue of being a Hawks-Grant comedy in 1952 couldn't help but be a film implicitly about aging—a theme that Hawks then made an explicit subject of the film (as he would with John Wayne in his final two westerns). This was not, and could not be, another *Bringing Up Baby*. It was 1952, not 1938, and Hawks and Grant were different, older people, and their art was going to reflect that whether or not they complied—although in *Monkey Business,* they do. Gerald Mast compares the way the film returns to the issues of *Bringing Up Baby* 14 years later—"in a wiser, older, softer, more wintery way"—to the way that "Shakespeare's late romances, written some dozen or fourteen years after his youthful comedies, return more soberly to the world and issues of those earlier plays." Hawks watches the new manner in which his partner in crime moves through his film's world: "Grant, his voice far slower and lower than in

Bringing Up Baby, his glasses even thicker, his movement more enervated, less staccato, more vacant, more languid, becomes the film's physical image of middle-aging in deliberate contrast to the exuberant Grant we remember in films like *Bringing Up Baby*." *Monkey Business* almost acts as a critique of *Bringing Up Baby*; whenever a character in the former takes the youth formula, they revert to a spastic immaturity that resembles nothing so much as the way characters act in the latter. The film speeds up and slows down in accordance with the taking of the formula, and when the characters are their sober selves the film is slower, more at ease than any other Hawks comedy save his last, *Man's Favorite Sport?*; the opening meta-gag with Grant first opening the door too soon (Hawks' own voice softly chastising him off-screen), then forgetting to be on the outside when closing it, is a perfect encapsulation of the patience and increasing simplicity of Hawks' comedy at this stage of his career. The Hawks of *Monkey Business* seems to assert that the youthful zaniness of *Bringing Up Baby*'s characters is all a bit foolish, and that the wisdom of age isn't worth trading in for it. The film ends with one of the most conventionally mature moments in all of Hawks, the reaffirmation of Grant and Ginger Rogers' marital love as the pleasure that no dreams of youth can tarnish or outdo. "I'm beginning to wonder if being young is all it's cracked up to be," Grant's character says at one point in the film. "We dream of youth, we remember it as a time of nightingales and valentines. And what are the facts: maladjustment, near idiocy, and a series of low comedy disasters. That's what youth is. I don't see how anyone survives it." In many ways this will be the working thesis, or one of them, of Hawks' late films.

Late Hawks will be a continuous search—serious but not without humor—for a definition of maturity, for a way of being in the world that achieves the integrity proper to one's station in life; the proper actions and attitudes for a man or woman to have in their relation to themselves and others. *Rio Bravo* is perhaps the richest, densest, most beautiful articulation of this theme. Hawks claimed the film was a riposte to Fred Zinnemann's *High Noon* (1952), a film he saw as being about a sheriff too scared to do his job and therefore not receiving the help he asks for. *Rio Bravo*, then, would be a film about a sheriff calmly doing his job and therefore receiving help without asking for it. Hawks, the consummate professional, loved nothing more than a man doing his job and doing it well; Luc Moullet would write that, in Hawks, "a man is a sheriff the same way he's a laborer or a subway contractor." *Rio Bravo* wouldn't simply present a story, or even characters, but nothing less than a way of being: the way of being a sheriff, the way of being a woman, the way of being a friend. The stance that one takes toward the world. John Wayne's signature contrapposto pose, relaxed yet poised, is a standing allegory for the film itself: self-assured, calm, collected, ready. Wayne's unspoken gestures of love for Dean Martin's recovering drunk speak profound volumes about what the actions of a man toward his fellow man should look like. The way Hawks shifts the burden of meaning from plot to character, from story to *being*, is representative of the attitude toward entertainment and art—i.e., the entire complex business of movies and their meaning—that the late films will demonstrate, and which *Rio Bravo* so deftly previews.

Especially formally, structurally; Hawks had determined that little in the way of plot was needed any longer—simply "more characterization and the fun of just telling a story." The vast majority of *Rio Bravo* is essentially downtime, the patiently observed interstices of an already minimalist plot set in motion by a moment of inciting violence for which motivation is sparse and the victim unidentified; it's much more a pretext for what the film becomes than a moment of dramatic meaning in and of itself. There's no rush to get anywhere; the film seems like it could go on forever, and its characters/actors are such relaxed and sympathetic company that you wouldn't mind if it did. Many people will rightly remember the duet of "My Rifle, My Pony, and Me" that Dean Martin and Ricky Nelson sing in full while they whittle away time holed up in the jail, but it's sometimes forgotten that Hawks then allows a second song—a variation on the folk song "Cindy" in which Walter Brennan joins in—to also play in full in immediate succession. The simple joy of good company is a staple pleasure of Hawks' cinema, but the late films will often raise it to a level of near non-narrative bliss. Manny Farber later went so far as to note the film's resemblance to one of the most radical modernist films, Chantal Akerman's *Jeanne Dielman, 23 quai du Commerce, 1080 Bruxelles* (1975): "There's no action…. *Rio Bravo* is a film of interiors, people speaking, very little action. Surfaces."

Hawks' increasing plotlessness around this time can be historicized by retracing his steps in the years between *Land of the Pharaohs*[1] and *Rio Bravo*, the longest gap between films in his career. Despite his claims that he had quit the film business for a while to reassess what kind of films he wanted to make after what he saw as the disappointment of *Pharaohs*—a reassessing that admittedly did happen to some degree—McCarthy reveals that Hawks in fact "aggressively, even desperately tried to get films made all through this period." Nevertheless, Hawks had a small revelation when he returned to the states from Europe in late 1956 and belatedly discovered the burgeoning medium of television. With a barrage of

---

[1] In an article about the 1978 publication *Hollywood-sur-Nil*, a French-language book written by second unit director Noël Howard about his experience on the film, Bill Krohn writes about *Pharaohs* as simultaneously fulfilling the plottedness of Hawks' past and predicting the plotlessness of his future: "Insofar as *Land of the Pharaohs* does have a complicated melodramatic plot—one of the most beautiful of any film epic—it represents the past, but what I have called 'the real film,' the self-reflecting narrative of the pyramid, already sets up a system that will culminate in *Hatari!*: a plotless film about a hunting season in Africa, in which Hawks filmed the actors actually capturing a series of wild animals and devised a story to fit as he went along. What we see, then, in *Land of the Pharaohs* is both the final form of a certain classicism—that was the business of Faulkner and his collaborators—and the birth of a certain modernism, one whose progeny extends from Jancsó to Straub, and that is the story that Noel Howard tells in his invaluable book." While, contrary to what their differing reputations would suggest, *Rio Bravo* does have things in common with *Pharaohs*—e.g., the rich, amber warmth of the films' interior lighting—the later film is mostly loose and langugorous where the earlier film is wound-up, tight.

series and episodes now being beamed into American homes on a daily basis, Hawks saw in this an oversaturation of plots; audiences knew all of the possible plots, and were therefore tired of all of the plots. Hawks intuitively recognized that the best way to keep the interest of these modern audiences was to keep them from knowing the plot, instead stringing them along via character work that would drive the story. The example of television made such an impression on Hawks that he would even experiment in *Rio Bravo* by using a wordless, opening pre-titles sequence, an allusion to the pre-commercial teaser that commonly opened television episodes. But while drawing inspiration from the small screen, *Rio Bravo* was also the ultimate big screen coup, a glorious and beautiful last-gasp of Hollywood classicism at the end of the evolutionary 1950s and right before the revolutionary 1960s. "If I were asked to choose a film that would justify the existence of Hollywood, I think it would be *Rio Bravo*," wrote Robin Wood, and with reason. The film would be a commercial success after a shaky decade box office-wise for Hawks, setting his mind at ease that his new, reassessed trajectory—of returning to well-trod scenarios and situations while further loosening the narrative reins—was indeed the right path for him, as a craftsman and business-minded entertainer, to be taking.

But the feel and flow of *Rio Bravo* leads one to regard it as something of a self-contained offering from Hawks—something that both summarized the nature of his work up to that point and prophesied the nature of his work to come. Hence why I separate it from the final five late films in my accounting of Hawks' career. Fernando Villaverde writes that "everything seems to gravitate around *Rio Bravo*: the natural evolution of his career leads to this film, and once he achieved this degree of precision and formal rigour, he had nothing left to do but to break with it." Still, neat organizations like this can't capture the messiness of an artistic life lived, especially in a place like Hollywood; the idea for Hawks' next film, *Hatari!*, had in fact come a few years before *Rio Bravo* but had fallen apart then only to be resuscitated now. Hawks had first come up with the basic idea for an African film about catching animals while on the continent making *Land of the Pharaohs,* and deals were brokered toward that goal with Hawks' old friend Gary Cooper in mind to star. Cooper agreed pending approval of a script, but eventually decided he wasn't interested in it; backers Warner Bros. pulled out of the deal as a result, which led Hawks to sue the company in May 1956 for reneging on their deal, a deal they believed to be dependent on Cooper's involvement. When the film finally went into production in 1960, it was as a cash-in on Hawks' post-*Rio Bravo* bargaining power with the studios, and had evolved into a passion project for him that was to take precedence in his mind over any other film ideas. Hawks was to privately tell Elsa Martinelli, his leading lady on *Hatari!,* "This is a film I wanted to make for years and I wanted to make it like it was a vacation."

And make it like a vacation he would. The experiment of *Rio Bravo* a success, Hawks doubled down on plotlessness, characterization, and the fun of hanging out with a group—letting them *be* the story, rather than having them merely be in one. Go-to screenwriter Leigh Brackett attested to Hawks' total lack of interest in conventional stories at the time: "That was the year that Howard was not buying any story…. He didn't want plot, he just wanted scenes." The story, as much as there was one, was to go through a number of reinventions in the years leading up to the actual shoot. In an early incarnation the film's tone was rather heavy and melodramatic, recalling *Only Angels Have Wings* in both mood and situation, with the idea of casualties of the dangerous job being replaced as time went along à la earlier films like *Angels, The Dawn Patrol* and *The Road to Glory* (1936). Another scrapped idea was to have Wayne star opposite Clark Gable in a scenario recalling *A Girl in Every Port,* with one an alcoholic being taken care of by the other and both after the same girl. (Hawks was very attached to this idea in his late period, as it reappears variously in the Wayne/Robert Mitchum set-up of *El Dorado* [1966] and in a major unproduced 1970s screenplay.) The studio wouldn't pay the salaries for two stars of such magnitude, so Hawks changed the story again—essentially splitting Gable's character into two younger actors, Gérard Blain and Hardy Kruger. Gable himself would die around the time shooting began on *Hatari!*, but not before starring in his last film (Marilyn Monroe's as well), John Huston's *The Misfits* (1961), which contains similar animal-capturing elements to *Hatari!* but set in the modern American west; a comparison of the two films—each great in very different ways—would be instructive in showing just how uninterested Hawks was in making any kind of social statement with his films, especially one like *Hatari!* that he viewed as a vacation as much as a job.

Although he had never seen a script that he couldn't improve during the actual shooting of it, in his later years Hawks increasingly worked from scripts that were unfinished, fragmentary, or mere jumping-off points—to many they seemed not to exist at all. On *Hatari!*, Gérard Blain claimed that during the seven months of the shoot, he never read Leigh Brackett's script and Hawks never used it, constantly improvising instead; as can be gleaned from a later documentary capturing some of the filming of *Rio Lobo*, Hawks would carry a yellow notepad around with him on set for jotting down ideas and dialogue. Hawks' indifference toward scripts in his later years, or at least toward letting anyone see them, stemmed from not just his increasing willingness to discover situations and dialogue on set with his collaborators, but also a slight paranoia that leaks would result in his best material making its way onto television before his own films ever made it into theaters; he would go so far as to have two scripts prepared before filming—"one that I let people read, without a lot of the best stuff in it, and the other I keep for myself." A Howard Hawks set was an enclave in which actors, writers, and crew members gathered to do a job while shutting out the exterior world, and in the process creating their own; naturally, just like Hawks' no-producers-on-set rule, a script wandering out of this enclave didn't fit that tight-knit picture, and things like improvising scenes the day-of, reworking dialogue together, or temporarily abandoning work for play when circumstances permitted, very much did. It's easy to see that *Hatari!* is also a documentary of its own making, an allegory for itself: on location in Africa, Hawks & co. would wake up on any given day without knowing what they were going to be shooting, waiting for word on where animals could be found, and then driving out to the spot of reported sightings with their custom-built trucks rigged with cameras to capture the actual actors capturing the actual animals—just like John Wayne & co.'s outfit in the film. François Truffaut wasn't shy about considering the film to be disguisedly about the movie-making process, claiming it as an influence on his own meta-fictional film about filmmaking, 1973's *Day for Night*; Jean Douchet would call the film a "documentary… on [Hawks'] profession as film director. In it, he reveals the secret of his aesthetic and his morality, the determination to get as close as possible to reality, to capture it with the lasso of his camera like a daring sportsman attempting a difficult exploit." Outside of the animal-capturing scenes, dialogue scenes filmed on location were kept to functional, contextless material so that Hawks had as much freedom as possible when the filming of interiors commenced back in Hollywood.

Safari-themed films were common in early 1950s Hollywood, but the genre was past its heyday when Hawks joined in on the fun—none such picture had finished in the top 20 grossers since 1953 until *Hatari!* finished eighth almost a decade later. Among other reasons, this may have been a result of Hawks solving one of the main issues of the subgenre: the interlacing of documentary and non-documentary footage in the film's narrative. With the demand for realism in films growing, *Hatari!*'s ability to tear down this divide not only satisfied a public who were no longer "naïve" enough to accept the obvious effects-work of safari pictures of old, but also opened up bigger doors of realism—like the interweaving of the non-dramatic with the dramatic—that Hawks was eager to step through. The film is structured simply: high intensity animal-capturing sequences, followed by low intensity moments of downtime. Hawks was enamored enough with this structure to use variations of it in both of his next two films; *Man's Favorite Sport?* and *Red Line 7000* (1965) both follow up sporting sequences, of fishing and racing respectively, with downtime filled by drinking, conversation, and romantic hijinks at or around some central hub of socialization. Hawks would defend *Hatari!*'s construction by simply saying that "the form of the picture is a hunting season, from beginning to end. It's what happens when you get a bunch of fellows together to hunt." Although the film is predicated on the realism of its dramatic moments with the animals, it's the second, non-dramatic realism that Hawks is most interested in—the "what happens when…" of his statement. In the home base which houses all of *Hatari!*'s main characters Hawks observes *what happens when…*: what happens when a crew member is injured and a replacement is brought in, what happens when two young men vie for the heart of the same woman, what happens when that woman is in love with a different man than either, what happens when a female outsider infiltrates the group, what happens when that female falls for the leader of that group, etc. But all of these would-be sub-plots are treated with equal importance to anything else in the film, causing them to rise to the level of plot, the "what happens" that makes up a narrative feature film.

Hawks doesn't skimp on his observations; at two hours and 39 minutes, *Hatari!* is Hawks' longest film by far (and he claimed to have enough footage for another hour). To take just one example, a scene between Dallas (Elsa Martinelli) and Pockets (Red Buttons) early in the film is over five minutes of pure conversation, where the characters literally sit down and ask each other "What should we talk about?" and then proceed to talk about it. Nothing visually spectacular happens; they just sit in chairs next to each other. But one's attention is held fast—not just here, but throughout the entire lengthy film—because it's this *character stuff* that Hawks is so entranced with, and therefore we are too. Characters and their relationships. Hawks learned early on to trust his instincts in that if he liked a character, the audience would too, and that when that rapport is established they'll follow them anywhere, doing anything. *Hatari!* is full of such characters. The melding of actor with character and character with actor is so casual and complete (the lack of stand-ins for the dangerous hunting scenes contribute to this) that the audience participates in the pleasure that Hawks and his actors must have had in making it; Dan Sallitt writes that Hawks' late films, *Hatari!* most daringly so in its discarding of narrative, "liberate performance from story to a large extent, and wind up feeling like documentaries of actors hanging out on sets." *Hatari!* is a movie that really makes you believe Hawks when he says that art is the furthest thing from his mind, which paradoxically makes his artistry all the clearer. For the low-stakes fun of the film's hangout scenes, particularly when juxtaposed against the high-stakes danger of the animal-capturing ones, casually begins to take on a profundity that it couldn't have had were it to be deliberately sought after. Ultimately, Hawks is an artist because he isn't one. He doesn't think in those terms—he sees movies as delivery systems for character, story, action, fun, entertainment; films aren't art objects for him, but rather holistic things that morph from the script to the set to the edit toward the creation of a living, breathing motion picture designed to go over with a paying audience.

That didn't stop French actor Gérard Blain from accepting Hawks' invitation to be in the film without reading a single word of a screenplay for the reason that a film by Hawks was sure to be better than anything being made in France, a decision "not prompted by commerce but by art." This coming from an actor dubbed "the first face of the New Wave" by Ronald Bergan for his prominent role in early French nouvelle vague films, one of which—Claude Chabrol's *Les cousins* (1959)—being the film Hawks discovered him in, watched strictly for the purpose of looking for attractive new faces— Hawks turned the film off before finishing in order to request a voice test by the actor in English right away.[2] Blain would later compare Hawks' improvisatory filming methods to those of Godard, a comparison that helps break down preconceptions in the way classic Hollywood filmmaking is thought

---

[2] Blain was to become a filmmaker in his own right, making his debut feature in 1971 and making a handful of highly-regarded but little-known films before his death in 2000. It was on the set of *Hatari!* that Blain started experimenting more seriously with a 16mm film camera.

about contra the international new waves of "art" films that exploded in the 1960s; Godard for one was still a passionate Hawks partisan when making his early 1960s films, placing *Hatari!* at the top of his 1962 top ten list for *Cahiers du cinéma*, deliberately fashioning his debut *Breathless* (1960) as a kind of remake of *Scarface*, as well as creating a protagonist in *Contempt* (1963) meant to be "a character from *Last Year at Marienbad* [1961] who wants to play the role of a character in *Rio Bravo*." Set in the film world, *Contempt* also prominently features a poster of *Hatari!* as part of its scenery.

A closer look shows that *Hatari!* —like other late Hawks films—represents an experimentation with the classical logic of time and space on screen to a degree not so far removed from the more conspicuously radical films of the 1960s and '70s that co-participate in that great era of film history's generational crossover. Hawks plays with time, and what he chooses to fill it with, in a way that reflects his own languorous nature—a nature that seeps into the very fabric of the late films. Although known for the quick-talking, fast-paced films from earlier in his career (Hawks' early trick to perk up a flat scene was simply to have it done 25 percent faster) Hawks as a person was in fact an extremely slow talker and always moved at a deliberately relaxed pace. Actor Leo McKern, who met Hawks when being considered for a role in *Hatari!*, stated that he had "never met anyone who spoke or moved slower…. Not that there was any sense of weakness conveyed; on the contrary. I believe that it was simply that he had long ago decided that if anyone was going to come down with an ulcer, it was not H. H." The late films tend to take on this slowness, and in doing so reveal that Hawks' strength never lay in the pace of his films per se but rather in what that pace entailed in terms of the rhythms of character dynamics. The elder Hawks (65-years-old at the time of *Hatari!*'s premiere, for those keeping track) courted a different pace than the younger Hawks, one that prized less the snappiness of a humorous or romantic or dramatic interaction and more the materiality of it, the way it hung in the air and then settled on the ground, the way it forever bottled a specific word or gesture from a specific actor, the way it told in real time of an interaction between people that had value in and of itself *as* an interaction before it ever became, if indeed it ever did, a point along a plot. So when Hawks has his cast partake in a group singalong of "Whiskey, Leave Me Alone" over their radio transmitters—the second time the song had appeared in a Hawks film, after Kirk Douglas and Dewey Martin's rowdy saloon singalong in *The Big Sky* a decade before—he has no higher intentions for the moment other than to be a moment, a moment which simultaneously has no bearing on the story but also means everything in establishing the camaraderie of the group, and by extension establishing the camaraderie of the audience with that group; but even before that, it is simply pure human pleasure. The same idea applies, in a different tone, to the animal-capturing scenes. When Hawks follows the group in real time chasing one animal, capturing it, losing it, chasing it again, and finally capturing it again, he is showing the material reality of the job, the physical and emotional struggle it entails, in documentary detail. No less than Jean-Marie Straub, when asked a question about his own "austere, documentary" formal structure, answered that he is really no different from a Howard Hawks who, whether making a film about Al Capone or fliers or people catching animals, "is forced to know exactly how people can catch animals, that's all." Like many great and diverse filmmakers, Straub among them, Hawks is interested in the *matter* of life, the stuff that makes up the world and our interactions with it. In *Hatari!* this includes capturing animals, navigating love, playing with elephants, or simply the beauty of the African landscape—Hawks considered the film one of his Westerns, and German actor Hardy Kruger even fell in love with the area so much that he bought the farm the film is set at after filming was over.

At the heart of this film full to the brim with Hawksian pleasures: John Wayne, whose mere way of being is one of the Hawksian pleasures par excellence. His presence in the Hawks Westerns is as axiomatic as Cary Grant's presence in the Hawks comedies, and is a perfect companion for late Hawks in that the category of "late Wayne" begins around the same time. Late Hawks' laidback pace accentuates Wayne's gentle side in a way that his other common collaborators didn't always do. He's the ultimate representation of "man" for the older Hawks, the good-humored, hard-working, uncomplaining leader but also the stubborn, unperceptive, often romantically incompetent social creature, yet above all the man of constant, composed, and unwavering integrity, which emanates from him silently and invisibly, and at times even antagonistically, in the form of love for his fellow compatriots. Despite the utmost respect and high regard he holds for Wayne in the late films, Hawks is always also having fun at his expense, most embarrassingly so in the romantic entanglements he sends his way. Wayne is never a womanizer in Hawks, but because of his integrity and offbeat charm (and Hawks' own personal and directorial preference for how he liked women to act, it should be said) he becomes the one being wooed, chased after by a woman who, despite seeing his flaws more clearly than anyone, still can't manage to resist him. This courtship reversal is directly established early on when Dallas is told straight off by Pockets that the only way her goal is going to be achieved is if she herself makes it happen. Hawks had begun this woman-chasing-Wayne trope in *Rio Bravo* with Angie Dickinson on his trail, and the same concept would be the meat of the plot in his next film, with Paula Prentiss chasing Rock Hudson around in *Man's Favorite Sport?*; of course, this is a deeply Hawksian trope that goes back much further than the late films— *Bringing Up Baby* is the 100-miles-per-hour ne plus ultra of it—but late Hawks treasures it in a way that demonstrates the essentially *comic* nature of his last handful of films.

In the early 1970s, Hawks noted that "especially in the last ten or twelve years, every time I can get some comedy into a scene, I'll do it." Although Hawks had always had a humorous streak, the days of heavier-toned films like *The Dawn Patrol, The Road to Glory,* or *Only Angels Have Wings* was mostly long gone—even *Red Line 7000*, the main exception to Hawks' comment, has a poppier, self-ironic register that ultimately becomes something more complex than a straight designation of drama can contain. All of the later films share in this complexity, however, and despite each in turn appearing more comic or more dramatic than their neighboring films—even their neighboring scenes, so wildly and easily can Hawks veer from one to the other within the same film—are not easily classified as either comedy or drama. But the same thing could be said of life. Robin Wood, writing about *Rio Bravo* but applicable to most of Hawks, said that "there is a continual sense of the contrapuntal interaction of the various levels of seriousness and humor, so that great complexity of tone often results." Tone is one of those things that often gets late films in trouble with critics who expect or want a film to adhere to one easily digestible register, and the more tonally complex a film is the less many critics know what to do with it—the knee-jerk reaction then is often to dismiss it. It especially doesn't help when the tone is primarily comedic, which to many viewers immediately frames a film as silly rather than serious, and before it's even given a chance they've decided to look for mere laughs rather than any kind of profundity; and if the film doesn't conventionally deliver on those—as late comedies often dissonantly don't—such a viewer will receive as empty a film that is in fact full, just in a different, unconventionally complex way. *Man's Favorite Sport?* has been one of the many victims of such a mode of perception, a comedy of great tonal complexity that's filled with Hawks' movie-intuitive sense of humor, a sense, alas, that was formed and matured in a vastly different era from the 1964 of the film's release. Hence, dissonance and anachronism ensue. "*I* don't know why a thing is funny," Hawks would say. "It just happens to be funny, but the poor damn critic has to write about it. But, actually, very few critics, in my opinion, know what the hell it's all about."

Just who those few critics were we don't know, but Hawks certainly had a growing contingent of critics and fans who were following in the footsteps of his 1950s devotees into the 1960s in taking his work seriously. News of Hawks' passionate embrace by the French was slowly trickling into American film culture, largely through the efforts of critics Eugene Archer and Andrew Sarris who—with the help of their younger friend Peter Bogdanovich—convinced the New Yorker Theater to hold a program called "The Forgotten

Film" in January of 1961, a series of films over a third of which were ones by Howard Hawks. Many of the films hadn't been shown in years, and many were hits with new audiences. Bogdanovich kept the ball rolling by engineering a near-complete retrospective of Hawks' films (27 of the then 35) at the Museum of Modern Art in New York the next summer, which curator Richard Griffith agreed to host only if Bogdanovich could convince Paramount (the studio behind *Hatari!*) to pay for it; as their promotional campaign for *Hatari!* was the studio's largest ever to that point, they agreed. Bogdanovich travelled to Hollywood to interview Hawks for the series' accompanying monograph he was to pen. Writing on Hawks' films in general—much of it from the auteurist perspective adopted from critical forebears in France—picked up aplenty, and the Hawks bug reached England as well; *Movie*'s December 1962 issue, dedicated to a whole slew of writings on Hawks and with an image from *Hatari!* on the cover, helped further the cause by translating Rivette's 1953 "Genius" article into English for the first time.

But Hawks showed little sign that this newfound adulation had any effect on him or the kind of films he was making, reacting only with mild bemusement. For their December 1963/January 1964 double issue on American cinema, *Cahiers du cinéma* sent a survey out to a plethora of directors working in America—including Hawks—the answers to which were to be published in the issue. Six questions were given, with subjects ranging from current projects, conditions of production and distribution, to how Hollywood had changed in the last decade; Hawks responded by sending back a single still from the upcoming *Man's Favorite Sport?* of Rock Hudson up to his neck in a lake, with nothing written except his signature. On the one hand it's a supremely Hawksian joke, but on the other it's also an honest testament to Hawks' unpretentiousness when it came to his own status as a filmmaker. George Kirgo, one of the writers on *Red Line 7000*, would recall that whenever somebody sent Hawks a copy of *Cahiers*, he would laugh and say "I just aim the camera at the actors… and they make up all these things about me." To keep perspective, however, it must also be mentioned that Kirgo thought this a pose and, despite his love for Hawks, found him to be "the most self-involved, self-obsessed man I've ever met." Another person who claimed to see through Hawks' unpretentious-craftsman image was François Truffaut, who in the 1970s wished a book-length interview with Hawks could be done similar to his own with Alfred Hitchcock (a wish fulfilled by Joseph McBride's *Hawks on Hawks,* published in 1982). "He is one of the most intellectual filmmakers in America," Truffaut would write toward the end of Hawks' life. "He often speaks in terms of film concepts. He has many general theories. He doesn't belong to the school of instinctive filmmakers. He thinks of everything he does, everything is thought out. So somebody ought to tell him one day that despite himself he is an intellectual and that he has to accept that." Truffaut may have had a point, that behind Hawks' veneer of anti-intellectualism was a thinker deeply invested in solving the problems of his chosen craft, one who simply adopted for convenience the general viewpoint that that craft, Hollywood filmmaking, couldn't possibly be worth calling an art.

Man's Favorite Sport?, however, certainly wouldn't convert anyone to the "Hawks the intellectual artist" camp who wasn't already a member. A romantic comedy about a ridiculously persistent woman chasing around a befuddled man who's engaged to someone else, the unavoidable "*Bringing Up Baby* 25 years later" label immediately brings to mind not just the obvious similarities between the two films but perhaps more so the distance separating them—for many critics, the distance separating the over-the-hill fatiguedness of *Man's Favorite Sport?* from *Bringing Up Baby*'s lightning-in-a-bottle vigor. But to say that *Bringing Up Baby* is "better" than *Man's Favorite Sport?* is to slip back into an unedifying consumerist mindset that has nothing to do with late style's perspective of meeting the artist where they are rather than where they once were, or where we would like them to be. Hawks is still Hawks—the unapologetic reworking of *Bringing Up Baby* and his common woman-chasing-man plot makes that obvious—but the Hawks of 1964 is not the same Hawks of

1938; and, obvious though it may be, 1964 itself is not 1938. Hollywood is different. The world is different. For a simple example, when Hawks repeats the same ripped-dress gag from the earlier film we see the woman's bare back rather than one clothed with undergarments. Rock Hudson is not Cary Grant (Hawks' first choice for the role, but who turned it down on the basis of his unwillingness to play the romantic lead with such young women)—this much is obvious. But despite the similarity of the role to Grant-led Hawks comedies of yore, it does no good to pay attention to the non-Grant-ness of the role rather than the Rock Hudson-ness of it. Hudson isn't Grant, and he doesn't need to be—the bumbling charm hidden under his suave front makes the role Hudson's own, as it did in the actor's comedic performances in a handful of other films. The same could be said for Paula Prentiss in the Katharine Hepburn role; she need only be herself, molded by Hawks' universe, to become a perfectly suitable Hawksian character—someone who recalls other Hawks characters while still being entirely themselves. In the same way, *Man's Favorite Sport?* recalls other Hawks films while still being entirely itself. Which just so happens to be the foundational fact behind not just the idea of cinematic authorship that goes by *auteurism* but that of late style in cinema as well, whose investigation-triggering question pertains to the exact nature of the "entirely itself" of that equation.

The pleasures are different: for example, where *Baby* is fast, *Sport* is slow. Where in *Baby* they talked a mile a minute and a new gag was introduced seemingly every few seconds, *Sport* luxuriates in its jokes and bits and gags, letting them play out in all their banal, out-of-time, "unfunny" glory. "Unfunny" because it's the same 1930s material but in a modern 1960s setting: "mostly old stuff—trouble with the tent, the foot in the bucket, etc." as Donald Willis put it. The anachronistic content of the gags, however, is re-imagined in the form of 1960s Hawks, a form more willing to let a thing play out in real, untampered time; similar to more modern comic performers like Jerry Lewis[3] or Jacques Tati, Hawks stretches out a gag almost to its breaking point, to the edge of being funny, sometimes even over the edge, which ironically makes it even more funny while also letting a hint of poignancy creep in to each gag that a more rapid-fire style wouldn't necessarily have room for. So rather than *Bringing Up Baby*, the Hawks film *Sport* most resembles is *Hatari!*; it almost plays like Hawks plucked the main romantic comedy element out of that film and stretched it into its own feature-length variation, with the same day's work/evening social play structure, the danger of the hunt traded in for the comedy of the fishing interludes, and then an enclosed social environment in which the film completely and languorously becomes about little more than relationships between characters. Hawks' plans for *Sport*'s runtime were also similarly ambitious. The film went into its first preview in a 145-minute cut, which Hawks reported to be a smashing success; the studio, however, wished it trimmed down to fit in more daily showtimes, which when done and previewed got less successful results; panicking, instead of restoring it they decided to cut it down even further to its current two-hour runtime. Hawks claimed this sabotaged the film—essentially eliminating all of the contextual "plant" scenes which were needed to make the remaining scenes funny—and led to his dissatisfaction with the ultimate result. But even without the excised time, *Sport* is still Hawks' slowest-paced comedy by far. Fernando Villaverde notes that the comedy doesn't follow a classical model, but rather that its "drawing out" of its gags for comedic effect was "something palpable that occurs within the scene, where repetition and failure produce a certain discomfort in the spectator, which is cranked up until it is finally released with laughter. This produces a much more physical relationship with time." As such, *Sport* continues the modernist play with time of *Hatari!* rather than retreating to the classical manner of its more ostensible precursor *Bringing*

---

[3] Lewis, big man on the lot at Paramount at the time, would cameo in *Red Line 7000* as one of the race car drivers (it is impossible to tell which) for which Hawks paid him scale for the day.

Up Baby, and does it specifically in the realm of comedy. "In slowing down the tempo," Erich Kuersten even claims that "Hawks ushers the film onto a postmodern pedestal, turning it this way and that until the tired old gags become positively Brechtian in their museum-light luster."

Despite appearances, *Man's Favorite Sport?* is no staid studio comedy past its sell-by date. In addition to its experimentation with the gag, it can also easily be called Hawks' most surrealist film. Hawks' early comedies, despite their incredulity (a natural screwball staple), never quite leave the realm of possibility, and only the science-fiction elements of *Monkey Business* and *The Thing from Another World* (1951) show Hawks venturing into the realm of the truly unreal, although even there the unreality is remarkably integrated with the otherwise functional realism of the proceedings. *Sport* offers a few things that are too outlandish or cartoonish to easily fit with Hawks' usual level of realism, such as a bear that Hudson encounters while riding his motorbike—after crashing, Hudson sees the bear take over his place on the bike and casually ride away like it was a normal occurrence—or the extra-filmic visual punctuations of trains crashing together inserted after Hudson and Prentiss kiss (a surprising device because used nowhere else in Hawks), or the simple fact that Hawks' sets have gotten phonier, more cardboard, more obviously built on studio backlots. The general feeling of the film is one of quaint ridiculousness, where anybody can be anybody and anyone can do anything for no other reason than the fact that they exist inside a screwball comedy, which nobody seems to realize hasn't been a popular type of comedy since the 1930s and '40s. Miscommunications and misunderstandings proliferate to the point of absurdity. This gives Hawks the chance to throw his characters together in situations and conversations which exist only to further their relationships with each other and with the audience, in a screwball variation on *Hatari!*'s downtime scenes. The actual words and actions matter little as the actors perform a dance around a feeling or a confession that we know must eventually be said but that no one wants to say. David Thomson has written of the "dazzling battles of word, innuendo, glance, and gesture" between Hawks couples, including Hudson and Prentiss, that "are Utopian procrastinations to avert the paraphernalia of released love that can only expend itself. In other words, Hawks is at his best in moments when nothing happens beyond people arguing about what might happen or has happened." One gets the sense that nothing would ever happen in a Hawks film if there wasn't a girl around to get the ball rolling, a theme prevalent in the last two Hawks films as well as the raison d'etre more or less for both *Sport* and the first full articulation of the theme in *Bringing Up Baby*. Both contain parallel quotes about how the love impulse in man shows itself in conflict, stating the theme of these twin films out loud. But the outrageous difficulty of actually getting anywhere via that impulse, as shown to the hilt in *Baby*, is simplified a bit in the late *Sport*, where, as in *Hatari!*, the trick is simply for the girl to go up to the guy and casually ask him to kiss.

There's never any great reason behind the romantic impulse in Hawks, it's simply there, popping up organically in a character almost against their will. Prentiss can't explain to her friend why she's in love with Hudson and later Hudson can't explain, despite everything, why he nonetheless finds her "strangely attractive," almost liking her at times. Similarly intuitive, illogical reasoning rears its head throughout Hawks, and not just in romantic situations: when asked why they fly despite the danger it entails, the veteran pilots in *Only Angels Have Wings* search within themselves and find no good answer—they just fly. There is never any reason short of divine intervention or sheer dumb luck to account for how Rock Hudson is able to catch any fish at all in *Man's Favorite Sport?*, let alone win the tournament he's been entered in, and Hawks draws out such fishing sequences, twisting them into hilarious knots, to emphasize the absurdity of such an achievement. But the mysterious will animating Hudson's tournament victory could be said to be the same one drawing him toward Prentiss against his better judgment. As such, one half of the film offers a metaphor for the other: like catching a fish with your back turned, falling in love happens when you least expect it—without even realizing it, without knowing why it's happening, without any control over the situation. Or as a character in *Red Line 7000*—perhaps Hawks' ultimate statement on the illogicality and irrationality of love—says, "if love makes sense, then it isn't love." The eventually-discarded fiancées in both *Baby* and *Sport* live in an ordered, logical world and therefore demand explanations for their betrothed's behavior; the succeeding lovers don't—they simply feel the way they do, without being able to help themselves, and accept it on faith that therefore it is meant to be. Such a worldview is playful, childish, naïve, but in another sense awfully mature: Hawks respects life, and therefore respects the mystery.

This goes along with a Hawksian maturity that *Sport*, perhaps more than any other Hawks film, reveals: that the oft-spoken-of "Hawksian professionalism" he prizes in his characters is not, in fact, an end in and of itself; but rather that behind this trait is a deeper virtue that one might call *honesty of being*—a matching of external and internal being, an absence of hypocrisy, an integrity and wholeness of one's person. Despite being unimpeachably good at his job, it's clear that Rock Hudson's fishing gear salesman doesn't share in the Hawksian virtue that the professionalism of so many of his other characters causes them to possess. Hudson is a phony; he can't actually fish, and his expertise is entirely second-hand. By itself this is no crime. His advice to his customers is uniformly excellent. But his phoniness is still presented as a character flaw because his external self doesn't conform to his internal one, which for Hawks trumps a professionalism for professionalism's sake. The solution to this problem will eventually be Hudson's confession of ineptitude—importantly from his own willing mouth, rather than revealed by a poor tournament performance (the film goes to the length of miracles to not allow him to get off that easily)—which ironically causes him to get back the very job he had resigned from in shame. But he's still a fishing expert who can't fish! No matter, however, since his honesty resolves his external/internal discrepancy and earns him a Hawksian wholeness and integrity of character; his professionalism becomes an extension of his specific identity rather than a front of fakery. Along with *Monkey Business,* then, *Sport* has a seriousness underlying its comedy that's more visible in late Hawks than early. This goes along with the patient, amiable, durational elements of late Hawks, which *Sport*'s at-times uniquely contemplative moods couldn't quite exist without; whereas there's too much business constantly going on in *Bringing Up Baby* for any real moments of pause, in *Sport* both Hudson and Prentiss get full moments to mope or think or just be.

There are pleasures and profundities galore in early Hawks, but the late films display a quiet maturity that's an integral result of their unhurried, casual, unzeitgeisty temperaments. This is true even of a film that on its surface appears the loudest and most "hip" of the final Hawks films. *Red Line 7000* is ostensibly a thrilling picture about the lives and loves of modern racecar drivers, yet the majority of the film consists of remarkably hushed conversations in intimate spaces—quiet moments between friends or lovers in a bed, a car, an office, an empty courtyard, a hospital room, etc. Hawks takes a cast of young, fresh faces in a 1960s environment of hopping bars and roaring racetracks and somehow ends up making one of his most muted, mature, minor key films. It's also the most pertinent example of the way the classicalist, traditionalist side of Hawks productively clashes with his modernist impulses, or as Peter John Dyer put it, "it is the constant cross-graining of cliché and inventive detail which produces the shock of pleasure his best work provides." The late-career *Red Line* has an early-career counterpart in *The Crowd Roars* (1932), Hawks' previous racing picture, but one of the important ideas behind the film goes all the way back to 1921, from Hawks' earliest days in the motion picture business. His friend Marshall Neilan had directed a film called *Bits of Life* which was an anthology of four different short stories. Over the years Hawks kept the idea of making a film out of multiple stories and finally tested it with *Red Line,* which would weave together three storylines set within the same world. No script existed yet when Hawks sent out his second unit director to collect footage from NASCAR races, and when he sat down with his hired writers he didn't have much in the way of a story, just a few character ideas; they listened to him describe racetrack incidents from his past and scenes from some of his old movies. The structure that finally resulted from this dissatisfied him—he found that dropping one storyline for another just when the audience was getting interested ultimately made for a poor picture. But Hawks overstates the degree to which the storylines are truly separate, as the main characters—three guys and three girls—overlap into each other's stories enough to give the impression that it's ultimately one canvas we're looking at, not three. I use the word canvas intentionally, as what's created from the three converging semi-plots is the closest thing to an Art Object that Hawks ever made. Hawks didn't make Art Objects—he told stories on film. But the structure of *Red Line* allows the film to slip away from him a bit in that regard. The film, like an album of music or a triptych in painting, is an *accumulation*. Its wholeness isn't created by following the story of one group of people but by interlacing multiple stories, stacking scenes on top of scenes, weaving together a web of characters and relationships, plots and perspectives, that finally congeal to produce what the film ultimately *is,* in toto. So what Hawks saw as a classical weakness is actually a modernist strength; the experimental structure allows for multiple subjectivities to create a dialectical whole via Hawks' own relaxed take on cinematic montage.

Hawks had grown old enough to live into an era where the techniques of his youth could be mistaken for, or simply become, modernist gestures. In a culture that was coming to expect increased realism, Hawks films the racing sequences with techniques not very far removed from those used on *The Crowd Roars* a generation or two earlier: mostly a combination of second-unit documentary and stock footage with shots of the actors done in-studio using rear projection. The artificiality is clear and unconcealed. "Such moments," suggests Joe McElhaney, "bring the film more in line with the deliberately artificial car rides of sixties art cinema, epitomised by Federico Fellini's 'Toby Dammit' episode from… *Spirits of the Dead* [1968]." Or note, as Villaverde would have us, the shot of a flaming car that begins the film, "exactly the same as the one Godard would later use in *Weekend* (1967) to represent society's collapse." *Red Line*'s representation of the specificities of its contemporary setting tipped over, for some critics of the time, into an ugly commercialism, their ire targeted largely at the use of product placement in the film. Most noticeable in an outdoor scene between James Caan and Marianna Hill where the two talk over bottles of Pepsi retrieved from a vending machine, at closer inspection the scene is too charged and intimate for the obviousness of the Pepsi label on their drinks to register as anything but an ironic signifier of modernity—to prove the point, the Pepsi corporation wasn't happy with how the scene essentially eroticized its product. McElhaney clocks the use of advertising imagery as akin to what Michelangelo Antonioni would do in *Zabriskie Point* (1970) with advertising billboards—"elevating them to the level of graphic abstraction and rendering irrelevant what is being sold"—or to Andy Warhol's Pop Art, "with its frequent use of commercial logos multiplied and refracted in numerous ways, elevating this commercial raw material to the mythic and the ironic."

Red Line doesn't just have parallels in the world of art cinema, but according to Richard Thompson also deliberately clashes with the kinds of racing pictures commercial Hollywood was making around the same time. He points out that, à la Hawks making *Rio Bravo* in response to *High Noon,* so too *Red Line* offers a counter to such Hollywood racing films: "Hawks, who has never strayed from his commitment to casual (and as we'll see, causal) hipness, would hardly consider doing a picture about the high-brow Grand Prix world when its American-/Hawksian counterpart exists in stock car racing; but on the other hand, lacking the social and political orientation manifested in [Tom] Wolfe and *Thunder Road* [1958], and being more a documentarist than a legend maker for youth-rebellion heroes, Hawks must make it his own way. He chooses to make a practical, somewhat disillusioning statement of how it is in stock car racing without that legend stuff." As always, no matter the ostensible subject or genre, Hawks can do nothing but make a Hawks movie—that is, a movie which will be about characters and character relations before it's about anything else. But *Red Line* will be about this in a unique way because, unlike Hawks' other films, none of the actors are stars; they don't bring metaphysical baggage into their performances and, therefore, are free to be something like Hawksian models, to borrow a concept from Robert Bresson. (Some of whom weren't thrilled at being molded in this way.) The six main characters—all played by young, conventionally attractive 1960s actors—wander around the bar/restaurant or motel[4] sets falling in and out of love with each other in often disarmingly upfront sequences of emotional vulnerability; I'm hard pressed to think of a movie that contains more instances of "I'm in love with you" or variations thereof directly spoken in its dialogue. It may all seem a bit silly if you're not willing to be emotionally keyed in at the same serious tone as the film you're watching, a film with so many tears it may seem more like a soap opera than the melodrama it is (while it doesn't abandon comedy completely, it is the heaviest late Hawks by far), a melodrama in the same vein as something like *Only Angels Have Wings,* which along with other early Hawks films is the precursor for *Red Line*'s dramatic stakes of men courting death in order to do their jobs. And to the potential heartbreak of a woman—Jean Arthur in *Wings* is the '30s prototype for the three '60s women of *Red Line* who argue with themselves over whether it's worth being in love when the possibility of that love being snatched away is inches away every time their man steps into his speeding machine. Even Arthur's climatic yell of "Heyyyy!!" upon belatedly realizing Cary Grant has asked her to stay is updated here to a hospital scene between Laura Devon and John Robert Crawford, who

---

[4] Another small difference between early and late Hawks: the bar/ restaurant is usually the same location as the hotel in famous sets like that of *Only Angels Have Wings* or *To Have and Have Not*; it is also worth noting that Red Line's bar/restaurant/nightclub combination is supposedly what Quentin Tarantino based his Jack Rabbit Slim's *Pulp Fiction* set on; Tarantino wrote that film's script in Amsterdam where in the evenings he attended a running Howard Hawks retrospective that was going on in the city.

has lost his hand in a crash. Faced with his emasculated reluctance to voice his desire for her, she gets up to walk out of the room in order to force him; he finally asks her to stay, and then she turns and embraces him in a fit of tears. (A casual, wonderfully Hawksian cut swiftly puts Crawford back in a racecar, a hook for a hand.)

Hawks begins the film the same way he often does to establish the dramatic stakes: with death or injury as a result of the profession we are about to watch an entire film of people doing. *Red Line 7000* is the ultimate expression of Hawks' foundational dramatic impulse, which he himself succinctly summarized in an interview: "There is no action when there is no danger. It follows that if you achieve real action, there must be danger. To live or to die! What drama is greater?" Life or death stakes are emblazoned all over *Red Line*; the tension created by the possibility of death seeps into every moment of downtime—the roar and excitement from the racetrack echoing into all those hushed, intimate scenes—in a way that it doesn't in another late film like *Hatari!*, where even though danger lurks ("hatari" literally means "danger" in Swahili) it isn't as much of a constant, explicit fear as it is in *Red Line.* It creates a thrillingly complex, and modern, mood and atmosphere. The film follows the same A-B-A-B… structure of activity/downtime as the previous two late films, but the downtime is haunted by the nearness of death. Every race presents not only the possibility of death for one of the men, but the possibility that one of the women will have to grieve said death. The woman played by Gail Hire[5] embodies this to the extreme, as her character is given the burden of believing, because of past events in her history, that her falling in love with a driver is literally akin to a death sentence for him. She and the other women have plenty of logical reasons not to get involved with these men, to refuse the relationships, but—as

---

[5] A one-time-only performance from a girl Hawks discovered by seeing her on a billboard and ordering someone to find her and screen test her; it's one of the great one-offs in film history, as to these eyes no other Hawksian woman came so close to Hawks' favorite of them all, Lauren Bacall.

in the other late Hawks films that respect the mystery of this film's "it's not love if it makes sense" line—love trumps logic, and chooses to stare death in the eye rather than abandon its object. Just as in *Man's Favorite Sport?*, the sport the men go off to do by themselves serves as a metaphor for the love games that happen when they return to home base. Hawks loves both dangerous situations and communal spaces, and their juxtaposition is the engine behind the films' drama: the masculine urge to go off and do something potentially dangerous that makes you feel alive, and then to return home to the bar, restaurant, club, whatever—the site of drinks, conversation, and, most importantly, the female. The latter things are a release from the former things, yes, but they also present a different kind of danger—that of relationships, where despite appearances you have just as little control over what happens as out in the field of danger: you could be victorious, but you could also get burned. Things are just going to happen how they're going to happen. In this, *Red Line* is an incredibly adult picture; true to love and heartbreak, life and death, and more.

The issue of the curse felt by Hire's character comes to a head in a scene between her and Charlene Holt, a slightly older, maternal figure in the film. "I always thought it was God who decided who lived or died," she says sharply to Hire. "And you don't look a bit like God to me." This brief religious interjection comes as a surprise at the tail end of a filmography largely absent religious sentiment. But this also gives it a unique power, and a brief pondering of the statement quickly reveals it as an explanation of almost all of Hawks, the unspoken reason why his characters are able to accept death and move on the way they do. It's relevant to note that one of the only other such explicitly religious statement in Hawks— in *Red River*, when Wayne reads over the grave of a departed member of his cattle drive—is identical in meaning as the one spoken in *Red Line*: "We brought nothing into this world, and it's certain we can carry nothing out. The Lord gave and the Lord hath taken away. Blessed be the name of the Lord. Amen." Even though this kind of moment is rare in Hawks (who himself, though raised Protestant, was not particularly religious), it attests to a religious feeling that's buried deep in the films but usually only comes out via implication, mired in the stuff of life, in how the acceptance of things and their mysteries—of love, of death—is necessary in order to survive. Hawks' characters accept, or learn to accept, their not-God status. From the "Who's Joe?" coping mechanism routine early in *Only Angels Have Wings,* to Harry Carey Jr.'s burial in *Red River,* to *Red Line*'s opening funeral—attended casually, like it's just another part of the job[6]—Hawksian professionalism always contains an undertone of submission to a divine will. One wonders how much this theme emerges accidental to the overall Hawksian attitude, or whether it arises more, if not intentionally, then subconsciously from Hawks himself: one can recall, for instance, that Hawks lost his younger brother Kenneth early in his own directorial career to an aviation stunt accident.

Red Line 7000 clips along at a patient yet breezy pace, shot with a Hawksian, unemphatic straightforwardness that *captures* the charged, tense energy of its individual scenes rather than needing to create it; these scenes then casually dissolve one into the next, and by the end of the film we've already reached the beginning of a new racing season—contrary to Hawks' usual condensed timelines, he has made *Red Line* into one of his rare elliptical movies, like *Red River* or *Land of the Pharaohs* (albeit in miniature), without us even noticing. Hawks ends with a beautiful moment of female solidarity: the three women at the racetrack watching, hoping, loving, seated together as they watch their men embark on another year of courting death—as we are reminded in an abrupt and shocking final shot of a car crashing out of a race, returning us to the film's beginning. This rare moment of feminine camaraderie in Hawks comes as an assertion of what could be called his late period's newfound openness to the female perspective (the late

---

[6] A too-good-not-to-mention contemporary parallel to *Red Line*'s theme and treatment of love and death in the line of racing duty is *Ferrari* (2023), the latest film from Michael Mann, a modern master to Hawks' classical one.

films consistently have more prominent female roles: two in *Hatari!*, *Sport,* and *El Dorado,* three in *Rio Lobo,* and four in *Red Line* compared to the usual one in earlier Hawks films) as well as additional evidence for feminist readings of Hawks that sprang up in the 1960s and '70s. It also anticipates *Rio Lobo*'s use of its female cast members as important pillars of its peripatetic plot. Hawks' casting choices with his young actors have taken a fair share of criticism—having prided himself on being a kind of unofficial talent scout since the beginning of his career, his failure to launch the careers of any female actors with his late films is used as evidence of his failing powers—but what these fresh faces lacked in conventional old-Hollywood charisma they made up for in sheer Hawksian presence, modern figures molded into statues of classical beauty with whom Hawks could populate his stories-written-on-cinema. Their unique energies also charged Hawks' images in a way older, more familiar, more classically trained presences couldn't. James Caan (the only new face in late Hawks who went on to a traditionally successful acting career) in *Red Line 7000* is the supreme example of this, a ferociously modern performance trapped in Hawks' classical frames, a barrel of pent-up energy eked out in mumbles and whispers, a gamut of emotions from melancholy acceptance to full-on rage all coiled up inside this short, curt man. He epitomizes the modernism of *Red Line* at the same time as he makes visible the classical parameters Hawks still functioned within. In this we see one of the many paradoxes that define Hawks' late style.

Robin Wood wrote that *Red Line 7000* "is perhaps, in Britain at least, the most underestimated film of the sixties." He saw in it an experimental modernism that completely belied Hawks' stated disappointment with the film; some other (mostly auteurist) critics agreed. But this was not the majority opinion whatsoever. Nonetheless, the case for the genius of Howard Hawks continued to be pushed by a small contingent in the 1960s and '70s as he wound down his career, and if critics were able to do so it was often on account of their ability to adopt Hawks to their own modernist purposes. Thus a magazine like *Cahiers du cinéma* could stick with Hawks into the 1960s despite editorial shakeups and changing emphases within the magazine; Hawks could be claimed by both the classical vein of '50s *Cahiers* and the more modernist one of the '60s. Late Hawks appealed to auteurists across the globe of the 1960s and '70s in a similar way as artists like Beethoven appealed to Theodor Adorno and Edward Said in their writings on late style. Such artists could be seen as possessing an unconscious modernism despite working within a classical framework; their works were ripe for recruitment into the cause of artistic modernism because they operated "against the grain" of their mediums' contemporaneous conventions. No matter that such adoption was itself anachronistic, quite literally in Beethoven's case and in Hawks', given he was unlikely to have had any aspirations to modernist art, clearly a case of going beyond artist intention. Which there's nothing wrong with—in both cases perceptive thinkers sought to relate such artists to the *now,* which it is possible to do with all great art, and especially so with great late art, because it represents a clash between past and present that pushes it into the realm of the timeless and ever-relevant.

As Hawks was still alive and working, his increasing reputation as a hidden master of Hollywood cinema coincided with the releases of the final films of his career. So while writing continued to pour forth from both French and English language sources—a January 1963 issue of *Cahiers* dedicated entirely to Hawks, an interview conducted by the young duo of Serge Daney and Louis Skorecki in 1964, two French monographs published in 1966 and 1971, the twin 1968 publications of Robin Wood's monograph and Andrew Sarris' *The American Cinema* (in which Hawks was designated a "pantheon" filmmaker), as well as the 1972 critical anthology *Focus on Howard Hawks*, to name just a few things—Hawks was also a living figure that cinema fanatics could rub shoulders with. French publicist and general man-about-cinema Pierre Rissient befriended Hawks and shot screen tests for him in Europe and introduced him to many actresses; Peter Bogdanovich became something of a mentee to Hawks, interviewing him often, visiting his film sets to watch him work, and even teaching a class on his films at UCLA in 1969. Young filmmakers of the next generation like Bogdanovich and Martin Scorsese would excerpt Hawks films diegetically into their own early work—*The Criminal Code* (1931) in *Targets* (1968), *Red River* in *The Last Picture Show* (1971), *Rio Bravo* in *Who's That Knocking at My Door* (1967)—synchronously with the release of Hawks' own, final films.

But the question in the air amidst all this homage and rediscovery was whether this was all a case of nostalgia for the great Hawks films of ages past or whether the contemporary Hawks was still making films worthy of such attention. Or to return to the original proclamation given by Rivette (who had launched his own career as a filmmaker by this point): was the evidence on the screen *still* proof of Howard Hawks' genius? It's no secret that many then, and many now, would answer in the negative. But someone looking through the eyes of late style might answer differently. Rivette's dictum that you only have to watch *Monkey Business* to know that it's a brilliant film was always a kind of tautology that spoke past certain viewers, which raises the question of just what kind of viewer he *was* talking about. Most likely it was those in the early auteurist camp, whose sensibilities opened them up to receiving more from a film like *Monkey Business* than other viewers, with less radical or mystical approaches to cinema, were able to. As the concept of late style performs a similar, parallel reorientation of the viewer, so too are those looking through this lens able to receive more from a film like *Red Line 7000* than those who aren't. In other words, *how* you see a film will affect *what* you see. So a late stylist is just as capable of saying, or at least meaning something similar to, a sentence like "you only have to watch *Red Line 7000* to know that it is a brilliant film."

Suffice it to say, however, that the only perceptions Hawks really concerned himself with were his own and his (commercial) audience's—and films like *Man's Favorite Sport?* and *Red Line 7000* satisfied neither. Hawks had a mind to beat a retreat to a more dependable, more comfortable kind of film for both himself to make and for an audience to enjoy: a Western. With *El Dorado* and *Rio Lobo*, Hawks would close the lid on his career with a double dose of the same potion that had resulted in *Rio Bravo,* one of his most artistically and commercially successful recent films. And given that he had the formula that had worked for that film, why not use it again? Hawks had always unashamedly borrowed and pilfered ideas from his own past films, but besides the literal remake of *A Song Is Born,* the two late Westerns would be Hawks' most explicit "remakes" of his career. When asked by interviewers about repeating himself, Hawks would often (repeatedly) turn to sporting analogies. "If a quarterback throws a touchdown pass, he should quit now because he's already done it? If it was good once, it can be good again." Or "if a man, a good boxer, hits somebody with a left hook, he doesn't stop left-hooking in the rest of his fights. And anybody who is any good—any writer—is always going to repeat himself, so that you're going to know who wrote the thing." Hawks even liked it when someone said he repeated himself—"Because if they can remember that long, the scene must be pretty good." Hawks had a sense of humor about these things; repetition, unlike some other aspects of his artistry, could not be totally confused for a subconscious impulse—it was intentional. Bogdanovich relates a story from the set of *Rio Lobo* when Hawks made a rare announcement to the entire cast: "Now, if there's anyone here today… who recognizes certain lines or situations. Anyone who finds some of these things familiar…"—Hawks paused, hands still on hips, and looked Bogdanovich straight in the eye—"… He can just damn well shut up about it!" Wayne, who knew Bogdanovich, laughed at the joke as he knew Hawks was also ribbing himself when he said it.

But that said, Hawks didn't view *El Dorado* and *Rio Lobo* as remakes. He even cited his friend Ernest Hemingway in artistic defense of stealing from himself, while saying that although the two later Westerns share similarities of style with *Rio Bravo,* they shouldn't be confused for having the same story. This is true in some ways and untrue in others. (A flip of Hawks' take would be closer to the truth: though the later Westerns share similarities of plot with *Rio Bravo,* they shouldn't be confused for having the same style.) *El Dorado*'s whole first hour of plot is without parallel in *Rio Bravo*, and *Rio Lobo* takes even longer to settle down into something resembling its predecessors. Yes, the character set-ups are similar—Wayne as the head of a group of four men in a situation involving a jail and prisoner exchanges—but the way Hawks involves women in each is significantly different, character attributes get inverted (Nelson's sharpshooting into Caan's incompetent gunmanship) or shaken up (the sheriff becomes the drunk), and most importantly each film represents a shift in *style*. Those who insist on *El Dorado* and *Rio Lobo* as unoriginal copies of *Rio Bravo* reveal themselves as viewers who focus on plot at the expense of form; while anyone could study the three films' stories and make a list of similarities and differences, it's when viewing the films *as* films that their essential originalities come to light. And yet the fact that they are all indeed variations on the same general subject remains important, for this allows a greater understanding of both Hawks' approach to originality—he variates enough to challenge himself but not enough to become uncomfortable—as well as where he is an artist at any given moment in time. Greg Ford compares Hawks' run of related Westerns to artists such as Henri Matisse, who "painted his odalisque figure in the same reclining position throughout his life, but from ever-changing angles and with varying degrees of formal abstraction"; or William Faulkner, who "recapitulated his tale of Jack Houston's murder a total of three times, and on each occasion emphasized new aspects of the killing, highlighted new areas of concern"; or Wallace Stevens, who wrote a series of rhymes called "Thirteen Ways of Looking at a Blackbird." Why can't Hawks, asks Ford, do a series of Westerns "which, taken together, might easily be designated '3 Ways of Looking at a Male Friendship'?" Hawks always fed off his previous work and relished the chance of recontextualizing it in the mode of the present, and the last two Westerns attest to that in their very being; Jean-Pierre Coursodon labels Hawks' late period as "one of self-exploitation, with Hawks distorting and degrading his own formulas in his effort to revitalize them."

Like a chef experimenting with his own recipes, Hawks was after new tastes but with the same dish.

If repeatedly remixing his own hits with an aging John Wayne wasn't unfashionable enough, Hawks was also making Westerns in a world where the Western itself had fundamentally changed. As the 1960s inched closer to the 1970s, the genre's status as a staple of classical Hollywood was beginning to decline, and many new Westerns reflected that in a dying-of-the-West metatextuality. John Ford's *The Man Who Shot Liberty Valance* (1962), which looked ambivalenty on the myths of the West that were implicitly believed in by most of the classical Westerns from the decades before, was just one of many films that seemed to serve as an elegy for the entire genre. Meanwhile, the genre underwent a diversification in the form of Spaghetti Westerns, Euro-Westerns, and Exploitation Westerns—as well as Hollywood entries less beholden to (increasingly slackening) censorship—where amidst cross-cultural experimentation things generally got dirtier, grimier, and bloodier. Hawks, however, showed little sign of being influenced by any evolutions in the genre outside of the ones he himself was undergoing. The most that can be said is that the gradual elimination of the production code led to a slight rise in the viscerality of his violence, but even that was nothing compared to a film like Sam Peckinpah's *The Wild Bunch* (1969), which Hawks wasn't shy about disliking. Rather, Hawks' late Westerns, in their adherence to the classical makeup of the Western at a time when it was disappearing, brought to the fore the intrinsic fakeness of the classical genre: the fake punches, fake shooting, and fake sets (Sallitt: "in the eight years between [*Rio Bravo* and *El Dorado*], Hawks had become less interested in disguising his sets as anything but a set, and his actors as anything but friends") were all more obvious in the increasingly realist paradigm that was coming to reign in the 1970s. In this, Hawks' Westerns participate more generally in the "lateness" inherent to the genre itself in the 1960s, '70s, and beyond. *El Dorado* opened in the U.S. in the summer of 1967 soon after *For a Few Dollars More* (1965), the second film in Sergio Leone's trilogy of Italian Westerns;

Rio Lobo opened in December 1970 the same week as Arthur Penn's *Little Big Man* (1970), a film that plays up the ridiculousness of Western myths from a socially conscious angle. Neither comparison could have made Hawks' Westerns seem very modern or exciting in the context of the late 1960s and early 1970s revolutions in cinema. Hawks, who at this point in his life preferred watching TV and reading magazines, rarely visited the cinema, and it's no surprise that his finger had slipped off the pulse of the American moviegoing public. But the resulting dissonance now makes Hawks' films of the era in many ways more fascinating than other films that seemed newer or more exciting at the time.

Hawks may not have set out to make any elegies or grand statements about the West when making his final Westerns—he was too unsentimental for all that—but if the films still offer a meta-textual resonance, it's largely because of the aging, end-of-an-era status of both Hawks and, more immediately, John Wayne. In the years between *Hatari!* and *El Dorado* Wayne had been diagnosed with cancer, resulting in the removal of one of his lungs; it slowed him down, and with Hawks getting into his seventies himself (and having suffered two leg injuries while shooting *Rio Lobo*, one while shooting a train set piece and one while biking off-set), their final two collaborations reflect a physically wearier (yet no less spiritually buoyant) temperament that turned down the dial on the more "athletic" films of *Hatari!*, *Man's Favorite Sport?*, and *Red Line 7000*. Age became not just a physical concern, but very much a thematic one as well. As it happens, the Hawks-Wayne partnership had begun 20 years earlier with Wayne cast as an older man in *Red River*—"just watch me," was the then-50-years-old Hawks' advice to Wayne on how to play it. Now he didn't have to act. But as Luc Moullet has written, old age "was to become the principal motif of Wayne's art"; despite mostly ignoring it in his own personal productions, he allowed his two closest collaborators in Hawks and Ford to give shape to this rich thematic vein. After *Red River*—supposedly the film that made Ford realize Wayne could really act—Ford immediately made him up even older in *She Wore a Yellow*

Ribbon (1949). Wayne's taste of Oscar gold finally came in *True Grit* (1969), a film explicitly playing up the old-man angle to a near-stereotypical degree, and he would don the eye-patch again in *Rooster Cogburn* (1975) for another go at the character, this time alongside Katharine Hepburn. Wayne gave in completely to the metatextual nature of the theme in his final film, Don Siegel's *The Shootist* (1976), playing an aging gunslinger dying of cancer—significantly, a film whose backstory-setting opening credits sequence includes black-and-white excerpts of Wayne from *Red River, Rio Bravo,* and *El Dorado.* Hawks himself was no stranger to the age theme, which was hardly exclusive to his late films: Thomas Mitchell's "Kid" in *Only Angels Have Wings* losing his sight and therefore losing his wings, James Robertson Justice's Vashtar in *Land of the Pharaohs* going blind while building the pyramid to free his people, *Red River*'s generational drama with Wayne in search of an heir, and of course the central issue of *Monkey Business* all revolve around the body/spirit contrasts arising from the effects of time. But *El Dorado* and *Rio Lobo* approach the same theme from a lighter, more comfortable point of view—age brings not sadness, but serenity. Hawks later said that "I'm not very interested in making pictures about old men." Despite this, or because of it, Hawks' vision of age is neither sentimental nor cynical. Rather, as with any of his other films about any other age group, his last Westerns find a profundity in people acting according to their station in life, accepting their lot and getting on with it. Wayne's diminishing agility and unsuitability for any kind of womanizing by the time of *Rio Lobo* finds Hawks compensating by endowing him "with greater apparent dignity and self-respect," according to Greg Ford. His status at this late juncture is near mythic: "Here Wayne seems to be some apotheosized exaggeration of a Hawks-hero, possessing the size and noble air of an earth-bound Olympian." One dissatisfaction Hawks felt with both *Hatari!* and *Rio Lobo* was that, without a Robert Mitchum or a similarly statured figure to play alongside him, Wayne's presence blew everyone off the screen. But part of the pleasure of such films is seeing the cross-generational camaraderie kicked up between Wayne and his younger co-stars. A film like *Red Line 7000* focused on youth, and *El Dorado* more on the older folks (besides James Caan, who's banter with Wayne is a great source of fun, particularly as, per Hawks, Caan didn't know he was playing a comic character); but a film like *Rio Lobo* (or earlier *Rio Bravo* and *Hatari!*) mixes them, creating a juxtaposition that allows Hawks a more holistic look at, and embrace of, the differing phases and roles of a man's (and woman's) life.

The late Westerns continue, therefore, Hawks' interest in characters, despite locating them in more traditionally plotted material relative to his more experimental work in the previous few films. "As usual," Bogdanovich writes about *El Dorado*, "the story is simply an excuse to look at some characters that interest Hawks, and to play some evocative variations on themes he has been elaborating and deepening for more than forty years." *El Dorado* was originally based on Harry Brown's *The Stars in Their Courses* (1960), a novel that attempted a Western riff on ancient Greek literature; Leigh Brackett's adaptation was, despite her protestations, deemed too grim and downbeat for Hawks' current tastes, the story too full of "losers," as Hawks termed them, so besides keeping an inciting incident (Wayne's shooting of the boy) they started from scratch and soon enough Hawks essentially went, Hey — why not do *Rio Bravo* again, but different? "When I finish a script," said Hawks, "I deliberately go over it to see how it would work if it was done the opposite way." Hawks had also kept notes while doing *Rio Bravo* and had stockpiled enough good unused material for a whole other film; so with a little remixing and reversal, they made it. One intentional variation relevant to age being that, where in *Rio Bravo* none of the good guys get hurt, in *El Dorado* Hawks leaves them all a little worse for wear. But it takes *El Dorado* until halfway through the film before it repeats *Bravo*'s inciting incident which eventually gets them into the jail; in *Rio Lobo* it takes even longer, only initiating the jail-centered set-up toward the end of the picture. *Rio Lobo*, like *El Dorado*, wasn't originally initiated as a *Rio Bravo* riff. Hawks had envisioned it rather as a Western variation on the set-up of *A Girl in Every Port*, a film that

Hawks had optioned the rights to in 1965 and remained a story idea that he'd play around with for the rest of his life—*El Dorado* itself partakes in the set-up by having Mitchum and Wayne play old buddies who have a history with the same girl, and *Rio Lobo* was originally set to follow in its footsteps until the studio couldn't pay for Mitchum, causing Hawks to throw out the story and whip up a new one. The result bears the markings of a scenario created via a hodgepodge of Hawksian ideas sketched out and strung together—an opening civil war section, with a train heist set piece based on Hawks' remembrance of how planes were landed on the first flattop aircraft carriers (by a hook attached underneath the incoming plane picking up ropes with sandbags on each end to slow it down); the introduction of a girl in trouble, who shoots her pursuers through a table with a hidden gun like Bogart in *To Have and Have Not*; a change of scene to the titular town of Rio Lobo, where villainous bullies are causing land ownership disputes à la *El Dorado*; and finally some business with holing up in a jail, a proposed prisoner exchange, and a climatic shootout that wraps things up on a variation of *Rio Bravo*. As Dan Sallitt has noted, "Hawks' penchant for recycling familiar dialogue and situations from his previous films starts to take on a ritualized, automatic quality at this point in his career. And the careful interweaving of events that was so impressive in *Rio Bravo* has given way… to the most naked, barely motivated setups, as if Hawks no longer cared a whit about hiding behind the curtain or pretending that events are motivated by forces within the film universe."

Hawks' last stories are instinctive, almost unconscious creations—which was part preference, part necessity, as Hawks' scripts continued to be more working outlines than strict reference guides; Todd McCarthy relates that Hawks only had 18 pages of material when cast and crew first arrived on location for *Rio Lobo,* and that actor Ed Faulkner said it wasn't a script but a "fragment." Robert Donner, a regular actor in late Hawks (and husband of William Wellman's daughter Cissy, a good friend of Hawks), attested to a similar situation on *El Dorado*'s set, saying that "the script was written in sand." But none of this stressed Hawks, who had become accustomed to his methods and reveled in the fun and play of it all, remaining as relaxed as ever on set. To Hawks, making a Western with John Wayne was near impossible to mess up, and he referred to them as "wheelchair jobs"—so easy to direct that you could do it as an invalid. Hawks' penchant for rewriting dialogue on location forced actors to memorize pages of dialogue on the spur of the moment, something that Wayne especially had an innate ability to easily do. But his actors still regularly showed up on the Western sets not just without a script but with no idea what the story was even going to be. Bogdanovich relates a great anecdote about Hawks calling up Robert Mitchum to ask him to be in *El Dorado*, who when agreeing asked what the story was going to be, causing Hawks to answer "quickly and sharply, with a touch of bored irritation: 'Ohh—no *story*, Bob…'." By the time of *Rio Lobo*, for Wayne it was simply a matter of coordinating his schedule with Hawks' and then showing up; he greeted Hawks on location with the question, "Do I get to play the drunk this time?" Wayne's authority was second only to Hawks; Bogdanovich relates that he would sometimes direct the other actors himself to the acknowledged approval of Hawks ("Isn't that right, Mr. Hawks?" "Sure, Duke."). Actor Johnny Crawford recalled the pace on the *El Dorado* shoot as "totally relaxed and ponderous." It was an environment of fun and friends; John Ford even visited the set, fresh off shooting his final feature *7 Women* (1966)[7]. The atmosphere of a Hawks set was open and inviting and playful all while remaining perfectly professional—except the time that Hawks failed to show up one Monday morning, causing the company to scour the set and anyplace they could think to locate him; they found him lounging poolside at his hotel, having lost track of time and believing it a Sunday. Another Monday found the whole cast and crew—horses included—

---

[7] Interestingly, if one combines the names of Wayne's characters in *Hatari!* (Sean Mercer) and *El Dorado* (Cole Thornton), one gets Sean Thornton, the name of Wayne's character in Ford's *The Quiet Man* (1952), one of Hawks' all-time favorite pictures.

sporting celebratory eye-patches upon Wayne's return from winning the Best Actor Oscar for *True Grit.* Despite money issues preventing him from being in the film as planned, Robert Mitchum took the time to visit the set and his son Chris—"the less expensive Mitchum" that Hawks had gotten instead. Hawks even opened the set to journalist and media personality George Plimpton, who made his visit to the set of *Rio Lobo* the subject of the television special *Plimpton! Shootout at Rio Lobo*, one of a number of participatory journalism specials he did that aired on network television. Hawks claimed that the show "typifies the way we work more than anything else that's been made," and indeed nowhere else does one get such a good idea of the relaxed mood of a Hawks' shoot. Plimpton steps in to plays the role of "4th Gunman," and between insights into the making of Westerns, the Eastern-bred journalist is subjected to playful ribbings from Hawks and Wayne as they chat about this and that related to the film. The punchline comes when Hawks, to everyone's laughter and Plimpton's good-natured befuddlement, at the last minute rewords Plimpton's sole line of gun-toting dialogue that he's been nervously practicing all day from "This here's yer warrant, mister" to "I got a warrant right here, sheriff."

All this casualness at work prevents either late Western from slipping into a particularly elegiac mode, even though the greater context of the films and their makers lends a twilight profundity to even the simplest things like someone cocking a rifle, getting on a horse, or just opening a door. Each film begins with an opening credits sequence that sets up a meditative, reflective tone—the eponymous Edgar Allan Poe-inspired theme song set against Western-themed paintings by Olaf Wieghorst in *El Dorado,* the austere, moody close-ups of a finger-picked guitar theme being played in *Rio Lobo*—only to mostly do away with it once the proceedings begin, but not without leaving a lingering sense that the entire film is meant to be read in the shadow of these overtures. The films continue the interlacing of comedy and drama that Hawks had been perfecting throughout his career. In *El Dorado,* a scene like the unintentional shooting of a young boy and the deliverance of his body back to his family sits next to scenes of antiquatedly cartoonish slapstick like Mitchum being bonked over the head with a frying pan, or a Rube Goldberg gag in which a shotgun-wielding Caan misses his target only to hit a sign that falls down to knock the man out (Hawks: "That's really going back to the Keystone days")—a disparate collection of scenes that somehow gets across without any apparent tonal inconsistency. One of the most dramatic, spiritually stirring aspects of *Rio Bravo*—Dean Martin's alcoholism—gets reworked in *El Dorado* as a largely comedic, physical affair with Robert Mitchum, yet it's still able to retain the underlining moral seriousness of the idea that Hawksian integrity requires a man to be sober, even when he's drunk. "In *Rio Bravo*," writes Robin Wood, "Hawks used Dude's lack of physical control—his trembling hands, etc.—consistently to express a spiritual condition; in *El Dorado* the emphasis is far more on the outward signs of physical degeneration for their own sake: Harrah's unshaven and bleary face, the size of his paunch, his stomach-clutching. The 'cure' is basically physical, too, not moral as in Rio Bravo, where there is no equivalent for Mississippi's horrific concoction of gunpowder and mustard." But both characters get a moment to turn the tables on the laughing townsfolk in a manhunting saloon scene—Wayne: "I hope you're good enough"; Mitchum: "I hope I am too"—which becomes similarly spiritually redeeming, a chance for a Hawksian character to stand up straight *as* a Hawksian character.

Lest Hawks' laidback approach, his focus on character, or his reputation for functional craftsmanship lead one to believe that he didn't care about the visual side of things, just witness the beauty of *El Dorado*'s largely evening-set lighting scheme, of the yellow amber light pouring out of doors and seeping through windows into the Western night. Hawks had instructed cameraman Harold Rosson—younger brother of Richard and Arthur (both Hawks collaborators of yore) who came out of retirement to shoot the film—to study the nocturnal paintings of Frederic Remington to see how light slashed onto the street out of saloon doors. The warmth of the cinematography matches the relational intimacy of the film as well as tinting the proceedings with a venerable glow. Partially as a result of Hawks' slowing production rate in the back half of his career, partially because of his distaste for earlier color processes, he only made nine films in color, which only accounts for about one quarter of his career. But Hawks adapted quickly and with originality, making eye-popping, energetic use of color in *A Song Is Born* and *Gentlemen Prefer Blondes* and experimenting with its abilities in CinemaScope, before settling in to the rich autumnal palette of *Rio Bravo* that would define the earthy, bold colorings of the late films. Hawks was a sensitive visual stylist in his black-and-white days too, but his light and shade and mise-en-scène work really pops in the color films in a way it inherently couldn't before, especially in his patented indoor scenes. Any number of moments come to mind: Martinelli toward the end of *Hatari!* holed up in her room with the lights off, silhouetted against the window slats and evening night; Hudson and girls early in *Man's Favorite Sport?* talking in a piano museum framed against colorful stained-glass windows when the lights go off; or the intimate scene between Caan and Hill in *Red Line 7000* inside a little cross-slatted shade spot in a motel courtyard, where Hawks does magnificent work with shadows, rare close-ups, and two bottles of Pepsi. But for Hawks his images are never posed toward ostentatious artistic effect, using them rather to create moods and define relationships, to highlight character moments, character gestures, looks, postures, the way someone stands in a room, the way someone looks at someone else, the way someone simply exists. Hawks—the sturdy craftsman of unpretentious external action—is secretly one of the most incisive inner-life artists; and it's because of exactly that unpretentiousness. There's no affected pausing on actors emoting; he reaches emotions in a different, more invisible way, almost without you noticing he's doing it, so organic is his way of harmonizing his character's external actions with their internal feelings.

Even with an infusion of new young actors (few of whom he much liked, thus perhaps why the "hangout" vibes of *Rio*

Lobo are noticeably lower than the other late films), Hawks had a way of immediately adopting them with his camera into his world of internal/external cohesion, new elements in an old paradigm. And despite his preference for the familiar, late Hawks still showed his willingness to give the new a try—in *Rio Lobo*, a score by Jerry Goldsmith as adventurous and distinct as any in Hawks outside of Henry Mancini's stringless, exotic one for *Hatari!*, as well as the repeated use of zooms as a formal tool, short shots of a quickly advancing or receding viewpoint to dynamically establish new scenes or moments; and in *El Dorado*, a more noticeably direct approach to violence, a film made just before the already-weakened Production Code was abandoned for good. Despite deploring Sam Peckinpah's gory, slow-motion theatrics, Hawks' late violence can at times explode onto the screen in a similar way—just less gory, and in real time, short and curt and over and done with, a shotgun blast and a slumped figure undwelled upon. *El Dorado* participates in a lineage of movie violence at a pivotal moment in film history: just two months after its U.S. release in the summer of 1967, *Bonnie and Clyde* arrived on the scene. "The American spectator," Fernando Villaverde writes, "could practically have heard Mississippi's shotgun firing almost simultaneously with the shots that killed Bonnie (Faye Dunaway) and Clyde (Warren Beatty), thereby keeping the echoes of violence resounding in movie theatres." An echo which could be traced all the way back to another Hawks movie, *Scarface*, which had been a hot point for the censorship of movie violence in the early 1930s as well as a specific reference point for *Bonnie and Clyde*'s infamously bullet-riddeled ending (via Jean-Luc Godard, whose stylish *Breathless* was a connecting point between Hawks' radical entertainment and Arthur Penn's New Hollywood big bang.)

Another, straighter line can be drawn from *Scarface* to Hawks' final film, *Rio Lobo*, in the form of the literal scarred face that travels across 40 years of film history from Paul Muni to the cheek of Sherry Lansing, received at the hands of the film's male villains as punishment for giving shelter to Wayne & co. upon their arrival in town. Susana Dosamantes' character is beaten for helping as well; Jennifer O'Neill's has to defend herself from a murderous posse come to fetch her before she can report their crimes. Roger Greenspun writes that the women of *Rio Lobo* "carry a greater burden of pain than in any other Hawks movie," are "specifically victimized," and "are therefore more fully integrated into the conditions of their world, and the special beauty of *Rio Lobo*... lies in its acceptance of women's tears in the catalogue of valuable human responses." Along with *Red Line 7000*, no other Hawks movie so directly involves multiple female characters in its emotional stakes. In one scene, Hawks gives Jennifer O'Neill room to deliver a moving personal monologue about how, having spent time working in a saloon after her husband got himself shot, she's tired of being pawed at by men. "Do you know what it's like to work in a saloon?... They never leave you alone. *Never.*" Even if the kind of female empowerment Hawks' displays in such scenes might be deemed too clumsy, too awkward, or, well, too Hawksian—O'Neill ends up kissing Jorge Rivero anyway (after having instigated her speech with his pawing); "Didn't you want me to do that?" "Of course I did, sure I did, but I am generally the one who starts it." "Well that's why I started it, 'cause now I know when it'll stop."—it's still moving to see Hawks allow such sentiments to be voiced, and in a beautiful close up with Goldsmith's stirring score quietly underscoring it. Although Hawks' women were always relatively autonomous compared to the rest of Hollywood's, the late films, especially *Rio Lobo,* display an awareness of feminine suffering far beyond anything in earlier Hawks, perhaps suggesting an evolution in Hawks' aging perspective (that, for what it's worth, just so happens to coincide with the years of second wave feminism.) The shifting role of women also parallels the shifting role of John Wayne, trackable throughout his last four roles for Hawks, from romantic lead to sexless, "comfortable" old man. O'Neill, chilled during a night under the open sky, goes to find warmth next to Wayne rather than Rivero, because he's older, therefore safer. Wayne, although predictably embarrassed, mostly takes his newfound status as the comfortable old man in stride, comically cognizant of it throughout the film but living without bitterness. But less opening for romance means more for friendship—the kind of relationship Hawks always prized more anyway. Thus Hawks' final film ends with a limping Wayne and a scarred Sherry Lansing[8] walking off together, leaning on each other in mutual support, two souls moving forward in Hawksian fellowship.

El Dorado had ended in mostly the same way, Wayne and Mitchum both hobbled but walking in stride down the street together, a Hollywood film closing not on a romantic embrace but on the rather more banal image of two old men attached at the hip via unspoken friendship. This, ultimately, is Howard Hawks' great theme: *philia*, the Greek word for the kind of love we translate as friendship or affection, but which has an invisible strength to it which only connotation can capture. "There's probably no stronger emotion than friendship between two men," Hawks would boldly say in an interview. The late films begin to extend this emotion to women as well, but in the final Westerns Hawks asserts the primacy of friendship over romantic relationships—even *in* romantic relationships. Charlene Holt in *El Dorado* is clearly set up as Wayne's love interest, but it's the mutual understanding between them, their bond of affection— rather than any great romantic sentiment—that defines the relationship. Hawksian relationships are "based on a balance of equality between free men," writes Robin Wood. "There are those who can see no more to this theme of close friendship between men in Hawks's films than the endorsement of a hearty, superficial matiness: nothing could be further from the truth. These relationships in Hawks almost invariably embody something strong, positive, and fruitful: at the least (*The Thing*) a warmth of mutual response; at the most (*Rio Bravo*) the veritable salvation of a human being." Contrary to *Rio Bravo,* where relationships are either

---

[8] Given the last action in Hawks' last film—the killing of the corrupt sheriff—Lansing would walk away from her own short-lived acting career and later become a hig-ranking executive at multiple major Hollywood studios, as well as marrying William Friedkin (who had previously dated Hawks' daughter Kitty).

long-time givens or have time to simmer and grow, in the last Westerns one notices the intuitive, almost comical ease with which such bonds are established. In *Rio Lobo,* Wayne strikes up a quick friendship with Jorge Rivero and Chris Mitchum despite having been fighting on opposite sides of the Civil War just days prior; Rivero and Sherry Lansing's casual rapport is established from the second he barges into her home, despite them being strangers and her without a shirt on; and in just their second scene after meeting, Wayne and Jack Elam are bantering like they've known each other for 30 years. In *El Dorado,* Hawks shows that sometimes friendships exist even where one has never been established, simply by the mutual webbing of people and goals: Mitchum doesn't even know who Caan is until he asks it for the third or fourth time, well after they've begun working alongside each other. Hawks' characters always remain individuals even when part of a group—often with a defining accessory, like all the different hats given to the supporting cowhands of *Red River*—but in Hawks that individuality is never complete until it's found its place in the ecosystem of a community, be it two men or a whole town. The strong camaraderie that organically springs up between people in Hawks suggests that though friendship can be built on as little as a shared feeling or goal, in the end it can have inestimably large or veritably life-saving power. Or to put it another way, in pointed words from Ernest Hemingway's novel *To Have and Have Not*: "a man alone ain't got no bloody fucking chance." Yet late Hawks' casual storytelling—especially as embodied in his endings, which organically wrap things up without seeming to dwell on any profundities—doesn't go out of its way to inspire grand thematic pronouncements or extolment as high art. And maybe that's just as well. Writing about Hawks in 1969, Manny Farber suggested that "rating these close camaraderie films, teeming with picturesque fliers-punks-pundits and a boys' book noble humanism, in the Pantheon division of Art and giving them cosmic conceptions is to overweight them needlessly." Indeed, the pleasures of late Hawks are too tied up in the genial nature of the films, their characters, and their stories to stubbornly insist on any solemn reading that would cause anyone to lose out on participating in that.

Despite never making another picture, Hawks still very much considered himself an active filmmaker in the 1970s. He would often view his stops at film festivals, either as part of juries or as an attendee of retrospective showings of his work, as promotional stops where he could get new projects off the ground. Once, serving as jury president at the San Sebastian Film Festival in 1972, Hawks put in a word to get a Russian film a special award and was subsequently approached to make a film there (Leonid Brezhnev loved Westerns), but it didn't pan out. Nevertheless, Hawks still exercised his storytelling muscles by becoming an eager and willing interview subject for anyone who was interested in talking to him (as many were with his increasing critical reputation), leaving behind a veritable oral history of his career. Just like in his films, Hawks liked to repeat himself, telling many stories again and again, sharpening them as time went by. (He liked a good story so much that on occasion they weren't even true.) Hawks dabbled with a number of prospective ideas for films—among them a *Don Quixote* with Cary Grant, a film about the WWII friendship between Ernest Hemingway and photographer Robert Capa, a Vietnam film, and a couple of ideas for a Western—but the film he spent the most time on (over a decade) and came closest to making was a remake of *A Girl in Every Port* known variously as *When It's Hot, Play It Cool*; *Now, Mr. Gus*; or just *Mr. Gus*. It was to be a globe-hopping comedy following two oil riggers around the world getting into scrapes and fighting over the same girls. At one point he eyed Clint Eastwood and Steve McQueen for the roles, but "every time I think about some of the scenes and how funny they are, and I think about those two guys in 'em, I get sick. Because neither of them is a bit funny." Hawks wrote a full first draft himself in 1976 and envisioned shooting interiors in Spain while sending someone else off to do the location work, but he never did end up approaching anyone to do it. Today we're left merely with the tantalizing possibilities of the project, as it promised to be another Hawksian treatise on male friendship, as the final scene attests: the two men both accidentally falling into the same bed back-to-back, both making a pact to kick out their imagined intruder, and then one ending up thrown out on the floor— "Never mind," the other one says, "you can sleep with me." Hawks lived in the present tense even when those around him saw him as a thing of the past; he never thought to have his papers, gathering dust in his garage, collected into an archive until James D'Arc from Brigham Young came around asking. Hawks became a mentor figure to a number of young film-makers: Peter Bogdanovich of course, who he tried to set up a deal producing films for which fell through; William Friedkin, who was living with Hawks' daughter Kitty in the early '70s, and who Hawks claimed as the recipient of his advice to make something with a good car chase in it; Max Baer Jr., son of a boxer and actor Hawks knew from the old days, who got Hawks to help him write, produce, and even edit Richard Compton's *Macon County Line* (1974); as well as Leonard Schrader (brother of Paul), who approached Hawks for advice on a story that eventually became Shinji Sômai's *P.P. Rider* (1983). Hawks hung out with old friends as well, spending time with John Ford in his last days in 1973 swapping stories about all the picture ideas they stole from each other. Time had finally made Hawks respectable enough for the Motion Picture Academy, who gave Hawks an honorary Oscar (along with Jean Renoir, who didn't attend) at their 1975 ceremony— never mind that Hawks had stopped voting and being an active member of the Academy for a decade already, reportedly because of their poor track record of actually choosing the best picture. John Wayne presented the award, and started going off the stage in the wrong direction after Hawks had made his speech; it wasn't a flub—Hawks had told him to do it before-hand, creating one tiny last gag in his final piece of on-screen directing. Hawks would live two and half more years, finally dying at the age of 81 on December 26, 1977, due to complica-tions from a fall he took tripping over his dog at home alone. In one final, fitting irony, the long under-the-radar master filmmaker was relegated to page two news: Charlie Chaplin had died the day before.

Charles Chaplin

"CHAPLIN CHANGES! CAN YOU?" Emblazoned in large blue lettering at the top of posters advertising 58-year-old Charlie Chaplin's latest work, *Monsieur Verdoux* (1947), these words acted as a last-ditch marketing attempt to reinvent the conversation around a film that had been fighting an uphill battle with America's press and public from the get-go. Chaplin hadn't released a new film in seven years, and when *Monsieur Verdoux* received its world premiere in a New York theater that April, the results were so underwhelming that Chaplin and his distribution company United Artists pulled the film from exhibition after just six weeks. It was relaunched at the end of September starting in Washington, D.C., but four months' time and a new marketing campaign could do little to stymie a near decade's worth of increasingly sour public relations for the Chaplin camp; the poor critical and commercial reception of *Monsieur Verdoux* was just the icing on the cake. (Although it's worth noting that the film did decent business in areas of the country where conservative political groups weren't pressuring theaters to cancel showings, and would win Best Film as awarded by the National Board of Review.) The list of Chaplin's perceived infractions against his adopted home of America was long. His last production, *The Great Dictator* (1940), which directly satirized Hitler and World War II-era European fascism, had ruffled feathers for being planned, produced, and released at a time when America had yet to abandon its isolationist stance, and although it was a hit with audiences, critics were less than pleased with Chaplin's supposed trading-in of entertainment for political speechifying in its final, direct-address sequence. Chaplin repeated the film's speech to a radio audience of 60 million for Roosevelt's January 1941 inauguration, but even when his antifascist sentiments became officially sanctioned with the U.S.'s entry into the war that December, an accident of fate in May 1942 led him to continue his speech-giving career under a new banner, this time subbing in for the former Soviet Ambassador Joseph E. Davies, out ill, at a San Francisco gathering for Russian War Relief. Chaplin spoke strongly in favor of opening a second front in the European war to aid the Soviets in their battle against the Nazis. Despite being an official ally, Soviet Russia was associated with communism, and therefore Chaplin now was, too. He continued to be vocal in his support, giving more speeches, and in the process brought upon himself more accusations of having "Red" sympathies—which were bolstered even further by Chaplin's opposition to the postwar probings of the House Un-American Activities Committee (HUAC). Red-blooded Americans also challenged Chaplin on his unwillingness to become an official American citizen, his associations with leftist émigrés in Hollywood, and his general nonconformist nature. To top it all off, from the early- to mid-1940s Chaplin was embroiled in a highly publicized paternity suit brought by a young actress named Joan Barry, whose relationship with Chaplin had begun as a potential collaboration on an adaptation of Paul Vincent Carroll's 1937 play *Shadow and Substance* and had ended in a drawn-out legal battle—which eventually forced Chaplin to support her child, despite scientific evidence (inadmissible at the time) proving it wasn't his.[1] To many, this only went to show once again that Chaplin was a social menace, especially as far as young girls were concerned, having already married and divorced two of them to calamitous effect earlier in his life and fresh off a third unsuccessful marriage to boot.[2] And

---

[1] What happened between these two points is complicated, disputed, and written about enough elsewhere, but for our purposes it's clear that Chaplin and Barry had a physical relationship along with their professional one, both of which Chaplin attempted to dissolve as Barry's behavior became increasingly unbalanced. The ordeal from start to finish kept Chaplin in a state of high stress and anxiety for the better part of three years and was one of the main elements in this inflection period of his life, personally and above all publicly.

[2] Chaplin's first marriage in 1918 was to Mildred Harris, her 16 and he 29; they had one son, Norman, who died at three days old, and divorced in 1920. His second was to Lita Grey in 1924, her 16 and he 35; they had two sons, Charles Jr. and Sydney, and divorced in 1927. Both marriages were highly unsuccessful and ended acrimoniously. His third marriage to Paulette Goddard (her 26, he 47), although much more pleasant on the whole, only lasted from 1936 to 1942. (However, the official status of their relationship was kept private for much of their time together, and it's possible they were never technically married.)

when Chaplin stole away to marry 18-year-old Oona O'Neill in 1943 while the fiasco was still raging, they expected more of the same, and soon.

All of this commotion gave the Chaplin name a much more ambivalent, if not downright negative, connotation in 1947 than it had ever had before. It was certainly a far cry from the time when Chaplin had been the most popular and widely beloved film artist in the country. Yes, Chaplin had changed — but America had, too. One depression and a world war later, the social and political landscape of the country looked vastly different. A general rightward shift politically had occurred between the pre-war depression and the postwar boom, and what had been a bipartite spectrum between left and right was now closer to a tripartite one, with the dangerous poles of communism on the left and fascism on the right being held at bay by good ol' U.S. democracy in the vital center. Any straying from that, or criticism of it, was seen as a betrayal of the good and threatened to give evil the upper hand, and Americans from the government on down were on high alert to anything that might reek of dissident thinking. Chaplin, still one of the most famous men in the world and a longtime foreign resident of the States, was apt to be scrutinized every which way. Thus when he released a new film that not only did away with the beloved Tramp figure that'd made his name but also explicitly criticized society via the perspective of a serial murderer, it's no surprise that the film didn't exactly take. *Monsieur Verdoux* made almost everyone, from audiences to critics to government officials, supremely uncomfortable. While they wanted him to stay simple, Chaplin had become complex; while they wanted him to stay silent, Chaplin had opened his mouth; while they wanted him to stay funny, Chaplin had grown serious. Author Charles Maland writes of the "aesthetic contract" that had developed between Chaplin and his audience over the first decades of his career, the idea that Chaplin had essentially taught his viewers to expect an artistic comedy with humor, romance, pathos, and light-hearted engagement with serious themes, starring himself as his loveable alter ego — this is what made a Charlie Chaplin film "a

Charlie Chaplin film," a self-created genre that belonged only to him. If *The Great Dictator* had slightly wavered from that formula, *Monsieur Verdoux* was a near-complete betrayal of it. Chaplin had broken his aesthetic contract, and people knew it, and people did not like it. His late period in itself would do little to make people forgive him for it.

In many ways, this break was a long time coming, and all that preceded and prophesied it makes the pinning down of *Monsieur Verdoux* as the "true" beginning of Chaplin's late period only as useful as an educated understanding of his evolution will show it to be, rather than an uncomplicated line in the sand. What brings Chaplin from the instinctive and immediately iconic entertainer of the one- and two-reel Keystone shorts to the wizened film artist-philosopher-king of *Monsieur Verdoux* is a journey that takes us across a number of important thresholds in Chaplin's maturation as an artist and thinker—his increasing artistic ambitions, the longer gestation periods between films, the dawning of the sound era, and the abandonment of the Tramp persona, among other things. Chaplin's almost instantaneous worldwide acclaim had made him wealthy enough to become perhaps the only true independent artist in Hollywood, able to avoid the changes that came with the consolidation of the studio system; his partnering with Douglas Fairbanks, Mary Pickford, and D. W. Griffith in the formation of United Artists in 1919 to distribute their own pictures both gave him additional autonomy while, ironically, introducing a period of artistic anxiety that would foreshadow Chaplin's changing concerns over the rest of his silent era— this because Chaplin still contractually owed four films to the First National Exhibitors' Circuit, and his restlessness to start producing films for United Artists was becoming palpable. There were already stirrings that Chaplin had "lost his touch" after the release of *Sunnyside* (1919) later that year; his ambitions to create longer and more complex work, as shown by *The Kid* (1921), were mostly being thwarted by his current circumstances; and the bouts of not feeling funny that would dog Chaplin throughout his career were being felt acutely as he shared with friends his lack of interest in finishing *Pay Day*

(1922). The Tramp was becoming a burden to Chaplin, and feeling himself outgrowing its strictures he confessed to an interviewer that he was suffering from a "disgust of the character that circumstances… forced [him] to create." Finally free of his First National contract and eager to spread his wings with his first project for United Artists, Chaplin would, for the first time in his career, abandon the Tramp. In fact, Chaplin wouldn't appear in the feature film at all (outside of an unrecognizable, blink-and-you'll-miss-it cameo as a porter). *A Woman of Paris* (1923), its subtitle *A Drama of Fate* making plain its serious artistic ambitions, would include a title card explaining to audiences Chaplin's absence from the film, but no explanation could convince audiences that a film without Chaplin was must-see viewing, so for the most part they stayed away. It was immensely influential on numerous filmmakers, arguably groundbreaking in its subtle behavioral realism, and anticipated Chaplin's later attempts at more ambitious and dramatic work. But it was also a "flop," and in short order Chaplin resurrected the Tramp for his next, and remaining, silent features.

The coming of sound in the late 1920s presented Chaplin with an artistic dilemma that cut to the core of who he was, and who he was going to be, as a performer and director. *The Gold Rush* (1925) and *The Circus* (1928) had built on the combination of comedy and sentiment in *The Kid* ("A picture with a smile—and perhaps, a tear.") in setting a template for what a feature film starring and directed by Chaplin was like. Now came the decision to either continue making silent films—and become an immediate anachronism in an industry that was quickly moving on—or switch to sound and say goodbye to the Tramp, as Chaplin saw him as an essentially silent figure. Having the Tramp talk was "unthinkable, for the first word he ever uttered would transform him into another person. Besides, the matrix out of which he was born was as mute as the rags he wore." At the time, Chaplin wasn't shy about his distaste for the new sound paradigm, which he variously commented upon as something that was "spoiling the oldest art in the world, the art of pantomime," "ruining the great beauty of silence," and "defeating the meaning of the screen." Ever the independent, he would solider on—*City Lights* (1931) would be silent. But in point of fact Chaplin never did make a fully silent film in the sound era, as one thing he did unequivocally love about the introduction of synchronized sound was the ability to exhibit his films with the same soundtrack everywhere, a luxury the all-consuming artist and music lover didn't previously have; Chaplin himself would compose the score, on top of his innumerable other roles.[3] *City Light's* soundtrack would also contain a number of comic sound effects, marking Chaplin's early interest in the role of sound in his films regardless of the lack of dialogue.

Exhibitors were lukewarm about the prospect of showing a silent film, even if it was a Chaplin, but audiences showed up in droves and dampened Chaplin's fears of irrelevance for the time being. But it wasn't long before he again felt distressed about his position in the movie industry, and in the world at large. After *City Lights* premiered, Chaplin had taken off for a world tour, visiting faces and places everywhere from his home country of England to faraway Japan, seeing the people flock to his appearances and rubbing shoulders with the rich and famous. The combination of taking in the global effect of the Great Depression and being treated like an important artist by everyone he met contributed to something of a political and artistic awakening for Chaplin, who returned home believing

---

[3] This was a laborious but ultimately rewarding process for Chaplin that for most of his career was filled with a revolving door of musical collaborators, as Chaplin himself had little actual knowledge of musical composition and was a notoriously difficult musical collaborator; an amateur (left-handed) violin player, Chaplin's proficiency on the piano was limited to three fingers, so his composing process largely consisted of attempts to get his collaborator to translate his humming or playing into actual musical notation and scoring through trial and error. Despite never learning the rudiments of composition and rarely ever working with the same person twice (until Eric James became his regular collaborator late in life), Chaplin's scores are all resolutely his and display a remarkable mind for music that impressed his collaborators, even if they had difficulty in being asked to read it (his mind, that is).

it was his destiny to align his art with his politics and deliver a film that critiqued society and inspired humanity all in one go—his new film would be called *The Masses.* But the question nagging him day-in and day-out remained: silent or sound? Choosing the former would further alienate him from an industry that was increasingly considering him old-fashioned, a has-been; besides, he said, "although a good silent film was more artistic, I had to admit that sound made characters more present." He couldn't decide. "As I walked the boulevards I began to deliberate whether I should retire, sell everything and go to China. There was no further incentive to stay in Hollywood. Without doubt silent pictures were finished and I did not feel like combating the talkies. Besides, I was out of circulation." The film, however—eventually to be called *Modern Times* (1936)—had to be made, and while still of two minds about it, Chaplin prepared for the prospect of making it as a sound film by building enclosed roofs for his studio. Production went forward, but Chaplin only lasted a day—it would be a silent picture after all. But ultimately the film is a mélange of silence and sound, punctuated by sound effects along with some occasional disembodied talking, including the Tramp's audio debut via a song sung entirely in a parodic version of foreign languages of Chaplin's own invention. A strange beast straddling film's two eras, *Modern Times* was the crowning achievement of Chaplin's comedy template with a greater human and political significance than ever before, while at the same time its hesitant incursion into the realm of sound only highlighted its antiquated nature as a film; more or less a few self-contained Chaplin one-reelers strung together in the shape of a feature narrative, little about its performances, framing, or use of cinematic space bore any resemblance to the films being made in the 1930s. Even more than *City Lights, Modern Times* is knowingly late relative to both Chaplin's body of work at the time and the industry around him. But Chaplin weaponizes this self-awareness in an astounding symbiosis between his own anachronistic tools and the resolutely modern nature of his subject matter, which he then synthesizes by offering, in the film's last image, a final note of universal, individualistic optimism that doubles as a farewell to both the Tramp and the silent paradigm that had nurtured him.[4]

From the jump Chaplin knew his next picture would finally take him into the world of sound for good. Now 50,[5] he was being confronted with the challenge of learning to make films in a new way while at the same time facing the pressures of a project that was more politically ambitious and of-the-moment than anything he'd made before. Chaplin's old-fashioned, ingrained filmmaking techniques jumping into the sound era would ultimately make *The Great Dictator* a rather schizophrenic film. It's a film caught between silence and sound, between his signature sentiment and his newfound political bluntness, between looking back and looking ahead (both formally and thematically), and most of all between two mirrored characters both played by Chaplin: one an obvious variation on his Tramp character, the other his hateful alter ego—a not-at-all veiled showdown between Charlie Chaplin and Adolf Hitler, two world-historic figures born just four days apart who'd both risen from poverty to unimaginable fame/infamy, the toothbrush-mustached face of good and evil respectively.[6] What makes the film a fascinatingly schizo-

---

[4] Note Chaplin's repeated, iconic use of the image of the Tramp walking off into the distance in previous films like *The Tramp* (1915) and *The Circus* (1928), and *Modern Times'* knowing repetition and revision of it to include a partner, Paulette Goddard's "gamine," who here could easily be said to be a stand-in for everyone in the audience who had been on this silent journey with him over the years or indeed anyone who was simply in need of hope.

[5] "Do not believe all those people who tell you life begins at forty," Chaplin would later say. "Life begins at fifty. At forty, you begin to lose the tensions and worries of youth. At fifty, you begin to settle down and live in the present and enjoy life. Now that I have celebrated my fifty-eighth birthday, not only have I forgotten all the troubles of the past but I am enjoying every single precious moment of the immediate present."

[6] This would be the ne plus ultra of Chaplin's interest in doubles, which was a notable element in films both made—*The Floorwalker* (1916), *The Idle Class* (1921)—and unmade—a Napoleon project with the idea that he'd escaped his second exile via the aid of double, and an adaption of David Leslie Murray's *Regency: A Quadruple Portrait*

phrenic (and rather late) work is the way it seems split in two via its crosscutting between the Jewish barber, still largely trapped in a silent paradigm, and the dictator, in a sound one—granted, one less like the carefully articulated world of words that is *Monsieur Verdoux,* and more an extrapolation upon the mock language of Chaplin's *Modern Times* song. Underneath the political messaging, the film can in some ways be productively read as a metanarrative about Chaplin's switch to sound: the barber getting knocked out in World War I and waking up in the World War II era unaware of the past 20 years could easily be a metaphor for Chaplin's inability to fully give up the world of the silents and adjust to new technology. Even on a simple material level, one adjustment Chaplin had to make ironically involved a decrease in noise: the "click, click, click of those good, old-fashioned, hand-cranked cameras" was dearly missed, as Chaplin had been able to "hear the beat of the camera and time every one of [his] movements to its rhythm." Also missed was the comforting laughter of the crew as he performed for the camera, as "now everything had to be acted out in a silence so dead you could hear a pin drop."[7] Chaplin's son Sydney relates how his father once excitedly called up his friend and fellow director Lewis Milestone to show him how he'd mounted a camera on a crane to get a moving overhead shot, only for Milestone to respond, "Charlie, they've been doing that for years." But *The Great Dictator* funnels all of its specific silent/sound circa 1940 Chaplinian oddness toward its final speech by the barber-mistaken-for-the-dictator that both reconciles the film's ostensible contradictions and transcends its bounds altogether, a speech in which Chaplin—Chaplin, not just his character— "weeps over primary truths," per François Truffaut. The speech is an intervention into the rhythms of the

---

in which he considered playing both the regent and the lower-class outlaw that a girl would be emotionally caught between.

[7] Still, Charlie Jr. relates that "it wasn't long, however, before Dad began to realize that talkies weren't the bugaboo he'd been picturing them. And presently he was enjoying the medium so much that he even started speaking regretfully of not having made *Modern Times* with sound."

film, stopping it dead against the dictates of good dramaturgy. Chaplin considered it a wig-off moment, a curtain speech, in which he could break the fourth wall and directly address his audience about the fact that, though he hoped they enjoyed the film, there was still a terrible tragedy going on in the world. The speech is remarkable for any number of reasons filmic and extra-filmic, but for our purposes mainly because it marks the tipping point for Chaplin's late period. He abandons the silence of the Tramp and asserts the primacy of words, all while retroactively giving voice to the humanist principles that the little fellow had come to silently stand for. It is past, present, and future Chaplin in one four-minute moment.

In the almost ten years between the start of production on *The Great Dictator* and the premiere of *Monsieur Verdoux*, Chaplin experienced an extended inflection point in his life and career that would strongly mark him as he moved deeper into the back half of his life. As mentioned before, public opinion was on a drastic downswing because of the Barry case and his wartime speeches in support of Soviet Russia. Furthering the loneliness he felt was the loss of his best (and in some ways only true) friend Douglas Fairbanks, who died in 1939 at the age of 56. But while his public life was taking a turn for the worse, his private life started going in the opposite direction once he met and married Oona O'Neill, daughter of the playwright Eugene, who had come out to Hollywood to explore an acting career but instead fell into the arms of Chaplin, where she would devotedly remain until his death 35 years later. Friends and family expressed the belief that Chaplin was happy for the first time in his life. Artistically, too, Chaplin was entering a new world, one devoted to sound and words and serious ideas to be expressed in a post-Tramp environment amidst changing industry standards. Chaplin would betray his new preference for words in a 1942 rerelease of his classic silent film *The Gold Rush,* which he trimmed and revised while adding his own spoken narration in place of intertitles.[8] Work on *Monsieur Verdoux* would begin in 1941

---

[8] While no doubt losing some of the magic of the original, the rere-

and continue until its filming in 1946, a sign of the increasingly leisurely gestation periods for Chaplin's later films that was partially a new necessity; a postwar rationing of film stock meant that Chaplin could no longer afford to shoot hundreds of takes as he experimented on set like in the past, nor could he have off days during shooting to think things over—organization and planning were now paramount. (*Verdoux* was shot in 80 days as opposed to *The Great Dictator*'s nonconsecutive 170, and 1952's *Limelight* would only be 59.) As unions gained more traction in the industry, the costs of running a studio also mounted, forcing Chaplin to rent his out when he wasn't using it as well as having to staff more people, many of which Chaplin neither wanted nor understood the use of. A script girl? A makeup man? A film cutter? It was all perplexing to the man who had been working in Hollywood since the early do-it-yourself days. Adding to the stress was the death of Chaplin's longtime studio manager Alf Reeves in 1946, whose replacement John McFadden (who no one much liked and was promptly fired after filming was over on *Verdoux*) instituted a precise shooting schedule and kept a much stricter watch on budget and time constraints than Chaplin was used to. Yet these dictates of economy ultimately made for one of the smoothest shoots of Chaplin's career.

"The world needs ideas," Chaplin would write at the time of *Monsieur Verdoux*. "The baggy trousers are gone and will never come back.... I cannot be a clown all my life. There is too much to be done.... Time is short, and the world needs ideas. Adult ideas. Otherwise... Kaput. Finis. Finito." Chaplin was upfront about the fact that with his new film he'd be asking his audience to engage with his work in a new, more serious, more adult way. While still to be a comedy, *Verdoux* was born from the gravest of subject matter: in 1941, the

---

lease version is moving in its own altered, truncated way as an expression of where Chaplin was at circa 1942 as he continued to attempt to bridge the silent and sound eras. One also gets the sense that the film is Chaplin, who often impulsively narrated private viewings of his work to family and friends, merely regaling us with a kind of cinematic bedtime story.

young Orson Welles (in the middle of taking Hollywood by storm with *Citizen Kane*) approached Chaplin about the idea of playing French serial killer Henri Désiré Landru in a film. Although accounts by the two men differ about how exactly it happened and whether or not a script was involved, it's likely that, while interested in the idea, Chaplin was less interested in being directed by someone other than himself; therefore he offered Welles $5,000 to be clear of obligations to him (with the added proviso that Welles could request screen credit later).[9] But Welles' idea may have merely prodded loose older, more subconscious interests of Chaplin's, who'd actually been in Europe during the original Landru trial in September 1921 and shared headlines with him as the two biggest news items on the continent. An early French biographer of Chaplin's even shares the information that when in Paris later in 1931, he'd insisted on meeting some of the crime reporters who'd been present at the trial. Chaplin had a general fascination with crime, the macabre, and death; he loved to read pulp detective magazines and was also interested in prisons. On his return trip from Europe in 1921, he stopped off in upstate New York to visit Sing Sing prison and got a personal tour of the facility, even sitting in the electric chair. A glimpse of a man facing execu-

---

[9] Too interesting to go unmentioned is Welles' potential secondary role in helping kick off Chaplin's late period, as told by Jane Scovell in her biography of Chaplin's wife, *Oona, Living in the Shadows*: "One of [Oona O'Neill's earlier] escorts was the film colony's youngest resident genius, twenty-six-year-old Orson Welles. The charismatic Welles escorted Oona to a nightclub on their first date and volunteered to read her palm. He took her upturned hand in his, gazed at it intently, then raised his head and, looking deeply into her eyes, declared that he saw a love line which led directly to another, older man. The Boy Genius further proclaimed that he knew who this man was. In the very near future, predicted Orson Welles, Oona O'Neill would meet and marry Charlie Chaplin. Was Welles' forecast a bona fide prophecy or a damn good guess? According to British drama critic Kenneth Tynan, Welles did make the prediction. Welles himself referred to it later in a televised interview with David Frost, and when she was asked to verify the story, Oona Chaplin answered that while she did not recall the incident she supposed it could have happened. In any event, she did not want to stand in the way of a good story."

tion had a great effect on Chaplin—"Tragic, appalling! I shall see that face until I die." The subjects of *Monsieur Verdoux* had cast a spell on Chaplin long before they were ever realized on film. In 1967, Chaplin also claimed the influence of Joseph Kesselring's 1941 play *Arsenic and Old Lace,* a comedy in which two spinsters take to murdering lonely old men. But in the end, the duality at the heart of *Monsieur Verdoux* is probably most succinctly summed up in a remark by Charlie Chaplin Jr., who recalled that his "father might read Spengler and Schopenhauer for edification, but for sheer relaxation he chose murder mysteries"—thus the high-low combination that fuels *Verdoux,* one foot in pulp and the other in philosophy, the low "comedy of murders" (the film's working title) sublimated into the realm of high ideas political, ethical, and moral.

David Bordwell suggests that the film could be linked with "murder culture" and read as "a perverse contribution to the serial-killer film cycle of the 1940s," with Chaplin's outsized fame and culturally dense image provocatively weaponized at the center of it. In the early 1920s sculptor Clare Sheridan had made a bust of Chaplin, upon contemplation of which he had mused, "It might be the head of a criminal, mightn't it?" The remark is a nice foreshadowing of the way criminal and philosophical impulses are intertwined in *Monsieur Verdoux,* a film in which Chaplin satirizes real-life tragedy—as he had done before with the Donner party in *The Gold Rush* and Nazi Germany in *The Great Dictator*—but this time from an angle both vulgar and cerebral. Neither angle, though, was likely to appeal to fans of the simple, optimistic, down-to-earth Tramp of Chaplin's past, fans who surely looked askance at the intellectual, cynical, enigmatic creation that was M. Verdoux. It was this betrayal of the *spirit* of the Tramp, rather than the disappearance of the Tramp himself, that offended them the most.[10] Given that audiences had long (mis-)associated

---

[10] Clearly audiences had forgotten the earliest, most primitive version of the Tramp of Chaplin's first shorts, who in his pinching and prodding and general anarchic tomfoolery could be quite a nasty character. Cf. especially Chaplin's athletic, proto-Verdoux performance as a money-hungry seducer/conman in *Tillie's Punctured Romance* (1914).

Chaplin the man with the Tramp character in his films, it was only too instinctively easy for them to transfer that association (after the public relations nightmare of the 1940s) to the criminal misogynist of his latest film. In some ways Chaplin must have known what he was inviting, choosing a plunge into the polar opposite corner of his cinematic imagination rather than meeting his audience in the middle with, say, a gradual transition to new characters and themes (and at least giving new, younger audiences who hadn't grown up with the Tramp a decent foothold). Chaplin had axed the Tramp for good in a way totally dissociated from the sweet sendoff at the end of *Modern Times,* and closer to the devilish self-assassination hinted at in a 1931 four-panel photograph by Edward Steichen, in which Chaplin mimes shooting a bowler hat with a cane as his gun. Longtime cameraman and associate Rollie Totheroh noted a change in Chaplin that belied his desire to "be distinguished" now, a result of more contact with deeper thinkers and less with common people; Chaplin's pencil mustache in *Verdoux* was for the first time a real growth; and the usual "Charles" Chaplin denomination in the film's opening credits no longer seemed overly formal. Chaplin had leapt to a point that many weren't prepared to follow him to. Rather than for simple personal or political reasons, however, French filmmaker Jean Renoir (at that time living and working in America) believed that attacks against the new Chaplin had a more primal cause: "I think rather that the trouble is their panicked terror before total change, before a particularly long step forward in the evolution of an artist."

Evolve as he might, Chaplin was still the product of an earlier era, and his increasingly idiosyncratic film style betrayed a refusal to shoot and edit in any other way than the way he long liked. He disliked eccentric camera movements, unorthodox angles, excessive close-ups, fancy lighting, and showy editing; he prized the performer above all, and therefore preferred unobtrusive camera positions that allowed the full revelation of his and his actors' movements through space. "I act with my feet as much as my head," Chaplin once said in defense of his insistence on having his full figure being framed in almost every shot. (Also: "I am the unusual and do not need camera angles.") The clash of stylistic ideas between Chaplin and his (mostly younger) collaborators was nowhere more apparent than in his relationship with associate director Robert Florey, who would go on to call Chaplin "the irreconcilable enemy of all that is photographic composition." The Frenchman Florey was a well-established filmmaker in his own right, someone who had written about films in France (including a book about Chaplin) and then directed them in Hollywood without, however, ever making a big name for himself—yet he was happy to accept a demotion of sorts for the chance to work with the great Chaplin, who besides being impressed by Florey's passionate feedback on *Verdoux* in pre-production was interested in having his technical advice for the French settings. But Florey's suggestions for spicing up shots was mostly dismissed by Chaplin as "Hollywood chi-chi." Technical gaffes like a visible microphone shadow in a shot or miscellaneous continuity errors were brushed away by Chaplin as unimportant when brought to his attention. And on a set where it was Chaplin's way or the highway, Florey and others had to swallow sometimes contradictory camera instructions; they'd adapt by shooting scenes (knowing they'd be retaken numerous times) with every different camera lens available in order to give the vacillating Chaplin choices in the rushes. Although blessed with many great collaborators throughout his career, Chaplin had a habit of alienating them with his occasionally dictatorial on-set temperament, and Florey was no different; Chaplin's promotion of his half-brother Wheeler Dryden to the same position of associate director (and an on-screen credit that appeared before Florey's) was the cherry on top of his experience, which he later memorialized in not one but two French-language books detailing what he saw as the duality of Chaplin's personality, the charming entertainer vs. the vindictive tyrant.

Be that as it may (and statements from others more than back it up), Chaplin's power as writer, director, producer, and star was wielded not for its own sake but for the purposes of his art. His style may have been ridiculously antiquated and technically deficient, but in his dedication to his own specific vision at the expense of all else Chaplin created a style that was very distinctly and dissonantly his. In his autobiography, he would briefly speak to the criticisms that hounded him throughout his late period: "I am surprised that some critics say that my camera technique is old-fashioned, that I have not kept up with the times. What times? My technique is the outcome of thinking for myself, of my own logic and approach; it is not borrowed from what others are doing. If in art one must keep up with the times, then Rembrandt would be a back number compared to Van Gogh." Despite a three-dimensionality to Chaplin's cinematic spaces that hadn't been seen since *A Woman of Paris* (no longer having to yield the screen to silent Charlie's front-and-center pantomime), *Monsieur Verdoux* still looked rather theatrical when placed next to the deep focus stylings of a Hollywood Welles or William Wyler or the in-the-world neorealism of international offerings, a fact that had thematic implications—per Andrew Sarris, "*Verdoux* is neither slick enough for the dream merchants nor sincere enough for the humanists." What might appear as some kind of anti-cinema, though, is really just Chaplin's unique implementation of cinematic artifice for his film of ideas that operates at an ironic remove from traditional emotional strategies. When Chaplin cuts to a stunning medium shot of Verdoux staring out of a balcony window at a beautiful full moon, the obvious fakeness of the lunar backdrop provides the moment a highly specific, faux-romantic, comic-poetic atmosphere as we prepare for the implied offing of one of Verdoux's female victims that a more "realistic" style couldn't. Similarly, the repeated insert shots of spinning train wheels signifying Verdoux's travels is less a monotonous, expedient shorthand than it is an elegant and economical visualization of the film's interest in destiny, thematically and dramatically—most of the film's tension is in the *how* and *when* of Verdoux's death, as it has been plainly foretold at the outset. Chaplin's unshowy cutting merely takes us from moment to moment, scene to scene, with an ultra-simplicity that could be confused as unremarkable; however, filmmaker Jean-Marie Straub—himself a great admirer of *Monsieur Verdoux* and expert cutter—considered Chaplin the best editor in the history of cinema because he "knew precisely when a gesture begins and when it ends, so he knew precisely when to cut."

This simplicity, however, had usually been paired with the ever graceful and balletic little Tramp, who skipped his way across the screen with perfectly calibrated imperfection—everything in place, all proceeding with elemental ease, cinema at its smoothest and sweetest. Yet this was a deception: Chaplin and his collaborators worked gruelingly for months on end to create these fine-tuned illusions, their apparent ease actually the result of blood, sweat, tears, and endless trial and error; Chaplin, often in the throes of the human struggle for a good idea, would retire to his dressing-room and "go into the Gethsemane," as he told those around him. With the shortage of film stock and tighter schedules of the postwar sound era, the highly manufactured effortlessness of his early films gave way to a more mundane, earthbound sense of movement and rhythm. Part of this resulted also from the loss of a silent filmmaking technique known as undercranking, where the cameraman would deliberately crank the film camera at a slower rate than the standard 16 to 18 frames per second; when projected at the standard rate, this gave the actors an unreal agility and speed integral to many of the visual jokes of silent slapstick. Film historian Ben Model notes that "one of the biggest concerns Chaplin may have had in moving into sound was this entire layer of gags…. His dexterity, the split-second timing, the agility, that was so much a part of the Tramp's character on screen, would have to go away." Besides simply having to use their voices, "comedians and action stars… were now moving in real time."[11] But the differences of *Verdoux* and Chaplin's subsequent sound films can't be chalked up as failures to repeat the artistic successes of the silent films, because in no way was Chaplin attempting to replicate them. From the jump, Chaplin

---

[11] However, Chaplin would still utilize the concept for a few flourishes in the sound films, such as the amusing scene in *Verdoux* showing Chaplin rifling through a stack of paper money with inhuman agility.

attended to sound cinema *as* sound cinema. A 1947 interviewer relayed that Chaplin "likes dealing with sound, which he asserts has its own elements of poetry, in comedy as well as drama." "The ideal talkie has not been made yet," declared Chaplin. "It won't be until we discover the *limitations* of sound. We can't say the formula is less talk and more action, or more talk and less action, or anything else. It depends on what the subject matter calls for." Chaplin's perfectionist bent quickly extended to sound, too, and he attacked the problem with a surprising outpouring of on-screen verbosity, naturally unexpected from cinema's premier silent star. Contenting himself with what sound had to offer him in his evolution as an artist, in *Verdoux* Chaplin doesn't hold back on the talking front, weaving words together in scene after scene not just for the sake of their meaning but to delineate precisely who Verdoux is as a person and as a conman, with his highfalutin romantic phraseology and overly dignified politesse. Chaplin's diverse set of skills allowed him to be as adept at stringing sentences together as he was at pantomime; Ignatiy Vishnevetsky writes of Chaplin's voice as "a beautiful instrument, delicate but rich, with diction so crisp that you could hear the punctuation marks…. Verdoux's pretentious flattery, misunderstood asides, and ad-libbed deceptions play like comic music." Suddenly, all the comedic ability of Chaplin specific to his voice—already known to friends and acquaintances via his impromptu entertaining at parties—was at his cinematic disposal.

Thus, the intricacies of Chaplin's performance (vocal and otherwise) give the lie to the criticism that *Verdoux* is dull and didactic—what it is, rather, is dialectical. The character of Verdoux is simultaneously Chaplin's embodiment of the tragicomic endpoint of modern geopolitics as well as the mouthpiece used to criticize them; in other words, Verdoux has some good points but is also, at the same time, full of it (and himself). Unlike Chaplin's silent films, which in theory could be dipped into and out of at any point and have each moment be enjoyed much the same, *Monsieur Verdoux* is explicitly constructed on the accumulation that comes with narrative succession, building from beginning to end toward what it ultimately *is.* The dialectical idea at the heart of the film isn't necessarily visible on a scene-by-scene basis. Although Chaplin was clear as to what his film finally was about: in a telegram he sent to a HUAC official preempting the committee's questions, Chaplin wrote, "In order that you may be completely up-to-date on my thinking I suggest you view carefully my latest production, *Monsieur Verdoux.* It is against war and the futile slaughter of our youth. I trust you will not find its humane message distasteful…. I am not a Communist. I am a peacemonger." While truly not a communist in any real sense, it's likely that Chaplin had been swayed further left in the 1940s by his new set of artist-intellectual émigré friends, which included the likes of Salka Viertel, Lion Feuchtwanger, Thomas Mann, Hanns Eisler, and Bertolt Brecht. Eisler and Brecht in particular claimed to have "radicalized" Chaplin, not by words and arguments but simply by consistently laughing harder at the Chaplin jokes that had "a strong political thrust." It's therefore easy to see—given the film's emotional distance, biting political critiques, and neglect of cinematic realism—how *Verdoux* very much parallels Brecht's ideas of social satire for the theater. (Feuchtwanger: *Monsieur Verdoux* "is a great ethical lecture, and makes the relationship between crime and the general economic situation clearer than a thousand essays.") But as a "progressive" work marooned in a political valley between the 1930s, when such ideas were more acceptable, and the 1960s, when they regained popularity, none of this went over very well with audiences—it wasn't until 1964, when the film was re-released in New York to record-setting turnouts, that people began to see how ahead of its time *Verdoux* had been, a forerunner to the social disaffection of America's rising youth culture, the political satire of Stanley Kubrick's *Dr. Strangelove,* and the black humor of novelists like Kurt Vonnegut and Joseph Heller.[12] Contra the

---

[12] To say nothing of its anticipation of the modern obsession with true crime, of a culture fascinated by society's worst creations without a balancing interest in the underlying causes, dwelling only on the microcosmic, titillating facts.

machine-age Chaplin of *Modern Times,* this was now atom-ic-age Chaplin, and *Verdoux* was a film birthed by the tumultuous first half of the 20th century that saw two world wars and a depression in between; although set in the years leading up to World War II, it is implicitly a post-bomb film, as well as a post-Holocaust one. James Agee, one of the film's only American defenders upon its original release, noted that it was a film "so cold and savage that it had to find its public in grimly experienced Europe."[13] The film ends in a brutal, austere scene of Chaplin as Verdoux walking off to the gallows after saying his last words (this verbose film knowing exactly when to shut up and return to silence), a starkly bleak endpoint that's all the more shocking for the way it offers a sardonic twist on the classic Chaplinian ending of the Tramp walking off into the distance, here with optimism traded in for its grim opposite.[14] Chaplin kills the killer; to return to the dialectic, this act is Chaplin's final repudiation of his creation that he had allowed to speak for him to a point, but no further. It's an earlier scene that most succinctly and dramatically shows us the crossroads

---

[13] Agee famously wrote multiple articles about *Monsieur Verdoux* and was also present at the film's press conference where Chaplin was hounded about his political beliefs (Agee interjected with an earnest yet not entirely coherent comment in Chaplin's defense). They eventually became friends when Agee came to Hollywood to write scripts for John Huston, although Agee had believed his and Chaplin's destinies intertwined before this, having already written an entire script for Chaplin that would resurrect the Tramp as the (initially) lone-surviving figure in a post-atomic, apocalyptic New York City. Agee later helped Chaplin translate his prose into a workable screenplay for *Limelight,* was shown a rough cut of the film, and came to see Chaplin off on the morning of his departure for England in 1952; he didn't find him, despite Chaplin waving from a porthole window (where he was hiding from process servers). It was the last time Chaplin would see Agee, who died in 1955 at the age of 45.

[14] Chaplin flips familiar Tramp-isms on their head elsewhere in the picture, too, like in a twist on the gag (seen in *The Gold Rush,* for example) where Chaplin gazes with romantic longing at a girl who seems to be looking at him but is in fact looking at someone behind him, here recreated with Chaplin's romantic aspirations replaced by Verdoux's amoral, "business" prospecting.

at which the film's ideas are perched: Verdoux's meeting of a young, down-and-out girl played by Marilyn Nash, in which an intended trial run of an untraceable poison becomes a test of Verdoux's philosophy—which he fails, instead sending the girl off with a renewed faith in life and people. The scene is essentially Verdoux's worldview crumbling in contact with Chaplin's own; the film posits the simultaneous existence of great horror and great beauty in the world (it's important that Verdoux is an aesthete), yet Chaplin's ultimate belief in the intangibles that make life worth living is driven home in the final glimpse we get of Nash's character, a brief but affecting cut to her face (our main connection to humanity in the picture) as she listens with sadness to Verdoux's self-justifying courtroom speech.

Verdoux was by far Chaplin's most complex creation up to this point, and his ability to make audiences feel simultaneously both empathy and revulsion (along with a gamut of other things, emotional and intellectual) for him is a testament to Chaplin's newfound interest in *characters*—fully-embodied literary creations, rather than just cinematic *types*. Verdoux is the first; not even the Tramp, whose identity and personality accumulated film to film, ever truly escaped being a type in any given film (hence the lack of a name). *Monsieur Verdoux* is otherwise rounded out by a cast of types and caricatures, figures who represent something to us and Verdoux rather than having much autonomous personhood. That would change with Chaplin's next film, *Limelight,* a story set in the London of Chaplin's youth in which almost every character in the film is an actual *character,* and the film in which Chaplin's increasing literary ambitions are most obvious; not least because rather than begin by writing a traditional script, Chaplin embarked on the project by penning an entire novella. In *Footlights,* as the film too was originally to be titled, Chaplin wove a literary tapestry detailing the present and past lives of his two main characters—Calvero, an aging clown whose glory days are behind him, and Theresa, a young girl whose dancing career has stalled due to a kind of psychosomatic paralysis—as well as the atmosphere and environment of London's music hall scene of the early 1900s. In some ways it was a dry run for Chaplin's ultimate literary achievement a decade hence, the writing and publication of *My Autobiography* (1964), which like all of his writings of the period was birthed via a complex process of dictation, longhand corrections, typing, and retyping until Chaplin was satisfied with the final result (a result which was then subject to further revisions). Chaplin's first stirrings as a writer may have come during his 1931 world tour (hand-in-hand with his political stirrings), from which came the travel memoir *A Comedian Sees the World*, published periodically from 1933-1934 (although this had been preceded by an earlier work, 1922's *My Trip Abroad*, covering his 1921 voyages[15]). As Chaplin grew into his self-made role in the 1930s and '40s as an armchair philosopher, economist, politician, etc., it naturally translated into his newly wordy film work: the final speech of *The Great Dictator*, upon which the rest of Chaplin's sound work could be seen as riffs with varying degrees of irony or sincerity; *Monsieur Verdoux*, which despite everything was nominated by the Academy of Motion Picture Arts and Sciences for Best Screenplay; and now *Limelight*, which continued Chaplin's interest in the art of the word from its conception to completion. It must have been an obvious irony that this literary uptick was coming from a man who had not just fought long and hard to avoid the talkies but had actively denigrated them as an art form when they first appeared.

Although not intended for publication, *Footlights* was Chaplin's way of working himself into the settings and moods of his next film before translating it into a script and then onto the screen. Chaplin was now in his sixties, and the film would use the thinly veiled stand-in of the clown Calvero to explore Chaplin's changing relationship with his audience (whose goodwill he had mostly lost with *Monsieur Verdoux*) in a setting that called back to his roots in the English music hall tradition. It would be Chaplin's most explicitly personal film, and a deliberate reversal of his current trajectory as a public "peacemonger"—a *memory* film rather than a message one.

---

[15] Records show, however, that a ghostwriter was hired for this book.

Chaplin began pulling back on his political outspokenness around 1950, several world events having given him pause and, more pressingly, with a distribution company on the verge of bankruptcy in United Artists. He couldn't afford to alienate audiences any further. The decision to make himself (the apolitical, Tramp-coded version, that is) and his own history the focus of *Limelight* also stemmed from Chaplin's general feelings at the time, which included a homesickness for his birthplace of England clearly exacerbated by the increasingly exhausting treatment he was receiving in the U.S. "I think my father must have been the loneliest man in Hollywood in those days," Charlie Jr. would write. Chaplin spent the three years of *Limelight*'s creation in a deeply introspective mood, often lost in melancholy reverie about his London past and sharing remembrances with anyone who would listen. The thought of retiring after the film was finished was on Chaplin's mind; he expected the film would be his last and his best.[16] As though he meant it, Chaplin poured a lifetime's worth of memories and wisdom and autobiographical-adjacent material (during the longest pre-production of his career) into a film with story elements that had been percolating inside him for years—hints of a 1920s idea for a film about a clown, 1930s notations for a story about a dancer, and all set in 1914, the year Chaplin burst onto the scene in Hollywood; the film is implicitly a kind of alternative history imagining a Chaplin that didn't go into movies and strike it rich. This epic self-portrait of one of the most complex and famous men in history would also spring from one of the simplest dramatic clichés: what's more inherently pathos-ridden than an old, sad clown?

Asked in a 1950 interview whether his new film was autobiographical, Chaplin responded casually: "Everything is autobiographical… but don't make too much of that." Almost every aspect of *Limelight* has some basis in Chaplin himself,

---

[16] Granted, as Charlie Jr. related, "that talk of retiring has been periodic with my father ever since those Keystone days. I can't recall his finishing a single big picture without telling me it was his last, that he was through for good."

his relationships, and his recollections, but the translation of these things into fictional characters and situations results in little that can be identified as related to one thing only; rather, most elements have multiple potential referents, the film being a highly specific and complex swirl of memory, history, imagination, and fantasy. Chaplin not only cast himself but also his son Sydney, in the prominent role of the composer, as well as the rest of his family in bit parts: son Charlie Jr. as a clown in the ballet, half-brother Wheeler Dryden as a doctor, and three of his kids with Oona (Geraldine, Michael, and Josephine) as street urchins. The character of Calvero is obviously a self-portrait of Chaplin himself—in more ways than one *Limelight* is the story of an old comic, who has ceased to be able to make audiences laugh, trying to make an artistic comeback—but also shares a likeness with his father Charles Chaplin Sr., who had worked the music halls and died a penniless alcoholic at age 38. In his autobiography, Chaplin also cited the names of American stage comic Frank Tinney and the Spanish mime Marceline as inspirations for the character, both having lost their public standing at the end of successful careers. Chaplin feared the same fate for himself, not just in a public sense but a private one as well—his mother had gone insane, and Chaplin spoke to those close to him of a belief that the same thing would happen to him. *Limelight* and its source novella were Chaplin's way of speculating about the lives and relationships of both his parents, who while central to Chaplin's emotional makeup remained enigmas to him. Hannah Chaplin also inspired the composite creation of Theresa, played by Claire Bloom, along with a mélange of other probable women in Chaplin's life: Chaplin's maternal grandmother (who had also gone mad), who she's named after; Hetty Kelly, Chaplin's first love before he left for America; silent film actress Florence Deshon, lover of Chaplin's friend Max Eastman (and likely Chaplin as well) who died from a gas oven suicide at age 26 like the one Bloom survives in the film; Paulette Goddard, who like Terry (as Theresa is called in the film) was given a masculine nickname, Peter, by Chaplin; and above all Oona

Chaplin, who Claire Bloom more than slightly resembled[17] and whose devotion to the much-older Chaplin in real life was, similarly, the shining silver lining of his late life (although Chaplin denies Calvero this romance in deference to a younger suitor of Terry's, despite her protestations).[18] Bloom herself, like Oona and the fictional Terry, came from a family broken by her father, and came to see Chaplin as the adopted father she thought she deserved; in another mirror of the film, Bloom was also a little bit in love with both Chaplin and Sydney, each in their own way. Much of this emotional history that Chaplin filled *Limelight* full to bursting with wouldn't have been visible to the average viewer; but the cultural history of Chaplin himself as a public artist definitely would have been. Theodore Huff's 1951 biography of Chaplin had just been released (kicking off a publishing industry of Chaplin books that continues to the present day), and the increased scrutiny of Chaplin's private life surely led many to be curious as to what, deep inside, made the man tick.

Reporting on *Limelight*'s first preview showing, writer Sidney Skolsky declared it irrelevant the degree to which one liked the film, because it "is no ordinary picture made by an ordinary man. This is a great hunk of celluloid history and emotion, and I think everybody who is genuinely interested in the movies will say, 'Thank you.'" Indeed, most immediately astonishing about *Limelight* is its unvarnished capturing of the body and face of a Chaplin that audiences had never seen before: old, weary, clean shaven, embodying the memory of his past screen persona while at the same time emphatically present as the person he now was. Chaplin, carrying nearly 40 years of film history with him, had never seemed so vulnerable on screen. It was clear now that the Tramp had at least partially

---

[17] Oona even appeared as a stand-in for Bloom in some retakes.
[18] Bloom: "Chaplin had already decided upon every last detail of every garment I was to wear. He remembered the way his mother had worn such a dress and the way his first girlfriend had worn such a shawl, and I quickly realized, even then, that some composite young woman, lost to him in the past, was what he wanted me to bring to life."

been a kind of mask, and that *Limelight*—in a completely different way from *Monsieur Verdoux*—was Chaplin's removal of it. Once asked by German millionaire Wolfgang Schleber (Pola Negri's lover at the time) why he had developed the Tramp character, Chaplin replied, "Herr Schleber, if I was as tall and handsome as you, there never would have been a tramp. You see, there would have been no need to hide." In the 1950s Chaplin settled into his post-Tramp screen self, his characters in both *Limelight* and his next film *A King in New York* (1957) merely simple variations on his own, relatively banal persona—in the former at least spiced up by literary characterizations, in the latter skewing toward non-characterization altogether. *Limelight* is dotted with bleak, haunting close-ups of Chaplin's face—for the first time ever, sans mustache— including a moment where he removes his stage makeup in real time to reveal his entirely plain, old-man's visage that, because of its simplicity and banality, is as special and casually moving as anything in Chaplin's work. Despite the film's focus on the past and the way it presses on the present, *Limelight* is a resolutely anti-nostalgic work. "If anybody else says it's like old times, I'll jump out the window," says Buster Keaton's character, and Keaton and Chaplin's on-set attitudes were similarly present-facing; far from being a nostalgic retread of the glory days, the *Limelight* set saw Buster and Charlie not speaking about the old times but merely getting down to business as two professionals doing work on a new film. The old pros had both had their ups and downs—Keaton's personal and professional decline after his artistically independent silent days had been a steep, alcohol-fueled one[19]—but that was all in the past when they set to work on their comedy act, improvising together and sharpening themselves against each other. Chaplin was still so sure of their abilities as performers that

---

[19] When hiring Keaton for the role, Chaplin expected him to be a wreck grateful for a job—in fact, Keaton was arguably happier and healthier than Chaplin at the time, having recovered, remarried, and renewed his fame through the means of television, where he often appeared as a guest as well as having his own show in L.A. Chaplin, who wouldn't own a TV until late in his life, had no idea.

he included no audience laughter on the soundtrack for their scene together, expecting theater audiences to provide it themselves; viewed at home decades later, this gives the scene an eerie, austere feeling that actually ends up suiting the haunted atmosphere of the film.

It's also suitable, in fact, because it's basically irrelevant whether you find their act funny at all, or whether you do so in a way that prompts any actual laughter. *Limelight* is about comedy without being a comedy, at least not in any traditional sense as demonstrated by all of Chaplin's other films, minus one.[20] *Limelight* is above all a dramatic reverie, a literary dream, a meditation on beauty as uniquely defined by Chaplin: "an omnipresence of death and loveliness, a smiling sadness that we discern in nature and all things, a mystic communion that the poet feels—an expression of it can be a dustbin with a shaft of sunlight across it, or it can be a rose in the gutter. El Greco saw it in our Saviour on the Cross." This is explicitly a film by Chaplin the Artist, wherein every last fiber of his artistic being is splayed across the screen, the awkwardness of his "primitive" formal and technological knowledge straining—and succeeding, in its own touching, handmade way—to express a lifetime of wisdom and emotion. The literary shape of the story leads Chaplin to spend the first, hefty chunk of the movie entirely in the building where Calvero and Terry live, exiting only via plaintive dissolves to memories, flashbacks, and dreams that shade in the characters' inner lives. The rest of this time, and much of the rest of the film, is dedicated to simple conversations between Terry and Calvero; Chaplinian dialogue spoken with a Chaplinian lilt, these scenes combine the heightened best of both theater and cinema in developing the pair's complex, nurturing relationship. Chaplin shares his hard-won wisdom in poetic turns of phrase that surely seemed

---

[20] *A Woman of Paris,* that is. Although pertinent to a discussion of Chaplin's late style is that none of his late films are traditional comedies in the sense that his silent ones are: *Monsieur Verdoux* a black comedy, *Limelight* not really a comedy at all, *A King in New York* a tragicomic satire, and *A Countess from Hong Kong* (1967) a realist comedy where the actors don't know they're in one.

grating to those irritated by Chaplin's real-life pontificating, yet the character of Calvero—and by extension Chaplin—has a self-awareness about his own gooey verbosity: he's constantly undercutting his own flights of philosophical fancy by remembering he's forgotten to make breakfast or do this or that or the other thing, but he also knows there's a kernel of truth buried somewhere in what he's saying, hidden underneath the inflated sense of poetry gifted to him by the life he's led. Added to *Limelight*'s already dense self-awareness, then, are these light, casual jabs of comedy thrown in at his own fading expense.

At times Chaplin even seems to be weary of his own voice, and by extension what sound cinema—even cinema itself, period—was asking of him. Sydney Chaplin remembered his father still saying that he preferred silent films to talking ones (the "dialogue just gets in the way in films") and Charlie Jr., hearing his father talk so often and so nostalgically about his old part as Billy the Shoeshine Boy in "Sherlock Holmes," suspected that "secretly he might have preferred the stage to pantomime and the movies." Naturally, the stagecraft-centered *Limelight* interrogated these feelings. Chaplin had actually been steeped anew in theater in the late 1940s thanks to Los Angeles' Circle Theater, a group of passionate young people putting on plays for a pittance in a small theater that had been started in 1946 by Jerry Epstein. Sydney's joining of the group led to Chaplin's interest, and his presence at the theater turned into a casual mentorship of the players and the impromptu leading of long, intense rehearsal sessions. Although his involvement went unadvertised, Chaplin ghost-directed seven shows in all for the theater, and in the meantime he honed his philosophy of acting, performance, and gesture during rehearsals; Chaplin was a proponent of François Delsarte's 19th-century school of acting, which emphasized the connection between emotion and the physical expressions of the body. Founder Jerry Epstein impressed Chaplin, and their friendship evolved into Epstein's hiring as an assistant on *Limelight*; they would work together for the rest of Chaplin's life, Epstein taking on more and more responsibility as he proved himself to be the most consistent and dependable collaborator of Chaplin's late career (even to the point of moving to Europe at his behest in the 1950s). Chaplin's Circle Theater adventures would transfer directly to his work on *Limelight*. "That's the trouble with movies," Chaplin would say—"directors don't know their theater. Everything comes from the stage. Learn your theater first, and then you'll be more effective on screen." Sydney preferred his father as a stage director more than a film director, but noted how he shot his films as though he were the former and carried over his "old-fashioned style toward acting" to the *Limelight* set. Chaplin's preference for subtle, gestural acting often led him to demand that his actors not "act" at all. À la his forward-thinking approach on *A Woman of Paris* in dramatically toning down the theatrics of silent film acting, *Limelight* offers this specific kind of cinematic acting—subtle, small (because the screen will eventually project it large)—inside rather theatrical staging. Chaplin as a "serious" actor never had a greater show-case, giving a performance of sensitivity and pathos (based on the accrual of a half-century of work) that proved his comedy stylings had never been because of a lack of dramatic chops.

Limelight is the epitome of Chaplin's all-consuming desire to have his art be a total expression of himself with as little contamination from others as possible. Like many of his films, his laundry list of roles is comically long: actor, writer, director, producer, studio head, composer, editor, choreographer, casting director, wardrobe and makeup designer, prop man, and, at *Limelight*'s Hollywood preview, even acting as an usher and sound man. In an age of artistic compromise, negotiation, and collaboration within a hierarchical factory landscape, Chaplin's late films were the kind of total auteurist visions unheard of in Hollywood. As his own producer, and the owner of his own independent studio, Chaplin had final say on everything from who he worked with to what cut of the film would go out into the world. (Indeed, final cut had been a non-negotiable for Chaplin ever since Essanay managers had meddled with *Burlesque on Carmen* [1915] against his will after he'd left the studio.) More often than not, Chaplin used (or tried to use) his collaborators as vessels for his own ideas rather than as artistic contributors in their own right; anyone who ever visited a Chaplin set attested to his desire "to do it all," in the words of fellow director (and *City Lights* bit player) Robert Parrish, to play not just his own but all of the parts. "I don't think he ever fully accepted the idea of not being able to be behind the camera and in front of it at the same time." But he still tried. To Jerry Lewis, a student, fan, and later friend of Chaplin's,[21] he was the prime example of what he termed the "total filmmaker" — "[Chaplin] was totally in, on, and all over his films." This was the antithesis of quotidian Hollywood's modus operandi, and in a December 1947 interview Chaplin spoke of having "lost confidence" in the (to him, "dying") industry: "Hollywood is now fighting its last battle, and it will lose that battle unless it decides once and for all to give up standardizing its films — unless it realizes that masterpieces cannot be mass-produced in the cinema, like tractors in a factory." In this way *Limelight* is the result of a filmmaking philosophy closer to a Federico Fellini or a Robert Bresson than anything coming out of English-language cinema; formally and thematically, it's a film easier to read alongside international art cinema's looks at aging in contemporaneous films like Vittorio De Sica's *Umberto D.* and Akira Kurosawa's *Ikiru* (both 1952), or Ingmar Bergman's later *Wild Strawberries* (1957). If Chaplin could sometimes be "the great dictator" of his movie sets, the big boss of *Modern Times* that he ostensibly deplored, this tight control nevertheless sprang from a singular, uncompromising artistic consciousness that resulted in works, like

---

[21] Lewis first met Chaplin at a restaurant and then later visited him a few times in Switzerland. They loved each other's films; Chaplin was so impressed by *The Bellboy* (1960) that he exchanged a print of *Modern Times* for a print of Lewis's film. On one visit in 1963, they talked for hours about tempo, pace, and how to cut comedy. Much could be written about the way Chaplin's late films are in conversation with the films of Lewis as total, singular, against-the-grain self-expressions. Chaplin's daughter Geraldine relates that on a visit to him months before he died, she found him shaking with laughter at a Jerry Lewis film, a cycle of his films having been shown on Swiss television in the mid-1970s.

Limelight, that are nothing less than the total revelation of his vision.

But to the critics conditioned to the standards of "well-made" Hollywood entertainment or the collaborators who had to stomach the relegation of their own visions, Chaplin's artistic single-mindedness mainly seemed to manifest itself in effects that were "raw and naïve and outdated," as Claire Bloom termed them. But whereas Bloom was ultimately happy to be grafted into Chaplin's universe (and as a nervous performer new to film, to have Chaplin essentially give her performance for her via his direction), others were more apt to question Chaplin's bizarre and archaic stylings. Chaplin knew his reputation, though, and sometimes took steps to counteract it, like when he hired veteran cinematographer Karl Struss (DP of DeMille, Murnau, and Griffith pictures of years past) in a move to essentially replace long-time cameraman Rollie Totheroh, who, having been insulated in his services for so long, was unsatisfactorily proving no less old-fashioned than Chaplin himself.[22] Although Struss thought *Limelight* "the slightly more interesting of the two films photograph-ically"—he'd been brought on in similar circumstances for *The Great Dictator*, there bugging Chaplin with his desire for "mood" effects like shots with tree branches in them—he still found his wishes hindered by a filmmaker who, according to him, "had no knowledge of camera direction" and whose films "were completely 'theatre.' It was very routine work with him; you'd just set up the camera and let it go and he and the other actors would play in front of it." To save on time and money, Chaplin and Epstein even filmed multiple scenes without repositioning the camera and out of continuity. All the long shots in Calvero's apartment were filmed together,

---

[22] However, Jerry Epstein recalls an amusing irony here common to Chaplin's contradictions as a filmmaker: "At the end of shooting, we ran everything we had filmed. Charlie looked at some of Claire's close-ups and said, 'Oh, these are beautiful. They're the best in the whole picture.' These were the work of Rollie before he was taken off!" Totheroh was credited on the picture as a "photographic consul-tant."

Chaplin and Bloom merely changing costumes between takes, and then onto the medium shots, and then the close-ups all the same way; extensive rehearsals had made it easy for them to play scenes out of order. All of this was head-scratching at best—completely maddening at worst—for assistant director Robert Aldrich, who thought Chaplin "hopelessly old-fashioned," according to Scott Eyman. Aldrich was an experienced assistant and studio professional (his work for Jean Renoir on 1945's *The Southerner* had directly led to his recommendation by actor Norman Lloyd for *Limelight*) and would shortly thereafter go on to make a name for himself as a director in his own right, and a stylistically bold one at that. Chaplin reportedly hired Aldrich because he "wanted someone on set who would be like a cop," a part of his wish to economize the production in its usage of time perhaps, but Aldrich quickly learned that this role did not apply to the man himself: hearing Aldrich tell an aide that "if anything goes wrong technically give me a signal," Chaplin swiftly corrected him: "We'll stop if anything goes *esthetically* wrong." "He can't direct," Aldrich told Lloyd. "He's the greatest actor in the world, but he can't direct." Aldrich wanted more "artistic" shots and couldn't understand Chaplin's predilection for the simplest, most static of set-ups. But in a wondrous turn of events, Aldrich's skepticism evaporated in contact with the finished product. Jerry Epstein tells the story in his memoir: "After the preview, Bob came to Charlie, shattered, with tears in his eyes. 'I take it all back," he said. "You know exactly what you're doing. The picture was marvelous!' We were all touched, coming from this skeptic. But the greatest compliment Bob paid to Charlie was in his own film *Autumn Leaves* [1956], where he borrowed some of Charlie's own camera set-ups and lighting effects."

Chaplin had marshalled his "antiquated," theatrical camera style and "awkward," dialogue-heavy scenario into a paradoxically assured and unified work—the expansive sense of memory and the depth of feeling turning an almost miniaturist chamber drama into an emotionally intimate epic. Nothing about the rickety U.S. studio hodgepodge version of Old London scraped together with a shoestring budget of $900,000 (essentially bankrolled by the 1950 rerelease of *City Lights*) can diminish the essential richness of the project; in fact it rather enhances the sense of a world built solely from memory fundamental to *Limelight*'s creation. The film is literature, theater, and cinema nestled together. Although his camera was more active than most writing admits, Chaplin's preference for a static set-ups came from his view of the camera aperture "as a small proscenium" through which, like in the theater, the drama unfolds both right there with the audience and also in a magical world apart. Watching *Limelight,* one swims in its novelistic, theatrical, cinematic ambience, all two hours and twenty minutes of it (Chaplin's longest film by far), getting lost in the film and submitting to its unorthodox yet entrancing rhythms. André Bazin even admitted to boredom watching the film in 1952, but "I never wished for any shortening of this period of boredom. It was rather a relaxing of attention that left my mind free to wander—daydreaming about the images. There were also many occasions on which the feeling of length left me.... The film, objectively speaking a long one... and slow, caused a lot of people, myself included, to lose their sense of time." The sense of *Limelight* as a novelistic, three-dimensional world that the viewer wades through, drowns in, and loses their bearings on space and time during is one arguably particular to this film; as rich as other Chaplin films are, none are rendered on a plane of thought and action quite as deep and wide as this one. Helping in this regard is Chaplin's music—both the literal compositions as well as the musical rhythms of the film in general. He would often listen to his own score[23] before entering rehearsals so as to steep himself in the moods of the film and his performance, as well as having it in his head while he directed. His leading lady in *A King in New York,* Dawn Addams, later said that Chaplin directed like a "musical conductor," and sometimes suddenly became "a saxophone or a violin to give one the mood of the

---

[23] *Limelight*'s score is maybe Chaplin's best, and so good that it won Best Score at the Oscars 20 years later in 1973, having only become officially eligible for nomination with the film's 1972 rerelease. This resulted in the Academy changing its eligibility rules so an old film couldn't be nominated in this way again.

scene as the spectator will watch it." This carries over to Chaplin's exquisite filming of *Limelight*'s ballet sequences, where he gives the film over to them and simply basks in them via simple, elegant camera angles, capturing via dance (and in other scenes, music hall acts) the public magic of art, music, and the performer's relation to the audience, to their partners, and to themselves that is heightened and frozen in time by the cinema.

As a summative statement on Chaplin's art past and present, *Limelight* was Chaplin's apolitical olive branch to an American public that had soured on him post-*Verdoux*. Unfortunately, they would barely receive it—right-wing political groups were still actively promoting anti-Chaplin rhetoric, leading boycotts across the country against his new film that damaged not only the film's chances at a successful release but Chaplin's ego as well. Refusing to suffer the humiliation of the boycotts, Chaplin pulled *Limelight* from American distribution—it didn't even play one week in Los Angeles. But by this time Chaplin had plenty of reason to be bitter about America, having received the news, two days into his transatlantic voyage to premiere the film in London in the fall of 1952, that his re-entry permit had been rescinded, and that he'd have to face more bad faith questioning from U.S. immigration officers if he wanted back in. Chaplin had been having premonitions of a potential break with America for a few years now. Originally planning to shoot *Limelight* in his native England, he'd made plans for a 1948 trip with the dual purpose of showing Oona his homeland and scouting for his film; Chaplin's lawyer advised him not to go. As late as spring 1950 he still hoped to shoot the film overseas. And when he finally left with his family in tow in September 1952, the intention was to see the film to its October premiere, embark on a world tour, and return to California in spring 1955. But he mentioned to friends the vague possibility of not returning, willingly or not, and even added the name of the American-born Oona to his bank accounts as a safety measure. Ultimately, though, Chaplin's exile was a self-exile; his decision to stay in Europe, settle down, and live out his remaining years there was an assertion of his personal, political, artistic, and moral integrity rather than a submission to government mandate. "You're not going back, Charlie?" asked the American consul upon Chaplin's discarding of his re-entry permit. "No… I'm a little too old to take any more of that nonsense." The truth is, Chaplin could have re-entered the United States if he really wanted to; having searched for years for definitive evidence tying Chaplin to communist causes, they'd come up with a handful of nothing, therefore with no real case for barring Chaplin's return. Indeed, it was the moral case against Chaplin, rather than the political one, that primarily spurred the rescinding of his permit in the first place. But Chaplin was exhausted with his adopted nation long before this, and took it in stride as his opportunity to restart in a more peaceful environment. He was received heartily across Europe; *Limelight* became Chaplin's highest-grossing picture based on foreign receipts alone. Oona renounced her American citizenship in solidarity with her husband, and in 1953 the couple and their four (soon to be five) children settled into their new mansion in Switzerland, the 37-acre Manoir de Ban in Corsier-sur-Vevey.

The germ of an idea for Chaplin's next film travelled with him to Europe in the form of a recurring dream, about "an immigrant who arrives in the New World speaking an ancient language that the customs officials are incapable of understanding."[24] Chaplin was living through the second major relocation of his life, 40 years after the first, back to the

---

[24] This dream displays a strong similarity to an improvised comedic conversation between Chaplin and Bertolt Brecht during the McCarthy era, as remembered by Brecht's collaborator Ruth Berlau: "In the course of a conversation they improvised—each reacting to the words of the other—a story about Chaplin leaving America. He is already on the ship when the emigration officials appear. They want to establish whether he is a 'security risk' and begin to grill him, but nobody can understand the language in which he replies. They bring in a Chinese interpreter, then a Japanese one, then a Korean, and so on, but all come to grief. No wonder, since Chaplin is speaking a language of his own invention…. At the end, he showed us the emigration officials giving up the ghost. As the ship is leaving the harbor, Chaplin casts a look at the Statue of Liberty through a porthole and sees the goddess close one eye in a wink."

continent whence he originally came. There had never *really* been any doubt that Chaplin would return to filmmaking, and, following the heavily autobiographical *Limelight*, his ideas continued to circle around his own life circumstances: his exile, his adjustment to a new way of life, his emerging status as a kind of outmoded royal figure. The Manoir de Ban's location put Chaplin in the midst of a host of actual royalty, meeting deposed monarchs at social gatherings, rubbing shoulders with the likes of the former queen of Spain; he became intrigued by the stories of how they'd fled revolutions in their home countries. Holed up in his mansion and surrounded by fellow (rich) exiles, Chaplin's aristocratic airs had room to foment. As he grew older, Chaplin increasingly inhabited two headspaces to the exclusion of others: one, his present situation as a kind of exiled, aristocratic king,[25] and the other a melancholy, rose-tinted remembrance of his poverty-filled childhood—the pre-Oona years, the height of his fame, faded away more and more for him. "In old age," Francis Wyndham would write toward the end of Chaplin's life, "Chaplin has lost interest in the achievements of his prime. He is mainly concerned with what he will do next, and with that obscure period of his life before his genius had been given a chance to define itself. The tragedy of those days has acquired a poignant beauty for him with the passage of the busy years." Contra the poignant beauty of *Limelight*, his new film *A King in New York* would be firmly and bleakly set in the present, acting as a reflection on all the chaos he'd escaped for the more tranquil waters of Europe, and once again starring himself in a lightly fictionalized self-portrait that furthered the "mythic" idea of post-Tramp Chaplin. As the real Chaplin settled down into home and family life for the first real time in his life, he still understood, as François Truffaut wrote, "that the roles of 'settled' men were forbidden to him." Thus his King Shahdov, an in-between character trapped for a time in post-exile purga-

---

[25] His new company inaugurated post-exile was named Roy Enterprises, as in *roi*, the French word for king.

tory, searching for a state of being calmer than the crazy culture storming around him.

Appropriately, Chaplin would have to make the film in a similarly strange and unfamiliar environment. His new base of operations would be Shepperton Studios in England; he'd have to rent studio space for the first time in his life. The project had to be approached with a cost-efficient mindset, as there would be no plans for American distribution — given the satirical subject matter, it would almost certainly be a flop and, anyway, continuing tax disputes with the American government meant it was likely they'd confiscate any profits the film. Chaplin hired B-performers and stage actors for his cast and planned for what would be the shortest shoot of his career. Foreshadowing the way the film offered a specifically Chaplinian paraphrase of America, all of the actors were British despite the characters being American; as *Limelight* had been an American studio reproduction of London, so *A King in New York* would offer an English studio reproduction of New York. Besides assistant Jerry Epstein, Chaplin's usual studio people were no longer at his disposal, forcing him to work with an unfamiliar crew that, to Chaplin's chagrin, would mutiny without their afternoon tea breaks. Their different methods and unique approaches to the work had pros and cons for Chaplin — "They're slower, but more thorough," he would say. The best thing about it?: "that it cost 25 per cent less." (Chaplin was once again self-financing.) Yet the atmosphere was "frosty and strained," according to Jerry Epstein. "There seemed to be no heart at Shepperton. We felt we were *all* in exile." Despite all this Chaplin was eager to get to set every morning, full of energy and ready to have fun making a new film, as euphoric about the work as he had been while making *Limelight*. The bitterness of the subject matter did nothing to stanch the joy of Chaplin's creative outpourings, even though he was nearing 70 years old.

A King in New York was to be, as Chaplin told Clifford Odets, a "satire on Americans and the *modus operandi* of the day." Its comedy works through a series of gags satirizing contemporaneous trends — rock & roll music, widescreen

movies, progressive schools, television, plastic surgery,[26] etc.—
on its way to skewering its main target, the McCarthyism that
contributed to Chaplin's exit from the country. The prevalence
of screens comically (and ominously) anticipates modern ideas
of surveillance[27] and hyper-saturated commercialism.[28] Some of
Chaplin's satirical targets might look silly or cliché ("old-man-
dislikes-new-thing") from today's perspective, but this is a
shallow way of looking at a more complex phenomenon; just
because Chaplin makes a gag about loud music doesn't mean
he hates loud music; besides whatever inherent comedic value
it might have, it's a way of showing the changing times and
the new contexts in which people live. (Chaplin wasn't just
some aging dullard: presented with the Elvis phenomenon, for
example, he didn't dismiss it as a fad but recognized that there
must be *something* there if people liked it so much.) As should
be one's approach with late art, just because grandpa shows a
leery eye at new developments doesn't mean he doesn't have
a point; maybe he's lived long enough to tell when something
isn't the healthiest thing, or lived through enough to see something as the fad it is. And as the film's turn from more frivolous
matters to more serious, tragic ones indicates, the accumulation of gags demonstrating the mayhem of modern American
life has mainly served to create an atmosphere of appropriate
cultural exhaustion. When the film finally gets down to the
business of directly attacking America's petty political witch

----

[26] The face-lift scene was inspired by an experience of Jerry Epstein's,
who almost got a nose job on request from Eddie Constantine, the
French-American movie star known for playing detective Lemmy
Caution (used most famously in Jean-Luc Godard's *Alphaville* in
1965). In the 1950s Epstein had worked with Constantine, writing
scripts and directing a couple of movies for him; Chaplin would occasionally contribute uncredited gags.

[27] As does a fellow late film from Fritz Lang, *The 1,000 Eyes of Dr.
Mabuse* (1960), which also happens to star Dawn Addams. (Not to
mention Chaplin's own *Modern Times*, which prefigures George
Orwell's image of a surveilling Big Brother by over a decade.)

[28] Ironically, Chaplin's Los Angeles studio had been rented by Procter
and Gamble in the late 1940s for the production of some of the earliest
television commercials.

hunts, it's the bitter cherry on top of the chaotic disorder that Chaplin's King Shahdov has experienced New York as.

"Friends have asked me if I miss the United States—New York," Chaplin would write in his autobiography a few years later. "In candor I do not. America has changed; so has New York. The gigantic scale of industrial institutions, of press, television and commercial advertising has completely divorced me from the American way of life. I want the other side of the coin, a simpler personal sense of living—not the ostentatious avenues and towering buildings which are an ever-present reminder of big business and its ponderous achievements." Like *The Great Dictator* and *Monsieur Verdoux, A King in New York* was a film born out of anger, an explicitly political comedy expressing in no uncertain terms Chaplin's criticisms of the modern world. But *A King in New York* is loaded with a *weariness* absent from those previous pictures, the sense that Chaplin no longer had in him a vigorous, passionate rebuke but was instead simply worn out, intellectually and emotionally, and merely wished for all the hysteria to end, and soon. Faced with the ostensible climax of the film in Shahdov's appearance before the House Un-American Activities Committee, Chaplin opts not for a big speech à la *The Great Dictator* but for some old slapstick business with an uncontrollable fire hose, suggesting that HUAC is such a silly and stupid thing that it's not even worth giving a platform to for the sake of denouncing it. Chaplin's dramatic attention is instead directed toward the boy Rupert Macabee, played by his son Michael Chaplin, whose parents are under investigation by the committee and whose wish for their return results in him naming the names that his parents wouldn't, just to get them back. Shahdov's first run-in with the boy is at a progressive school where Rupert is discovered reading Karl Marx and then getting on his soapbox to preach a kind of anarcho-internationalist philosophy of political liberty. Viewers have been quick to put his words directly into Chaplin's mouth, as they did with Verdoux, but once again there is more of a dialectic going on, as Jonathan Rosenbaum points out: "Similarly, I would argue that those who reject *A King in New York* because they find

Chaplin's ideas in it too obvious, simplistic, or bitter are likely to be overlooking the fact that he places many of his own most cherished leftist and anti-nationalist sentiments in the mouth of an obnoxiously self-righteous and hectoring brat who often won't let Chaplin's title king get a word in edgewise when he holds forth. This implies a dialectical as well as a self-critical side to Chaplin—not to mention a certain intellectual depth—that few commentators are likely to concede about the man." (For all of Chaplin's post-*Dictator* films, it's always important to note who, i.e., what character, the words are coming from.) Yet the character of Rupert, having begun the film as a comedic character, ends it as a tragic one; Chaplin's final sympathies re-color our perception of the boy into someone who, as much as he might get carried away with childish hyperbole and righteous anger,[29] is ultimately the organic reaction to the society he's been raised in—a society to be regretted not just for what it's done to people, but for what it's made people do to other people; Chaplin's grand statement on the toxic paranoia of mid-century American life ultimately boils down to the image of crying child. And this is what he's tied his self-portrait to. "It's me," he would tell an interviewer in 1957. "I keep repeating what I am. The boy and I are human beings, that's all." Although on the surface more of a companion film to *Monsieur Verdoux*'s atomic age satire, *A King in New York* almost nudges closer to being a late career reimagining of *The Kid* (albeit with a stronger streak of bleakness; Jean-Claude Biette perceptively compares the heartbreaking character of

---

[29] Michael Chaplin would become something of a rebel himself, bucking under his father's strict yet detached parenting style, running away from school, and getting up to various misadventures across Europe. (He recalled his work on *A King in New York* as the only time he had a real relationship with his father.) A ghost-written autobiography of his life, datedly stylized in the countercultural patois of the 1960s, appeared in 1966 when he was just 20 years old as *I Couldn't Smoke the Grass on My Father's Lawn*. Chaplin tried to suppress its publication, and Michael joined in on the effort as he'd reconciled with his parents soon after its writing; it eventually appeared anyway, in an agreed-to revised text, after Michael withdrew his legal appeal.

Rupert to the child in Rossellini's *Germany Year Zero* [1948].) Shahdov ends up leaving the country for similar reasons that the boy has been crushed by it: it's all just too much, life can't be lived here, best to just skip town and get out of there. The ending of the film, an abrupt cut to Shahdov on a plane leaving the country, is Chaplin's clear self-commentary on his political and emotional situation: there may be things (or, at least, people) to like about America, but too much time there just gets exhausting. Chaplin even aborted a planned final shot that would show, in a bitter callback to *The Immigrant* (1917), the Statue of Liberty growing smaller and smaller in the distance as the plane flew away. In fact, the whole script of *A King in New York* had, "after considerable reflection," been decidedly toned down, according to Charlie Jr.—"the first draft of that script was far more biting than the one my father finally used for shooting." Perhaps the remnants of Chaplin's genuine feeling for the country, one that he had idealized more than any other "with its promise of freedom of thought and belief and its emphasis on the importance of the individual." In view of this, Chaplin's political hounding is all the more bitterly ironic, and must have stung all the greater; *A King in New York* is Chaplin's deeply human, and arguably compassionate, response.

Yet all these thematic resonances play out in a film that, at least on the surface, seems like a technically deficient, awkward, out-of-date series of C-tier gags. The comedy of *A King in New York* has little of the agile action humor of something like *City Lights,* for example, a fellow "city film" that sees Chaplin flying up, down, and around town (although some of the situational humor is reversed: there Chaplin walks into wealth for a time, and here Chaplin loses it) in a film that goes back to stringing together gags into a story rather than the complex narratives of his previous two films. Many of the film's posters—favorites of mine, as the cover of this book attests—see the 68-year-old Chaplin quaintly traipsing in front of a New York cityscape, and this is accurate to the pacing of the film, as well as the subjective nature of its anachronistic humor: some of it is uproariously funny (at least to me)—the riotous baptism-by-culture in the early going that includes the caviar pantomime gag, the widescreen movie trailers, and later the face-lift laughter scene—and some of it is like screwball at half speed, such as the elongated scene of Chaplin weaving his way through a crowd to escape an autograph hound he's mistaken for a government agent. In a foreshadowing of *A Countess from Hong Kong* (1967), much of the film involves the ostensibly dull and repetitive business of doors opening and closing and bells and telephones ringing, the characters unable to stay ahead of it all and forced to swim with the tide. But this slowed-down, geriatric kind of comedy is perhaps Chaplin's deliberate exploitation of the limitations of his person. He'd flirt with the idea of bringing back the Tramp around this time (the organization and re-release of three early shorts as *The Chaplin Revue* [1959] had reawakened the thought), but even if the matter of talking were ignored it was the physical handicap that ultimately made it impossible for him: the Tramp was defined by an athletic gracefulness that Chaplin no longer possessed. The bumbling inelegance of King Shahdov was an evolution, however, that allowed Chaplin to speak to new modes of being in his art and comedy—to "[use] the screen as his personal diary," as Andrew Sarris would put it, a tendency that made his late work "a study less in decline than in modal metamorphosis." There's more to comedy than eliciting laughter, Chaplin's late work seems to say; given the ease with which Chaplin produced reactions from his audiences in the past, François Truffaut would argue, "If we neither cry nor laugh at *A King in New York*, it's because Chaplin made up his mind to touch our heads instead of our hearts." Sticking with black and white and the traditional academy ratio, enacting the film's opening "revolution" (economically, hilariously) with just a dozen or so extras, or being released in the UK by a minor distributor known mainly for low budget British films and imports—none of this has any bearing (in fact it contributes to the spare directness of it all) on the film's final artistic value. Poet and screenwriter Paul Dehn observed that the film's "narrative may be incoherent, its cutting slack, its camera-work primitive and its décor (by glossy Hollywood standards) abominably shoddy, but it says more in its brief, tragic-comic compass than all this year's glossy Hollywood pictures laid end to end; and the more you see it, the more it will have to say...." As usual, Chaplin was adamant about his artistic priorities. Veteran French cinematographer Georges Périnal (films by Cocteau, Clair, Grémillion, Preminger, and Powell & Pressburger were on his résumé), slow to perfect the set-up of his lights one day, received this Chaplin broadside: "Turn all the lights on!... I have to give a performance! I don't give a goddamn about your artistic effects! It's a comedy! We need light!" Joe McElhaney has written of how many talented directors "remain attached to the idea that one must make *accomplished* films," whereas "the Chaplin of *A King in New York* could not care less about such matters. In fact, the great aging filmmaker possesses an assurance that is so internalised, it no longer needs to be insistently announced in every sequence. This is not the transparency of classicism but something else, as though both modern and classical forms are giving way to that which cannot yet be categorised."

A King in New York makes no concessions to the way movies circa 1957 were supposed to function; in this way we can agree with Roberto Rossellini's famous proclamation, essentially a more succinct way of saying the same thing as McElhaney, that *A King in New York* "is the film of a free man."[30] Even British critic Kenneth Tynan, who could hardly

---

[30] As reported by Jean-Luc Godard in more than one *Cahiers du cinéma* article (relatedly, the film would appear in first place on the magazine's list of the best films of 1957). The relationship between Chaplin and Rossellini is worth mentioning, two artists looking to express themselves in free and personal ways outside traditional mid-century models. They had first met in Los Angeles; Chaplin admired *Rome, Open City* (1945), Rossellini spent a day "venerating" *Monsieur Verdoux*. When Chaplin came to Europe in 1952, they met up again, talking through to the morning. Chaplin was taken to see *Europa '51* (1952)—"He cried from one end of the movie to the other, like a fool, completely without restraint," according to Rossellini's biographer Tag Gallagher. "It was the story of my mother," Chaplin would explain. "She was unusual, she had ideas for humanity; she died in a clinic too." Chaplin would later gift Rossellini the *Shadow*

be said to have liked the film, had to admit that "nobody has subjected the script to 'a polishing job,' which is the film industry's euphemism for the process whereby rough edges are planed away and sharp teeth blunted…. The result, in the fullest sense of the phrase, is 'free cinema,' in which anything, within the limits of censorship, can happen." *A King in New York* is Chaplin riffing, with the tonal freedom of a jazz artist, on the new modern times of the '50s and his own place in them. The film may have looked, or may still look, like something from a filmmaker who was irredeemably "behind the times" — but it's literally a film *about* being behind them, and trying to keep up with them. It's a late film about the very changes the world has undergone that *make* it a late film. Criticizing the Chaplin of *A King in New York* for being old-fashioned is a useless redundancy; he's already self-diagnosed himself, an artist cognizant of the world flying him by and asking questions about whether he even cares to chase after it. Where his other three postwar late films are all more or less the result of decades-long incubation periods, *A King in New York* is defiantly contemporary, a movie of the moment made in the moment, a stubbornly "un-hip" piece of cinema that from today's vantage point looks hipper than most everything else released in 1957 — hip to what the times were all about, hip to what wasn't so hot about them, and hip to what they meant contextually to his own artistry. Few were in a position to realize this at the time: most European filmgoers weren't fully aware of what McCarthyism had truly wrought, and American audiences could only react to the European reactions — the film wouldn't be shown stateside until 1973 (in a version slightly shortened, ironically, to appease a distributor wanting to fit it into the two-hour slots of television.)

The film was more apt to be appreciated in the political culture of the 1970s, but by then Chaplin had devolved into a mostly apolitical humanitarian. His personal politics had never been particularly coherent relative to any single ideology,

---

and Substance story he'd failed to make himself, and a few years later was moved again by Rossellini's film *General Della Rovere* (1959).

regardless of what he'd been accused of; indeed, his public mislabeling as a communist (or communist sympathizer, for many much the same thing) had been metaphorically foreshadowed by the scene in *Modern Times* where Charlie picks up a safety flag fallen from a truck only to get mistakenly arrested as the ringleader of a massive street protest. But the fact that a man who enjoyed the luxuries of wealth as much as Chaplin did could still be reasonably confused for a communist sympathizer was part and parcel of Chaplin's many contradictions as a man; his claims to the effect that he was just an apolitical peacemonger could be read as true or false depending on how casual your definition of politics is. The interest he evinced in the Soviet Union was less a show of admiration for their particular system than it a was a vote of idealistic hope in a different, and therefore possibly better, way of doing things. Chaplin admitted that the reason he never visited the Soviet Union was because he was "afraid I might be disillusioned"—better to remain ignorant on this count than lose faith in humanity altogether, he thought. But despite accepting the Communist-sponsored World Peace Council's World Peace Prize in 1954 (Chaplin gave away the prize money to the poor of London and Paris) and meeting Soviet leaders Nikita Khrushchev and Nikolai Bulganin at a Soviet embassy event in London in 1956, by this time Chaplin had privately lost enthusiasm for the Soviet project. He had never been exclusively loyal to one system of thought, but instead "enjoyed cementing together the odds and ends he had collected from various countries to create magnificent but utterly impractical utopias," per his son Charlie. If we really want to put a name on it, I'm inclined to apply to Chaplin James Agee's diagnosis of John Huston as, "like perhaps five out of seven good artists who ever lived... a natural-born antiauthoritarian individualistic libertarian anarchist, without portfolio." Yet Chaplin's interest in politics waned after *A King in New York*'s release, and in 1960 was quoted as saying, "I remain just one thing, and one thing only—and that is a clown. It places me on a far higher plane than any politician." By a decade later he'd mellow even further, in 1971 claiming no ill feelings toward

America and observing that "when you live as long as I have, all politics look pretty foolish." His focus had shifted completely toward his family and his work. "I don't think it matters how the world progresses," he'd say in 1972.

The aging Chaplin's decreasing interest in global matters was accompanied by an increasing turn inward: circa the turn of the decade, his most pressing subject was himself. After finishing work on the successful rerelease bundle *The Chaplin Revue* in 1959, Chaplin sat down to write his autobiography. Multiple years of uninterrupted effort—Chaplin led a disciplined lifestyle with dedicated time slots for writing and dictation—finally produced the highly anticipated book in 1964 under the title *My Autobiography* (a thick work that Chaplin, as late as 1963, had considered stretching to two volumes). In the age of ghostwritten celebrity biographies, Chaplin insisted on writing *My Autobiography* himself, and as a result it bore the distinct mark of its author's personality and peculiarities on both a word-by-word basis and on the level of its general construction. Chaplin's florid prose (also displayed, although not yet publicly at the time, in *Limelight*'s source novella) reveals a literary personality both highly mannered yet down-to-earth, thesaurus-dependent yet movingly poetic. Chaplin was proud of his autodidactic literacy, having spent most of his childhood outside of any consistent schooling and, because of that, always cautious about the extent of his grammatical knowledge—a copy of the Fowler brothers' 1906 usage and grammar book *The King's English* was his constant companion and guide while writing. Yet as to the general substance of the book his self-confidence was sturdy; Truman Capote, a Swiss neighbor at the time, was soundly rebuked by Chaplin for offering editorial advice on a manuscript he was meant only to read and enjoy. The autobiography earned admiring yet ambivalent notices that had to do with its essentially two-pronged structure: the first half a stirring, detailed, nigh-Dickensian recollection of Chaplin's hardscrabble London youth, the second—generally less and less detailed as it advanced closer to the present day—essentially a roll call of the many famous cultural, scientific, and political figures Chaplin had rubbed shoulders with throughout the 20th century. This in lieu of detailed discussion of his relationships, his collaborators, his films, or his filmmaking philosophy in general; titles like *The Circus* and *A King in New York* go almost completely unmentioned.[31] The book exposes, as the later films do, the perspective of a man who had completely skipped over the middle class, and had dedicated most of his mental space to the aforementioned duality of his early poverty and later fame. Critics generally loved the first part of the book, less so the second—perhaps in parallel to the reaction garnered by his increasingly unloved, "aristocratic" later films compared to his beloved early ones from his metaphorical filmmaking child-hood. Regardless, *My Autobiography* was a smashing financial success and remained a top-ten nonfiction bestseller for six months.

The success reinvigorated Chaplin. His obsessive drive to continue working and creating far exceeded any lethargy that might be expected from a man now well into his seventies, and fulfilled his self-made prophecy from 1916 that he expected to still "be at it fifty years from now." "Chaplin in his old age seems to feel physically forty-five," noted Penelope Gilliatt (even a bout of flu right before his next production that kept him from full strength didn't diminish this sense), yet in other ways looked like a man who'd clearly reached the other side of his life: "With his present white hair he looks almost like the negative image of his silent-film self." Death was claiming many of those closest to him: half-brother Wheeler Dryden in 1957, former leading lady Edna Purviance in 1958, and his brother Sydney who died on Chaplin's birthday in 1965; Rollie Totheroh would follow in 1967, as well as son Charlie Jr., prematurely at the age of 42, in 1968. Profiler Howard

---

[31] In the case of *The Circus* (despite its having won a special award at the first Academy Award ceremony), probably an effect of its making coming in one of the most difficult periods of Chaplin's life: his highly publicized divorce to Lita Grey (a relationship entirely unexplored in the autobiography, for the stated sake of their two children together), a fire that destroyed the set at the beginning of its filming, and a general state of affairs that caused him to suffer a mental breakdown.

Clurman had written in 1962 that, "For the first time in my long acquaintance with Chaplin, I had the feeling that he was not only an artist of genius, but a man who might be considered—or had become—wise. When I speak of 'wisdom,' I do not mean correct in opinion or even reliable in judgment. I mean that Chaplin's whole personality has become integrated and has attained the finest balance that his talents and nature could achieve...." Chaplin was eager to channel his creative energy into a new film, naturally, yet he was anxious about having to write a new screenplay—would an old one do? He ended up dusting off a script called *Stowaway* that he'd written in 1936 on the return from a trip to the Far East with Paulette Goddard (an idea perhaps first stirred on a previous visit to Shanghai in 1931), a bedroom farce about a former White Russian countess stowing away in the cabin of an American politician originally envisioned as starring Goddard and Gary Cooper. He went so far as to interview Cooper, whom Chaplin admired not for his acting ability per se but for his ability to *not* act. But Chaplin set aside the script in the late 1930s for the pressing matter of *The Great Dictator*. "How could I throw myself into feminine whimsey or think of romance or the problems of love," he'd later recall, "when madness was being stirred up by a hideous grotesque—Adolf Hitler?" The idea was partially resurrected in his mind by the election of John F. Kennedy; he believed the young, rich, handsome politician made the scenario topical again (although it was reworked to avoid overt parallels after his death). The film retitled as *A Countess from Hong Kong* would go before cameras at England's Pinewood Studios in 1966 as Chaplin's latest and last offering, characterized from the outset by its outlier status in Chaplin's filmography: starring not himself but rather two "bankable" (Chaplin thought the new-to-him word hilarious) stars in Marlon Brando and Sophia Loren, to be filmed in widescreen (the same format he'd satirized in his previous film), in color, and with his largest ever budget of just over $3 million—for the first time since his pre-UA days coming from outside financing, though Chaplin still retained final cut and complete creative control. If one is to compare the relative "lateness" of films, *Countess* is one of the latest—not by virtue of its director's age (his 77 years would be outstripped by decades by others), but by its sheer distance from everything that he'd built his fame and success on in the past. Yet even without the self-starring black-and-white Academy ratio foundation, we'll see that the film is still, remarkably, pure Chaplin.

It had been 44 years since Chaplin's last film he didn't star in, 1923's *A Woman of Paris*[32]; like that film, *Countess* would forefront a woman (who also takes up with a rich man after a fashion), but unlike it this new film would be a comedy—albeit a "realistic" one, per Chaplin's desire. It was to be, more accurately, a romance that didn't know it was a comedy. Despite an ostensibly comic set-up involving an uninvited female guest (Loren) and her tormented de facto benefactor (Brando) playing hide-and-seek with the ship's passengers and authorities, an absurd comic roundelay involving lots of doors and buzzers and staged proprieties, Chaplin would stop any of his actors if he thought they were trying to be funny. His dictum of actorly naturalism stood as strong as ever, if not stronger if he was to pull off the complex tonal tightrope he was envisaging. Chaplin insisted that he would never have hired Brando if he'd thought he was funny; his character Ogden Mears was supposed to be wooden, and therefore Brando was perfect in the role.[33] Critics past and present have begged (loudly, uncom-

---

[32] It's perhaps interesting to note Chaplin's predilection for stories of people in transit (immigrants, really): *A Woman of Paris*, *A King in New York*, *A Countess from Hong Kong*. The person-preposition-place title pattern is certainly indicative of a deeper fascination with the subject, apt for a man who could have had chapters of his life titled in the same way: *An Actor from London*, *A Man of Hollywood*, *An Exile in Switzerland*, etc.

[33] Brando rarely appeared in straight-up comedies, but his performance in 1964's (hilarious, neglected) *Bedtime Story* is indicative of the fact that he had genius for not just drama but comedy, too, as well as a self-awareness that allowed him to play against his own "serious" persona as the pouty victim of an elaborate, film-long cosmic joke. But both *Bedtime Story* and *A Countess from Hong Kong* also twist his comic persona into a facsimile of his dramatic one by their ends, lending their more serious denouements a weight they otherwise

prehendingly) to differ. But his performance is the epitome of Chaplin's ability to use his actors as vessels through which his own idea of the role is acted out (even at 77 Chaplin still acted out all the parts himself on set with panache); Brando's dour mien, sullen looks, stiff posture, and even some of his signature mumbled agitation combine to create a Brando *by* Chaplin—proof that though Chaplin may have used his actors as puppets, he also knew exactly what qualities each puppet was suited to represent. Brando's stuffiness is ideal for his role in the same way that Loren's broad and bawdy gestures, with her sparkling eyes and still face reflective of so much feeling, were ideal for hers. "The continuity of [Chaplin's] career is maintained even in the absence of his acting persona," wrote Andrew Sarris, "which proves that in the cinema feelings are expressed *through* actors, not *by* actors." Both Brando and Loren had signed on to the project without having read the script, such was Chaplin's living-legend status at this point. Loren and Chaplin got along famously, and she cherished the experience; Loren and Brando did not; but it was Chaplin and Brando's butting of heads that's defined reports on the film, a fact that has colored its reception as a failure and been used as proof of Chaplin's outmoded methods. Chaplin had no interest in the "method" acting style of Brando, yet Brando mostly took the copy-and-paste direction from Chaplin in stride; Jerry Epstein reports Brando saying, "This is the easiest picture I've ever made. I don't have to do anything. Charlie's doing it all!" Besides a few early clashes sparked by Brando showing up late to the set, the main catalyst of their disagreement was Chaplin's treatment of his son Sydney, playing Brando's friend in the film, who Chaplin had always been excessively critical toward on set going back to *Limelight* (perhaps a misguided attempt to appear to not be playing favorites with his own son). Brando found this cruel and tyrannical and took Sydney's side, wondering to him why he remained so submissive to his father's behavior. Brando became cold toward

---

wouldn't have had if Brando hadn't been game for the tonal acrobatics asked of him.

Chaplin and refused direct communication with him, although Epstein again reports that Brando later melted and became friendly with him again when they played Chaplin's cameo scene together. "I still looked up to him as perhaps the greatest genius that the medium has ever produced," Brando would later write in his memoir. "I don't think anyone has ever had the talent he did; he made everyone else look Lilliputian. But as a human being he was a mixed bag, just like all of us."

Chaplin's direction and on-set manner, as reports from all of his sets corroborate, could be alternately charming and domineering. Besides being reflective of the bipolar nature of the man himself, it was also perhaps evidence of the fact that, per Donna Kornhaber, "even the very idea of what it meant to 'direct' a film changed substantially between his early days on the Keystone lot and the conclusion of his career in the 1950s and 1960s." *A Countess from Hong Kong* certainly has anachronism written all over it. On the surface of things, one could easily imagine the film as the 1930s bedroom farce it was originally going to be, yet Chaplin directs it as if, per Joyce Milton, "the entire history of romantic comedy, from *It Happened One Night* [1934] to Cary Grant and Katharine Hepburn, not to mention Cary Grant and Audrey Hepburn, had never existed." Indeed, the film's set-up gives the impression of something contrived for an early Keystone one-reeler rather than a sound comedy from the 1930s, let alone the 1960s; it even bears similarities with the very first film Chaplin made while sporting the Tramp costume, *Mabel's Strange Predicament* (1914), in which Mabel Normand gets trapped outside her hotel room wearing only pajamas. Yet *Countess* is far from being a staid retread of earlier cinema decades past its due date, and in fact exists as a product of the 1960s in a way that productively complicates its anachronisms: note its cynical view of politics as a load of nice-sounding drivel spewed at reporters off the top of one's head, the forefronting of sex as a thematic element (cf. all the beds, bathrooms, pajamas, etc. and associated humor that litter the film), and its observation of the erosion of marriage as a meaningful contract—not just the failing marriage between Brando's character and his wife, played by a late-appearing Tippi Hedren (the idea of a divorce is temporarily axed for the sake of political propriety once he's assigned to a new ambassador gig), but in the fake marriage between Loren's character and Brando's valet Hudson that's merely a concession to the technicalities of a green card. The repeated harping on not having "consummated" the marriage by Hudson (as played brilliantly by Patrick Cargill) is on the one hand a funny gag that gets mileage out of its recurring innuendo,[34] while on the other it's a thematic comment on how marriage has been downgraded by the characters to a mere ploy with absolutely none of the pleasures or responsibilities that accompany it. Richard Brody has written of how, contrary to its perceived apoliticism, "Chaplin, the director—who had started his screen career, under the direction of Mack Sennett, in classic slapstick comedies—turned his last film into a social critique of slapstick, a moral analysis of the roots of comic indignity." *Countess* "has an underlying political context—two revolutions and American diplomacy—but its political perspective goes even deeper, to the long-standing and long-unchallenged moralism that results in pervasive hypocrisy." Or as Chaplin told an interviewer in 1960 as he looked ahead to his next project, the film would be "a satire on bigness."

But unlike his previous late satires, *Monsieur Verdoux* and *A King in New York,* the comedy (and whatever satirical bite it might have) of *A Countess from Hong Kong* comes less from the content of the scenario or its dialogue than the form of it—the way a line is said, for example, rather than what a line is saying. The satirical targets of those previous "message" films were massive in scale and explicitly political in nature (global militarism, national paranoia) whereas here what's on trial is little more than the human individual, or if you want to extrapolate from that, little less than life itself. (It's a resonance that

---

[34] "I've never done anything as funny as the valet Hudson," Chaplin would boldly say. "We took three weeks working out the fight scene in *City Lights,* and it was technically good—but it wasn't so funny as Hudson."

Chaplin couldn't have made if he himself were the star, and thus he merely gives himself a narratively irrelevant cameo as a seasick steward[35] in a bit of comic business that calls back to early shorts like *Shanghaied* [1915] or *The Immigrant*, never to show up again—a planned final shot of Chaplin sweeping up the ship's dance floor was discarded, an incredibly tantalizing what-if for its meta-thematic possibilities but also a potential obstruction to the kind of self-sufficient universal drama Chaplin was aiming for.) Journalist Penelope Gilliat reported from set that Chaplin "doesn't laugh at the lines in themselves; he laughs at the way they are executed. One has the feeling that when he wrote them he probably wasn't even yet amused. The chuckles must have come later, when the actors had gone through the lines mechanically, overemoted, lost their confidence, learned their moves backwards, broken through some sort of actors' sound barrier, and eventually found the work as easy as breathing."[36] The way Chaplin directed his actors on *Countess* is instructive in this regard: when acting out performance details for them, he would invariably use nonsensical filler like "blah-blah-blah-blah-blah" rather than their actual dialogue. Donna Kornhaber makes the argument that, rather than a final disappointment, *Countess* actually fulfills the promise of Chaplin's silent work in a way that the other sound films don't: "Chaplin here refigures speech to a point of ontological equivalency with action, stripping it of meaning in its content and leaving it only functional importance. Late into the sound era and near the end of his life, he thus finds a means of returning to the filmic priority once given to space and movement and to the position of aesthetic instability that had first defined his style and his approach to making films."

Countess proceeds with a strong rhythmic elegance, a symphony of movement and dialogue and surprise and

---

[35] A tribute to his recently departed brother Sydney, who had been on a number of oceanic voyages in their youth.

[36] Cf. this with the non-emotive, second-nature acting philosophies of other filmmakers: an older guard figure like Robert Bresson, the new-on-the-scene duo of Jean-Marie Straub and Danièle Huillet, or the contemporary David Fincher.

complicated tonal shifts as it makes its way in and out of and then back into room after room via door after door, the sporadic yet consistent buzz of the doorbell marking the syncopated beat. Chaplin throws in his musical score as emotional counterpoint and then seemingly undercuts it by the repeated absurd suggestion that it's actually diegetic, sourced by the room's radios. Somehow Chaplin keeps the motor running on the this-way-now-that labyrinth of a scenario while also introducing a sense, surely accentuated by the lateness of the film itself, that there's something profound about watching these people scramble in and out of rooms trying to figure out their lives. Pedro Costa has spoken of the way the ostensibly disposable happenings of *Countess* actually speak to something greater: "Even if there are only two or three doors, and two big stars, Chaplin is able to put them in their place, making them act like idiots, like the rest of us—people who are simple and a bit stupid, who open and close doors. That's life, opening and closing doors. That's what he's telling us, and it's of the greatest simplicity." Something similar is going on with Chaplin's occasional dissolves to the surrounding sea, ostensibly a simple way of indicating the passing of time before the next scene begins. But these interstitial, transitional shots of the nocturnal waters give one the impression of a profound contrast: that between the everlastingness of the sea and its waves toiling away beneath the moon every night,[37] and the petty, screwball meanderings of this small hodgepodge group of people trapped aboard the ship—a visualization of fate as potent, in its own way, as the churning train wheels of *Monsieur Verdoux*. It also contributes to the sense of the film as existing in a kind of cinematic nether-realm between reality and fantasy, its main events blocked and staged in the theatrical, not-wholly-three-dimensional way Chaplin often did and littered with obvious stock exterior shots and rear-screen projection that make no attempt to hide its status as a studio-bound fiction (the gag with the music underscores this,

---

[37] Chaplin, p. 26 of *My Autobiography*: "My first sight of the sea was hypnotic. As I approached it in bright sunlight from a hilly street, it looked suspended, a live quivering monster about to fall on me."

too). It wasn't an oversight or a technical deficiency; Chaplin was sensitive to matters of form that mattered to him, like the film's color, for example. "Chaplin had very definite ideas for the color grading of his first color motion picture," writes Jeffrey Vance. "In the way a painter might adjust a palette to reflect certain moods, Chaplin enhanced the colors for some scenes while intentionally muting the colors in others." In a way, *A Countess from Hong Kong* could be considered Chaplin's pure artist's statement in a way that none of this other late films can: no political or satirical messages (though they're there), no autobiographical elements (though they can be found), and no self-referential subtext or historically significant subject matter—per Éric Rohmer, Chaplin "finally gives us his pure *mise-en-scène.*"

Chaplin bristled at what reviewers said about the film, many of whom did little to hide their belief that Chaplin was over the hill and his film old-fashioned. "Old-fashioned? What's old-fashioned about the story? It's about a multi-millionaire who gives up his lovely wife to marry a whore. What's so old-fashioned about that? I think it's rather current." Like *A King in New York*, *A Countess from Hong Kong* is actually quite modern in its concerns; but since it's delivered in a formal package that on the surface has more in common with the antiquated studio productions of Chaplin's heyday, the idea that it might be in conversation with the alienated relational modernism of, say, Michelangelo Antonioni is laughed out of the room. Brando's acting *must* be stilted, one thinks to oneself, because this simple romantic comedy doesn't have the energy one expects from the genre—but maybe this is a sign that something else, something not so simple, is going on here. Tim Hunter writes that "Chaplin's treatment of [Brando's] character forces us to question his capacity for love, and look for other less romantic motives for his behavior." What to some viewers might look like a simple romance, and—given that the main characters come together in the end—one with a happy ending, Chaplin in interviews made it clear he didn't agree: "Between you and me and the gatepost," he said in one of them, "it's a very sad story. This man who leaves his icicle of a wife for a girl who's a whore. I think the end, where they're dancing, is tragic. Perhaps his love for her is just a passing thing, as happens to us all." Chaplin would know; in a way the film is a self-criticism of his younger, philandering self, and is clearly the work of an older man who had been happily married for almost a quarter century. A closer look at the story's contextual building blocks reveals the tragic contours Chaplin noted: Brando's character is uptight, shallow, exhausted, cynical, unhappy, the love between him and his wife gone (if it was ever even there), barely a façade remaining; Loren's character is a child of unhappiness, her parents dead at 13, then the mistress to a gangster, then a prostitute in Hong Kong, who just wants to escape it all for the chance at a better life. It's a story of two sad people crossing paths, frustration turning into infatuation, their love less for one another than what each represents to the other in the way of "happiness." Chaplin still sees them as two human beings, their passions real and understandable, but ultimately also rash and ephemeral. You never get the sense from the ending that this is a relationship built to last for either of them, but more likely a pitstop on the way to their next destination in life, one just as happy or unhappy as this one, only in a different way. Chaplin remains non-judgmental enough to leave room for ambiguity and nuance here; in one of the most stunning compositions of his career, Loren looks longingly from land out of a ballroom window at the fading cruise ship she believes Brando to be on, the reverse shot a luminous close-up that words can't do justice. ("The most important thing," Chaplin told a 1967 interviewer, "is a close-up when somebody smiles or looks at somebody and it is real and it is the end of the world and the beginning of everything.") Yet evidence for the non-happiness of the ending—besides the fact that, after *The Great Dictator* (whose optimistic ending was rendered moot by the Holocaust), Chaplin had consistently ended his film on downbeats—is the way it parallels one of the opening images of the film, of men paying to dance with "the countesses of Hong Kong." Now it's just one man dancing with one countess, and although a lot of emotions have come and gone throughout the film, it's ultimately still just a man dancing with a prostitute. As harsh as that may sound, it's what Chaplin felt, and when the end credits dissolve onto screen over of the dancing couples exactly as the opening ones did to begin the film, a rush of complex emotion overcomes one—just like the bookending arrival and departure of *A King in New York*'s circular structure, we're back where we started, left to ponder the dismaying development of a human race that's as ripe for tragedy as it is for humor.

"I think it's the best thing I've done," Chaplin said about *A Countess from Hong Kong.* "I can be more objective about it than the pictures I've acted in, which can be very irksome and give me terrible inferiority complexes. It's full of invention…. it has great charm…. The critics now are terrified of being old-fashioned, but this picture is ten years ahead of its time." Chaplin had almost always claimed his latest film as his best after each of their releases, but his enthusiasm for *Countess* went further than usual, his emotional investment in it palpable even to visitors of the Manoir de Ban. "It's my best film," he assured one of them, even putting it above *City Lights,* the one he most liked otherwise. Suffice it to say that most critics disagreed. British detractors ("bloody idiots," Chaplin called them) and their English-language brethren across the pond had little nice to say about it—audiences there following suit to the tune of 62nd place for the year's box-office attractions—although thankfully the French didn't allow the film to pass wholly without praise. Issues at the press screening due to projectorial neglect (the special lens used to screen *Dr. Zhivago* [1965] hadn't been removed[38]) didn't help the film's cause, and Chaplin ended up shaving around a dozen minutes from it before it reached New York. The film epitomized the uphill battle faced by many a late film against a public and critical class unprepared to accept on its own terms a work of art that is moving just for existing in the specific

---

[38] Which is ironic, because Chaplin had disparaged the film in an interview despite his daughter Geraldine having a role in it; he surely thought her better utilized in his own film, where she has a small part as one of Brando's air-headed dancing partners.

historical, cultural, and personal circumstances that it does. Shifting aesthetic contexts and viewer priorities had little room for a Chaplin who was from a different era and going in a different direction. "The trouble is that as I get older," he'd say, "I get more and more interested in beauty. I want things to be beautiful. I'm wondering whether this isn't a moribund period of art. Aesthetics have gone into things like space and science—those beautiful airships; utility at its height. No artist could compete with that."

Though Chaplin would try to one more time. In the late 1960s he watched birds fly across his lawn in Switzerland and into his head sprouted the idea of a girl with wings. The film would be called *The Freak* and star his teenage daughter Victoria, a kind of tragicomic fantasy about a birdlike girl discovered by scientists in Argentina and taken to England, the tale of a fragile, nonconformist angel who finally ends up captured and put in a cage while the English courts debate whether she's an animal or a human. Victoria's elder sister Josephine would have a role, too (both had cameoed in *A Countess from Hong Kong* in tennis garb), and of course a bit part was written in for Chaplin, this time as a drunk who thinks his eyes are playing tricks on him when he sees the girl fly above him in the London skies. Victoria had studied ballet as a child and was eyeing the Royal Academy of Dramatic Arts in London for after the film was completed; Chaplin thought she had inherited his comic charm, even surpassing his own, and coached her while laboring over the script. Financing was a more difficult prospect. Jerry Epstein contacted United Artists to pitch the film to, and a pair of executives traveled to Switzerland to view the script and discuss things with Chaplin, leaving with a copy and the promise of hearing from them; weeks later a package arrived containing only the copy of the script and a note saying "with the compliments of...." Chaplin had been given the brush off. But Epstein kept at it, making the rounds, trying everywhere. (He truly was Chaplin's most loyal, dedicated soldier; Epstein remembered Penelope Gilliat describing their rapport on the set of *Countess* as "like watching a doctor in the operating theater with his assistant, shoving the right instruments into his hands without having to say a word.") Chaplin was resolving to put up the money for the picture himself when Epstein finally obtained financing and returned to the Manoir to share the good news. Storyboards under his arm, Epstein made his way to Chaplin's room when Oona stepped into the hallway and stopped him, saying quietly but forcefully: "There's no picture." Despite having urged Chaplin to make another film because he was happier when he was working, Oona thought the actual production of this one, with its difficult technical effects, would be too much for him and might kill him. (Chaplin had broken his ankle during post-production on *Countess*, putting an end to his obsessive tennis hobby and leading to weight gain and overall diminished health.) Oona and Epstein privately tabled the project, and as soon as Victoria learned it wasn't going ahead she ran off with her boyfriend Jean-Baptiste Thiérrée (famous for playing the son in Alain Resnais's *Muriel* [1963]) in 1969; they married and in 1971 fulfilled their dream of creating a circus together. Unaware that his wife had quashed the picture out of concern for him, Chaplin thought the project's demise due to Victoria's departure and was deeply wounded by what he saw as his abandonment by his favorite child, who he'd wanted to launch into a film career like he'd tried to do with Edna Purviance in *A Woman of Paris* or his older son Sydney in *Limelight*. Chaplin grew to accept Victoria's marriage and new profession in time, but he never truly gave up wanting to make *The Freak*. By 1972 he still planned to direct it, and writing and revising of the script continued as late as 1974. "I mean to make it one day," read the very last words of *My Life in Pictures*, a visual supplement to *My Autobiography* with small captions by Chaplin published in 1974. A home movie of Victoria, back in Switzerland years after the project fell apart and wearing the wings designed for the movie, offers a tantalizing glimpse of what beauties the octogenarian Chaplin may have been concocting. "Every time I read the ending, I wept," Epstein would later remember. "I was convinced it would have the same effect on an audience. To me it was Charlie's best film since *City Lights*. When I saw *E.T.* [1982] with Oona, I said to her *The Freak* was a combination of *E.T.* and *The Elephant Man.* She agreed."

One element from *The Freak* that did reach the public was the musical theme Chaplin wrote with his compositional amanuensis Eric James, which Jerry Epstein felt was the best thing Chaplin had ever written. "This," he recalls Chaplin saying, "is real Puccini!" The piece ended up becoming the theme for *The Kid*—a key element created for Chaplin's very last feature given to his very first. In 1969 Chaplin began revisiting all of his unscored First National shorts and silent UA films in order to compose and record official scores for them, to accompany their rerelease and any future showings. As time went by Chaplin leaned more and more on James to read his mind or simply compose fitting themes himself (even though he was forbidden from claiming credit), yet to the degree that they are Chaplin's final creative works they deserve attention as the late artistic statements they are. "The accompaniment that Chaplin created with James reflects the lush, *grandioso* musical style of Chaplin's days with Fred Karno," writes Jeffrey Vance. "The scores for the reissues of the feature films *The Circus, The Kid,* and *A Woman of Paris,* for example, are saturated with continuous, full waves of sound and only the occasional solo. This style of accompaniment is a departure from the popular songs of the 1920s and 1930s that permeate the scores for *City Lights* and *Modern Times,* and from the direct cueing that underscores the action of these films." In a sense, Chaplin's new scores retroactively turn these early films, as one views them today, into hybrid early/late films that touch on the dual ends of Chaplin's creative journey. This is especially prevalent in the version of *The Circus* available today, which begins with a little gem of a prelude involving the use of a looped image of actress Merna Kennedy on a trapeze swing (taken from later in the film) scored to the elder Chaplin singing his own composition "Swing Little Girl" with deep voice and music hall lilt. James had essentially tricked Chaplin into its inclusion; originally recorded by a different male vocalist, James suggested Chaplin record a version himself for his family's pleasure, all the while knowing he'd then realize it was the more fitting interpretation. Reissues of Chaplin's films were nothing new, as Chaplin had strategically deployed them ever since 1942's rerelease of *The Gold Rush* (often to draw attention away from his current self toward the image of the beloved Tramp), but a 1971 deal he made selling worldwide distribution rights to his films netted him not just an additional fortune but an opportunity to stay in the public consciousness. And the undemanding personal appearances he made to promote the screenings likely added years to his life.

Chaplin had an insatiable need to be working, to be creatively active. "I am still very ambitious," Chaplin had written at the end of *My Autobiography*. "I could never retire. There are many things I want to do; besides having a few unfinished cinema scripts, I should like to write a play and an opera—if time will allow." The opera was a proposed adaptation of Thomas Hardy's *Tess of the d'Urbervilles*, and besides *The Freak* Chaplin had publicly mentioned ideas for a spoof on Hollywood superproductions, a story about a condemned Kansas convict, and a slapstick comedy or a musical for Sydney to star in (he'd had great success on Broadway). Most of his late ideas were things for his children to act in, rather than stars or himself, constantly keeping alive the sentiment shared in *Limelight* by Calvero: "We're all amateurs. None of us lives long enough to be anything else." In his old age Chaplin received numerous requests to appear in other people's films, some of which he never even answered—Samuel Beckett's barrage of letters asking to cast him in his short *Film* (1965), for which Buster Keaton was subsequently recruited—and some of which tempted him—John Huston's attempt to cast him as Noah in his *The Bible* (1966), an idea he toyed with but ultimately rejected on the grounds that he still couldn't conceive of being in anyone else's picture (Huston would end up playing the role himself). Federico Fellini originally hoped Chaplin would appear in his film *The Clowns* (1970), but that was a no go, too (the young Victoria Chaplin and her husband, however, do appear). Nonetheless, it was largely Chaplin's creative drive that kept him active and alive. "To work is to live," Chaplin was quoted as saying shortly before his death, "—and I want to live."

It also helped that, having weathered the lifelong roller-coaster of public opinion, Chaplin's reputation had finally made a mostly complete shift from "political pariah" to "persecuted genius." Festivals and awards bodies promptly took note and began showering him with laurels. The 25th edition of the Cannes Film Festival awarded him a special prize in 1971; Venice followed suit in 1972, and after Chaplin's insistence on staying through the fight scene in *City Lights* led to him watching the entire movie, he and his family were "hustled into gondolas and taken down the side canals, which were lined with people who had reached out their hands and literally pulled the boats along." And after having been considered for knighthood as early as 1956 and denied the designation as late as 1969 (the British still feared what the Americans would think), Chaplin finally made the visit to Buckingham Palace in March 1975 to accept the honor from Queen Elizabeth II to the strains of *Limelight*. The failure of *A Countess from Hong Kong* had taken a toll on Chaplin—daughter Geraldine even saying that, privately, it "destroyed" him—but these awards appearances, combined with the rereleases of his work, kept him going, and waylaid his insecurities about not being remembered. The granddaddy of his career-capping prizes, however, was undoubtedly the Honorary Oscar he received in Hollywood in 1972. The subject had first been broached at a 1971 Paris showing of *Modern Times* that was kicking off Chaplin's new rerelease deal. He had interest, but it was tempered with fears—had America actually forgiven him? But when the official request later came and lined up conveniently with a celebration of his work at the Film Society of Lincoln Center in New York, he decided to accept and return to the country that had meant so much to his life, both good and bad. An official Los Angeles release for the prematurely-pulled *Limelight* was even planned to coincide with his appearance.[39]

---

[39] When *Limelight* won the Oscar for Best Score in 1973, a small irony occurred: Chaplin's Oscar statuette was damaged in the mail on its way to Switzerland, so they sent him a replacement. That replacement was the statuette Marlon Brando had won for his performance in *The Godfather* (1972), which he'd rejected via a political statement

When Chaplin and Oona arrived that April, it was only a few months shy of being exactly 20 years since his departure.[40] It was a fitting final twist of fate for a tempestuous life that seemed to happen in 20-year increments: Chaplin's arrival in 1912 for his second U.S. tour with Fred Karno's comedy troupe, which shortly led to his catapulting to global fame; his return in 1932 from his post-*City Lights* world tour, marking the height of his fame and the beginnings of his eventual slide into public disrepute; his 1952 exile to Europe near the low point of his reputational valley; and now his triumphant 1972 return to America, indicating his successful reclamation of the worldwide fame and glory that he'd once had and lost. The effect of that last 20-year gap on Chaplin can perhaps be measured by two portrait photographs taken by Richard Avedon in New York, one just before his departure and one just after his return; the first sees a spry, grinning Chaplin holding up fingers as devilish horns, whereas the second shows a noticeably heavier, wearier, and all-around more weathered Chaplin with only the slimmest of visible smirks. "This is my

---

read on stage by Sacheen Littlefeather, an activist for Native American causes.

[40] Technically, Chaplin had been on U.S. soil at least twice since his 1952 departure, one a refueling pitstop in Alaska in the early 1960s and the other a brief plane changeover in New York in transit from Jamaica to Switzerland later that decade. Michael Chaplin (or, rather, his ghostwriters) tells the amusing story of the first case: "Father was quite jolly as we jetted out of Europe and nosed over the North Pole, but the smile was suddenly wiped off his face when we landed to refuel at Anchorage, Alaska. No sooner had he set foot on the tarmac than it struck him that Alaska had recently become America's forty-ninth state. He was standing on U.S. territory! The realization so panicked him that he did a quick about-face and tried to scuttle back into the aircraft and sweat out the two hours' wait inside the cabin. No such luck, man. All passengers had to be cleared out of the aircraft for some technical checkout…. Father stared at the distant prospect of the immigration checkpoint and dug in his heels like a startled stallion. He was terrified lest they take away his passport, money, socks and braces, and toss him in the hoosegow. Making a great effort of will, he approached the checkpoint in a state of acute concern." But, "The duty officers couldn't have been nicer."

renaissance," Chaplin proclaimed at a New York event in his honor, reflecting on his complex relationship with the country that had given him his chance in life. "I'm being born again. It's easy for you, but it's very difficult for me to speak tonight, because I feel very emotional." Chaplin would go in and out of focus at times, lucid and charming one moment and then hazy the next. "Even when his remarks made sense," writes Kenneth S. Lynn, "his mind seemed to be floating on a faraway sea of remembrance." Chaplin's appearance at the Academy Awards ceremony in Hollywood was intentionally made the highlight of the night, given pride of place at the end of the show (an anomaly in Oscar history) and honored as the sole recipient (usually multiple honorary awards are given out each year). A tribute video assembled by Peter Bogdanovich and Richard Patterson gave way to a spotlighted Chaplin waiting on stage and the longest standing ovation in Oscar history.[41] A few words of simple thanks and an attempted bit of business with a hat and cane handed to him was all he could muster. "I cannot cope with emotions any more," Chaplin would say around this time. "It's very hard to respond to affection. I can respond to antagonism. But love and affection...."

Ultimately the only affection Chaplin needed was from his wife Oona, who dutifully attended to Chaplin, often at the expense of her own health, until the very end. A fall in 1972 that fractured vertebrae in Chaplin's back and a stroke that left him partially paralyzed in 1976 contributed to his increasingly inflexible need for Oona to be near him at all

---

[41] The moment is powerfully recreated in Richard Attenborough's *Chaplin* (1992), based on Chaplin's autobiography and David Robinson's authorized 1985 biography *Chaplin: His Life and Art*. Interestingly, Attenborough had been present at Chaplin's knighting and even makes the tiniest appearance in *A King in New York* in the background of a London exterior shot (standing in for New York) on a poster for the 1956 film *The Baby and the Battleship*, in which Attenborough starred as an actor. *Chaplin* takes its licenses but, as a film, is worthy of its subject, particularly in Robert Downey Jr.'s lead performance, the casting of Geraldine Chaplin as her own grandmother, and the dual role of Moira Kelly as Chaplin's first and last loves, Hetty and Oona.

times. She was his rock and helpmate for the second half of his adult life, an ambassador of goodwill both on his film sets and off (on *A Countess from Hong Kong*, "Whenever Charlie finished a take he would look to her for approval, and she would nod encouragement"), and was the example, with her "loving devotion and her quiet strength," according to Claire Bloom, "responsible for finally erasing the image of broken womanhood that his mother's suffering had imprinted on his artistic conscience." It's no surprise then that an accounting of Charlie Chaplin's late style could well and simply call his late period "the Oona years," such was the role she played in reshaping his life. A biographer of Oona's father Eugene O'Neill, Louis Sheaffer (who became a pen pal of hers), wrote to her this sentiment: "I'll always think of Charlie Chaplin as one of the most fortunate of mortals, not simply because of his international fame and his fortune but because at a time when you'd think his life's pattern was crystallized and he was on the downward slope of his life, he had you and his life began a second Springtime." Their marriage and family life wasn't perfect—with a total of eight children together and a demanding artist at its head whom Louise Brooks once called "the most bafflingly complex man who ever lived," how could it be? Sometimes Charlie and Oona's love for each other was so strong that there was little left to trickle down to their children; to say that Chaplin made for a difficult father is plainly an understatement. "Charlie is a half-and-half personality," Oona would say. "One half is difficult—the other easy. But I find we manage very happily." When Chaplin died in 1977 on Christmas day (a holiday he hated for its commercialism and the memories it brought back of his early poverty), at the age of 88, it was a devastating blow to the woman who'd spent her entire adult life attached to him. She never truly recovered and her drinking problem, begun years before Chaplin's demise, exacerbated her early death in 1991 at the age of 66.[42] But a

---

[42] Jane Scovell's 2009 biography of Oona is essential for the way it asserts Oona's autonomy as a person, someone who indeed happily and willingly submitted to being Chaplin's other half yet also a woman

fitting final image for the late Chaplin saga comes to us rather from Richard Patterson's *The Gentleman Tramp* (1975), an intimate documentary that Chaplin described as "like reading one's own obituary": the film closes with 1974 color footage shot in Chaplin's Swiss backyard, of Charlie and Oona, together, hand in hand, walking away from the camera in a moving, autumnal recreation of the ending of *Modern Times.*

---

with a rich inner life and mind of her own, thoroughly complicating the superficial narrative that a quick glance at the couple's 36-year age gap might conjure up.

Alfred Hitchcock

The story, or so we're meant to believe, goes something like this: at some point in the early-to-mid 1960s, Alfred Hitchcock's artistic decline began. Some pinpoint *Psycho* (1960) as his last good picture, although more often today *The Birds* (1963) is singled out for that designation. *Marnie* (1964) is the classic "divisive" Hitchcock picture—some love it, some hate it. But after that the decline is undoubtedly precipitous: *Torn Curtain* (1966) and *Topaz* (1969) show a bored and tired Hitchcock unsuccessfully retreading his cinematic roots in the spy thriller. A return to British soil with *Frenzy* (1972) offers glimpses also of a return to form, but the ugliness of its subject matter and its treatment thereof renders it disagreeable on the whole. *Family Plot* (1976) might be lightly likable and, as Hitchcock's last film, able to coast on the goodwill accrued over a legendary career, but one wishes he'd been able to go out with more of a bang. Mention of these last films (if they're mentioned at all) often circles around choice moments where the "classic Hitchcock touch" is visible amongst material otherwise deemed substandard: the drawn-out killing of Gromek in *Torn Curtain,* the dress-spreading death of Juanita in *Topaz,* the camera backtracking down the stairs to imply a murder in *Frenzy.* But it hardly needs saying, if you've read this far in the book, that I not only "disagree" with this narrative of decline, but find it completely foreign to a view of cinema that appreciates films as art made by artists. Since the publication of early touchstones like Éric Rohmer and Claude Chabrol's *Hitchcock: The First Forty-Four Films* (1957), Robin Wood's *Hitchcock's Films* (1965), and François Truffaut's *Hitchcock* (1966), the Hitchcock publishing industry has exploded into a long-ago overwhelming body of literature—spend any significant amount of time immersed in it, and the consensus narrative recited above, or something very much like it, will quickly become a nauseatingly familiar one. As with any consensus, there were and are outlier voices challenging it—to take just one example, all of Hitchcock's last four films placed on Andrew Sarris' top ten lists in the years they were released.[1]

---

[1] Yet, ironically, Sarris considered *Marnie* on release to be "a failure by any standard except the most esoteric."

But even though new generations of writers and cinephiles have affected the narrative slightly—*Marnie*'s reputation has clearly fared better in the 21st century than the 20th—Hitchcock's last decade-plus of films are still overwhelmingly and unjustly overshadowed within the film-cultural consciousness by his earlier achievements, remaining strangely underdiscussed side curios despite their creator's immense stature and arguably unmatched popularity within the world of film and film publishing. But that's enough generalizing for now.

The career of Alfred Hitchcock offers an abundance of turning points: his ascent into the director's chair with *The Pleasure Garden* in 1925; his switch to sound films with *Blackmail* (1929), the British film industry's first talkie; his reuniting with producer Michael Balcon for *The Man Who Knew Too Much* (1934), which inaugurated Hitchcock's famous run of 1930s spy films and established the template for the kind of humor-infused suspense thriller that came to be known simply as an "Alfred Hitchcock film." Then, of course, there was Hitchcock's jump to America with the David O. Selznick-produced *Rebecca* (1940), where his art benefited from access to Hollywood's much bigger, and more expensive, electric train set; his first color film, *Rope* (1948), which along with *Under Capricorn* (1949) experimented with long-take cinematography under Hitchcock and friend Sidney Bernstein's short-lived independent production company Transatlantic Pictures, an attempt to reinvigorate his career post-Selznick; and shortly thereafter *Strangers on a Train* (1951), which, coming out of a period of wandering and self-reflection after the London-shot *Stage Fright* (1950), Hitchcock launched into with confidence, enthusiasm, and "unusual zeal." "During the first day of shooting on *Strangers on a Train*," writes Bill Krohn, "Hitchcock announced to cast and crew that none of his previous pictures counted—today was the real beginning of his film-making career." *Rear Window* (1954) was Hitchcock's statement picture to open up his legendary stint at Paramount—"About this time I felt that my batteries were really fully charged," he would later recall—a film that offered everything he wanted as an artist: a satisfying technical challenge, a chance to flex his artistic philosophies (forever after he would explain Kuleshov's montage theories to interviewers with reference to this picture), and a game cast of two Hitchcock stars par excellence—the ever-dependable and increasingly tortured James Stewart, and Hitchcock's ideal blonde beauty Grace Kelly, who'd been recently introduced into his world in 1954's *Dial M for Murder* (a 3-D film he'd coasted through on the winds of his ambitious plans for *Rear Window*, which he mused about to Kelly between takes). When television encroached on cinema's territory, Hitchcock was persuaded to branch out and conquer that realm, too. *Alfred Hitchcock Presents* made his image into an icon, his name into a brand, and for the next decade kept both of them in the minds and on the lips of viewers everywhere; his conscious self-marketing, begun long ago in print and on screen with his famous in-film cameos, had now paid off magnificently—and not just financially. His artistic autonomy in this era was higher than it had ever been before or ever would be thereafter. In 1956 he finally remade *The Man Who Knew Too Much*, something he'd been considering ever since landing in the U.S., which deserves obligatory mention if for no other reason than the neat example it gives of the way Hitchcock's mid-1950s American films are late relative to his mid-1930s British ones: "the first version is the work of a talented amateur, and the second was made by a professional," Hitchcock would declare.

Yet Hitchcock's next films betrayed artistic stirrings of a deeper kind than usual. *The Wrong Man* (1956), made without salary for his former studio Warner Bros. as a gesture of thanks, is essentially an American "art film" shot in a dispassionate, logistical black-and-white style that submerged Hitchcock's Hollywood expressionism beneath his version of documentary neorealism, all in a never-before-so-direct elaboration of his patented "wrong man" theme. *Vertigo* (1958) swings in the opposite direction stylistically, but it doubles down on the artiness that showed Hitchcock reaching for a cinematic modernism foreign to quotidian Hollywood productions: thematic ambiguity, oblique characterization, structural experimentation, heightened aesthetic moods, lack of traditional closure, etc. Such subversions foreshadow the path Hitchcock would audaciously tread in the 1960s and beyond. Donald Spoto writes that "a sudden shift occurred in Hitchcock's emotional interest and aesthetic concern, from the fundamentally warm and comic tones provided by John Michael Hayes's scripts" for the mid-1950s films, "to the obsessive fear of lost identity in the films now to come." Even *North by Northwest* (1959), easily the most buoyant of the films surrounding it, would participate in the representation of this fear. The film stands as something of a decade's-end culmination of Hitchcock's classical era, deliberately written by screenwriter Ernest Lehman as "a Hitchcock picture to end all Hitchcock pictures," the ultimate remix of the witty, thrilling, man-on-the-run spy picture as epitomized by *The 39 Steps* (1935) and its American counterpart *Saboteur* (1942)—films that exemplified the use of a barely-there "MacGuffin" (Hitchcock's term, borrowed from English screenwriter Angus MacPhail, for the plot-catalyzing whatsit that doesn't really matter at all) as a pretext to build a wondrous cinematic scaffolding on which Hitchcock simply *did cinema*. On the lighter side, this suave, almost self-parodic film previews the way Hitchcock would play around with his own iconography in the late films; on the darker side, the film's "cool adroitness," per Spoto, "...did not cover over the fact that it was a bittersweet farewell to glamour and romance." When Hitchcock returned the next year with the thrown bomb that was *Psycho* (1960), it was the sign of an artist who had grown, evolved, and become interested in a wider swath of thematic and aesthetic territory. "Style in directing develops slowly and naturally as it does in everything else," Hitchcock had once said, and later when questioned about his thematic "broadening out" he suggested, following François Truffaut's insistence that his American period was stronger than his English one, simply that "it's a natural tendency to be less superficial." These quaint statements merely hint quietly at something the films themselves would soon proclaim loudly.

Psycho would be Hitchcock's last film for Paramount, although when the studio balked at his desire to film Robert

Bloch's horror novel—unable to persuade him otherwise, they refused to fund it or make room for its filming on their lots—Hitchcock took it in stride and moved the production to Universal (already home to his television set-up and soon to be his permanent working residence), deciding to put up the $800,000 needed to film it himself and forgoing his salary for a percentage ownership of the negative. He'd film it cheaply, quickly, and intuitively with his television crew, with multiple cameras and in black and white.[2] Inspired in turn by Frenchman Henri-Georges Clouzot's *Les diaboliques* (1955) and the low-budget horror flicks being churned out by companies like Hammer Films and American International Pictures, Hitchcock salivated at the idea of using his talents to turn paperback shlock into cinematic gold. When released, *Psycho* wasn't only a cultural phenomenon and smashing financial success (with a helping hand from some cunning Hitchcockian promotional strategies) but a bold first leap into the experimental 1960s, a film unmoored from traditional narrative strategies. By killing off his leading lady Janet Leigh halfway through the picture, Hitchcock announced his renunciation of the classical star system as well as the typical comforts that came with having a strong audience-identification figure. The second half of *Psycho* leaves the viewer shocked, adrift, and straining for a satisfying solution to a twisted psychological narrative that doesn't have one. Bernard Herrmann's radical symphonic score only dug the knife of tension in further. Hitchcock "had reached a point in his professional life when he was ready for a totally different kind of picture," according to the film's screenwriter Joseph Stefano; but just what kind of picture *Psycho* was is up for debate—was it the pitch-black comedy that Hitchcock later claimed it was, or rather the expression of a man, as Stefano would suggest, grappling deeply with mortality and the fear of sudden death, coming as

---

[2] Parallels abound with Jean Renoir's late film *Le testament du Docteur Cordelier* (1959; known as *Experiment in Evil* in English), a similarly scaled-down experiment that used television techniques to film "low" genre material in black and white. Renoir and Hitchcock had both made their debut films in 1925.

the film did on the tail of Hitchcock's 1957 illness and his wife Alma's 1958 cancer scare?

The gap between *Psycho* and *The Birds* (1963) was the biggest of Hitchcock's career up to that point. He and Alma took a long vacation followed by promotional tours in America and internationally, taking the time to digest the impact of *Psycho* and assess his future. Hitchcock "was in a sense unsettled," according to biographer Peter Ackroyd. "His cheapest and quickest film had suddenly become his most successful." And when *Psycho* went home empty-handed at that year's Oscars ceremony, it only contributed to his unease about just what constituted artistic success or failure at this point in his career. A new project called *No Bail for the Judge* was discarded after detailed pre-production had been completed when Audrey Hepburn decided against playing the lead role she was slated for. Then an additional project was moved to the back-burner for reasons of casting trouble: *Marnie*, based on Winston Graham's 1961 novel, which Hitchcock was so keen on having be his next film that, after purchasing the film rights before it was even published, he became involved with the book's marketing in the U.S. Hitchcock was envisioning it as Grace Kelly's return to the screen. She had married Prince Rainier of Monaco in 1956 and hadn't acted since, and was herself keen to make her return under Hitchcock's wing. At the same time Hitchcock was being wooed by friend and agent Lew Wasserman to sign a contract with Universal (which was being bought out by Wasserman's talent agency MCA), and though Wasserman was skeptical of *Marnie*, he was reassured by Kelly's involvement enough to accept the project in order to finalize Hitchcock's move to Universal in 1962. But Kelly wouldn't be available that year—could Hitchcock wait? He decided to make *The Birds* next while he did.

Hitchcock set up shop at Universal in offices fit for a king. It was obvious from this "self-designed universe" on the studio lot (as described by later production president Thom Mount) that he was there to stay, and so he would. It was a natural home: it was there that he had made both *Saboteur* and *Shadow of a Doubt* (1943) on loan from Selznick, two of his signature early American films. It was also the site of his television series, a venture in which Hitchcock directed a smattering of episodes before the medium began to bore him in the early 1960s; his last offering for the small screen, and his only hour-long episode for the retitled *Alfred Hitchcock Hour,* aired in 1962. "Hitchcock privately had no illusion about the artistic limitations of the medium," notes his biographer Donald Spoto. "'In three days' shooting,' [Hitchcock] said, 'there can be no question of comparable quality. Television just can't match the scope of pictures.'" The scope of Hitchcock's pictures was indeed in its own category, and never more so than *The Birds,* which was set to be his most ambitious film yet. His writer for the picture, Evan Hunter, recalled Hitchcock declaring that "he was entering the Golden Age of his creativity," and that *The Birds* was going to be his "crowning achievement." It would also be his most expensive, his most technically detailed, and require his most extensive use of special effects to date. Daphne du Maurier's 1952 short story was merely the evocative jumping-off point from which Hitchcock and Hunter created their own American version of a coastal town beset by unexplainable bird attacks. Fleshed out around it, however, was an entirely original narrative that continued *Psycho*'s experiment with structural bifurcation—the highly-anticipated birds of the title only descend en masse in the second half of the film. The set-up involves some subtle psychological interplay reminiscent of romantic comedy, yet we watch it in an unorthodoxly distanced manner because we already know, before the movie even begins, that it's going to be undercut by a more cosmic drama. This unique structural ploy is only the beginning of Hitchcock's experimentation: no satisfying explanation is given for why the birds attack; the film ends open-endedly, without traditional closure; there is no musical score (Hitchcock and Herrmann instead collaborated with German music artists Oskar Sala and Remi Gassmann on a revolutionary, catharsis-less soundtrack that combined natural and electronic bird sounds)[3]; and the film's

---

[3] Hitchcock had experimented before with the idea of a scoreless film: *Jamaica Inn* (1939), *Lifeboat* (1944), *Rope,* and *Rear Window*

leads were a total unknown (Tippi Hedren) and someone in one of his first major roles (Rod Taylor). "Evan," Hitchcock told Hunter early on, "there will be no stars in this picture. I'm the star—the birds are the stars—and you're the star." Having discovered Hedren in a commercial while Hitchcock and Alma were watching NBC's *Today* show one day (an ad recreated by Hitchcock at the beginning of *The Birds*), he subsequently attempted to turn her into a star of his own making, another in the line of Hitchcock leading ladies. Their real-life relationship would later take a sour turn, but on screen, as an unknown in a star's role, she strikes the perfect dissonant note in Hitchcock's 1960s cinema of icy ambiguity—it's in the way she *isn't* Grace Kelly, or Ingrid Bergman, or any other Hitchcock leading lady other than herself, that the alchemical thing happening between her and Hitchcock's camera sings its own wonderful era-specific tune.

Hitchcock poured himself into *The Birds* in ways nobody, himself included, could have predicted. He found himself in an unusually emotional state during filming, his typical humorous mood dampened, retreating home distressed each night to pore over the scenario again and again (which he normally never did), moved by an inexplicable creative spark to become increasingly subjective with his characters—even to the point of improvising shots on set toward the goal of taking the audience deeper and deeper inside Hedren's Melanie Daniels. The psychological currents involving her familial trauma merge with the life-and-death concerns of the avian onslaught raining down from above to create an intense emotional storm. Federico Fellini called the film an "apocalyptic poem." In a career full of experiments—the single-location drama of *Lifeboat*, the fluid long takes and invisible cuts of *Rope*, the 3-D cinematic theater of *Dial M for Murder*, the neorealist drama of *The Wrong Man*, the cinematic rug-pull that was *Psycho*—*The Birds* was in many ways his most forward-thinking achievement yet. The mixture of German expressionism and Soviet

---

all contain no nondiegetic scoring outside their opening and closing moments.

montage he'd transplanted onto English-language cinema throughout his career was clearer and bolder than ever, but it was now seasoned with a healthy dose of the modern ambiguity coming from the European art cinema experiments of the late 1950s and early '60s. Before filming *The Birds,* Hitchcock had watched films by Ingmar Bergman, Alain Resnais, Jean-Luc Godard, and Michelangelo Antonioni. The almost obsessive screening of films (in his private projection room[4]) was nothing new for Hitchcock, and it was one he'd continue to the end of his life, but "the influence and importance of this European work in the early 1960s," writes Joe McElhaney, "clearly represented for Hitchcock a force to be reckoned with and in a way that he had not experienced since the 1920s." Coincident with his beginnings in the film industry during the last decade of silent cinema, Hitchcock had been a member and regular attendee of the London Film Society, where he both rubbed shoulders with leading British intellectuals and absorbed the cinematic avant-garde from places like Germany and Russia in the form of films deemed too uncommercial to be shown by British distributors. He was also a serious collector of modernist art (his favorite painter was Paul Klee) and, in his "self-indulgent" approach to cinematic form over content, compared himself "to an abstract painter." John Williams, his final musical collaborator in the 1970s, attested that Hitchcock was also extremely conversant in the musical concert repertory, both classical and modern; and after *The Birds,* perhaps inspired by the film's experimental electronic score, he "did develop an adventurous curiosity about new music and its cinematic potential," according to Jack Sullivan, ordering recordings of Karlheinz Stockhausen, Pierre Boulez, and other contemporary composers. Hitchcock's public image as an entertainer working in a self-contained universe without influence from, or interest in, the work of anybody but himself was a carefully constructed

---

[4] Hitchcock would also go to public movie theaters, a fact not relayed in biographies but one passed on by Bill Krohn from Gary Graver (prolific cinematographer and late Orson Welles collaborator), who worked at a small repertory cinema in Hollywood and reported that "Hitchcock and his wife Alma came almost every week."

myth. Now, in the 1960s, the "new waves" of European film were prodding Hitchcock to double down on his career-long ambition to create movies at the intersection of art and popular entertainment. Thus the gift of *The Birds,* whose ambiguous ending is only the most telling sign among many that Hitchcock was looking to contemporary arthouse conventions to shake up, and deepen, his art—he deliberately refused to have "The End" appear over the final shot (although the studio insisted on a closing "A Universal Release" logo image to prevent total audience disorientation), denying the closure so sought after by the moviegoing public.[5]

The Birds was the 1963 Cannes Film Festival's opening film. Earlier that year, the film's New York premiere had coincided with a retrospective of Hitchcock's films at the Museum of Modern Art organized by Peter Bogdanovich. And at the tail end of the summer before, in 1962, François Truffaut had sat down with Hitchcock and interpreter Helen G. Scott for dozens of hours of taped interviews that became the bulk of his book *Le Cinéma selon Alfred Hitchcock,* as it would be published in French in 1966, and later published in English in 1967 and now known simply as *Hitchcock/Truffaut.* That these

---

[5] Despite the lack of traditional closure (i.e., answers to questions like "Why were the birds attacking?," "Will they stop?," "Will the main characters make it safely to where they're going?," etc.) Hitchcock does provide what I consider a "solution" of sorts to the puzzle of the film's meaning in the form of the young Veronica Cartwright's line as the four principals quietly pile into their escape vehicle: "Can we take the lovebirds? They haven't done anything wrong." If *The Birds* can be said to simply represent the World in its fallen state, this feels like Hitchcock subtly suggesting that love is the answer, the meaning-maker, with which to morally combat it. Immediately after this a pale, traumatized Hedren lays her head against Jessica Tandy's mother figure, and in a short series of silent cuts Hitchcock films love as it appears between two characters who have seemingly solved their respective individual neuroses (one as it relates to mothers, the other as it relates to potential daughters-in-law). Here is the profound ending to the film proper, on its deepest level. The continued presence of the birds, and what may or may not happen with them on a narrative level, is rendered of secondary importance to the bond of love that unites the four members of the car driving away from them.

events came about during the post-production and release of *The Birds* is apt for a film that Hitchcock intended as a kind of calling card for a new age of artistic recognition. "While all of Hitchcock's later films… were also driven by Hitchcock's ambition to be taken seriously as an artist," writes Robert Kapsis in *Hitchcock: The Making of a Reputation,* "*The Birds* represents the first, the most ambitious, and certainly the most expensive project the filmmaker ever undertook for the purpose of reshaping his reputation among serious critics." The view of Hitchcock as a director of highly entertaining yet ultimately disposable genre fare in the English-language world was being challenged not just by Hitchcock himself in his new work, but also in a growing body of auteurist literature, originating in France but quickly crossing into his own culture, that claimed Hitchcock as an artist with as much of a right to that title as any of the great painters or writers. While Hitchcock would make joking remarks about his revered status amongst young French cineastes, there's no doubt that their recognition of his artistry—not just as critics but as fellow filmmakers[6]—touched him deeply: Hitchcock admitted to being moved to tears by Truffaut's original letter suggesting they collaborate on an interview book.[7] *Marnie,* Hitchcock's next project, would push even further his goal of making what were essentially art films filtered through the language of classical Hollywood, and of increasing his appeal to "art" audiences as a part of an overall publicity campaign to transform his image from entertainer to artist.

Having originally planned *Marnie* as his follow-up to *Psycho,* the film was never far from his mind even during

---

[6] And not just young ones—Bill Krohn shares the fact that upon Truffaut's request, "Hitchcock arranged a screening of *The Birds* for Jean Cocteau in Paris just before his death."

[7] Hitchcock and Truffaut would remain friends and correspond regularly until Hitchcock's death (Truffaut himself would die from a brain tumor only a few years after), sharing news of their works-in-progress, reading each other's scripts, and offering collegial feedback. Hitchcock never missed screening the new Truffaut film, often sending him a telegram sharing how much he and Alma had enjoyed it.

production on *The Birds.* Evan Hunter attests that "we discussed *Marnie* on the sixty-mile ride to and from location. We discussed *Marnie* during lulls in shooting and during lunch and dinner every night. We discussed *Marnie* interminably." Hitchcock's approach to scripting a film involved talk, talk, and more talk. Conferences with his writers involved discussion of just about every subject under the sun *other than* the film at hand, but when that main subject was finally, inevitably broached ideas had a way of evolving organically between writer and author—the real author being none other than Hitchcock himself, despite the fact that he never took any credit. Everyone who worked on a Hitchcock script knew that he was the sun around which their work revolved; the writers, in a way, *became* Hitchcock, and wrote from his frame of mind as much as, if not more so, than their own. As a visual thinker above all, Hitchcock leaned on his writers for areas like characterization, structure, and dialogue, often using multiple writers per film, each brought in independently of the others, and chosen for their specific literary strengths (for this reason Hitchcock preferred novelists or playwrights rather than screenwriters). As with his collaborators in any department, Hitchcock orchestrated their talents to his own ends: subsumed into his universe, "His collaborators gave him only what he wanted, or only what he would accept, and everything he demanded," per Donald Spoto. *Marnie* saw Joseph Stefano, Evan Hunter, and finally Jay Presson Allen all take a crack at a script that Hitchcock had a very specific vision for. The sense that Hitchcock knew he was embarking on a project of artistic importance for him is evidenced by the fact that he taped his conversation sessions with Hunter and production designer Robert Boyle. Not even the absence of Grace Kelly—who had to drop out due to the unfortunate timing of a political conflict between Monaco and France (due to the former's status as a "tax haven")—could totally stymie Hitchcock's eagerness to make *Marnie.* Tippi Hedren was recruited for round two. The intense subjectivity that had overcome Hitchcock's treatment of her and her character in *The Birds* was pushed to an extreme, via both the expressionism and abstraction of Hitchcock's mise-en-scène and his unhealthy attachment to her as an actress and woman—an attachment seemingly allegorized by *Marnie*'s near-feral depiction of fetishistic masculine desire and infringed feminine autonomy ("the camera was to come as close as possible, the lenses were almost to make love to her" were Hitchcock's directions to his cinematographer Robert Burks, according to Spoto).

But lest we turn *Marnie* into a symbolic Exhibit A in the villainization of Hitchcock and lose sight of the actual film at hand, it may be pertinent to note that this was the third consecutive film in which Hitchcock centralized a female point-of-view: *Psycho*'s Marion (alias Marie), *The Birds*' Melanie, and now Marnie (aliases Marion and Mary)[8] may all be subjected to physical and psychological violence, yet the way Hitchcock films them leaves no doubt as to his fervent empathy for these characters—each, by the way, the most sympathetically portrayed of their respective films. It's the stylized portraiture of these women as complex heroines of psychological suspense narratives that most aggressively reveals Hitchcock's art of the period as one of deep moral intimacy with his broken characters and, by refraction, his (and our) own broken selves. Hitchcock and DP Robert Burks went for bold, moody, and uninhibited choices that anachronistically melded classical studio era techniques with explosively symbolic art cinema aesthetics. The look of *Marnie* is defined by its heavy use of diffusion filters and nets (transparent materials used to soften the lensed image to hazy, glowing effect), devices popular in 1920s Hollywood but which by 1964 had long been out of fashion; the effect is one of jarring intensity, as a technique more common in classic black-and-white melodramas springs out at you in color for a tale of 1960s psychosexual alienation. As Hitchcock's interest in color symbolism was reaching a fever pitch in his late period, he also had Burks desaturate the film's

---

[8] Throw in *The Birds*' Mitch and Marnie's Mark on the male side, and Hitchcock's unproduced dream project *Mary Rose* to boot, and have fun formulating a theory about Hitchcock's heavy usage of "M" names in this period.

palette to emphasize yellows (the color of Marnie's handbag in the film's opening shot) and reds (the retraumatizing visual prompts of Marnie's memory flashes that Hitchcock has fill the screen in expressionistic bursts). This was in keeping with Hitchcock's philosophy of color that had begun as far back as the 1930s, when he was yet to work with color but very keen to—he was interested in it not for simple realism, but only for "dramatic and emotional effect, as a symbol of action and thought." And Bernard Herrmann's lurching, deliberately repetitive symphonic score frantically sweeps you up into all this aesthetic excess, never for a moment allowing you any objective distance from the proceedings. A more criticized anachronism was Hitchcock's continued use of rear projection and matte paintings, which had changed from an accepted economical technique to a slightly unreal "eyesore" with the shifting of audience expectations in the 1960s. A hulking matte-painted ship docked at the end of Marnie's mother's Baltimore street was a deliberate evocation of Hitchcock's memories of London docks with smokestacked ocean liners perched at the end of ordinary streets, as well as an attempt, per authorized biographer John Russell Taylor, "to recreate the unreal, dreamlike effect he had seen two or three times in his life, in Southampton, and again in Wellington, New Zealand, of ships looming surrealistically above the roofs of houses, with no evidence of water to explain them or give perspective." It was the logical expressionistic touch for a location that was in no way normal, or where a real person lived, but was rather the site of the outsized, operatic drama that is Marnie's trauma and its climactic recreation. Entreaties to redo the shot by his collaborators were nixed by Hitchcock, who at the time saw nothing wrong with it, and indeed likely knew perfectly well how its apparently flippant economy and paucity of realism served his hyper-emotional film.[9] (It was only later, *after* the

---

[9] Maurice Yacowar, in his 1977 book on Hitchcock's British period, offers a useful polemic relevant to this and other moments in Hitchcock's work: "Hitchcock's ironic detachment also explains those moments in his work where we see the seams of his craft, where his technical work may seem to be rough. One lesson which the British

film had been deemed a failure by the press, public, and—due partially to audience reaction and partially to his subsequent break with Hedren—Hitchcock himself, that he expressed regret at that "technical mixup.")

Every formal decision Hitchcock makes prioritizes Marnie's interiority and her highly subjective emotional relation to the material world. Despite its apparent lack of traditional Hitchcock suspense (there is no real threat of death in the film, for example) and plenty of dense dialogue scenes, *Marnie* is one of Hitchcock's "pure cinema" movies, where he strings images together to tell a story "like notes of music make a melody." Even *The Birds* capitulated, in a sense, to its titular creatures; *Marnie* is the story of Marnie the whole way. Everything is happening on the inside even as it's all happening on the outside, too, where Hitchcock's stark attention to material details only intensifies the sense of The World According to Marnie. The film's "denaturalized purism of style…," suggests Michele Piso, "recalls the geometrics of Mondrian, the cropped chasteness of Bresson, the angularity of Antonioni's techno-world. The image is cold, silent, intense; its restricted framing creates an abstract and disorientating relation to the body." Throw in the world-restructuring of Eisenstein's montage, too: Marnie's fall from her beloved horse leading to its fatal injuries—another moment often singled out for criticism for its unrealness—is filmed in a way that maximizes the drama of a pivotal emotional moment, extending a split-

---

films should teach us is that Hitchcock always knows what he is doing…. [W]here Hitchcock's technical work seems shoddy what we really have is not a craftsman nodding but an artist extending his resources. Where Hitchcock's craft seems loose, we usually find his technique subserving his content, his literal realism shading off into vibrant metaphor. To put it another way, it is safe to assume that what seems to be a Hitchcock error is likely our failure to work out what he is doing. In *The Lady Vanishes*, for instance, the palpably false opening shot and the unreal proportions of the departing train are typical of how Hitchcock extends his realism into expressionism— only to be charged with poor technique. This liberty came from the German cinema. Thus Fritz Lang inserts a jarring interlude of false scenery into a key moment of *Rancho Notorious*."

second event into an uncomfortably drawn-out series of cuts that chooses tormenting psychological poetry over naturalistic representation. "After all," Hitchcock would say before filming a montage scene on a later film, "the object of film is to annihilate time and space."[10] It's in statements like these that Hitchcock's artistic camaraderie with the new generation of modernist filmmakers is most evident. Indeed, in an early production conference Hitchcock expressed a desire to "cheat like they do in the Italian films and have nobody around" for the opening sequence in the train station, which he eventually did after passing on the idea of having it crowded. He almost made a further hat tip in a scene where Marnie was to rob a movie theater, having originally planned a parody of an Italian art film to be playing during the sequence—alas, it was cut from later drafts and never filmed.[11]

The electrifying dissonance between the film's old-fashioned qualities and its modernist ones is obvious from the first few minutes, where the aforementioned train station opening is juxtaposed with the credit sequence preceding it of a storybook's pages being flipped, like something out of a 1940s romance picture. But *Marnie* proceeds to undercut any traditional genre expectations: its obvious surface relation to the "woman's picture," or to classic melodramas, gets filtered through its twin relation to contemporary art cinema, and in the process the idea of "a Hitchcock picture" also gets upended. In line with his bid for serious critical consideration, Hitchcock set out to make a character study first, and only secondly a thriller. Yet what he ended up making was more than conversant with previous films of his: the film begins like *Psycho* (woman absconds with stolen money) and ends like *The Birds* (traumatized woman gets into car with ambiguous future), with a middle that combines the pop Freudianism

---

[10] Cf. the moment in *The Birds* when Hitchcock cuts between Hedren's terrified, frozen, impotent gaze and a path of flames as they scream toward a gas station; time expands beyond realistic proportions to escalate to expressionistic proportions a pivotal moment of the film's dramatic catastrophes.

[11] Shades of Orson Welles' *The Other Side of the Wind*, perhaps.

of *Spellbound* (1945) with the densely-riddled psychological textures of *Vertigo.* (Marnie is in some ways the active version of Stewart's passive victim of psycho-paralysis.) Yet these antecedents are all pushed to their breaking points; as much as *Marnie* can be read as the capper to an early 1960s trilogy with *Psycho* and *The Birds*—all films dealing with the effects of childhood trauma/mother issues—this last film is pitched at a psychological intensity that borders on the stylistically and thematically garish. But this is Hitchcock in pure movie land, operating at a deliberately operatic level where anything that might not pass muster with modern psychologists is justified by the overwhelming intensity of his cinematic vision. Having established Marnie's fear of thunderstorms, Hitchcock crashes a tree straight through a window near her during one; having made it clear that Marnie's scared of confronting the trauma of her childhood encounter with one of her mother's johns, Hitchcock stages a delirious memory interrogation at the same site to provoke her psychological catharsis. This last scene is played like the final battle in an ongoing psychological war between Marnie and her husband Mark (Sean Connery, his brutish charm played as potentially-to-actually predatory). "*Marnie* was *The Taming of the Shrew*," Hitchcock would later note, "but the public didn't notice." But what's so complex about the battle of wills between Mark and Marnie is that their relationship becomes a knotted mess of competing impulses of benevolence and perversion. Marnie resents Mark for his hold over her, yet in her weakest moments desperately wants help and knows she needs it; Mark loves Marnie and genuinely wants to help her, but in his weakest moments desperately wants her to act the part of a genuine wife and succumbs to forcing himself on her. It's this dialectical tightrope that allows the film to be described as both tender and dangerous at the same time, and in his walking of it Hitchcock turns in a film of savage power.

The strange mood that had overcome Hitchcock on *The Birds* had yet to dissipate, and along with bouts of ill health, fatigue, and anxiety throughout *Marnie*'s filming it may have contributed to the sense of the film as a fever dream—Truffaut called it a "great sick film." Hitchcock told actor and associate Norman Lloyd that "you might have to finish this one for me," such was Hitchcock's state at the time; yet doctors and specialists called in were unable to diagnosis any specific cause for his issues. It's likely, however, that no small part of it resulted from his relationship with Tippi Hedren, who more than any actress ever under contract to him had been subject to Hitchcock's obsessive concern over every element of her life, both on and off screen. Her performances, as an unknown model turned leading lady, were coached extensively by Hitchcock down to the smallest detail, and her simultaneously icy and emotive presence in both *The Birds* and *Marnie* suit those respective characters and films perfectly. Hedren was game for being clay in Hitchcock's hands on screen, but she understandably bristled at Hitchcock's hands-on approach to her offscreen life; being told what to eat, how to dress, or who to see socially wasn't so tolerable, especially when Hitchcock's attentions seemed to cross the line from the manipulations of a directorial puppet master to the pathetic efforts of an unrequited romantic. Tempers flared one day due to a disagreement over whether Hedren be allowed to take time off to accept an award in New York, and Hedren did the one thing nobody was allowed to do: insult Hitchcock's weight. According to Hedren, Hitchcock also sexually propositioned her. The controversy over this account is too complicated to relitigate here; suffice it to say, communications between the two took a turn for the worse, and Hitchcock completed the film with less vigor than he had started with.[12] Hedren's rejection, combined

---

[12] I lay no claim to special insight about what happened between Hitchcock and Hedren, but after absorbing a good amount of informational context, as well as a range of different perspectives regarding the issue, my own small theory is this: Hitchcock, like many directors, was known to play psychological games with certain of his cast members. How he treated his actors on set was often purposefully meant to provoke certain moods or attitudes, a kind of invisible direction for subconscious effect. Hitchcock's infamous comparison of actors to cattle was a front that hid just how deeply—yet subtly—he concerned himself with his performers. In Hedren's case, his attempt

with poor critical and audience responses to the film, marked an inflection point in Hitchcock's career—"Hitchcock was never the same after *Marnie*," Truffaut would later say, "and its failure cost him a considerable amount of his self-confidence."

The "failure" of *Marnie* would haunt the rest of Hitchcock's career, primarily in its effect on Universal executives who weren't interested in the commercial disaster that might result from letting Hitchcock make any more bizarre art films. His new contract in 1964 "made him a bird in a gilded cage," according to biographer Patrick McGilligan. "At Universal he would be worry-free financially, but creatively he had sacrificed his power and freedom." This didn't bode well for the film Hitchcock wanted to make next, a long-envisioned adaptation of *Peter Pan* author J. M. Barrie's ghost story *Mary Rose*, which had already been scripted by Jay Presson Allen after she'd finished her work on *Marnie* and was to complete a trilogy of Hedren-Hitchcock films. Even if Hedren was interested in working with Hitchcock again (she wasn't), Universal rejected the uncommercial project in no uncertain terms—ever after, Hitchcock would claim that it was specifically written into his contract that he could do any project he wished for under $3 million *except* for *Mary Rose*. Hitchcock's next films, caught between his competing commercial and artistic interests, would retroactively make clear that *Marnie* was the end of an era. As such, we can perhaps pause to consider a quasi-sci-

---

to isolate her, to keep her away from the touch of others, to alienate her, has obvious parallels with what her character in *Marnie* is meant to be like. Lewd joking was also a regular tool of Hitchcock's, meant to shock or humor (or even relax before takes) those he worked with in ways similar to the practical jokes he was fond of playing on them earlier in his career (which sometimes overstepped good taste). It's possible that the business with Hedren may have been Hitchcock's extreme attempt to provide fuel for her performance in *Marnie*, just taken too far and incurring serious offense; or at least that may have been his self-justification. But, again, this is simply educated conjecture I share due to its relevance to Hitchcock's late career, and I leave it to the reader to do any supplemental research for themselves. Ultimately, what truly happened, and why, was likely known only to the two people involved.

entific partitioning of Hitchcock's career: *North by Northwest* as the peak of classical Hitchcock, its culmination, the *most* Hitchcock a Hitchcock film could be; the abstract experimentations of *Psycho* and *The Birds* as evolutions, transitions, into *a* late period; and *Marnie* as both the logical conclusion of this period and, given its continued problem-child status in Hitchcock's filmography, a radical step into something beyond it—Hitchcock's late phase proper. Yet *Marnie* can't totally be lumped in with the films that come after it, all of which have the feel of an epilogue to a career that had, in multiple (non-artistic) senses, hit a dead end. As Hitchcock regrouped and navigated new commercial and industrial contexts, his art branched into new territories that, for those willing to follow him into the late style weeds, would prove as interesting and invigorating as anything Hitchcock had ever made.

Multiple paths forked in front of him in late 1964 and early 1965; it was only a matter of choosing which one to travel. Hitchcock contemplated his future during a European holiday with Alma at the end of 1964. Post-*Marnie*, he'd been "poring over short stories, crime novels, news reports, and even recent plays in search of a new film idea." Returning from his vacation, he came armed with plans for two films, with an eye toward doing whichever one came together easiest. The first was a comic thriller involving a family of Italians, a New York City hotel, and the mafia, to be called *R.R.R.R.* and written by the famed Italian duo Agenore Incrocci and Furio Scarpelli (Age & Scarpelli, colloquially), whose work on *Big Deal on Madonna Street* (1958) Hitchcock had enjoyed. The second was a contemporary serial killer movie that Hitchcock asked *Psycho* author Robert Bloch to write as a novel for him to adapt. Neither prospect flourished as Hitchcock had hoped: the Italian hotel film turned out to be too much of a cultural bridge to gap, and Bloch wasn't impressed by the deal Hitchcock offered him. But there was a third project percolating around the same time, a political thriller about a Cold War defector, for which Hitchcock had in mind some big names. Russian-American novelist Vladimir Nabokov was his first choice. In his letter to the writer, Hitchcock offered him the choice to work on either the spy film or the hotel film; Nabokov replied that he didn't feel fit for the former, and he wasn't able to devote energy to the latter as soon as Hitchcock would have liked.[13] Next on his list was the prolific Italian screenwriter Cesare Zavattini, who he was interested in having write a treatment for the spy film based on Hitchcock's original idea; however, he never did follow through with plans to contact him. That this was the case, and that Hitchcock did eventually choose this material for his next film, *Torn Curtain*, were both probable symptoms of studio pressures at Universal where, despite his mythic status, he was subject to more oversight than he'd had in years. After *Marnie*, the studio expected Hitchcock to tackle proven commercial material, with typical Hitchcock thrills and suspense, and with stars attached to guarantee an audience; under their scrutiny, he didn't have much choice in the matter. One of the few boosts to Hitchcock's damaged self-confidence in the mid-1960s was being asked to play master of ceremonies at Lyndon B. Johnson's 1965 inauguration, but other than that the signs weren't great: his TV show was dropped for low ratings at the end of its 1964-1965 season, and a slew of Hitchcock's treasured collaborators became unavailable to him. Longtime editor George Tomasini died of a heart attack in 1964; Hitchcock's speech writer James Allardice passed away in 1966; and cinematographer Robert Burks—who was unavailable to shoot *Torn Curtain* after suffering a nervous collapse—died along with his wife in a 1968 house fire. *Marnie* would also turn out to be Hitchcock's last collaboration with production designer Robert Boyle and, after a disagreement over the *Torn Curtain* score, composer Bernard Herrmann as well. That former producer David O. Selznick also died in 1965 made this all seem like the symbolic passing of an era.

---

[13] Hitchcock would approach Nabokov again to generate a script for 1972's *Frenzy*, but Nabokov declined under the pressure of his own writing schedule. The two weren't as different as it may seem: born just a few years apart, they were both English educated, both emigrated to America around the same time, and they had some overlapping thematic interests (*Lolita* being the site of many of them).

Hitchcock himself had now been a dominant cultural figure for long enough that, as an elder statesman in his mid-60s, films created in the shadow of his legacy were spawning left and right. But none of them were so globally successful as the James Bond series, which kicked off in 1962 with the Sean Connery-starring *Dr. No* and had three additional entries by the time Hitchcock released his next film in 1966. Hitchcock was friends with Bond producer Albert "Cubby" Broccoli and had been following Ian Fleming's literary career with interest (it's likely that George Sanders' character in 1940's *Foreign Correspondent* was loosely based on Fleming, who had worked as a reporter for Reuters); there was some mutual flirtation with the idea of Hitchcock directing a Bond picture, but nothing concrete ever coalesced. Yet the series' films were recognizable as light, globe-trotting variations on Hitchcock's spy pictures that didn't always take pains to hide the influence. The scene in *From Russia with Love* (1963) of Connery evading an attacking helicopter on foot, for example, seemed clearly modeled after *North by Northwest*'s Cary Grant vs. crop duster sequence. Hitchcock, ever the obsessive consumer of movies and intimately familiar with their conventions, always tried to build his own films *against* cliché—and when his innovations eventually became clichéd in turn (as with the Bond borrowings), he simply counter-innovated. *Torn Curtain* would be a reversal of what Hitchcock saw as the comic-book plotting and atmosphere of the Bond films; it would be a "realistic Bond," an anti-Bond, a spy picture à la *Notorious* (1946) that would thrust normal people into a pressurized geopolitical predicament. This would be evident formally and narratively—for example, in a scene that critiques the swift dispatches of the invincible Bond via a messy, drawn-out sequence meant to show how hard it is to actually kill someone—as well as thematically, in the way it subverts its genre concerns in being, as Murray Pomerance suggests, "not a spy film at all, but a film set in the context (and written to some degree in the language) of spying" toward the greater purposes of being "a film in which the human mind is a central protagonist against the human heart." Any political intrigue would be secondary. Hitchcock's inspiration for the story came less from the facts of the 1951 defection of British diplomats Donald Maclean and Guy Burgess than it did from the accompanying question of what effect it may have had on *Mrs.* Maclean's emotional world. Irish-Catholic writer Brian Moore (Graham Greene's "favorite living novelist"), far from an obvious choice for Hitchcock fare, was approached to write the script based on his reputation for sensitively-drawn female characters. (Moore didn't want to write for Hitchcock, but was advised by his lawyer to accept when the pay offer was doubled.) Other than *North by Northwest, Torn Curtain* would be Hitchcock's first film not based on preexisting material since the Ben Hecht-scripted *Notorious* 20 years earlier, and his fingerprints were all over it as usual; "I told him that for truth's sake," Moore later said, "the credits should read 'Screenplay by Alfred Hitchcock, assisted by Brian Moore,' but he said he never took writing credit." But it wasn't the happy collaboration of *Notorious*, and Moore claimed that if it had been one of his novels he'd have scrapped the whole thing and started over. Hitchcock brought in English screenwriters Keith Waterhouse and Willis Hall to polish the dialogue as filming began (often doing rewrites just hours before the scenes were to be shot), but ironically they weren't interested in having their names in the credits either.[14]

This rough start that left Hitchcock dissatisfied with his screenplay was exacerbated by his inability to delay production to fix it; Julie Andrews, the newly in-demand star that Universal insisted Hitchcock work with, had a schedule that prevented it. And with Andrews fresh off her star-making roles in *Mary Poppins* (1964) and *The Sound of Music* (1965), Hitchcock resented being made to work with someone who

---

[14] Hitchcock did want their names credited, even pushing for arbitration from the Writer's Guild (who, however, ruled against it). The duo had adapted Waterhouse's own novel *Billy Liar* for director John Schlesinger in 1963; it's here that Hitchcock saw Julie Christie, who he was interested in having play in *Torn Curtain*, before the role was given to a different Julie. (Truffaut would use Christie instead, in his film of Ray Bradbury's *Fahrenheit 451*.)

he claimed the audience would constantly be expecting to break into song. Matters were only made worse by Universal's choice for her male co-star, the method-trained Paul Newman, who Hitchcock was made additionally wary of by both a dinner gathering where he'd behaved indecorously (taking off his jacket at the dinner table, drinking canned beer instead of the selected wine) and memos Newman had sent him with concerns about the script (Waterhouse and Hall were subsequently tasked with keeping him out of Hitchcock's hair with satisfying-enough explanations). But the actors' worst crime was simply that their combined salaries were taking up 20 percent of the film's budget. Hitchcock hadn't had a true star at the center of one of his films since Cary Grant in *North by Northwest*, and one could make a convincing argument that *Psycho*'s shower scene, by metaphorically killing off the role of "stars" in Hitchcock's cinema altogether, marks the exact point at which Hitchcock's late style begins. After this, when we do get "stars" (Connery, Newman and Andrews) they are stars of a different breed, of a new generation, and employed in a slightly more complicated way than classical stars like Grant or Fonda had been, now too old to play the parts. Hitchcock utilizes but then subverts the marquee value of these new stars' names—they become puppets, models, of Hitchcock's formalist universe, subsumed into his stylistic paradigm, swallowed by his mise-en-scène. He weaponizes their qualities and abilities—Newman's bright blue eyes and edgy intensity, Andrews' gentle face and emotional tenderness—and inserts them into his splintered montage, where the performances are created just as much by their placement amongst the images and cuts as by any traditional "acting" that may be going on. As stars in a cinema that had moved beyond the need of them, and as actors believed miscast by a filmmaker for whom casting was half the job of directing actors, Newman and Andrews may not have "fit" *Torn Curtain*—but the dissonance of their presences produces something beyond what even Hitchcock may have envisioned. In a film where a more classical love plot competes with a more modernist decentralized narrative structure, a conventionally attractive young star couple provides an ideal locus around which the film can variously fulfil its romantic expectations or have them subversively crumble apart. *Torn Curtain*'s structure is trifold: the film begins from Andrews' perspective, shifts to Newman's, and then reunites the pair for the third act. Which is to say, it begins from a continuation of the three previous 1960s films' centering of the female perspective, and then foreshadows the three Hitchcock films that will follow it which lack centralizing viewpoints; *Torn Curtain*, split down the middle between its two protagonists, splits down the middle the last seven films of Hitchcock's career. It partakes in the emotional rhythms of classic melodrama (a genre Hitchcock explicitly didn't want Moore to avoid) while also overlaying the modern relational ennui of Antonioni's 1960s films, where rather than traditional performers the actors seem to have become formal pawns for the director to move around his cinematic chess board[15]—which isn't to disparage the performances of *Torn Curtain* at all (they already have been far too often). Andrews, for example, would later prove multiple times over her suitability for roles caught between love and espionage in films like *Darling Lili* (1970) and *The Tamarind Seed* (1974), both directed by her husband Blake Edwards (who she was dating at the time of *Torn Curtain*).

In fact, I can't think of many films this side of Robert Bresson that have a more cinematically rewarding usage of their actors. The whole drama of the picture is happening on Newman and Andrews' faces at every moment, even and especially when the film goes to East Germany and their faces *can't* betray the drama for fear of Newman's double agent status being exposed—yet it is still totally happening, under a layer of strained normalcy; little enough that the characters not in the know are kept there, but just enough that audiences are clued in to the drama happening on multiple levels (the A story of the scientist spies, the B story of the strained lovers) via

---

[15] It's been pointed out that, indeed, Antonioni's *L'avventura* (1960) had beaten Hitchcock's *Psycho* to the punch by a matter of weeks in radically dispensing with its main star long before the end of the film.

micro-expressions of their bodies and faces. Thus Hitchcock can get a lot out of silence and can use words, like Newman's prevarications about his actions to a confused Andrews, as verbal tells that add far more to the drama than their basic denotation. The suspense of *Torn Curtain*'s first half (before Newman and Andrews are reunited) is due less to the spy narrative than to what Ken Mogg calls a "suffer-in-silence" motif common to melodramas and Hitchcock films in which, like in *Torn Curtain,* neither character "has the opportunity to tell the other, or anyone else, the extent of their anguish," and "inasmuch as words are by definition not appropriate" suits a visual approach descended from silent cinema. Hitchcock allows no emotional breathing room—as soon as he's resolved the romantic drama by having Newman confess his role as spy to Andrews, he spends the rest of the film doubling down on the suspense wrought by their attempt to complete the mission and exit the country alive. As a late career reimagining of *Notorious, Torn Curtain* exists within an appropriately evolved formal schema while proffering a similar kind of romantic suspense: from the couple kissing casually and repetitively in an early scene, to the idea of two people together against the world teetering on the edge of failure as a couple and as agents. And like that film, *Torn Curtain* employs its spy plot not to make any direct political statements, but rather as one giant MacGuffin on which to hang the real drama of two people tested in love; in some ways the whole film is just the mini-drama spelled out in the opening bedroom scene (she wants to stop putting off their wedding, he's dissatisfied with his career trajectory) splayed out across an international geopolitical canvas. If Andrews doesn't decide to follow Newman to East Germany, the story is dead on arrival—there may be interest in the will-he-won't-he narrative of Newman's extraction of the formula (the idea of hinging a plot on the stealing of something intangible out of another man's head certainly has dramatic promise), but there'd be no emotional substratum from which the foundational complexities of *Torn Curtain* as it is might flower. "Relationships matter, not political secrets," is how Donald Spoto articulates Hitchcock's real thesis. The final image of Newman and Andrews covered by a blanket echoes our introduction to them in the same situation at the beginning of the film, circling back to reveal the film's priorities. Hitchcock's proposed ending would have made this point even clearer: after everything the pair had gone through to obtain it, he originally had Newman's character throw the scientific formula into a fire. "It speaks to the futility of it all," Hitchcock would argue, "and it's in keeping with the kind of naïveté of the character, who is no professional spy and who will certainly retire from that nefarious business." But even though commercial pressures led him to discard the subversive idea, the lack of any scene showing him handing off the formula to anyone, or being welcomed or congratulated by the Americans, communicates by absence that the main feeling of the ending is purely one of "we escaped (together)." It's like the film "forgot" what it was "supposed" to be about.

That Hitchcock couldn't have his downbeat ending didn't prevent him from constructing the entire picture with a formal approach that communicates a gloomier vision than a surface level viewing might suggest. His continued interest in diffused light received its most extensive expression yet: Hitchcock instructed cinematographer John F. Warren (a collaborator as far back as *Rebecca* and a regular DP on Hitchcock's television show) to put a gray gauze over his lens and set up white canvases of various sizes around the set to softly reflect the light back into the shooting area. Hitchcock used his usual DP Robert Burks' absence as an opportunity to experiment with a less glossy, less seductive, more realistic style in search of a photographic naturalism. It started from a foundational philosophical question—"What *is* natural light?" Hitchcock asked Warren in his office.

"Look at the way we're sitting here. What is the light like in this room? Are there black shadows anywhere? We're living in reflected light. In the office, as we sit here, there's not one bit of direct light on us, even from the window because the curtains have softened it. The colors are not shouting at us. Everything is soft and there is no artificial element of light in this room. Why can't we put the same effect on the screen in *Torn Curtain*?"

The attempt to use almost nothing but reflected light in photographing the film was a "drastic change," in Hitchcock's own words, and it made for a new experience for others, too. "The actors kept on asking, 'Where are the lights?'" The lights, rather than being trained directly on the actors, were being bounced off canvas reflectors in order to create soft, indirect, shadowless illumination that was diffused throughout the set. Light was reduced to approximately a quarter of what the usual Hollywood film employed, and no one besides the two leads wore makeup so that the texture of their skin was maintained by the soft light. The overall effect is one of painterly paleness, a look mirroring the subdued bleakness of story and setting and more than complemented by Hitchcock's detailed attention to the film's color. He had long felt that "color films were being photographed in almost the same manner as black-and-white films," with "a hangover from one to the other." But for Hitchcock, making color films that used color purposefully didn't mean garishly showing off color for color's sake. Following *Marnie*'s intense use of color symbolism, *Torn Curtain* similarly employs color to associative, subconscious effect but with its own unique palette: when the picture relocates from Copenhagen to East Germany, for example, the film is drained down to tones of grey and beige (with only dashes of dangerous red). It was a coordinated effort between Hitchcock, Warren, and production designer Hein Heckroth—from the use of grey diffusers (even on exteriors) to the grey-painted sets—to create a cohesive look that reflected the sinister, depressed mood of life behind the Iron Curtain for the film's American scientists. (It was also designed to imitate the muted, washed-out look of films made using the German color process Agfacolor from the 1930s on.) Heckroth was known for his work on Michael Powell and Emeric Pressburger films, and his contribution to the vibrant *Red Shoes* (1948) may have inspired one of the few the touches of bright color in *Torn Curtain,* a fiery scene at a ballet set to Tchaikovsky's symphonic poem *Francesca da Rimini* (whose story based on the fifth canto of Dante's *Inferno* has parallels with the trapped lovers scenario of *Torn Curtain*). The colors are one of the main visual-emotional indicators of the "ice and fire" motif—or to use the film's own twice-repeated words, the "combination of mathematical logic and romantic inconsistency"—that runs through *Torn Curtain* and its dueling formal and thematic impulses toward the coldness of scientific duty and the heat of love's passion. Some of the film's most artistically astounding moments seem to articulate both at the same time, like the shot of Newman and Andrews in their East German hotel room—him hunched in an unlit corner on the right of the screen, her facing the amber glow of the window on the left—that Andrew Sarris claimed "would inspire rapturous essays for its meaningful use of color if only it had popped up in an Antonioni film."

The motif is introduced from frame one in an experimental credits sequence designed by Mel Sattler and inspired by the Argentine kinetic artist Julio Le Parc, of flames licking the left side of the screen while moments from the upcoming film are superimposed amidst a shadowy, pale blue smoke on the right. Like the abstract title designs of Saul Bass for *Vertigo, North by Northwest,* and *Psycho,* the one for *Torn Curtain* signals a film that, while in some ways presenting itself as a traditionally entertaining genre film, will on a deeper level offer itself as an artistic object caught in a web of realism, poeticism, and abstraction. On the one hand Hitchcock will do his usual detailed research, even smuggling microphones into East Germany to record ambient sounds; on the other he'll shoot the entire film on a Hollywood soundstage and a handful of California locations, relying on matte paintings and rear-projection to get across his cinematic paraphrase of the film's real-world setting (footage from a German second unit sent to covertly capture the authentic thing was deemed substandard). Hitchcock's go-to matte painter for his post-1960 films, Albert Whitlock (originally a lowly sign painter for Hitchcock back on *The 39 Steps*), would almost wholly recreate a version of

East Berlin's Alte Nationalgalerie art museum for a drawn-out chase sequence, painting not just the walls but the painted pictures *on* the walls; Newman performed in a virtually empty space. (Newman: "What is my motivation for walking straight?" Hitchcock: "If you don't, you'll disappear behind the matte painting.") Another protracted, suspense-prolonging version of a chase scene is the climactic bus journey—scored by a slowly intensifying cue that imitates Ravel's *Boléro*—the couple takes on their way out of the country, which also partakes in abstraction via heavy rear-projection usage, here achieving "a notable expressive effect," according to Robin Wood, "intensifying the spectator's sense of the bus as a small enclosed world sealed off from the surrounding normality." If *Torn Curtain* is a movie torn between boundary-pushing artistic effects and its more mundane studio-bound techniques, the kerfuffle over its score is the perfect example of Hitchcock's increasingly conflicted stance toward the relationship between art and commercialism. Hitchcock wanted Bernard Herrmann—despite disagreements and minor ego-conflicts on the 1960s films up to that point, and Hitchcock's concern that Herrmann was self-plagiarizing his music for other films, Hitchcock still wanted Herrmann. It was a vote of loyalty for perhaps his greatest collaborator against a studio in Universal who saw Herrmann's music as old-fashioned and his name as a box-office liability. Hitchcock tried to find middle ground by asking Herrmann to write something catering to a new kind of audience that was "young, vigorous and demanding. It is this fact that has been recognised by almost all the European film-makers where they have sought to introduce a beat and rhythm that is more in tune with the requirements of the aforesaid audience." But when Herrmann turned in a heavy, dark, idiosyncratic score filled with unusual instrumentation, a few minutes of listening were enough for Hitchcock—after sticking his neck out for Herrmann, he felt betrayed, and promptly fired him. "What do you want from me?" Herrmann wondered. "I don't write pop music." They never did work together again, and Hitchcock hired composer John Addison to write a score that, at Universal's recommendation, would be popular enough and light enough to both sell records and help warm away some of the film's chilliness.[16]

A certain coldness does pervade the Hitchcock films of this era—at least until the more genial *Family Plot* in the mid-1970s—a coldness which matches descriptions of Hitchcock around the time as somewhat more morose than usual. Part of this moodiness likely stemmed from what he felt was the curtailing of his artistic ambitions, not just by Universal but by his own reputation amongst audiences and critics. Despite being one of 1966's top ten domestic grossers, *Torn Curtain* received frustratingly tepid reviews from English-language critics for a film that was being advertised as "Hitchcock's 50th masterpiece." So frustrating, in fact, that after some enthusiastic French notices came to his attention, Hitchcock had some sent clandestinely to US reviewers. But his position within both the modernizing cinematic landscape and Universal's business offices would come to a head with the project he proposed next: a stripped-down contemporary film about a New York City serial killer to be shot on location, in natural light, using hand-held cameras, experimental color, a cast of cheap unknown actors, and featuring ample violence and nudity. These new stylistic ideas were clearly inspired by a spate of recent French and Italian films that Hitchcock had

---

[16] Ironically, Herrmann's unused score is the more popular record today. (Elmer Bernstein first conducted a reconstruction of it in 1977.) One could say that it is memorable where Addison's is merely serviceable; no doubt it would have worked perfectly for the film had circumstances been different (between Hitchcock and Herrmann, between Hitchcock and Universal, etc.), yet the collaboration was not to be. (However, there is evidence suggesting that the Tchaikovsky piece used in the film was selected by Herrmann before his firing.) Herrmann spent the remaining decade of his life in England, ironically often scoring films made under the sign of Hitchcock by younger filmmakers like François Truffaut and Brian De Palma, whose *Vertigo* riff *Obsession* (1976) Herrmann called "the finest film of my musical life." Contrary to legend, Hitchcock and Herrmann did meet and speak again, but not in a way reflective of the sustained friendship they'd had prior to the falling out over *Torn Curtain*.

been blown away by—especially Godard's *Masculine Feminine* (1966) and the Antonioni films *Red Desert* (1964) and *Blowup* (1966). *Red Desert* had so impressed him ("White on white!" he exclaimed to his assistant Peggy Robertson. "There, you see! It *can* be done!") that he had a detailed query sent to Universal's Rome headquarters asking how Antonioni had achieved the film's colors. *Blowup* startled him even more; soon after he'd engaged novelist Howard Fast to work on his script for him, Hitchcock shared a rare admission of enthusiasm for another's work—"My God, Howard! I've just seen Antonioni's *Blow-Up*. These Italian directors are a century ahead of me in terms of technique! What have I been doing all this time?" Before Fast, Hitchcock had first turned to Benn Levy (a collaborator on the script for Hitchcock's *Blackmail* almost four decades earlier) to write the treatment for a film Hitchcock would variously refer to as *Frenzy* (not to be confused with his 1972 feature) or *Kaleidoscope*. The aggressively contemporary may have seemed like a strange playground for a man in his sixties, especially one who cultivated an old-world Edwardian air about him, yet Edward White writes of a Hitchcock who "remained fascinated by the times in which he lived, collecting files' worth of newspaper clippings about hippies, the Black Power movement, anti-apartheid and anticolonialism across Africa, the Weather Underground, the 'opening-up' of China, and third-wave feminism," even if nothing came of them. His idea for *Kaleidoscope* was to set the film among New York hippies and base his serial murderer on a version of English criminal Neville Heath (who'd killed two women in the summer of 1946) modernized by public domain accounts of more recent sexually-tinged homicides. Camera tests commissioned in New York to "compare different film stocks in low-light settings," according to Dan Auiler, resulted in "nearly an hour of silent footage" including "full mockups of actual scenes from the screenplay, using unknown actors and models."[17] Meanwhile, horrified Universal executives

---

[17] Fragments of the test footage and some tantalizing pre-production stills are available online, most comprehensively at the.hitchcock.

were doing everything in their power to persuade Hitchcock against making the film. Their repeated opposition to the idea culminated, after extensive pre-production work, in a July 1968 attempt by Hitchcock to present his test footage as a last-ditch pitch to go ahead with the production; the meeting left Hitchcock humiliated and in tears. The project that Auiler calls "an intended turning point in Hitchcock's career" was shot down, and Universal quickly rerouted him toward more palatable material for his next film.

In theory, Hitchcock may have been able to force the project ahead if he'd really wanted to — as a low-budget production, *Kaleidoscope* could easily have been budgeted for far less than the $3 million cap spelled out in Hitchcock's contract, under which he was supposed to have near-total freedom of material. But Hitchcock was worn down by all the voices telling him not to make it (even Truffaut wasn't thrilled with the idea), and his feeling of responsibility to those around him was too acute to barrel ahead just because he technically could. Asked by an interviewer why he couldn't just make anything he wanted to, this is how Hitchcock answered: "That's a privilege I have, but one mustn't take advantage of it. My contract gives me complete artistic control. I can make any film I like, up to three million dollars. But such privileges are a responsibility to the studios, which I obviously cannot, and would not, take advantage of. I don't have the right kind of conceit." Hitchcock's sense of financial and professional ethics kept him from indulging in his own ideas at the expense of betraying his producers or alienating his audiences[18] — even when he became one of Universal's largest stockholders in the 1960s, he didn't wave the fact around demanding a completely free reign. He maintained a tactful approach with the front office (after all, they *had* made him rich[19]) and remained cognizant of the vast amounts of capital that cinema played around with,

---

zone/wiki/Kaleidoscope.

[18] With *Kaleidoscope*, for example, Hitchcock mused about how far he could go in terms of nudity and violence without audiences leaving the theater saying to others "don't go."

[19] "… and they never let Hitch forget it." – Bernard Herrmann

analogizing filmmaking to the absurdity of handing a painter a \$750,000 canvas, a \$500,000 easel, a \$250,000 box of paints, an \$800,000 palette, and a \$500,000 set of brushes and then demanding they paint a picture that at least made the money back. Above all Hitchcock, who in his early days had held just about every position possible on a film set, harbored a great feeling for the film industry and the people that populated it, and looked at the workers coming in at six in the morning carrying their lunch pails as his personal responsibility—their livelihood depended on Hitchcock making fiscally responsible pictures. And yet Hitchcock also felt an attraction to a more artistic, and therefore inherently less commercial, cinema. His early (and to a lesser degree later) 1960s films palpably strain toward modernist currents in film, music, art, and literature as exemplified by the European art cinema of the time. But Hitchcock's commercial instincts kept him from taking too much of a leap, lest he make a film that "never get[s] beyond New York's East Side" and neglect "the power of film to reach a world audience."[20] Were he to make films in a vacuum with no one to please but himself, the films "would certainly be different from the ones you see on the screen," said Hitchcock. "They would be more dramatic, perhaps without humor, more realistic." And indeed Hitchcock "was eager to direct a different kind of film, but the studio prevented him," as his wife Alma told Andrew Sarris in 1972. But Hitchcock felt a prisoner of his own success and obliged to deliver the suspense stories his audience expected from him, and ones that avoided industry taboos at that. ("We have to avoid elderly persons and limit ourselves to youthful characters," Hitchcock grumbled to Truffaut; "a film must contain some anti-establishment elements; no picture can cost more than two or three million

---

[20] Thus why when holding up Hitchcock's late work to Edward Said's description of late style, Mark Goble believes it is only *Psycho*, *The Birds*, and *Marnie* that fit this idea of Beethovian self-exile, and that the films that come after it are merely self-conscious pastiches of better, earlier work. Hitchcock's "too-late style"?, he asks. I hope the introduction has explained why this approach demonstrates the necessity of redefining late style to be more inclusive.

dollars.") History encouraged this line of thinking: in the mid-1950s Paramount, anticipating the great success of *Rear Window* and *To Catch a Thief* (1955), had given him complete freedom for his next project; although a personal favorite of his and indicative of Hitchcock's sense of humor like nothing else, *The Trouble with Harry* (1955) was a box-office disappointment in America. Hence Hitchcock's continued attempt to thread the needle between commercial considerations and artistic ones—for example, his fluctuation between ridiculing the "plausibles" (i.e., those who cared about logic) and pleasing them—which was hard enough on its own *before* being complicated by his relationship with Universal head Lew Wasserman. Hitchcock's ambivalence toward front office types was nothing new (his earliest films had temporarily been held from release by executives who thought them too "artistic"), but Wasserman was a friend—his agent for many years and along with his wife a regular dinner and vacation guest. There was a trust there, yet at the same time Hitchcock was aware of an increasing power imbalance that resulted in annoying oversight; "what were once suggestions from Lew Wasserman," writes Dan Auiler, "now became instructions carried out by his second and third level executives." Throughout it all, however, Hitchcock was level-headed and realistic about the fact that the film business is "full of compromises…. All things considered I feel I am doing well if I get 60 [!] per cent of my original conception onto the screen."

From the very beginning Hitchcock's next film would be among his most compromised, but it also afforded him a prime opportunity to practice what he tried "to make my first rule of direction—flexibility." Leon Uris's 1967 best-selling spy novel *Topaz*[21] was suggested to Hitchcock by Universal after a period of inactivity and the shuttering of multiple never-to-be-made projects (two of which would have been among

---

[21] Uris novels had previously been adapted into Raoul Walsh's late *Battle Cry* (1955)—Walsh was around the same age then as Hitchcock was for *Topaz*—and Otto Preminger's late-ish *Exodus* (1960), another international epic that, like *Torn Curtain*, also starred an ostensibly "miscast" Paul Newman.

Hitchcock's most radical experiments); the desire to work, the lack of any more promising material (Universal's story department was somewhat provincial, but he was dependent on it for source literature), and the continued itch to get his idea for a "realistic Bond" right led Hitchcock to accept the assignment. But from the get-go he had an uneasy relationship with Uris, who was guaranteed first crack at the script as part of the rights-acquisition deal for his book, and he deemed the writer's screenplay unfilmable. This resulted in an unusual time crunch for a Hitchcock production: without a workable screenplay, and with an autumn 1968 production looming (it was essential that it be shot in the right season), he called in *Vertigo*'s Samuel Taylor as pinch writer. Taylor flew to Europe on 24-hours' notice and began writing scenes from scratch "a few days—and in many cases a few hours—before they were shot." With similarly last-minute casting and no prep time either, *Topaz* became a stressful improvisational act for a film-maker who claimed he only shot thoroughly prepared, "pre-cut" pictures—although research by Bill Krohn and other scholars has poked major holes in the myth that Hitchcock never improvised on set or shot more than he needed to, and in fact this was far from the first time Hitchcock started a shoot without a completed script (a similar problem occurred with Raymond Chandler's disregarded *Strangers on a Train* draft, for example). Besides, for someone who always asserted the image as more important than the text, shooting without a locked-down script was hardly the hurdle it would have been to less visually adept filmmakers, and Hitchcock was bolstered by regular crew like production designer Henry Bumstead, costumer Edith Head, and visual effects man Albert Whitlock as well as returning collaborators: Taylor of course, but also producer Herbert Coleman from the Paramount glory days, editor William Ziegler (*Rope, Strangers on a Train*), and cine-matographer Jack Hildyard, who was an old acquaintance from Britain's Elstree Studios. Flying by the seat of his pants, working from what he considered substandard material, and making (another) spy film after the genre's mid-1960s boom had begun to dissipate, *Topaz* became Hitchcock's ultimate example of pure mise-en-scène, a film with which he demonstrated "how an entire moral universe [is] elaborated on the basis of this form and by its very rigor," per Claude Chabrol and Éric Rohmer, who had closed their 1957 book with the claim that "in Hitchcock's work form does not embellish content, it creates it." Hitchcock was too much of an artist, in other words, to let a project like *Topaz* pass by without doing his utmost to infuse it with his signature, to redeem—or transcend—whatever kind of material it might be via his stylistic treatment of it.

"The older he got," writes Edward White, "the more Hitchcock professed that for him filmmaking was about the perfection of form. 'As far as I'm concerned,' he avowed in the 1960s, 'the content is secondary to the handling; the effect I can produce on an audience rather than the subject matter' was the chief interest." In *Topaz*, Hitchcock at times even seems to be making a wry comment on the superfluous nature of scripted dialogue by peppering *Topaz* with long, near-wordless sequences like the opening setpiece of the defectors escaping Copenhagen or a later scene of two characters hashing out a plan to steal secret documents, shot from behind a glass window and without sound. Striking, painterly imagery seems to abound in the film's silent crevices, some perhaps inspired by the paintings of Johannes Vermeer, books of whose work Hitchcock simply left "lying around, knowing that his set decorator and lighting director would flip through them while on break." (One shot of the defector's daughter at a piano seems an obvious recreation of Vermeer's *The Music Lesson.*) More soft, diffused lighting and more experimental color symbolism—especially useful in a convoluted film in which a myriad of characters of different nationalities come and go—continues the aesthetic path being carved out in late Hitchcock, but the picture's steady-trot tempo and matter-of-fact editing add a new flavor appropriate to the film's tonal originality. By doing away with classical dissolves and transitioning scenes only via hard cuts, Hitchcock creates the sense when cutting to an entirely different country that we're merely going to a different room. (The cutting within actual rooms is no joke either; a late conference room scene in France is a visual masterclass in staging and decoupage.) Exotic, international intrigue isn't the point—the form mirrors the bureaucratic soullessness of the narrative. Despite being Hitchcock's lengthiest film, little is dwelt upon; even though we're shuffled fairly briskly from one location to the next, the two hour and twenty-three minute *Topaz* moves like a long, convoluted swamp of a movie. What on successive viewings is actually a pretty legible, linear delineation of a simple spy plot set during the Cuban Missile Crisis (a Russian official defects to America; he tells them of Soviet plans in Cuba and a secret spy ring in the French government; a French agent helps the Americans suss it all out) still feels like a complicated tangle of motivations caught between the personal and the political. More than any of the genre-defining spy films Hitchcock had made since the 1930s that *Topaz* seems to deconstruct, the film—in style and subject—harks back most to Hitchcock's wartime shorts *Bon Voyage* and *Aventure malgache* (both 1944) that he made about the French Resistance for the British Ministry of Information, in French. Even with short runtimes, the films (only widely seen decades later) are easy to get lost in, curt experiments in non-linear style that leave one with the lingering sense of the intelligence game as a largely unfulfilling one of confusion and betrayal. *Topaz*'s experimental structure is by necessity broader—its hopscotching narrative has been compared by Charles Derry to no less than Luis Buñuel's *The Phantom of Liberty* (1974)[22]—but it results in a similarly deromanticized view of intelligence work. The film could be productively lumped with other late, bleak spy movies like Anthony Mann's *A Dandy in Aspic* (1968) or Otto Preminger's *The Human Factor* (1979).

---

[22] Buñuel was one of the few filmmakers who Hitchcock publicly professed admiration for late in his life, having screened many of his films in the weeks leading up to George Cukor's 1972 luncheon celebrating Buñuel's visit to Hollywood. He was notably impressed by *Tristana* (1970) (especially the scenes after Catherine Deneuve has lost her leg to illness), and told Buñuel as much—"Tristana's false leg...." he kept murmuring.

Hitchcock's unglamorous view of spycraft in *Topaz* was also modeled for him by 1965's John le Carré adaptation *The Spy Who Came in from the Cold* (directed by frequent Paul Newman collaborator Martin Ritt), a film he and his staff watched several times; Hitchcock reportedly admired it on a technical level and for its Bond-repudiating realism, if less so on a story level. But contrary to "the tortured intensity of Le Carré's vision," writes Michael Walker, "*Topaz* is quieter, sadder, and without hatred. But it is a film with a terrible sense of emptiness under the surface." Just like underneath *Torn Curtain*'s geopolitical machinations lay the film's main romantic drama, the spy plot in *Topaz* is merely the narrative scaffolding for Hitchcock's real concerns: the emotionally numbing atmosphere of espionage life, the bleakly perfunctory nature of modern political actions, and love as the only meaningful object. The film's dispassionate elegance—what some viewers have mistaken for plain dullness—keeps it on a formal wavelength that accurately reflects the mood of its proceedings. This is one of several strategies Hitchcock uses to simulate for his audience the emotional distance felt by his characters. Another is his casting: with the picture's international scope calling for foreign actors (and still smarting from his *Torn Curtain* wounds), Hitchcock deliberately decentered the film by not using any stars—and in the process decreasing subjectivity, frustrating audience sympathy, and signaling the "bereftness" (as Ken Mogg puts it) that the film is about. An international cast assembled from diverse sources: Swedish actors Per-Axel Arosenius and Sonja Kolthoff as the husband and wife defectors (suggested by Ingmar Bergman on a Stockholm visit while Hitchcock was in Europe for pre-production); French actress Claude Jade (recommended by Truffaut fresh from his *Stolen Kisses* [1968]); French actor Michel Subor as her husband (famed for his part in Godard's *Le petit soldat* [1963] and, later in life, Claire Denis films); German actress Karin Dor as the Cuban Juanita de Cordoba (a Bond girl in 1967's *You Only Live Twice*); the American John Forsythe (a Hitchcock veteran from *The Trouble with Harry* and his final television episode "I Saw the Whole Thing" [1962]);

and staples of French art cinema, Philippe Noiret and Michel Piccoli. Alongside them, Hitchcock chose as his nominal lead the Austrian actor Frederick Stafford, who'd come to Hitchcock's attention playing a French riff on James Bond in the *OSS 117* series and was selected as an approximation of a Cary Grant-as-realistic-Bond type. Yet like other actors called on by Hitchcock to approximate the real thing, a new specimen was created in the process—Stafford, in his European stiffness, becomes the perfect avatar for the film's free-floating emotional repression, Hitchcock's Bressonian "model" (his largely inexperienced, non-Hollywood-trained cast led him to direct their physical movements in unusual detail) who calls to mind what one writer notes about Italian action cinema of the era vis-à-vis George Lazenby's performance in *On Her Majesty's Secret Service* (1969): "It's all look and movement."[23] It's Stafford's appropriately blank face that's cut to every so often, flying on a plane from one part of the narrative to the next (and accompanied by the well-life-goes-on lilt of Maurice Jarre's zither-utilizing theme music[24]), that gives us the drama of each section of the story in miniature, the sense of espionage as a joyless game that changes little except for making those involved "older, tired and a little less capable of being happy," in the words of Vincent Canby.

If it feels like *Topaz* is less interested in traditional surface elements like its plot or its actors, it's in its uptick in detailed formalism, its continuation of *Torn Curtain*'s subversive genre story of spies suffering unheroically, and its unusual perspectival remove from its protagonists that makes the film feel like

---

[23] Both *Topaz* and *On Her Majesty's Secret Service* were released in December 1969; the latter could be read as a kind of parallel film where the emotional cost of espionage is examined in greater depth relative to the average Bond film.

[24] "Hitchcock wanted counterpoint, not sugar on a cake like most Hollywood directors," said Jarre. Originally, Hitchcock had ambitiously desired to seek out Russian composer Dmitri Shostakovich to score the film after being so impressed by his "Babi Yar" symphony. But these inquiries were deemed unfeasible due to the film's implications involving Soviet communism.

Hitchcock, at the end of the experimental '60s, has jumped from the modern to the postmodern: left adrift trying to grab onto traditional Hitchcock elements that just aren't really there, for the viewer it quickly becomes sink or swim. Paula Marantz Cohen suggests that "it is also possible to see *Topaz* as a film pushing against the limitations that narrative film poses in its allegiance to representational realism, and as pointing toward other genres that deal more effectively in abstractions: either abstract design, that allows the viewer to take over (as in abstract art or certain strands of avant-garde film) or the abstraction of ideas, where the specificity of visual representation is left behind (as in philosophy and critical theory)." Or to take a simpler approach, the fact that traditional investment is harder to come by watching *Topaz* is the sign not of directorial indifference (as some have accused) but rather Hitchcock's sardonic, semi-tragic comment on the '60s spy film craze. In 1969, *Topaz* was far enough removed from the novel's basis in the 1962 Cuban Missile Crisis (a fictionalized account of the real-life "Sapphire" affair that scandalized France) for viewers to have lost general interest in something that they already knew the outcome of, leaving Hitchcock the task of reigniting it to his own ends: for example, toward the literal end(s) of the film, all of which are bleakly ironic and withholding of traditional audience satisfaction. (The debacle resulting in multiple endings will be explored momentarily.) It's almost as if the international setting of the film led Hitchcock to abandon as much Hollywood conventionality as he could in favor of a new, global cinematic ambience. Slavoj Žižek asks the compelling question of what would happen "if we re-perceive *Topaz* as a *European art film*—with its complex love triangles, 'cold' marriages where affairs are tolerated, echoes of the old camaraderie of the Resistance, chamber-drama atmosphere, and strangely twisted non-linear narrative? This shift allows us to appreciate the film's qualities properly." Hitchcock's interests and influences were spread so widely by the end of his seventh decade that it makes sense to view his later work in a more artistically and culturally cosmopolitan spirit than one might view his earlier, more distinctly British or American films, and having lived through so many different eras with different emphases explains why Hitchcock's late work can feel dissonant or anachronistic in its layering of ostensibly discordant elements, for example his continued reliance on rear-projection in *Topaz* existing side-by-side with the film's distinctly contemporary interest in political and emotional malaise. It's here one recognizes the aptness of Gilles Deleuze's statement about Hitchcock, that "you might equally well say that he's the last of the classic directors, or the first of the moderns." Sometimes Hitchcock's methods in his later years seemed to stem from nowhere but his own enigmatic self, like his increasingly obsessive attention to "unnecessary" details and miscellaneous minutiae that often puzzled his collaborators—for example, on *Topaz,* holding up filming a French dinner scene "until he could make contact with a Parisian restaurateur to confirm the precise amount in a single serving of pâte de foie gras." Likely originating in a childhood fascination with maps and timetables, this precision resulted in everything from the ambient Greenwich Village street traffic recorded for *Rear Window* and the specificity of Jimmy Stewart's *Vertigo* apartment (he'd had his art director research the homes of single, retired policemen in the San Francisco Bay Area for an acceptable model) to the seemingly trivial details of which airlines depart from where on a given day, the distance between city landmarks, or, on 1972's *Frenzy,* requesting during postproduction "that a member of his team take a trip to the Colburg hotel, one of the film's settings, and record the noise of its elevator in operation, lest any erroneous whirring and clunking make its way onto the soundtrack."

Some, like Brian Moore, have accused Hitchcock of focusing on such trivial matters as a cover for his "profound ignorance of human motivation," and also of having no interest in the stories' political implications for the Cold War-set *Torn Curtain* and *Topaz*. There's a much better case to be made for the latter charge, although the *implications* of political situations didn't totally escape Hitchcock even if the situations themselves did. As Richard T. Jameson has written, "*Topaz* isn't 'about' the Cuban missile crisis, any more than *Notorious* was about uranium ore in wine bottles. At a time when streets, campuses, and 'youth movies' were filled with rants against 'the Establishment', Hitchcock filmed a supremely lucid, supremely disenchanted critique of just what Establishments, Governments, and Powers were up to, and how much it cost in individual human suffering…. There was no finer political film in that turbulently politicized era [than *Topaz*].") There's a running theme in the film of how the brunt of that suffering falls on the shoulders of those lowest on the political totem pole, everyday people conscripted to do the dirty work of bureaucratic button-pushers thousands of miles away. A character in Hitchcock's final, unproduced script *The Short Night* voices a similar critique: "Spying and espionage. Everybody suffers from it. The gains are vague and abstract. And the losses are all personal." So while Hitchcock did take pains to capture something realistic about politics and spying in *Topaz*—having been criticized by Uris for being out of touch with the realities of spy work, Hitchcock arranged for a number of intelligence briefings on the subject, including one from former deputy inspector general of the CIA George Horkan—it was all toward the goal of saying something about the personal, individual consequences of ideology in action. (The ultimate modern example of which had marked Hitchcock deeply, as he'd played a role in organizing footage of the Nazi concentration camps at the end of World War II.) Even though an ostensibly anti-communist film in line with the average political perspective of other Hollywood Cold War items, Michael Walker writes that "*Topaz* is the first spy film I've seen which is written from a pro-Western angle and then directed so that this is cancelled out in our overall sympathy for the protagonists, and the universal sense of suffering and loss." Indeed, when Uris was writing his first draft of the script, Hitchcock had instructed him "to write the intelligence agents *and* the revolutionaries as human beings, without regard to politics." This is perhaps another indication that for Hitchcock his spy films were never really just spy films (whether partaking in the atmosphere of '30s or '40s European fascism or the '60s Cold War), but rather melodramas filtered through them—their scenarios of pressurized situations, tested loyalties, and emotional suspense a convenient arena for life-and-death reflections on love. "Hitch, in the late winter of his life, didn't care about politics, only passion," wrote screenwriter David Freeman, who worked with Hitchcock near the end of his life. "He never said it to me, at least not in words, but I think he thought of the political content of the story as a great, cosmic MacGuffin; the idealogues were the dullards, those who fought for love were vital and worth our concern."

The final shot of the film—of a newspaper announcing the end of the crisis superimposed with glimpses of the film's victims' tortured faces and then indifferently tossed aside—is a succinct encapsulation of *Topaz*'s main emotional idea.[25] But this shot, depending on which version of the film you're watching, is preceded by one of three different endings that all color with slightly different shades the closing frames of this downbeat movie: 1) a pistol duel set in an empty French sports stadium in which the Topaz spy ring's leader (Michel Piccoli) gets taken out by a hidden sniper; 2) a dual departure on an airport tarmac, Stafford and Piccoli waving goodbye to each other as they get on separate planes, the latter headed for Moscow[26]; or 3) a cobbled-together shot of Piccoli entering his apartment, with a gunshot implying his suicide. Hitchcock's preferred ending by far was the duel, an idea inspired by a striking image he'd seen in a magazine of a duel being fought on the field of an empty stadium with nothing but product advertisements looking on. Exhaustive research had revealed that clandestine duels still took place in Paris and Hitchcock studied the exact protocol for the ritual, which he viewed as a logical continuation of the film's theme of espi-

---

[25] A shot actually filmed by a second unit headed by Claude Chabrol, who Hitchcock had asked to shoot the film's French exteriors (according to his explicit instructions/storyboards) after he felt too ill to come to France himself. Chabrol and his cinematographer Jean Rabier began but after a few days Hitchcock recovered enough to come to France and do the work himself.

[26] Which contains a cheekily meta final line spoken by Stafford: "Anyway, that's the end of Topaz."

onage as a chivalrous yet bloody game. (A moment shot but never used showed a groundskeeper washing the blood out of the stadium grass afterwards.) But this scene that Hitchcock had devoted more attention to than any other part of the film was laughed off the screen by a San Francisco preview audience, a group which had largely been culled from fans of Uris's book (where no duel appears). Despite some positive responses from other parts of the audience, the producers at Universal got spooked and implored Hitchcock to drop the duel and settle for another ending. Yet the ending Hitchcock filmed to replace it—of Piccoli boarding a plane for Moscow, which at least maintained some of the dramatic irony of the duel ending—was then subjected to concerns about French censorship, the government's touchy attitude toward the material already having been made evident by President Charles de Gaulle's public lambasting of the book and by a temporary delay at the start of filming caused by cultural minister André Malraux's withdrawal of the film's shooting permit on anti-Gaullist charges. To let a communist spy and French traitor walk away without punishment was deemed too risky. The suicide ending was devised by someone at Universal as a way of avoiding the issue, even though the footage needed to do it technically didn't even exist—the only shot they had of a man entering Piccoli's apartment wasn't of Piccoli but rather of Philippe Noiret, so only some tight trimming and contextual editing get the idea across. A "four-month standoff" (according to Bill Krohn) between Hitchcock and Universal ended in Hitchcock giving in, tired and dispirited. "I could have fought the decision," he later said, "but it didn't seem worthwhile." The film was released in different forms in different places, some getting the suicide and some the plane ending, and in some countries with around 20 minutes trimmed from the film (another capitulation to the studio). Hitchcock maintained that the suicide ending was a "horrible compromise," something he viewed during post-production as an in-emergency-only solution that he even tried to have assistant Peggy Robertson hide so it wouldn't be used. The only reason we have Hitchcock's preferred duel ending today is because he smuggled the footage out of Universal and stashed it in his garage, enabling it to eventually be found after his death by Richard Franklin (the future director of *Psycho II* [1983], who along with Peter Bogdanovich and Curtis Harrington had been invited onto the *Topaz* set) and included along with the other two endings on home video releases of the film. Yet even today, as Bill Krohn has pointed out, a complete "Director's Cut" of *Topaz* that truly deserves the name isn't available on DVD, as a replaced music cue and a few minutes of missing footage keep it from matching the 148-minute preview version, "which the director liked enough to cut the negative before the screening, with his original ending."[27]

Hitchcock's embarrassment about the whole fiasco led him to essentially disown the film (as he often casually did with films of his that he saw as containing compromising elements), which hasn't helped *Topaz*'s reputation any more than the slew of negative critical appraisals have. But at the very least, "Hitchcock, his composer, and his sound technicians were all proud of the European ambience and elegance of their creation," according to Jack Sullivan, and Hitchcock's cameo in the film—as a man being wheeled in a wheelchair who suddenly rises to stand on his own—seems to suggest Hitchcock thumbing his nose at those who'd been accusing him of senility during his late period. His cinematic agility was still intact, thank you very much, no matter that he'd been prodded into tackling less-than-thrilling material by producers who just wanted him to repeat former successes. Bill Krohn passes along the theory courtesy of film writer Ronnie Schieb that with *Topaz* (and *Torn Curtain* to a degree) Hitchcock was offering allegorical commentary on his own situation: "Be cold, do your job" is what he was being told after the passionate, extravagant "failure" of *Marnie,* just like

---

[27] Apparently the full preview cut (although still with the music cue that replaces Jarre's end-credits theme with a Russian military march) is available on a 1987 laserdisc release, according to Bill Krohn, whose article in the August 2001 issue of *Video Watchdog* remains the most detailed accounting of *Topaz*'s post-production drama and resultant versions.

Stafford (i.e., Hitchcock) is essentially told to do in *Topaz* when receiving assignments from John Forsythe (i.e., Lew Wasserman). But regardless of whether Hitchcock's next film was to be chosen by him or assigned to him, one thing was certain: it would have to be cheaper. At around $4 million, *Topaz* was his most expensive film ever, and it failed to justify its budget either at the box office or with the critics. Hitchcock spent 1970 reading and viewing endlessly and extensively: trips to the theater; an avid diet of books that ranged in subject matter from biographies, fiction, and politics to technical/scientific matters and legal history; and a packed screening schedule that included everything he could get his hands on, from awards contenders, Disney films, and—dutifully—everything produced by Universal, to foreign pictures, works from aging colleagues, and even blaxploitation and youth-exploitation movies (Antonioni's *Zabriskie Point*, for example). Anything that might spark his inspiration. When all was said and done, Universal put out a story that claimed Hitchcock "had worked his way through fourteen hundred projects" before deciding to make what would become *Frenzy*. Although still hoping to avoid irritating Universal with his choice, Hitchcock had regained some creative bargaining power by trading the rights to both *Psycho* and his television series for a controlling stake in the company, making him the "third- or fourth-largest stockholder," according to Dan Auiler. Thus his ability to make *Frenzy*, a choice that didn't thrill Universal—it was a different project from 1967's axed *Frenzy/Kaleidoscope*, but it had obvious parallels in subject and brashness of approach—but one they acquiesced to on the provision that it be made cheaply and quickly. Hitchcock's cost-cutting decision to shoot it in a British studio and on location in London was therefore a gesture of economy more than a matter of latent homesickness, and it also conveniently provided an Atlantic Ocean-sized swath of relative independence. The new-old environment led to one of the least turbulent productions Hitchcock had had in a while: a fast preproduction, a smooth collaboration on the script, and a shoot halving the expenses of *Topaz* that was marked by the familial atmosphere of British crews (often gathering for a drink at the pub after the day's work) and the professionalism of well-trained and unpretentious London stage actors.

Hitchcock's homecoming was treated with all the appropriate fanfare, but he wasn't back to revel in some idealized version of the city he grew up in. *Frenzy* would be a reprisal nearly a half-century later of 1927's *The Lodger* (subtitled *A Story of the London Fog*), the film that put Hitchcock on the map as the biggest name in British cinema, and it begins similarly with the discovery of a dead body on the side of the Thames before proceeding to draw a (nastier, more contemporary) picture of a city in the grips of a Ripper-like killer. In the words of Edward White, Hitchcock was back "telling the world that despite all this talk of a new, swinging London, this was the same glorious and rotten place it had always been, the greatest shithole on earth." The material—based on Arthur La Bern's 1966 novel *Goodbye Piccadilly, Farewell Leicester Square* and scripted by Anthony Shaffer of recent *Sleuth* fame (simultaneously being made into Joseph L. Mankiewicz's final movie)—was decidedly unsexy, and the film that came from it grimy in every way that, say, Hitchcock's '50s Paramount films had been elegant. Characters are mired in the quotidian disorganization of city life rather than standing aloof from the studio-ized version of it; in the place of a prim and proper Grace Kelly or a Cary Grant in a perfectly cut suit, there's Jon Finch sweating and raging in an old-fashioned, leather-patched suit coat. He's the "innocent man" on the run whose story is woven together with Barry Foster's "itinerary of a killer" (as François Truffaut termed the two types of Hitchcock films he experimentally combines here), but to riff on another British Hitchcock film shot at Pinewood studios that begins with a body being washed up on shore—1937's *Young and Innocent*—Finch's character is presented to us in a way that makes him seem not so young and not entirely innocent. *Frenzy* is a "wrong man" film like *Young and Innocent* or *The 39 Steps* but modernized in a way that recognizes the nearly 30 years of intervening British film production, from the postwar industry and Hammer horror to the British New Wave and its attendant "kitchen-sink" realism. Hitchcock had kept tabs on all of it, and *Frenzy* is the work of a filmmaker confident in his ability to shift settings and styles and to absorb—and then outdo—the very work being made in those modes, while still retaining his Hitchcockian essence. Peter Hutchings makes the additional point that another "important part of British film production in the 1960s and early 1970s was the work of, among others, Losey, Kubrick, Peckinpah, Polanski,[28] and Antonioni," all foreign directors whose British work seemed to push the boundaries of cinematic representation (often in the guise of exploitation films). Hitchcock, who "himself made *Frenzy* as a tourist rather than as a permanent resident," could be counted among them despite his British roots.

Yet Hitchcock's three decades of Americanization had merely complicated his Britishness rather than ever coming close to erasing it, and the British connection loomed especially large at the end of his career: excepting *Topaz*, every film he made from *The Birds* on was either based on a British text or scripted by a British author. From the very beginning, however, Hitchcock had had one foot in both industries: his initiation into filmmaking had come at the Paramount-precursor Famous Players-Lasky branch in London, where the studio had an American atmosphere and the personnel were mostly Americans. Even when he made the move to America in 1939, of his first four films in his new country, three (*Rebecca, Foreign Correspondent,* and *Suspicion*) were more British in setting than American—inaugurating the new Anglo-American tonal mixture that Hitchcock's middle career would flourish under, sometimes leaning more one way than the other depending on the project. While certain elements of Englishness stuck with him (he maintained the practice of the director of photography being in charge of lighting and framing shots and leaving the actual operating to the camera operator), other aspects of himself demonstrated a more American spirit—for example, Hitchcock never really

---

[28] Whose *Macbeth* (1971) featured Jon Finch in his most important role pre-*Frenzy*.

"got" the British honors system, and was knighted seemingly as an afterthought (of both England's and his self's) just months before his death in 1980. The fact that he only became an American citizen officially in 1955—five years later than his wife Alma, and exactly halfway between his departure from England and his return for *Frenzy*—neatly suggests the way both national atmospheres played their role in forming Hitchcock's identity, cinematic and otherwise. But *Frenzy* (his first fully British-shot film since 1950's *Stage Fright*) naturally leaned heavily British, and Hitchcock populated his crew with British collaborators from his past: sound recordist Peter Handford (from *Under Capricorn*); cinematographer Gil Taylor, who had recently shot a string of films for Roman Polanski but had been a clapper boy way back on Hitchcock's *Number 17* (1932); and actress Elsie Randolph, who has the distinction of appearing in two Hitchcock films 40 years apart, having played in *Rich and Strange* (1931) before being brought back as the hotel manager in *Frenzy*.

The Britishness of the film, however, is a peculiar one particular to Hitchcock himself. Rather than shoot an objective contemporary London, Hitchcock sought out the London of his mind, one that had been left largely unchanged since the pre-war days. "The London here is an alternate reality," writes Edward White, "one in which the fog has lifted, fashions and technology have moved on, but in every other respect it has been frozen in 1939." *Frenzy* became an exercise in deliberate anachronism, a reflection of his own status as "a Victorian relic in the thick of the twentieth century" (Hitchcock still showed up to work every day in his usual dark suit and tie) and an experiment in untethering story and setting from concrete temporal markers. Newer locations like the London Hilton hotel and New Scotland Yard that Hitchcock agreed to incorporate clash with the childhood sites he was adamant about including, like the Old Bailey courthouse (which had been recreated for 1947's *The Paradine Case*) and Covent Garden fruit-and-vegetable market, which Hitchcock wanted to get on film before its scheduled 1974 relocation. The latter was long-familiar to Hitchcock—his father William, a greengrocer who died in 1914, had often taken him there. (This sense of history was amplified while shooting in Covent Garden by a man who came up to Hitchcock and claimed to remember his father.) On scouting trips, Hitchcock was consistently drawn to older spots he was familiar with, locations with old-world character—he spoke about how newer pubs just felt wrong, for example, that for the film they needed a good pub with dark wood in it. The most noticeable anachronism of all, however, was the film's dialogue, which Arthur La Bern (no fan of the film made from his book) criticized as "a curious amalgam of an old Aldwych farce, *Dixon of Dock Green* and that almost forgotten *No Hiding Place*." (Low comedy stage plays from the 1920s and '30s and two 1950s and '60s television police shows, respectively.) But Hitchcock "was intractable about not modernizing the dialogue of the picture," recalled Anthony Shaffer, "and he kept inserting antique phrases I knew would cause the British public a hearty laugh or even some annoyance." Far from the slips of an old man, it was intentional: assistant Peggy Robertson later recalled that the deliberate use of "an outdated language" by the main character was because he "was living in the past." It's more of a symbolic gesture than a realist one—Finch's divorced, down on his luck ex-RAF man could just as easily *not* speak that way—and thus part of a complex fictional tapestry that Hitchcock is weaving together as a movie. Joseph Sgammato has proposed that "perhaps the Hitchcock of this late film in a long career is like the Cervantes of the last part of *Don Quixote* [published in 1615, when Cervantes was in his late sixties], where a deepened awareness of form becomes part of the form itself, and the line between reality and Don Quixote's imagined version of it becomes harder for the reader to distinguish since they are, for him, both fictional, and where Cervantes is no longer simply writing, nor the reader simply reading, a story any more."

Frenzy runs the tonal and stylistic gamut with a similar disregard for conventional cohesiveness, melding silent cinema techniques with contemporary realist trends, documentary naturalism with heightened "murder noir" touches, unflinching drama with edgy black humor. The opening of

the film announces this contrapuntal tendency via an incon-
gruously fanfaric musical theme seemingly out of place for
what we know—and will immediately be proven—to be a
"dark" movie.[29] But this darkness manifests itself not only in
the sordid dramatic details of the film's crimes but in what is
easily the darkest humor of Hitchcock's career, not just dotted
throughout in wonderfully uncomfortable comic interludes
(the exotic homemade dinners between the police inspector
and his wife, for example) but suffusing the whole narrative
to cosmic, darkly ironic ends, from the plight of Jon Finch's
character who can't catch a break to save his life to the film's
final moments: an abrupt comic reversal where, à la *Dial M
for Murder*'s ending, the ghastly proceedings are cut short by
an anticlimactic confrontation (and a cheekily subversive final
shot of a dropped suitcase). *Frenzy*'s tour de force setpiece,
of Barry Foster desperately trying to retrieve his missing tie
pin from a corpse in the back of a potato truck, takes Hitchcock's traditional suspense to new, blackly humorous levels.
John Belton writes of how "Hitchcock carefully calculates his
effects" here and then "brilliantly pushes them beyond traditional aesthetic limits," resulting in a "horror more grotesque
than that in any other Hitchcock film; its humor blacker and
more perverse." Hitchcock viewed *Frenzy* as an opportunity
to experiment with humor again after two films where he felt
held back by the awkwardness of having foreigners speak
English (indeed, *Torn Curtain* and *Topaz* are among the least
humorous of Hitchcock's works). It was the black humor
of *Alfred Hitchcock Presents* taken to the grisly extremes of

---

[29] Ron Goodwin's score was directed by Hitchcock's detailed tonal
instructions. "If Hitchcock hadn't directed me, I would have written
something with a macabre lilt to it. But he wanted no hint of the
horror to come." In other words, he would have written the kind
of music supplied by Henry Mancini, who was originally hired for
the score and then subsequently replaced after Hitchcock wasn't
thrilled by his musically severe offerings—offerings written without
instructions, according to Mancini, who had given Hitchcock what
he thought he wanted, only to find out later that Hitchcock really
wanted a lighter pop score that provided contrast.

post-Code, 1970s filmmaking; the film's obsessive (and darkly comic) interest in food may very well have been anticipated by a 1958 episode of the show called "Lamb to the Slaughter," a favorite of Hitchcock's that had *Vertigo*'s Barbara Bel Geddes cook and then serve the murder weapon (a frozen leg of lamb) she used to kill her husband with to unsuspecting police investigators in her kitchen.[30] For the intensely physical, material, and suffocating film, Hitchcock utilized the freedoms offered him by the Production Code's recent demise to get up close and personal with his perpetrators and victims—in scenes like the potato truck episode or, even more flagrantly, the early rape-murder of the protagonist's ex-wife, where the crucial benefit of the extra detail relates to "see[ing] the killer at work," per Hitchcock. It was part of his continuing on-screen dissection of the serial killer mind, this time one inspired by the English rapist-killer John Christie (who strangled at least eight women in the 1940s and early '50s[31]) and informed by Hitchcock's extensive reviewing of medical and psychological literature on sexual pathology. But this newfound explicitness wasn't the betrayal of principles that many criticized it as; Charles Barr (author of *English Hitchcock*) writes of tending "always to revert to the idea that Hitchcock was the supremely calculating exploiter of the full range of the medium's possibilities," and yet also recognized that the "freedoms of post-1960 allowed him to widen his canvas, as it were, without renouncing the eloquently allusive methods that he had been using and refining throughout his career." Despite the violence and nudity in *Frenzy*'s most talked about scene, it's still meticulously cut together—like *Psycho*'s shower scene—in a way that gives the *impression* of violence more than it actually shows it, and thus making clear two things: that accusations of Hitch-

---

[30] *Frenzy* might also be the closest Hitchcock came to making his idea for a "food film" that would follow the entire process from cultivation to consumption to disposal of a city's food supply.

[31] The husband of one of Christie's victims, Timothy Evans, was falsely charged with his wife's murder and hanged for the crime in 1950, which further parallels *Frenzy*'s wrong-man plot. The case was a major impetus for the UK's abolishing of the death penalty in 1965.

cock getting off on the explicitness are false (if set reports of Hitchcock hating having to shoot it weren't enough), and that in *Frenzy* his sympathies are entirely with the female victims. That he shoots the next murder—or rather chooses *not* to shoot it at all—in a completely "eloquently allusive" manner speaks volumes about what Hitchcock was trying to do with the movie; the famous reverse track away from Barry Foster and Anna Massey—whose presence explicitly links *Frenzy* with Michael Powell's proto-slasher *Peeping Tom* (1960)[32]— down the stairwell and (via an invisible cut à la *Rope*) into the streets simply triggers our memory of the first murder and leaves us with a sympathetic, totally non-voyeuristic pit in our stomach.[33]

---

[32] Powell's highly personal solo film came out just months before Hitchcock's *Psycho* and was similarly groundbreaking as a kind of London giallo, although where *Psycho* sent Hitchcock to even greater heights of fame *Peeping Tom* essentially spelled the beginning of the end of Powell's career. Massey, who plays the young female protagonist in *Peeping Tom*, was the daughter of actor Raymond Massey and the goddaughter of director John Ford, who had given her her first movie role in his own British film, *Gideon's Day* (1958), retitled *Gideon of Scotland Yard* in America. (In his autobiography Raymond Massey recalls that he was on the set of Ford's *The Hurricane* [1938] when he first got news of Anna's birth and turned to the first person he saw to ask him to be godfather, and it happened to be Ford.) Also noteworthy is Susan Travers (in the miniscule, thankless role of the final victim), who had a role in *Peeping Tom* as well and was the daughter of actress Linden Travers (who had acted in Hitchcock's *The Lady Vanishes*).

[33] Reams of feminist criticism have been written on (and usually against) *Frenzy*, yet it feels significant to me that, even though some of them get offed, the women are by far the nicest, most sympathetic, and most productive characters in the film. (The inspector's wife could be credited for the only real justice done in the film, having theorized Finch's probable innocence while cooking for her husband.) Hitchcock's realism is in efficiently making the women three-dimensional characters, with Anna Massey and Barbara Leigh-Hunt especially the kind of nice ladies who aren't overly this or that but simply want the best for Finch (that they love or have ever loved him is sufficient evidence that he can't be all bad), and therefore as victims emphasize the unmotivated misogyny and male psychopathy of Foster's killer.

The experimental sound work on this second murder—the ambient noises of London street life flooding back onto the soundtrack as the camera descends, implicitly drowning out the victim's cries—is just one of the many small ways Hitchcock shapes *Frenzy* into the "realistic nightmare" he was aiming for. He explicitly told DP Gil Taylor that "despite the gruesome story, [he] had no desire to make a 'Hammer horror'." They shot on the less glossy Eastmancolor film stock and leaned into the vitality and chaos of London city life, capturing the garish explosion of color and objects and faces and dirt of Covent Garden and surrounding locations, only to contrast them more vividly with the blackness of the night scenes. The film's visceral realism was a step beyond anything else in Hitchcock's career, a reminder that, despite his reputation as a world-creating expressionist, his early British films had been praised for their world-capturing realism; that this documentary impulse was still within him was perhaps demonstrated by his narration of 1969's *Hitchcock on Grierson,* a 45-minute Scottish television special paying tribute to influential documentarian John Grierson. *Frenzy* certainly gains something from its location work that one can't imagine being recreated on a soundstage (although even Hitchcock's sets had their usual termitic detail—the Hilton hotel's people were amazed by the dead-on copy of one of their rooms upon visiting.) John Orr has written of how *Frenzy*'s homage is not to the early German expressionism so important to Hitchcock's work but rather the social realist "New Objectivity" movement that emerged to counter it: "*Frenzy* is a naturalistic horror film that dispenses with distorted POV shots or subjective impressions. It shows an actual world in no way hallucinatory, one that on the surface of things would be mundane and ordinary were it not for the existence of a serial-killer and another wrong-man solution from the dilatory arm of the English Law. This is rape and serial killing without any melodrama at all." The dissonance between this pressurized, quotidian realism and the film's anachronistic world-creation tips *Frenzy* just off-balance enough to leave the viewer without traditional bearings, thus turning the experience of watching the film into the discomfiting moral endurance test it is.

Not helping matters is the fact that Hitchcock once again leaves us stranded without a star, or a sympathetic principal character, or anybody else to latch on to for the film's duration other than a disgruntled and belligerent middle-aged man. (Though Finch was just under 30 at the time of filming, he's meant to be playing older; the book's protagonist is nearing 50.) All we're able to do is witness blankly as he's driven to wit's end by a psychopath he then swears bloody revenge on, and then is only saved from committing the actual murder he's in jail for by a one-two punch of bleakly ironic facts: the person he bludgeons in their sleep isn't the killer, it's a girl; and the girl isn't sleeping, she's already dead. Hitchcock termed Finch's character a "loser" and a "nonhero." Thomas Leitch writes that "Hitchcock's turn from the psychological exploration of sympathetic principals reaches a logical extreme" in *Frenzy*, continuing the pattern of disillusioned identity from *Marnie* to *Torn Curtain* to *Topaz*. The protagonists of these late films are closer to being antiheroes than heroes, characters meant to subvert the traditional qualities of leads toward more oblique narrative or thematic ends. In *Frenzy*, the most basic subversion is of Hitchcock's very own "wrong man" trope: Finch, playing unlikeable from the jump, is a long way removed from Henry Fonda's morally upstanding patriarch in *The Wrong Man*. By using non-stars, and casting performers that aren't classically beautiful (more or less everyone is middle-aged, with the expressive physiognomies of character actors[34]), Hitchcock once again asserts himself as the main attraction of his film (an assertion borne out by the film's advertising). "When passers-by at Covent Garden asked me who the star of the film was," recalled Jon Finch, "I told them 'Alfred Hitchcock.'" Indeed, Finch and Hitchcock butted heads on set in

---

[34] "[Hitchcock] said, late in his life, that film 'begins with the actor's face. It is to the features of this face that the eye of the spectator will be guided, and it is the organisation of these oval shapes within the rectangle of the screen, for a purpose, that exercises the director.'"

ways that made it fairly obvious Hitchcock was deliberately playing it up for the sake of Finch's performance, keeping him ever so slightly alienated and on his toes as matched his character. But the idea of late Hitchcock protagonists as completely unsympathetic shouldn't be overplayed; they all have reasons for their behavior, and to the degree that those reasons reflect complex human characteristics, they are indeed sympathetic. As *Frenzy*'s Richard Blaney, for example, Finch is playing a kind of early-mid-life crisis version of the "angry young man" of the British New Wave—not entirely likeable, but not entirely unsympathetic either, just a complicated human being faced with obstacles that don't always bring out the best in him. In *Frenzy* he's cursed with rotten luck and has little to work with other than a writhing discomfort at his own place in life. "Life has been very hard on him," Hitchcock was quoted as saying in one interview, a phrase that despite the film's abrasiveness suggests a genuine tenderness toward the character, a man simply caught up in a world that—to use the words of *Shadow of a Doubt*'s final line—"seems to go crazy now and then."

Frenzy became Hitchcock's biggest success in years, premiering to a standing ovation at the 1972 Cannes Film Festival and providing evidence (to those who still felt they needed it) that the "Hitchcock touch" hadn't completely disappeared. But Hitchcock was never one to rest on his laurels, and 1972 and 1973 brought on another bout of home reading, film screenings, and the like in search of inspiration for his next picture. After a studio lunch with Hitchcock, two young television writers recalled the title of a recent book Hitchcock might be interested in, English author Victor Canning's *The Rainbird Pattern* (1972); the copy subsequently sent to their house passed muster with Alma, who recommended it to her husband, who now had the story ingredients for his new film. Some colleagues were slightly puzzled by Hitchcock's choice in material, which seemed to go in multiple directions (as one couple tries to track down the long-lost illegitimate nephew of an old woman, another carries out kidnappings for hefty jewelry ransoms on another plane of the story), but this playful, two-pronged structure was exactly what most attracted Hitchcock—"the idea of two separate and distinct stories slowly moving towards each other and eventually meeting and becoming one story," according to Ernest Lehman, who, after Hitchcock's plans to reteam with Anthony Shaffer fell through, was recruited to write the script. Eventually retitled *Family Plot* and released in 1976, it would be Hitchcock's most intricate structural gambit in a late period full of them: *Torn Curtain*'s POV-flip and eventual synthesis, *Topaz*'s international baton-passing, *Frenzy*'s interweaving of killer and wrong man. The last had been a furthering of Hitchcock's career-long interest in the "double" motif most strongly represented by *Shadow of a Doubt* and *Strangers on a Train*, and *Family Plot* in some ways "doubles" the double by mirroring couples rather than individuals. It also "doubles" the story in a way similar to *Psycho*'s narrative bifurcation, except instead of making a clean split down the middle, *Family Plot* slices its two stories up into little pieces and weaves them via crosscutting and cinematic gamesmanship. The experiment of it, however, is to keep the two strands separate—to keep the couples unaware of their doubles—until the very end of the film, which provides Hitchcock ample space to play up the kind of dramatic ironies he relishes; meta-narrative humor abounds. Both of Hitchcock's 1970s films partake in this kind of overarching, newly postmodern Hitchcockian humor despite their polar opposites moods: what's played as deeply black humor in *Frenzy* is, in *Family Plot,* played as what you might in turn call "white humor," a kind of pleasantly devilish, smirking sense of comedy that offers its own unique tonal magic. *Family Plot* is defined by a lightness of tone that Hitchcock variously compared to *The Lady Vanishes* (where he treated serious matters in a comic register), the idea of Ernst Lubitsch making a mystery thriller, and Noël Coward's *Blithe Spirit* (1941; David Lean's film adaptation came in 1945), whose bubbly spiritualist played by Margaret Rutherford offered a template from which Hitchcock created his own comic-realist version of the character type.[35] With a tonal kookiness more akin to *The Trouble with Harry* than anything else in Hitchcock, *Family Plot* is an experiment in what could be called "humor noir" (a phrase Vladimir Nabokov used in comparing his and Hitchcock's work). The film's performances—from Bruce Dern, Barbara Harris, William Devane, and Karen Black in the lead roles—adroitly straddle the line between seriousness and slapstick, and the film almost takes on a self-parodic tone—perhaps aptly, as Lehman had also written the self-aware capstone of Hitchcock's late middle period, *North by Northwest*. A scene with Dern and Harris careening their way down a mountain highway (their car's brakes having been sabotaged), for example, quickly moves from straight suspense into a ridiculous and hilarious Hitchcockian parody of it recalling the drunk driving scenes in *Notorious* and *North by Northwest*, Harris trying to hold onto Dern for dear life so rabidly that it makes it more difficult for him to drive; repeated cuts from a POV shot of the road back to the couple find Harris in increasingly contorted positions, her feet somehow having made their way up to Dern's face.[36] "We've passed the point of believability," writes Carlos Valladares, "and we're into a realm of fantastic parody that bests Mel Brooks's weak imitations in *High Anxiety* [1977]"—a film, by the way, that Hitchcock was "so flattered" by that "he sent Brooks a case of Château Haut-Brion."

A London *Times* reviewer noted that *Family Plot* "has the geometric ingenuity of the later American work, along with the delight in quirky character that marked Hitchcock's British period." It's this strangely generative mixture that gives the film its bounce and vigor as—alternatively, simultaneously—

---

[35] Hitchcock had just seen some of Coward's final plays on Broadway in 1974, a year after the latter's death, presented as *Noël Coward in Two Keys.*

[36] Contributing to both the comic surreality and the sense of self-parody is the obvious use of rear projection—which technically wasn't rear projection, but rather "an experimental technique [Universal] was developing which optically composited the background into the film frame."

a rigorous art object and a laid-back character piece. Voicing his fears that Hitchcock was losing himself in his "obsession with structure" as they worked on the script, Lehman was countered by a Hitchcock proclamation: "This film is going to be made by its characters!" It became true in more ways than one. For starters, the cast—culled from the new generation of actors, and none of them big enough names to offend Hitchcock's budget (as the Universal-floated Al Pacino or Jack Nicholson would have)—all brought their own playful peculiarities to outside-of-the-box roles: New Hollywood mainstay Karen Black played against her counter-culture type as a wig-wearing femme fatale; as her partner, William Devane—Hitchcock's first choice for the role, but who only became available after he let go of his second choice mid-shoot—is one of Hitchcock's best villains, a smilingly sinister, almost polite antagonist in the mold of *North by Northwest*'s James Mason who savors the film's sparkling black comedy more than anyone; Bruce Dern, who'd already played a small role in *Marnie*, probably "got" Hitchcock more than any other actor of the late period, and parlayed that understanding into some delightfully offbeat choices[37]; and Barbara Harris's spontaneity and creativity led Hitchcock to single her out—"of all the actors he had ever worked with"—as the one who "had made the most important personal contribution to the film of elements he had never even thought of, without any need for urging or obvious 'direction' from him." But what really allowed the characters

---

[37] The strength of their relationship stemmed from Dern's treatment of Hitchcock not as an unapproachable God-like figure, but as a regular human being: on the first day of shooting he made the bold movie of sitting right next to Hitchcock and pronouncing, "I don't give a shit if you like this or not, but I'm sitting next to you for ten weeks." His temerity was rewarded. A young Laura Dern (Bruce's daughter and future actress) visited the set and was treated with great generosity by Hitchcock; she later recalled that the experience "was a real turning point where I saw the relationship between a filmmaker and an actor. You guys had such an incredible shorthand that I fell in love with. I think I didn't really understand acting, and necessarily the process of storytelling, but I fell in love with the way a director and an actor work together and come together."

to make the film was the fact that Hitchcock, inspired by his actors, *encouraged improvisation*, and even began to improvise some of his shots based on what the actors were doing. Dern intuitively understood that Hitchcock's intense pre-planning created not an iron cage, but a pliable architecture under which everyone was then free to make interesting choices: "He's as flexible a director as anybody that I have ever worked with. He just is flexible *in his form.* In other words, he has a very strict form, but his form is so good and so right it enables an actor who is willing to take a few chances a certain amount of safety features. You can afford to fail with Mr. Hitchcock, because you're in a pretty darn good form. The architecture is designed so that you can try to do things within it as long as you're within his design." Having witnessed firsthand, Dern knew how far this Hitchcock was from the Hitchcock of *Marnie,* where ad-libbing was frowned upon, the storyboards reigned supreme, and the power of a star close-up was still key. Hitchcock's cinema had long outgrown the need for star personae—there aren't even "parts that would have lent themselves to these personae," notes Paula Marantz Cohen—and instead he relied relaxedly on the pleasure and professionalism that emanated from working with engaging, distinctive, and baggage-free performers. "I never know what you're gonna do next," Hitchcock told Dern. "I know that the frame is perfect. I know the shot works perfectly. All I want is to be entertained." Hitchcock sometimes took pressure off his actors by detailing aloud to them the exact number and location of cuts he'd use in the editing room for a scene, leaving even veteran crew members amazed by his grasp on cinematic minutiae. But the greatest shock of *Family Plot*'s shoot was watching Hitchcock make what "may be the only film in history made 'against' its storyboards," according to Bill Krohn. "It is not just a matter of detail: the storyboards are from a different film—a film by 'Alfred Hitchcock'. In *Family Plot* Hitchcock overturns the principles of his cinema and makes a film that belongs to the cinema of the eternally young, along with *Seven Women* (1966), *A King in New York* (1957), and *Le Petit Theatre de Jean Renoir* (1970)."

The storyboard with Hitchcock's usually detailed camera moves as drawn by Tom Wright *was* on set, but as reported by eyewitness John Russell Taylor in his 1978 biography of Hitchcock, "I never saw Hitch himself refer to it during shooting." Hitchcock instead freed himself from "the determinism of his own storyboards" (Krohn) and switched to a method privileging the capture of performance, favoring long shots and medium shots over close-ups, and introducing a wonderfully invigorating use of pans and zooms that constantly recontextualize his cinematic space.[38] A newly abstract space, too: having transposed Canning's novel from rural England to California, but tired of the hackneyed use of San Francisco ("I think if I see one more car chase bouncing over those hills I shall scream"), Hitchcock instructed his assistant director Howard Kazanjian (soon to be a producer for Lucas and Spielberg) to remove all signs and names that located the story in northern California—"I want it no city." In reality it would be a blend of Los Angeles and San Francisco, but by eliminating all the signifiers from Hollywood and its north Californian brother Hitchcock and cinematographer Leonard South (longtime camera operator for Robert Burks) created a strange, postmodern American geography perfect for this geometric tale of cars and graves and diamonds. The resultant formal play is most obvious in a scene where Dern chases a potential source of information through a cemetery, captured in a long overhead shot deliberately modeled on the late abstract paintings of Dutch artist Piet Mondrian. A "living Mondrian," as he called it.[39] Elsewhere, in the opening séance scene set in an old

---

[38] Although never to this extent, Hitchcock had used zooms before, like the one in *Frenzy* zooming up to a woman on a balcony overlooking the park where the wanted protagonist is residing, or the one in *Strangers on a Train* zooming in on Robert Walker watching Farley Granger at the tennis club, which was one of the earliest uses of a zoom lens in Hollywood history, according to Bill Krohn.

[39] Appropriately for Hitchcock's latest film, this art world reference to Mondrian is to one of the most popular examples of late style in the existing literature; Mondrian switched from a more figurative style to an abstract one of pure line and space and color toward the end of his life.

Victorian sitting room, Hitchcock specifically asked South to light it like a Rembrandt painting, and they shot it repeatedly trying to achieve the effect. It's a real mood-setter, as helped by the addition of John Williams' impressionistic female chorus on the soundtrack—a cue inspired by Hitchcock's interest in Claude Debussy's *Sirènes,* as well as a nod to the ghostly reverberations of the never-made *Mary Rose.* Williams' score (sandwiched between his more famous work on *Jaws* [1975][40] and *Star Wars* [1977]) is the most distinctive of Hitchcock's post-Herrmann period, an appropriately playful fusion of classical and modern elements—including electronic ones, perhaps the echo of Hitchcock's consideration (that Williams persuaded him against) of a heavy synthesizer-based score. This fusion is apparent in more than just the music, here and elsewhere in late Hitchcock, and in *Family Plot* the spirit of 1930s cinema strongly infuses a film that is still nevertheless very much of the 1970s: light cursing and swearing dots the picture, and the romance motif central to much of Hitchcock's work is replaced by a casual sexual openness. "In the films of the 1970s (and here I include *Topaz,* released in 1969)," writes Paula Marantz Cohen, "Hitchcock attempted to create a new lexicon that no longer relied on nostalgia for gender complementarity or even on psychological symbolism as a structural or atmospheric resource. Very different from each other in theme and imagery, each of these films can be viewed as a variation on a postmodern idea."

---

[40] As a Universal stockholder, Hitchcock made a small fortune from the ultra-successful *Jaws,* but when director Steven Spielberg tried to sneak onto the *Family Plot* set to meet Hitchcock, he was escorted off the premises. (Spielberg had tried a similar tactic—with similar results—as a 19-year-old on the set of *Torn Curtain.*) As told by Bruce Dern, Hitchcock claimed he felt ashamed around Spielberg because he'd taken money to be "the voice of the *Jaws* ride" (likely referring to the Universal Studio Tour which passed through several sets from the film via tram). "They paid me a million dollars. And I took it and I did it. I'm such a whore. I can't sit down and talk to the boy who did the fish movie. I couldn't even touch his hand."

Hitchcock's late work is constantly operating in ways that dispel the notion that he is out-of-touch, uninterested, or impervious to evolutions within his own art. *Family Plot*—made in his mid-seventies—is the final proof of this, even if the outward signs of his life seemed to point to someone coasting on his last legs. Hitchcock's health was becoming a more pressing concern: the increasing burden of his weight, the pacemaker he'd had installed in 1974, the pain he suffered from his arthritis, and the drinking he did to numb it. Mortality was often in the forefront of his mind. Alma herself had suffered a stroke in 1971 during the filming of *Frenzy*, and a second, more debilitating one came in 1976. Shooting during the making of *Family Plot* ended promptly at 4:00 p.m. each day, and when it wrapped most of the post-production tasks had to be delegated to others. Health issues forced Hitchcock to get creative on set, sometimes having his car driven right onto the studio stage where a chair awaited him nearby, sometimes directing remotely from the back seat; production head Thom Mount recalls that some of Universal's production people even customized an old Cadillac convertible by cutting off the sides and back of it, fitting a platform on the back, and putting a chair on it in which Hitchcock could move himself around in any direction, or be driven anywhere. But gossip that Hitchcock was checked out from the film and at times "couldn't be bothered to get out" of his car was patently false and uncontextualized, as explained by biographer Charlotte Chandler. "He cared desperately" about the film, "but by then he was in constant physical pain. His legs no longer supported him, and he was afraid of falling. He believed a director could not direct if he lost his dignity." Yet the delightful energy radiating off *Family Plot* from frame one gives no hint of this, and the film buzzes with colors, movements, and rhythms that display a filmmaker totally in love with his characters and their eccentricities. This all comes to a head in the film's final sequences, as Hitchcock breezily wraps things up in a nearly non-confrontational climax that borders on the pleasantly absurd. First, the film's two strands finally meet in a scene of comically crossed wires: Harris knocks on Devane's door to give him the good news that he's to be made heir of his aunt's fortune, but he and Black are in the middle of leaving to collect the ransom for the bishop they've kidnapped. Finally meeting as the garage door opens, in the middle of sharing her news Harris is yanked into their drama when the unconscious bishop spills out of the backseat of their car; she's promptly stowed away in the soundproof basement lair built for their kidnapping victims. When Dern arrives, Hitchcock stacks the suspense indicators—Dern stealthily wandering around the house, taking his shoes off to sneak past an unsuspecting Black, and discovering Devane attending to Harris in the basement lair—only to hilariously subvert expectations of any kind of fight by having Dern and Harris (only pretending to be unconscious) plan to seal Devane and Black in their own lair, which they carry out upon their return without a hitch: moral order is restored as the good couple replaces the bad couple, the latter immediately shut out of the picture (the solidity and soundproof-ness of the wall erasing face and voice), which then goes straight into cathartic epilogue mode as Hitchcock proceeds to set up his final punchline. To Dern's amazement, Harris "discovers," using her "psychic powers," the diamonds she's overheard the villains talking about hidden in the chandelier, and, sitting on the stairwell, *winks directly into the camera.* The End. This glitch in the cinematic reality, the breaking down of the wall between film and audience, had been prefigured by the cameos Hitchcock had been making his whole career; his films had always been made with a knowing illusionism, and he'd never been afraid to clue his audience into his movies' movie-ness. The wink is a modernist, cherry-on-top gesture of rapport between a filmmaker and his audience, made impossibly moving by its placement at the very end of Hitchcock's very last film. What paradoxically makes the wink even more moving and meaningful is the fact that *it wasn't scripted*—Harris had playfully added it at the end of her final take, without being asked to, and Hitchcock loved it. That he kept it in the film—and even made it a central part of the film's advertising (Hitchcock's winking face is seen inside a crystal ball on the film's poster)—is an inspired testament to the genial openness of Hitchcock's final film, as well as the never-dulled instincts of an artist who'd spent his entire career finding new ways to challenge and delight his audiences.

Nostalgia was never Hitchcock's thing: as early as 1936 he was remarking in a British *Film Weekly* article called "My Screen Memories" that "my most interesting picture is always my next one. I have enjoyed delving into the past in these reminiscences. But the future is more fascinating." The barrage of valedictory awards, medals, and other honorary items that fell upon him in the 1960s and '70s meant little to Hitchcock compared to the continued satisfaction of "apply[ing] glue" to the seats of his audience; in fact, most of the awards felt condescending, as though he were already retired or dead—"regarded more as a historical monument than as a vital part of living cinema," in the words of John Russell Taylor. He had no intention of retiring. When asked if he did he would trot out variations on a resounding "no": "Retire? What would I do? Sit in a corner and read a book?," or "I have lots of ideas… and something always comes up, some new story…. I warn you, I mean to go on forever!," or the more succinct "I retire when I die." (Besides, he claimed, he still technically owed Universal two more movies on his contract.) Thus it wasn't too long after *Family Plot* had come and gone that Hitchcock started to work on his next proposed project, an adaption of Ronald Kirkbride's espionage thriller *The Short Night*, crossed with the nonfiction account of an escaped double agent, *The Springing of George Blake* (written by Sean Bourke, who'd engineered Blake's escape). Hitchcock had been interested in the property since obtaining the rights in 1968, and had even scouted locations in Finland while in Europe for *Topaz* around that time. It would offer Hitchcock a third stab at a Bond-adjacent, realistic cold war thriller while also providing one of the most morally knotty premises he'd ever tackled, of a man falling in love with the wife of the man he's waiting to kill. (Even the ailing Alma, always his first critic and collaborator on any project, was rapt at Hitchcock's telling of it.) Different stars circled the production at different times: Catherine Deneuve and Walter Matthau at one point, Liv Ullmann and Sean Connery at another;

Hitchcock even had lunch with Clint Eastwood. Multiple writers were turned to, including Ernest Lehman again, before scriptwriter David Freeman was brought on board in autumn 1978 and from whom Hitchcock received a finished script in spring 1979. Storyboards were drawn, locations were scouted, but time was running out and Hitchcock—perhaps sensing the picture would never be made—didn't seem in a great hurry to move past the pre-production phase (it had always been his favorite part of moviemaking). Plans were made for Norman Lloyd to lead a second unit to shoot locations if Hitchcock wasn't well enough to travel, which it seemed would almost certainly be the case. But in May 1979 Hitchcock abruptly cancelled production and announced the closing of his office. He would make no more movies. Perhaps it was apt that *The Short Night* was never put on film beyond the screen of Hitchcock's imagination, as he had always claimed (whether true or not) that to him the actual shooting of a film was an unnecessary afterthought; one can certainly read the script, as published in David Freeman's book *The Last Days of Alfred Hitchcock* (1984), and imagine a film as morally and visually provocative as anything he'd ever made. The script was later offered to such Hitchcockian descendants as François Truffaut, Claude Chabrol, and Peter Bogdanovich (who'd offered to shoot the Finnish location work from Hitchcock's storyboards while the project was still alive, to no avail) but none of them took it on. In the end, it was just Alfred and Alma. "I beg permission to mention by name only four people who have given me the most affection, appreciation and encouragement, and constant collaboration," Hitchcock said upon receiving the AFI's Life Achievement Award in 1979. "The first of the four is a film editor, the second is a scriptwriter, the third is the mother of my daughter Pat, and the fourth is as fine a cook as ever performed miracles in a domestic kitchen, and their names are all Alma Reville." Hitchcock died on April 29, 1980, and Alma followed on two years later. "Do you think about posterity?" Hitchcock had once been asked. His wry answer? "What did posterity ever do for me?"

Concluding Note: Late Style as a Way of Life

Loath as I am to turn a book of art philosophy/film criticism into any kind of self-help pamphlet, even in the form of a very brief concluding note, I feel compelled to offer one last thought as it relates to both late style and the way thinking about late style has affected the way I think about life in general. I've come to believe that everyone has a late style — whether that means the way we traditionally think about it in terms of the final phase of a life or career, or simply as a *later* style as it applies to all ages and stations of life. To the degree that I am a different person, and go about both my life and the work I do in it differently than I did at an earlier time in my life (whether six months ago or ten years), I have a late style. To the degree that you are a different person than you were at an earlier time in your life, you have a late style. Everyone has a late style. It doesn't matter what you do: you could be a film director, a chef, a stand-up comic, a teacher, an engineer, a hair stylist, a crossing guard, an athlete, an activist, a parent, an employer, an employee, or simply a human being. To the degree that you are a product of change over time, you have a late style. We all participate in lateness in some form or another, and indeed are constantly doing so as residents of the present, who moment by moment live at the latest point in time that we have ever lived, just as everyone who's ever lived and everyone who ever will live has done and will do. On the precipice of the future where we all constantly hover, what's to be done? To the artist (and I include in my definition of artist those who express themselves creatively via any and all outlets): make art from your own point in life and history. And make it in a way that relates or doesn't relate to the era you're operating in — that goes against it, or around it, or toward it, or through it — according to your own personal proclivities, in a manner unafraid to "fail" relative to the conventions of your practice, and in a way that remains uncompromised even when faced with the inevitable compromises that come with reality's contingencies. Make art from your own position in history, and appreciate art from all positions in history. Contain multitudes in who you are as both person and artist. Pedro Costa has talked about how a film director needs to be "twenty and eighty at the same time…. all the feelings of a life must pass through your shot." Using Chaplin as an example, he says to beginning filmmakers that "you must keep a bit of *The Tramp* in you, and you must have begun already to have a bit of *A Countess from Hong Kong* in you too." Pulling back to a more universal viewpoint, anyone who's witnessed family members or friends age and evolve through life can use the paradigm of late style thought to appreciate the idiosyncrasies of the way they express themselves or simply the way they carry themselves and how those changes contribute to the fullness of who they are as a person. Late style looks at where you are, whether in art or life, and says that this—not anything in the past, not anything in the future—is the most important moment. It's a perspective that threads the needle between shallow nostalgias and destructive anxieties; it keeps you grounded in the present, lost in the moment, doing the work. Hal Hartley's most recent film *Where to Land* (2025)— his first in over a decade and a beautifully late one to be sure— ends movingly somewhere in this philosophical vicinity, with the suggestion of life as a kind of eternal present from which one continually operates anew. The sentiment is hidden in a family lullaby borrowed from Cat Stevens' 1972 song "Silent Sunlight" —

> *Sleepy horses, heave away*
> *Put your backs to the golden hay*
> *Don't ever look behind at the work you've done*
> *For your work has just begun*
> *There'll be the evening in the end*
> *But till that time arrives*
> *You can rest your eyes—*
> *And begin again*

A list of my 100 favorite late films
(one film per director)

Abraham Lincoln (D. W. Griffith, 1930)
The Greatest Show on Earth (Cecil B. DeMille, 1952)
Limelight (Charles Chaplin, 1952)
Anatahan (Josef von Sternberg, 1953)
Silver Lode (Allan Dwan, 1954)
French Cancan (Jean Renoir, 1955)
Man Without a Star (King Vidor, 1955)
Beyond a Reasonable Doubt (Fritz Lang, 1956)
The Bravados (Henry King, 1958)
Good Morning (Yasujirô Ozu, 1959)
A Private's Affair (Raoul Walsh, 1959)
Two Rode Together (John Ford, 1961)
Gertrud (Carl Theodor Dreyer, 1964)
Red Line 7000 (Howard Hawks, 1965)
Torn Curtain (Alfred Hitchcock, 1966)
A Dandy in Aspic (Anthony Mann, 1968)
A Time for Dying (Budd Boetticher, 1969)
The Private Life of Sherlock Holmes (Billy Wilder, 1970)
Tristana (Luis Buñuel, 1970)
Trafic (Jacques Tati, 1971)
Blaise Pascal (Roberto Rossellini, 1972)
Un flic (Jean-Pierre Melville, 1972)
Ludwig (Luchino Visconti, 1973)
Lancelot du lac (Robert Bresson, 1974)
Dersu Uzala (Akira Kurosawa, 1975)
The Last Tycoon (Elia Kazan, 1976)
A Matter of Time (Vincente Minnelli, 1976)
The Other Side of the Wind (Orson Welles, 1970-1976; 2018)
Hardly Working (Jerry Lewis, 1980)
Rich and Famous (George Cukor, 1981)
White Dog (Samuel Fuller, 1982)

The Osterman Weekend (Sam Peckinpah, 1983)
A Passage to India (David Lean, 1984)
Beyond the Clouds (Michelangelo Antonioni, 1995)
The Devil's Own (Alan J. Pakula, 1997)
Eyes Wide Shut (Stanley Kubrick, 1999)
The Company (Robert Altman, 2003)
The Hunted (William Friedkin, 2003)
A Talking Picture (Manoel de Oliveira, 2003)
Do You Like Hitchcock? (Dario Argento, 2005)
Match Point (Woody Allen, 2005)
Red Eye (Wes Craven, 2005)
Star Wars: Episode III—Revenge of the Sith (George Lucas, 2005)
Before the Devil Knows You're Dead (Sidney Lumet, 2007)
The Romance of Astrea and Celadon (Éric Rohmer, 2007)
Youth Without Youth (Francis Ford Coppola, 2007)
Around a Small Mountain (Jacques Rivette, 2009)
Bellamy (Claude Chabrol, 2009)
The City of Your Final Destination (James Ivory, 2009)
My Son, My Son, What Have Ye Done (Werner Herzog, 2009)
Another Year (Mike Leigh, 2010)
The Ghost Writer (Roman Polanski, 2010)
How Do You Know (James L. Brooks, 2010)
Road to Nowhere (Monte Hellman, 2010)
Unstoppable (Tony Scott, 2010)
Like Someone in Love (Abbas Kiarostami, 2012)
Hard to Be a God (Aleksei German, 2013)
Goodbye to Language (Jean-Luc Godard, 2014)
Squirrels to the Nuts (Peter Bogdanovich, 2014)
The Assassin (Hou Hsiao-Hsien, 2015)
Blackhat (Michael Mann, 2015)
Paris Can Wait (Eleanor Coppola, 2016)
Paterson (Jim Jarmusch, 2016)
Rules Don't Apply (Warren Beatty, 2016)
Submergence (Wim Wenders, 2017)
Twin Peaks: The Return (David Lynch, 2017)
The 15:17 to Paris (Clint Eastwood, 2018)
Ladies in Black (Bruce Beresford, 2018)
The Man Who Killed Don Quixote (Terry Gilliam, 2018)

Monrovia, Indiana (Frederick Wiseman, 2018)
Ready Player One (Steven Spielberg, 2018)
Domino (Brian De Palma, 2019)
A Hidden Life (Terrence Malick, 2019)
The Irishman (Martin Scorsese, 2019)
To the Ends of the Earth (Kiyoshi Kurosawa, 2019)
The Salt of Tears (Philippe Garrel, 2020)
Benediction (Terence Davies, 2021)
Fabian: Going to the Dogs (Dominik Graf, 2021)
The Souvenir: Part Two (Joanna Hogg, 2021)
Three Floors (Nanni Moretti, 2021)
Zeros and Ones (Abel Ferrara, 2021)
Dead for a Dollar (Walter Hill, 2022)
Irma Vep (Olivier Assayas, 2022)
Master Gardener (Paul Schrader, 2022)
Stars at Noon (Claire Denis, 2022)
Thirteen Lives (Ron Howard, 2022)
The Lost King (Stephen Frears, 2022)
Close Your Eyes (Víctor Erice, 2023)
in water (Hong Sang-soo, 2023)
Napoleon: The Director's Cut (Ridley Scott, 2023)
The Old Oak (Ken Loach, 2023)
Seven Veils (Atom Egoyan, 2023)
The Empire (Bruno Dumont, 2024)
Furiosa: A Mad Max Saga (George Miller, 2024)
Here (Robert Zemeckis, 2024)
The Room Next Door (Pedro Almodóvar, 2024)
The Shrouds (David Cronenberg, 2024)
28 Years Later (Danny Boyle, 2025)
Highest 2 Lowest (Spike Lee, 2025)
Where to Land (Hal Hartley, 2025)

Notes

Late Style in Film: An Introduction

3 "When a man…": quoted in Gordon McMullan, *Shakespeare and the Idea of Late Writing: Authorship in the Proximity of Death* (Cambridge: Cambridge University Press, 2007), 173.

3 "the idiosyncrasies of…": quoted in ibid.

6 "It is impossible…": Mark Cousins, "Widescreen," *Prospect*, 19 May 2001, https://www.prospectmagazine.co.uk/culture/56262/widescreen.

7 "Up until the…": quoted in Roger Ebert, "Remembering John Wayne," *RogerEbert.com*, 14 December 2012, https://www.rogerebert.com/interviews/remembering-john-wayne.

8 "in modern biography…": Michael Millgate, *Testamentary Acts: Browning, Tennyson, James, Hardy* (Oxford: Oxford University Press, 1992), 204.

8 "Monographs which lovingly…": Thomas Dormandy, *Old Masters: Great Artists in Old Age* (London: Hambledon and London, 2000), xiv.

9 "almost invariably…": Jonathan Rosenbaum, "Reel Life: Richard Pena's Film Center Testament," *Chicago Reader*, 13 May 1998, https://jonathanrosenbaum.net/2024/06/reel-   life-richard-pena-s-film-center-testament/.

9 "vital, existential intrigue…": J. Kim Murphy, "Karina Longworth on Late Style, Unfashionable Auteurs and Season 20 of Her Film History Podcast 'You Must Remember This,'" *Variety*, 24 April 2025, https://variety.com/2025/film/news/you-must-remember-this-podcast-karina-longworth-late-style-1236376721/.

9 "subset of cinephiles…": Karina Longworth, "Fritz Lang 1959–1970 (The Old Man is Still Alive, Part 2)," *You Must Remember This*, 21 January 2025, 1:00:00.

12 "Some may disagree…": Maynard Solomon, *Late Beethoven: Music, Thought, Imagination* (Berkeley: University of California Press, 2003), 1.

13 "The materials of…": Gordon McMullan, "Constructing a late style for David Bowie: Old age, late-life creativity, popular culture," *Creativity*

in Later Life: Beyond Late Style (New York: Routledge, 2019), edited by David Amigoni and Gordon McMullan, pp. 61-76. 65.

14 "People love to love…": Isiah Medina, correspondence with author, 2 October 2025.

15 "In this light…": Cobi Chiodo Powell, "The Final Cut: On Contemporary Cinematic Late Style," *The Culture We Deserve*, 26 July 2024, https://theculturewedeserve.substack.com/p/the- final-cut.

15 "It appears that…": Amir Cohen-Shalev, *Visions of Aging: Images of the Elderly in Film* (Eastbourne: Sussex Academic Press, 2009), 17.

16 "In the cinema…": Lawrence Garcia, "Ways of Worldmaking: Hong Sang-soo's Late Period," *MUBI Notebook*, 20 May 2024, https://mubi. com/en/notebook/posts/ways-of- worldmaking-hong-sang-soo-s-late-period.

17 "Who knows what…": quoted in Joshua Stecker, "Quentin Tarantino on When He'll Retire: 'I Don't Want to Be an Old-Man Filmmaker,'" *The Hollywood Reporter*, 15 November 2012, https://www. hollywoodreporter.com/news/general-news/quentin-tarantino-hell-retire-i-390963/.

18 "elucidating late style…": Gordon McMullan and Sam Smiles, "Introduction: Late Style and its Discontents," *Late Style and its Discontents: Essays in Art, Literature, and Music* (Oxford: Oxford University Press, 2016), edited by Gordon McMullan and Sam Smiles, pp. 1-14. 12.

20 "introspective… austere… difficult…": Joseph N. Straus, "Disability and 'Late Style' in Music," *The Journal of Musicology*, vol. 25, no. 1 (Winter 2008), pp. 3-45. 12.

20 "late style is…": quoted in Michael and Linda Hutcheon, "Late Style(s): The Ageism of the Singular," *Occasion: Interdisciplinary Studies in the Humanities*, vol. 4 (31 May 2012), https://shc.stanford.edu/sites/default/files/2012- 06/OCCASION_v04_Hutcheons_053112_0.pdf, 11.

20-21 "a *discourse of lateness*…": McMullan, *Shakespeare and the Idea of Late Writing*, 5.

22 "to fruitfully define…": Bailey Trela, "Pole Dancing: On J. M. Coetzee's Late Style," *Cleveland Review of Books*, 26 September 2024, https://clereviewofbooks.com/jm-coetzee-the- pole/.

24 "An important precondition…": Amir Cohen-Shalev, *Both Worlds at Once: Art in Old Age* (Lanham: University Press of America, 2002), 38.

25 "a work is good…": quoted in François Truffaut, *The Films in My Life* (New York: Simon & Schuster, 1978), translated by Leonard Mayhew, originally published in 1975, 2.

25 "Undoubtedly everyone has…": André Bazin, *What Is Cinema?: Volume II* (Berkeley: University of California Press, 1971), edited and translated by Hugh Gray, 130.

26-27 "In any case…": Éric Rohmer, *The Taste for Beauty* (Cambridge: Cambridge University Press, 1989), edited by Jean Narboni, translated by Carol Volk, originally published in 1984, 174-175.

27 "The type of criticism…": William D. Routt, "L'evidence," *Continuum: The Australian Journal of Media & Culture,* vol. 5, no. 2 (1992), https://freotopia.org/readingroom/5.2/Routt.html.

27 "like Beethoven's last quartets": Jean-Luc Godard, *Godard on Godard* (New York: Da Capo Press, 1986), edited by Jean Narboni and Tom Milne, translated by Tom Milne, originally published in 1968, English edition 1972, 232.

27-28 "is a perfect case…": James Schamus, *Carl Theodor Dreyer's Gertrud: The Moving Word* (Seattle: University of Washington Press, 2008), 9.

28 "the recognition that…": Robert Savage, "The Polemic of Late Work: Adorno's Hölderlin," *Language Without Soil: Adorno and Late Philosophical Modernity* (New York: Fordham University Press, 2010), edited by Gerhard Richter, pp. 172-194. 193.

28 "of 'debunking'…": Theodor Adorno, "Alienated Masterpiece: The *Missa Solemnis,*" originally published in 1959, translated by Duncan Smith, *Essays on Music* (Berkeley: University of California Press, 2002), edited by Richard Leppert, pp. 569-583. 570.

28-29 "I'm not trying…": quoted in Ryan Gilbey, "'Dead white men are what I'm legitimately interested in': film's foremost podcaster on resurrecting the classics," *The Guardian,* 3 April 2025, https://www.theguardian.com/tv-and-radio/2025/apr/03/dead-white-men-are-what-im-legitimately-interested-in-podcaster-karina-longworth-on-the-forgotten-work-of- hollywood-titans.

30 "paradigmatic (perhaps synecdochic…": McMullan and Smiles, "Introduction: Late Style and its Discontents," 11.

32 "Whether Homer existed…": Hermann Broch, introduction to Rachel Bespaloff, *On the Iliad* (Princeton: Princeton University Press, 1947, pp. 9-33. 26.

32 "The Greeks had…": McMullan, *Shakespeare and the Idea of Late Writing,* 194.

32 "sorrow for the hand…": quoted in Cohen-Shalev, *Both Worlds at Once,* 26.

33 "the shift he makes…": McMullan, *Shakespeare and the Idea of Late Writing*, 209, 211.

33 "that even God…": Ben Hutchinson, *Lateness and Modern European Literature* (Oxford: Oxford University Press, 2016), 11.

33 "the emancipation of artists…": Carel Blotkamp, *The End: Artists' Late and Last Works* (London: Reaktion Books, 2019), 114.

34 "in art history…": Cohen-Shalev, *Both Worlds at Once*, 26.

34 "very different from…": quoted in Hutchinson, *Lateness and Modern European Literature*, 25.

34 "old artists became…": Philip Sohm, *The Artist Grows Old: The Aging of Art and Artists in Italy, 1500–1800* (New Haven: Yale University Press, 2007), 8.

34-35 "three stages that…": ibid.

35 "structural backbone…": Bryan Gilliam, "Between Resignation and Hope: The Late Works of Richard Strauss," *Late Thoughts: Reflections on Artists and Composers at Work* (Los Angeles: Getty Research Institute, 2006), edited by Karen Painter and Thomas Crow, pp. 167-182. 167.

35 "Before the romantic period…": Karen Painter, "On Creativity and Lateness," *Late Thoughts*, pp. 1-14. 2.

35 "the Romanticism of…": McMullan, *Shakespeare and the Idea of Late Writing*, 138.

35-36 "When genius became…": Rüdiger Safranski, *Goethe: Life as a Work of Art* (New York: Liveright Publishing Corporation, 2017), translated by David Dollenmayer, originally published in 2013, 134.

36 "the idea of the…": McMullan, *Shakespeare and the Idea of Late Writing*, 2.

36 "the highest level…": quoted in Hutchinson, *Lateness and Modern European Literature*, 10.

37 "climax of his…": Margaret Notley, *Lateness and Brahms: Music and Culture in the Twilight of Viennese Liberalism* (Oxford: Oxford University Press, 2007), 37.

37 "from the time…": Safranski, *Goethe*, 135.

37 "typical of Goethe's…": ibid., 496.

37-38 "subject to extensive…": Anthony Barone, "Richard Wagner's 'Parsifal' and the Theory of Late Style," *Cambridge Opera Journal*, vol. 7, no. 1 (March 1995), pp. 37-54. 43.

38 "gradually receding…": quoted in John Deathridge, "Richard Wagner's Unfinished Symphonies," *Late Thoughts,* pp. 145-166. 145.

38 "constituted a distinctive…": McMullan and Smiles, "Introduction: Late Style and its Discontents," 3.

38 "several of the greatest…": quoted in Sam Smiles, "Artists over 50: better late than ever?," *The Guardian,* 2 September 2014, https://www.theguardian.com/artanddesign/2014/sep/02/artists-over-50-better-late-than- ever-turner-matisse.

39 "These new formal…": Sam Smiles, "From Titian to Impressionism: The Genealogy of Late Style," *Late Style and its Discontents,* pp. 15-30. 19.

39 "the discourse of…": Hutchinson, *Lateness and Modern European Literature,* 20.

39 "what may be…": Barone, "Richard Wagner's 'Parsifal'…," 45.

39 "a 'baroque' elaboration…": Stephen Katz, *Cultural Aging: Life Course, Lifestyle, and Senior Worlds* (Peterborough: Broadview Press, 2005), 108.

40 "The maturity of…": Theodor Adorno, "Late Style in Beethoven," originally published in 1937, translated by Susan H. Gillespie, *Essays on Music,* pp. 564-567. 564.

40 "In the history…": ibid., 567.

40 "over the course…": Hutchinson, *Lateness and Modern European Literature,* 269.

40 41 "it is worth noting…": ibid., 112.

41 "that Adorno's Beethoven…" Richard Leppert, commentary, *Essays on Music,* 520.

41 "is peculiarly resistant…": Hutchinson, *Lateness and Modern European Literature,* 262.

42 "To be an essayist…": Edward Said, *On Late Style: Music and Literature Against the Grain* (New York: Vintage Books, 2006), 81.

42 "late work without…": quoted in Michael Spitzer, *Music as Philosophy: Adorno and Beethoven's Late Style* (Bloomington: Indiana University Press, 2006), 62.

42 "In his influential…": Karen Painter, "On Creativity and Lateness," 5.

43 "a sort of high priest…": Edward Said, *The Selected Works of Edward Said, 1966–2006* (New York: Vintage Books, 2019), edited by Moustafa Bayoumi and Andrew Rubin, 415.

43 "The artist thus graced…": Broch, introduction to *On the Iliad*, 12.

43 "Thus if German Romanticism…": McMullan, *Shakespeare and the Idea of Late Writing*, 277.

43 "attributes the rekindled…": Cohen-Shalev, *Both Worlds at Once*, 28.

43-44 "transhistorical line of…": McMullan, *Shakespeare and the Idea of Late Writing*, 278.

44 "there are anthologies…": Aldous Huxley, foreword to *The Complete Etchings of Goya* (New York: Crown Publishers, Inc., 1943), 7.

45 "Said's interest in…": Michael Wood, introduction to *On Late Style*, 11.

45 "beginnings are usually…": Edward Said, "Adorno as Lateness Itself," *Apocalypse Theory and the Ends of the World* (Oxford: Blackwell Publishers, 1995), edited by Malcolm Bull, pp. 264-281. 264.

45 "artistic lateness not…": Edward Said, "Thoughts on Late Style," *London Review of Books*, vol. 26, no. 15 (5 August 2004), https://www.lrb.co.uk/the-paper/v26/n15/edward- said/thoughts-on-late-style.

45-46 "the intellectual trajectory…": Said, *The Selected Works*, 503.

46 "notion of tension…": ibid., 437.

46 "uncooptable into one…": Said, *On Late Style*, 47.

46 "far from being…": Moustafa Bayoumi and Andrew Rubin, introduction to *The Selected Works*, xlii.

46 "last decade of…": Timothy Brennan, *Places of Mind: A Life of Edward Said* (New York: Farrar, Straus and Giroux, 2021), 317.

46 "seems to be composed…": Said, *The Selected Works*, 503.

46 "provided the foundations…": Bayoumi and Rubin, introduction to *The Selected Works*, xlvii.

46 "bothered": Brennan, *Places of Mind*, 360.

47 "Their approaches are…": Sam Smiles, "From Titian to Impressionism," 30.

47 "Since the 1970s…": Karen Painter, "On Creativity and Lateness," 5.

47-38 "The late-style trope…": McMullan and Smiles, "Introduction: Late Style and its Discontents," 11.

48 "late style is less…": McMullan, *Shakespeare and the Idea of Late Writing*, 62-63.

48 "To offer a critique…": McMullan and Smiles, "Introduction: Late Style and its Discontents," 6- 7.

50 "the evidence…": David W. Galenson, *Old Masters and Young Geniuses: The Two Life Cycles of Artistic Creativity* (Princeton: Princeton University Press, 2006), 160-161.

51 "'Still I'm learning'…": Dormandy, *Old Masters,* 231.

52 "drew a picture…": Huxley, foreword to *The Complete Etchings of Goya,* 14.

51 "From the age…": quoted in Timothy Clark, "Late Hokusai, backwards," *Hokusai: Beyond the Great Wave* (London: Thames & Hudson, 2017), edited by Timothy Clark, pp. 12-27. 21.

51 "every time I see…": quoted in "'Let us hold out together for the sake of movies' – Read Akira Kurosawa's letter to Ingmar Bergman," *Far Out,* 16 December 2020, https://faroutmagazine.co.uk/akira-kurosawa-letter-to-ingmar-bergman/.

51-52 "I rather like…": quoted in Peter Cowie, *God and the Devil: The Life and Work of Ingmar Bergman* (London: Faber & Faber, 2023), 349-350.

52 "O, but they say…": William Shakespeare, *Richard II,* Act II, scene I.

52 "various challenges of…": Linda and Michael Hutcheon, *Four Last Songs: Aging and Creativity in Verdi, Strauss, Messiaen, and Britten* (Chicago: The University of Chicago Press, 2015), 108.

52-53 "both narratives tend…": Katz, *Cultural Aging,* 107.

53-54 "arguably an ethical…": McMullan and Smiles, "Introduction: Late Style and its Discontents," 12.

54 "affinity for particular…": Richard Brody, "Last Film, Best Film?," *The New Yorker,* 7 April 2016, https://www.newyorker.com/culture/richard-brody/last-film-best-film.

55 "harmonious synthesis": Adorno, "Late Style in Beethoven," 567.

55 "splendidness and tonal…": Adorno, "Alienated Masterpiece," 573.

55 "definition of old-age…": Erin J. Campbell, "Old-Age Style and the Resistance of Practice in Cinquecento Art Theory and Criticism" (doctoral dissertation, University of Toronto, 1998), 53.

55 "definition of literary…": ibid., 209.

55 "This is the prerogative…": Said, "Thoughts on Late Style."

55 "Robert Frost's famous…": Cohen-Shalev, *Both Worlds at Once,* 154.

55 "chronological 'homelessness'…": Carl Dahlhaus, *Ludwig van Beethoven: Approaches to his Music* (Oxford: Clarendon Press, 1991), translated by Mary Whittall, originally published in 1987, 219.

56 "shadows": quoted in Cohen-Shalev, *Visions of Aging*, 90.

56 "tower above the…": quoted in Rudolf Arnheim, "On the Late Style of Life and Art," *Michigan Quarterly Review*, vol. 17, no. 2 (1978), pp. 149-156. 156.

56 "characteristic of a…": Dahlhaus, *Ludwig van Beethoven*, 219.

56 "catastrophic commentator": Said, "Thoughts on Late Style."

57 "There is first…": Edward Said, "Untimely Meditations," *The Nation*, 14 August 2003, https://www.thenation.com/article/archive/untimely-meditations/.

57 "being at the end…": Said, "Thoughts on Late Style."

57-58 "late style, for…": Hutchinson, *Lateness and Modern European Literature*, 79.

58 "when I see...": Matthew Wilder, "In Praise of Late Woody: Darkness, Lightness and Other Anxieties of Influence," *Talkhouse*, 29 August 2016, https://www.talkhouse.com/praise-late-woody-darkness-lightness-anxieties-influence/.

58 "Allen's films move...": Richard Brody, "Contrarian Blogger Strikes Again," *The New Yorker*, 21 September 2010, https://www.newyorker.com/culture/richard-brody/contrarian-blogger-strikes-again.

59 "Crocodile tears over…": quoted in Jay Scott, "Master of meaning and magic," *The Globe and Mail*, 1 May 1980, https://the.hitchcock.zone/wiki/The_Globe_and_Mail_(01/May/1980)-Master_of_meaning_and_magic.

59 "Art demands of us…": quoted in Maynard Solomon, "Beethoven: Beyond Classicism," *The Beethoven Quartet Companion* (Berkeley: University of California Press, 1994), edited by Robert Winter and Robert Martin, pp. 59-76. 74.

59 "a life in art…": J. M. Coetzee and Paul Auster, *Here and Now: Letters 2008-2011* (New York: Viking Penguin, 2013), 88.

59 "You have to change…": quoted in Richard Shiff, "Willem de Kooning: Same Change," *Last Thoughts*, pp. 37-54. 37.

60 "the kind of simplification…": quoted in Galenson, *Old Masters and Young Geniuses*, 115.

60 "the kind of purified…": Richard Brody, "The Secret Fuel that Makes 'Ferrari' Such a Triumph," *The New Yorker*, 5 January 2024, https://www.newyorker.com/culture/the-front-row/the-secret-fuel-that-makes-ferrari-such-a-triumph.

60 "If… youth is…": Cohen-Shalev, *Visions of Aging*, 14-15.

61 "To the young…": Dormandy, *Old Masters*, 217.

61-62 "had such a…": Cohen-Shalev, *Both Worlds at Once*, 25-26.

62 "cleaning showed that…": Richard Smith, "Is there such a thing as 'late style'?," *Richard Smith's non-medical blogs*, 10 October 2016, https://richardswsmith.wordpress.com/2016/10/10/is-there-such-a-thing-as-late-style/.

62 "the predication of…": McMullan and Smiles, "Introduction: Late Style and its Discontents," 1.

63 "In depending on…": ibid., 7.

63 "critical complicity with…": McMullan, *Shakespeare and the Idea of Late Writing*, 16.

63 "there has not…": McMullan, *Shakespeare and the Idea of Late Writing*, 183.

64 "Late style may…": Max Norman, "Does 'Late Style' Exist?," *The New Yorker*, 13 January 2020, https://www.newyorker.com/books/page-turner/does-late-style-exist-in-art.

64 "the way in which…": Said, "Thoughts on Late Style." "no generalized late-style…": Hutcheon, "The Ageism of the Singular," 4.

66 "Any counter-measure…": McMullan, *Shakespeare and the Idea of Late Writing*, 109.

67-68 "might be useful…": Joseph N. Straus, "Disability and 'Late Style' in Music," 7, 11.

68 "An air of…": Robert Spencer, "Lateness and Modernity in Theodor Adorno," *Late Style and its Discontents*, pp. 220-234. 222.

68 "Critics preoccupied by…": ibid., 223.

69 "brought before the…": McMullan, *Shakespeare and the Idea of Late Writing*, 16.

70 "With 'late style' discourse…": Michael M. Bilandic, "Ulli Lommel's Last FreeK Off: A Conversation with Frank Dragun," *Screen Slate*, 27 July 2025, https://www.screenslate.com/articles/ulli-lommels-last-freek-conversation-frank-dragun.

71-72 "Like many modern…": quoted in Robert Kapsis, *Hitchcock: The Making of a Reputation* (Chicago: University of Chicago Press, 1992), 117.

72 "the applicability of…": Cohen-Shalev, *Visions of Aging*, 14.

72-73 "While the cinephilia…": Joe McElhaney, *The Death of Classical Cinema: Hitchcock, Lang, Minnelli* (Albany: State University of New York Press, 2006), 14.

73 "Every visit to…": Theodor Adorno, *Minima Moralia: Reflections on a Damaged Life* (New York: Verso Books, 2005), originally published in 1951, translated by E.F.N. Jephcott in 1974, 25.

73 "The current belief…": Detlev Claussen, *Theodor W. Adorno: One Last Genius* (Cambridge: Harvard University Press, 2008), originally published in 2003, translated by Rodney Livingstone, 172.

73 "inaugurated the final…": Said, *On Late Style*, 82.

73 "puzzling break in…": ibid., 86.

73 "back into a…": ibid., 83.

73 "is not in the end…": ibid., 97.

74 "The question of…": James Morrison, "George Cukor's Late Style: *Justine, Travels with My Aunt,* and *Rich and Famous,*" *George Cukor: Hollywood Master* (Edinburgh: Edinburgh University Press, 2015), edited by Murray Pomerance and R. Barton Palmer, pp. 28-42. 28-29.

75 "with it…": André Bazin, *The Cinema of Cruelty: from Buñuel to Hitchcock* (New York: Seaver Books, 1982), edited by François Truffaut, originally published in 1975, translated by Sabine d'Estrée with the assistance of Tiffany Fliss, 25.

77 "was generally dismissed…": Peter Bogdanovich, *Who the Devil Made It* (New York: Alfred A. Knopf, 1997), 11.

77 "Some directors who…": Laura Mulvey, "The Metaphor of the Beautiful Automaton Reanimated: Artifice, Illusion, and Late Style in *Vertigo,*" *Haunted by Vertigo: Hitchcock's Masterpiece Then and Now* (New Barnet: John Libbey Publishing Ltd., 2021), pp. 219-233. 219-220.

77 "where things start…": Karina Longworth, "Fritz Lang 1959-1970," 28:00.

78 "New Hollywood *was*…": Quentin Tarantino, *Cinema Speculation* (New York: HarperCollins, 2022), 161.

78 "hindsight reveals that…": Morrison, "George Cukor's Late Style," 29.

78 "an institutionalized avant-garde…": Andy Rector, "MY KINGDOM FOR (1985)," *Kino Slang,* 29 October 2024, https://kinoslang.blogspot.com/2024/10/my-kingdom-for-1985.html.

79-80 "In simpler times…": James Morrison, "The Old Masters: Kubrick, Polanski, and the Late Style in Modern Cinema," *Raritan,* vol. 21, no. 2 (Fall 2001), pp. 29-47. 30-31.

80 "how a perceived…": Morrison, "The Old Masters," 31-32.

81 "on the subject…": Bogdanovich, *Who the Devil Made It*, 11-12.

82 "Whereas many of…": McElhaney, *The Death of Classical Cinema*, 5.

83 "could impatiently and…": Miguel Marías and Peter von Bagh, "The Wondrous 60s. An e-mail exchange between Miguel Marías and Peter von Bagh," *Comparative Cinema*, April-May 2013, http://www.ocec. eu/cinemacomparativecinema/index.php/en/inicio-eng/15-n-2- forms-in-revolution/134-the-wondrous-60s-an-e-mail-exchange-between-miguel-marias- and-peter-von-bagh.

83 "without any sort of…": ibid.

84 "Auteurism said that…": Routt, "L'evidence."

85 "systematic doctrine…": ibid.

85 "this cannot be…": ibid.

85 "discover the virtues…": Rohmer, *The Taste for Beauty*, 175.

85-86 "We were thrilled…": Serge Daney, *Postcards from the Cinema* (New York: Berg, 2007), originally published in 1994, translated by Paul Douglas Grant, 73.

86-87 "although the movement…": James Naremore, *An Invention Without a Future: Essays on Cinema* (Berkeley: University of California Press, 2014), 24.

87 "for the way…": Daniel Fairfax, *The Red Years of Cahiers du Cinéma (1968–1973): Volume II—Aesthetics and Ontology* (Amsterdam: Amsterdam University Press, 2021), 511.

88 "suffused by love": Routt, "L'evidence."

89 "Packed in the…": Brody, "Last Film, Best Film?"

90 "We cannot say…": Rohmer, *The Taste for Beauty*, 136.

90 "the recognition of…": Brody, "Last Film, Best Film?"

90-91 "as a kid…": Matthew Wilder, "omg gramps u r totes mbrsng me :)," *Shadowplay*, 4 December 2013, https://dcairns.wordpress.com/2013/12/04/omg-gramps-u-r-totes-mbrsng-me/.

91 "whether the 'wrong end…": Adrian Martin, message to a_film_by discussion group, 8 January 2005, https://www.fredcamper.com/afilmby/0020601.html.

92 "relationship to contemporary…": Joe McElhaney, "Contemporary Cinema?," *Lola*, August 2011, http://lolajournal.com/1/contemporary.html, originally published October 2010.

93 "formula for the…": Richard Brody, "What It Takes to Make a Great Movie," *The New Yorker,* 20 September 2012, https://www.newyorker.com/culture/richard-brody/what-it-takes-to- make-a-great-movie.

93 "mass-consumer forms…": Said, *On Late Style,* 97.

94 "No writer enjoys…": Kenneth Clark, "The artist grows old," *Daedalus,* Winter 2006, https://www.amacad.org/publication/daedalus/artist-grows-old?utm, originally published in 1972.

94 "as privileged over…": Cohen-Shalev, *Both Worlds at Once,* 39.

95 "So it perhaps…": McMullan, *Shakespeare and the Idea of Late Writing,* 230.

95-96 "at their best…": Galenson, *Old Masters and Young Geniuses,* 184.

97 "further[ed] the microsystems…": Rector, "MY KINGDOM FOR (1985)."

97 "it is not…": Morrison, "The Old Masters," 46.

97-98 "the more distinctive…": ibid., 33.

98 "With your career…": David Bordwell, *The Way Hollywood Tells It: Story and Style in Modern Movies* (Berkeley: University of California Press, 2006), 23, 25-26.

99 "like late Yeats…": quoted in McMullan, *Shakespeare and the Idea of Late Writing,* 77.

99 "that which cannot…": McElhaney, "Contemporary Cinema?"

99 "are marked by…": Powell, "The Final Cut."

100 "grow in popularity…": ibid.

100 "While late style…": ibid.

101 "even when it's not…": quoted in Will Sloan, "Free Men: Jean-Luc Godard's *Every Man for Himself* and Jerry Lewis's *Hardly Working,*" *In the Mood,* no. 6, https://www.inthemoodmagazine.com/issue-6/jean-luc-godard-jerry-lewis.

102 "I started late…": quoted in Jordan Cronk, "Manhattan in Retrospect: Kent Jones on 'Late Fame,'" *MUBI Notebook,* 2 October 2025, https://mubi.com/en/notebook/posts/manhattan-in-retrospect-kent-jones-on-late-fame.

103 "Mr. Oliveira, force…": Dennis Lim, "Centenarian Director's Very Long View," *The New York Times,* 9 March 2008, https://www.nytimes.com/2008/03/09/movies/09lim.html.

104 "the question of…": Karen Leeder, "Figuring Lateness in Modern German Culture," *New German Critique*, no. 125 (August 2015), pp. 1-29. 24.

105 "The importance of…": Katz, *Cultural Aging*, 116.

105-106 "the ancient Persians…": C. S. Lewis, *Letters to Malcolm: Chiefly on Prayer* (New York: Harcourt, Brace & World, Inc., 1964), 45.

106 "It is a quirk…": Garcia, "Ways of Worldmaking."

107 "Perhaps this is…": Lecia Rosenthal, "Between Humanism and Late Style," *Cultural Critique*, no. 67 (Autumn 2007), pp. 107-140. 124.

107 "late-style criticism invites…": Notley, *Lateness and Brahms*, 38.

107-109 "After trying to…": Dormandy, *Old Masters*, 316-317.

109 "he who does not…": quoted in Hugo Munsterberg, *The Crown of Life: Artistic Creativity in Old Age* (New York: Harcourt Brace Jovanovich, Publishers, 1983), 12.

112 "exact stylistic beginnings…": Michael Spitzer, "Notes on Beethoven's Late Style," *Late Style and its Discontents*, pp. 191-208. 192.

Howard Hawks

115 "The evidence on the screen…": Jacques Rivette, "The Genius of Howard Hawks," *Cahiers du Cinéma: The 1950s: Neo-Realism, Hollywood, New Wave* (Cambridge: Harvard University Press, 1985), edited by Jim Hillier, translated by Russell Campbell and Marvin Pister [Joseph McBride], 126.

115 "the greatest American artist": Jean-Luc Godard, *Godard on Godard* (New York: Da Capo Press, 1986), edited by Jean Narboni and Tom Milne, translated by Tom Milne, originally published in 1968, English edition 1972, 29.

115 "one cannot really love…": Éric Rohmer, *The Taste for Beauty* (Cambridge: Cambridge University Press, 1989), edited by Jean Narboni, translated by Carol Volk, originally published in 1984, 131.

116 "When people discuss…": quoted in Michael Sragow, "*Only Angels Have Wings*: Hawks's Genius Takes Flight," *Criterion Current*, 12 April 2016, https://www.criterion.com/current/posts/4005-only-angels-have-wings-hawks-s-genius- takes-flight.

117 "each shot has a…": Rivette, "The Genius of Howard Hawks," 128-129.

119 "to let them handle…": quoted in Todd McCarthy, *Howard Hawks: The Grey Fox of Hollywood* (New York: Grove Press, 1997), 381.

119 "first cut represents…": McCarthy, *Howard Hawks*, 395.

120 "the confident foregrounding…": Dan Sallitt, "I Was a Male War Bride," *Thanks for the Use of the Hall*, 29 July 2010, https://sallitt.blogspot.com/2010/07/i-was-male-war-bride.html.

120 "in a wiser…": Gerlad Mast, *Howard Hawks: Storyteller* (Oxford: Oxford University Press, 1982), 134.

120-121 "Grant, his voice…": Mast, *Howard Hawks*, 163.

122 "a man is a sheriff…": quoted in Andy Rector, "Luc Moullet part one…," *Kino Slang*, 10 February 2007, https://kinoslang.blogspot.com/2007/02/luc-moullet-part-one.html.

122 "more characterization…": quoted in Peter Bogdanovich, *Who the Devil Made It* (New York: Alfred A. Knopf, Inc., 1997), 356.

123 "There's no action…": quoted in Bill Krohn, "*My Budd* by Manny Farber," *Rouge*, 2008 http://www.rouge.com.au/12/farber_krohn.html, originally published in 1988.

123 "Insofar as *Land of the Pharaohs*…": Bill Krohn, "Hawks at Work: The Making of LAND OF THE PHARAOHS," *Kino Slang*, 20 March 2009, https://kinoslang.blogspot.com/2009/03/hawks-at-work-making-of-land-of.html, originally published in 1990.

123 "aggressively, even desperately…": McCarthy, *Howard Hawks*, 539.

124 "If I were asked…": Robin Wood, *Howard Hawks* (Detroit: Wayne State University Press, 2006), originally published in 1968, 29.

124 "everything seems to gravitate…": Fernando Villaverde, "Echoes of Violence: Howard Hawks and the End of the Production Code," *L'Atalante*, no. 28 (July-December 2019), pp. 77- 92. 80.

125 "This is a film…": quoted in McCarthy, *Howard Hawks*, 580.

125 "That was the year…": quoted in McCarthy, *Howard Hawks*, 572.

126 "one that I let…": quoted in Joseph McBride, *Hawks on Hawks* (Berkeley: University of California Press, 1982), 152.

127 "documentary… on [Hawks']…": Jean Douchet, "Hatari!," originally published in 1963, translated by John Moore, *Howard Hawks: American Artist* (London: British Film Institute, 1996), edited by Jim Hillier and Peter Wollen, pp. 77-82. 82.

128 "the form of the picture…": quoted in McCarthy, *Howard Hawks*, 572.

129 "liberate performance from…": Dan Sallitt, "Rio Bravo," *Thanks for the Use of the Hall*, 21 May 2013, https://sallitt.blogspot.com/2013/05/rio-bravo.html.

129 "not prompted by…": quoted in "Hatari!," *AFI Catalog*, https://catalog.afi.com/Catalog/moviedetails/19931.

129 "the first face…": Ronald Bergan, "Gérard Blain," *The Guardian*, 19 December 2000, https://www.theguardian.com/news/2000/dec/19/guardianobituaries.filmnews.

130 "never met anyone…": quoted in McCarthy, *Howard Hawks*, 574.

131 "is forced to know…": quoted in "The Cinema of Jean-Marie Straub and Daniele Huillet," https://www.straub-huillet.com/wp-content/uploads/2016/05/brochure-cinema1.pdf, 6.

132 "especially in the last…": Howard Hawks, *Howard Hawks: Interviews* (Jackson: University Pres of Mississippi, 2006), edited by Scott Breivold, 80.

133 "there is a continual…": Robin Wood, *Howard Hawks* (London: British Film Institute, 1981), originally published in 1968, 128.

133 "*I* don't know why…": quoted in McBride, *Hawks on Hawks*, 148.

134 "I just aim…": quoted in McCarthy, *Howard Hawks*, 611.

135 "the most self-involved…": ibid.

135 "He is one of…": quoted in McBride, *Hawks on Hawks*, 5.

136 "mostly old stuff…": Donald Willis, *The Films of Howard Hawks* (Metuchen: The Scarecrow Press, Inc., 1975), 40.

137 "drawing out…": Villaverde, "Echoes of Violence," 80-81.

138 "In slowing down…": Erich Kuersten, "Fear of Fishing: Closets and Product Placement in Hawks' *Man's Favorite Sport?*," *Bright Lights Film Journal*, 1 May 2007, https://brightlightsfilm.com/fear-fishing-closets-product-placement-hawks-mans-favorite- sport/.

138-139 "dazzling battles of…": David Thomson, *The New Biographical Dictionary of Film* (New York: Alfred A. Knopf, 2014), sixth edition, 463.

141 "it is the constant…": Peter John Dyer, "Sling the Lamps Low," *Focus on Howard Hawks* (Englewood Cliffs: Prentice-Hall, 1972), edited by Joseph McBride, pp. 78-93. 81.

142 "Such moments…": Joe McElhaney, "*Red Line 7000:* Fatal Disharmonies," *Howard Hawks: New Perspectives* (London: Palgrave, 2016), edited by Ian Brookes, pp. 189-201. 196.

143 "exactly the same…": Villaverde, "Echoes of Violence," 81.

143 "elevating them to…": McElhaney, "Fatal Disharmonies," 197.

143 "Hawks, who has…": Richard Thompson, "Hawks at Seventy," *Focus on Howard Hawks*, pp. 139-146. 142.

145 "There is no action…": Hawks, *Interviews*, 7.

148 "is perhaps, in Britain…": Wood, *Howard Hawks*, 140.

151 "If a quarterback…": quoted in William Wellman, Jr., "Howard Hawks: The Distance Runner," *Focus on Howard Hawks*, pp. 8-12. 11.

151 "if a man…": quoted in Richard Schickel, *The Men Who Made the Movies* (New York: Atheneum, 1975), 113.

151 "Now, if there's anyone…": quoted in Bogdanovich, *Who the Devil Made It*, 253.

152 "painted his odalisque…": Greg Ford, "Mostly on *Rio Lobo*," *Focus on Howard Hawks*, pp. 150- 162. 151.

152 "one of self-exploitation…": Jean-Pierre Coursodon, *American Directors: Volume 1* (New York: McGraw-Hill Book Company, 1983), 165.

153 "in the eight years…": Dan Sallitt, "Golden Years," *Moving Image Source*, 4 June 2008, https://movingimagesource.us/articles/golden-years-20080604.

154 "was to become…": Luc Moullet, "John Wayne: Towards Decrepitude," originally published in *Politique des acteurs* (*Cahiers du cinéma*, 1993), *The Seventh Art*, 26 May 2020, https://theseventhart.info/2020/05/26/john-wayne-towards-decrepitude/, translated by Srikanth Srinivasan.

155 "I'm not very interested…": quoted in McBride, *Hawks on Hawks*, 118.

155 "with greater apparent…": Greg Ford, "Mostly on *Rio Lobo*," 153.

156 "As usual…": Peter Bogdanovich, "*El Dorado*," *Focus on Howard Hawks*, pp. 147-149. 148.

156 "When I finish…": quoted in Bruce F. Kawin, *Selected Film Essays and Interviews* (London: Anthem Press, 2013), 114.

157 "Hawks' penchant for…": Dan Sallitt, "Hatari!," *Thanks for the Use of the Hall*, 10 June 2008, https://sallitt.blogspot.com/2008/06/hatari.html.

157 "fragment": quoted in McCarthy, *Howard Hawks*, 456.

157 "the script was…": quoted in McCarthy, *Howard Hawks*, 621.

158 "wheelchair jobs": quoted in "Howard Hawks Interview 1972 San Sebastian," https://www.youtube.com/watch?v=fR7YSl3GSDo, uploaded 29 July 2015.

158 "quickly and sharply…": Bogdanovich, *Who the Devil Made It*, 245.

158 "Isn't that right…": quoted in McCarthy, *Howard Hawks*, 638.

158 totally relaxed…": quoted in Scott Eyman, *John Wayne: The Life and Legend* (New York: Simon & Schuster, 2014), 423.

159 "the less expensive Mitchum": Lee Server, *Robert Mitchum: "Baby, I Don't Care"* (New York: St. Martin's Griffin, 2001), 436.

159 "typifies the way…": quoted in McBride, *Hawks on Hawks*, 39.

160 "That's really going back…": quoted in Richard Schickel, *The Men Who Made the Movies*, 112.

160 "In *Rio Bravo*…": Wood, *Howard Hawks*, 157.

162 "The American spectator…": Villaverde, "Echoes of Violence," 89.

163 "carry a greater burden…": Roger Greenspun, "Film: 'Rio Lobo' Has Hawks's Unmistakable Touch," *The New York Times*, 11 February 1971, https://www.nytimes.com/1971/02/11/archives/rio-lo-bo-has-hawkss-unmistakable-touch- wayne-seeks-traitors-in.html.

164 "There's probably no…": quoted in McBride, *Hawks on Hawks*, 139.

164 "based on a balance…": Robin Wood, *"Rio Bravo," Focus on Howard Hawks*, pp. 118-134. 129.

165 "a man alone…": Ernest Hemingway, *To Have and Have Not* (New York: Scribner, 1937), 225.

165 "rating these close…": Manny Farber, *Farber on Film: The Complete Film Writings of Manny Farber* (New York: Library of America, 2009), edited by Robert Polito, 656.

166 "every time I think…": McBride, *Hawks on Hawks*, 155.

167 "Never mind…": quoted in McCarthy, *Howard Hawks*, 653.

Charles Chaplin

175 "disgust of the…": quoted in Kenneth S. Lynn, *Charlie Chaplin and His Times* (New York: Simon & Schuster, 1997), 268.

175 "unthinkable…": Charles Chaplin, *My Autobiography* (New York: Simon & Schuster, 1964), 366.

175-176 "spoiling the oldest...": quoted in Charles J. Maland, *Chaplin and American Culture: The Evolution of a Star Image* (Princeton: Princeton University Press, 1989), 113.

177 "although a good...": Chaplin, *My Autobiography*, 366.

177 "As I walked...": ibid., 378.

178 "Do not believe...": Charles Chaplin, "My New Film," reprinted in DVD booklet for *Monsieur Verdoux* (Criterion Collection: Spine #652, pp. 13-15), 13.

179 "click, click, click...": quoted in Lynn, *Charlie Chaplin*, 403.

179 "now everything had...": Charles Chaplin Jr., *My Father, Charlie Chaplin* (London: Longmans, 1960), 220.

179 "it wasn't long...": ibid., 222.

179 "weeps over primary...": François Truffaut, *The Films in My Life* (New York: Simon & Schuster, 1978), translated by Leonard Mayhew, originally published in 1975, 56.

181 "The world needs...": Chaplin, "My New Film," 15.

182 "One of [Oona O'Neill's earlier]...": Jane Scovell, *Oona: Living in the Shadows: A Biography of Oona O'Neill Chaplin* (New York: Warner Books, 1998), 102-103.

193 "Tragic, appalling!": quoted in Jerry Epstein, *Remembering Charlie* (London: Bloomsbury, 1988), 20.

183 "father might read...": Chaplin Jr., *My Father*, 71.

183 "a perverse contribution...": David Bordwell, "MONSIEUR VERDOUX: Lethal Lothario," *Observations on film art*, 28 July 2017, https://www.davidbordwell.net/blog/2017/07/28/monsieur-verdoux-lethal-lothario/.

183 "It might be...": quoted in Lynn, *Charlie Chaplin*, 442.

184 "be distinguished...": quoted in Donna Kornhaber, *Charlie Chaplin, Director* (Evanston: Northwestern University Press, 2014), 255.

184 "I think rather...": Jean Renoir, "Chaplin Among the Immortals," originally published in 1947, *Kino Slang*, 27 September 2019, translated by Andy Rector, https://kinoslang.blogspot.com/2019/09/chaplin-among-immortals-by-jean-renoir.html.

184 "I act with...": quoted in Kornhaber, *Chaplin, Director*, 145.

185 "I am the...": quoted in Jeffrey Vance, *Chaplin: Genius of the Cinema* (New York: Harry N. Abrahams, Inc., 2003), 269.

185 "the irreconcilable enemy…": quoted in Lynn, *Charlie Chaplin*, 448.

185 "Hollywood chi-chi": ibid.

186 "I am surprised…": quoted in Vance, *Chaplin*, 341.

186 "*Verdoux* is neither…": Andrew Sarris, "Films," *Village Voice* (16 July 1964), 13.

187 "knew precisely when…": quoted in Jack Miller, "A Portrait of the Artist at Work: *Unknown Chaplin*," *Establishing Shot*, 26 April 2021, https://blogs.iu.edu/establishingshot/2021/04/26/a-portrait-of-the-artist-at-work- unknown-chaplin/.

187 "go into the…": quoted in Francis Wyndham, introduction to Charles Chaplin, *My Life in Pictures* (London: The Bodley Head, 1974), 28.

187 "one of the biggest…": Ben Model, "A Study in Undercranking," video, *The Kid* (Criterion Collection: Spine #799).

188 "likes dealing with…": Philip K. Scheuer, "From Rags to Riches," *Charlie Chaplin: Interviews* (Jackson: University Press of Mississippi, 2005), edited by Kevin J. Hayes, pp. 98-102. 101.

188 "The ideal talkie…": quoted in ibid.

188 "a beautiful instrument…": Ignatiy Vishnevetsky, "*Monsieur Verdoux:* Sympathy for the Devil," *Criterion Current*, 26 March 2013, https://www.criterion.com/current/posts/2708-   monsieur-verdoux-sympathy-for-the-devil.

189 "In order that…": quoted in David Robinson, *Charlie Chaplin: His Life and Art* (London: William Collins Sons and Co., 1985), 545.

189 "radicalized… a strong…": quoted in Lynn, *Charlie Chaplin*, 440.

189 "is a great ethical…": quoted in John Wranovics, *Chaplin and Agee: The Untold Story of the Tramp, the Writer, and the Lost Screenplay* (New York: Palgrave Macmillan, 2005), 4.

190 "so cold and…": quoted in ibid., 85.

193 "I think my…": Chaplin Jr., *My Father*, 352.

193 "that talk of…": ibid., 22.

193 "Everything is autobiographical…": quoted in Vance, *Chaplin*, 283.

195 "Chaplin had already…": quoted in ibid., 284.

195 "is no ordinary…": quoted in Robinson, *Charlie Chaplin*, 570.

197 "an omnipresence of…": Chaplin, *My Autobiography*, 459.

198 "dialogue just gets…": quoted in Vance, *Chaplin*, 286.

198 "secretly he might…": Chaplin Jr., *My Father*, 19.

199 "That's the trouble…": quoted in Epstein, *Remembering Charlie*, 66.

199 "old-fashioned style toward…": quoted in Vance, *Chaplin*, 285.

200 "to do it…": quoted in Lynn, *Charlie Chaplin*, 336.

200 "[Chaplin] was totally…": Jerry Lewis, *The Total Film-Maker* (New York: Random House, 1971), 158.

200 "lost confidence…": quoted in Joyce Milton, *Tramp: The Life of Charlie Chaplin* (New York: HarperCollins, 1996), 472.

201 "raw and naïve…": Claire Bloom, *Limelight and After: The Education of an Actress* (London: Weidenfeld and Nicholson, 1982), 101.

201 "At the end of shooting…": Epstein, *Remembering Charlie*, 90.

201 "the slightly more…": quoted in Eric L. Flom, *Chaplin in the Sound Era: An Analysis of the Seven Talkies* (Jefferson: McFarland & Company Inc., 1997), 198-199.

202 "hopelessly old-fashioned": Scott Eyman, *Charlie Chaplin vs. America: When Art, Sex, and Politics Collided* (New York: Simon & Schuster, 2023), 258.

202 "wanted someone on…": quoted in Alain Silver and James Ursini, *Whatever Happened to Robert Aldrich?: His Life and Films* (New York: Limelight Editions, 1995), 8.

202 "if anything goes…": quoted in Eyman, *Charlie Chaplin vs. America*, 254.

202 "He can't direct…": quoted in ibid., 258.

202 "After the preview…": Epstein, *Remembering Charlie*, 103.

203 "as a small…": quoted in Vance, *Chaplin*, 363.

203 "I never wished…": André Bazin, *What Is Cinema?: Volume II* (Berkeley: University of California Press, 1971), edited and translated by Hugh Gray, 132.

203-204 "musical conductor…": quoted in Vance, *Chaplin*, 318.

205 "You're not going…": quoted in Chaplin, *My Autobiography*, 481.

205 "an immigrant who…": Milton, *Tramp*, 487.

206 "In the course…": Ruth Berlau, *Living for Brecht: The Memoirs of Ruth Berlau* (New York: Fromm International Publishing Corporation, 1987), translated by Geoffrey Skelton, originally published in 1985, 143.

206 "In old age…": Wyndham, introduction to Chaplin, *My Life in Pictures*, 32.

206 "that the roles…": Truffaut, *The Films in My Life*, 62.

207 "They're slower, but…": quoted in Robinson, *Charlie Chaplin*, 592.

207 "that it cost…": ibid.

207 "frosty and strained…": Epstein, *Remembering Chaplin*, 137.

207 "satire on Americans…": quoted in Eyman, *Charlie Chaplin vs. America*, 302.

209 "Friends have asked…": Chaplin, *My Autobiography*, 490.

209-210 "Similarly, I would…": Jonathan Rosenbaum, "Rediscovering Charlie Chaplin," *Cineaste*, vol. 29, no. 4 (September 2004), https://jonathanrosenbaum.net/2025/04/rediscovering- charlie-chaplin/.

210 "It's me…": quoted in Ella Winter, "But It's Sad, Says Chaplin, It's Me," *Charlie Chaplin: Interviews*, pp. 119-121. 121.

211 "after considerable reflection…": Chaplin Jr., *My Father*, 360.

211 "with its promise…": ibid., 340.

212 "[use] the screen…": quoted in Kornhaber, *Chaplin, Director*, 263.

212 "If we neither…": Truffaut, *The Films in My Life*, 59.

212-213 "narrative may be…": quoted in Vance, *Chaplin*, 326.

213 "Turn all the…": quoted in Epstein, *Remembering Charlie*, 139.

213 "remain attached to…": Joe McElhaney, "Contemporary Cinema?," *Lola*, August 2011, http://lolajournal.com/1/contemporary.html, originally published October 2010.

213 "is the film of…": quoted in Jean-Luc Godard, *Godard on Godard* (New York: Da Capo Press, 1986), edited by Jean Narboni and Tom Milne, translated by Tom Milne, originally published in 1968, English edition 1972, 171.

213 "venerating… He cried…": Tag Gallagher, *The Adventures of Roberto Rossellini* (Tag Gallagher, 2018), revised edition, 497.

214 "nobody has subjected…": quoted in Milton, *Tramp*, 504.

215 "afraid I might…": quoted in Maland, *Chaplin and American Culture*, 347.

215 "enjoyed cementing together…": Chaplin Jr., *My Father*, 340.

215 "like perhaps five…": quoted in Wranovics, *Chaplin and Agee*, 89.

215 "I remain just…": quoted in Vance, *Chaplin*, 303.

216 "when you live…": ibid.

216 "I don't think it matters…": quoted in Eyman, *Charlie Chaplin vs. America*, 343.

217 "be at it…": quoted in Maland, *Chaplin and American Culture*, 18.

217 "Chaplin in his old age…": quoted in Eyman, *Charlie Chaplin vs. America*, 332.

217 "With his present…": Penelope Gilliat, *Unholy Fools: Wits, Comics, Disturbers of the Peace: Film & Theater* (New York: The Viking Press, 1973), 145.

218 "For the first time in my…": quoted in Robinson, *Charlie Chaplin*, 604.

218 "How could I…": quoted in Maland, *Chaplin and American Culture*, 166.

220 "The continuity of…": Andrew Sarris, *The American Cinema: Directors and Directions, 1929- 1968* (New York: Da Capo Press, 1996), originally published in 1968, 42.

220 "This is the easiest…": quoted in Epstein, *Remembering Charlie*, 186.

221 "I still looked…": quoted in Lynn, *Charlie Chaplin*, 517.

221 "even the very…": Kornhaber, *Chaplin, Director*, 16.

221 "the entire history…": Milton, *Tramp*, 513.

222 "I've never done…": quoted in Vance, *Chaplin*, 340.

222 "Chaplin, the director…": Richard Brody, "DVD of the Week: 'A Countess from Hong Kong'," *The New Yorker*, 18 December 2012, https://www.newyorker.com/culture/richard- brody/dvd-of-the-week-a-countess-from-hong-kong.

222 "a satire on bigness": quoted in Bosley Crowther, "The Modern — Mellower — Times of Mr. Chaplin," *Charlie Chaplin: Interviews*, pp. 122-128. 128.

223 "doesn't laugh at…": Gilliat, *Unholy Fools*, 146.

223 "Chaplin here refigures…": Kornhaber, *Chaplin, Director*, 21.

224 "Even if there…": Pedro Costa, "A Closed Door That Leaves Us Guessing," *Rouge*, no. 10 (2007), originally published in 2005, translated by Downing Roberts, https://www.rouge.com.au/10/costa_seminar.html.

225 "Chaplin had very…": Vance, *Chaplin*, 338.

225 "finally gives us…": Eric Rohmer, *Essays on Chaplin* (University of New Haven Press, 1985), with André Bazin, François Truffaut, and Jean Renoir, edited and translated by Jean Bodon, 80.

225 "Old-fashioned?…": quoted in Eyman, *Charlie Chaplin vs. America*, 334.

225 "Chaplin's treatment of…": Tim Hunter, "A Countess from Hong Kong," *The Harvard Crimson*, 25 April 1967, https://www.thecrimson.com/article/1967/4/25/a-countess-from-hong- kong-palong/.

225-226 "Between you and me…": quoted in Robinson, *Charlie Chaplin*, 617.

226 "The most important thing…": quoted in Richard Meryman, "Ageless Master's Anatomy of Comedy: Chaplin, An Interview," *Charlie Chaplin: Interviews*, pp. 129- 141. 133.

227 "I think it's the best…": quoted in Robinson, *Charlie Chaplin*, 616.

227 "It's my best…": quoted in Lynn, *Charlie Chaplin*, 518.

227 "bloody idiots": quoted in Eyman, *Charlie Chaplin vs. America*, 334.

228 "The trouble is that…": quoted in Robinson, *Charlie Chaplin*, 617.

228 "with the compliments…": quoted in Epstein, *Remembering Charlie*, 202.

228-229 "like watching a doctor…": ibid., 225.

229 "There's no picture": quoted in Scovell, Oona, 237.

229 "I mean to…": Chaplin, *My Life in Pictures*, 324.

229-230 "Every time I read…": Epstein, *Remembering Charlie*, 201.

230 "This… is real Puccini!": quoted in ibid., 152.

230 "The accompaniment that…": Vance, *Chaplin*, 348-349.

231 "I am still…": Chaplin, *My Autobiography*, 497.

231 "To work is…": quoted in Vance, *Chaplin*, 350.

232 "hustled into gondolas…": Scovell, *Oona*, 245-246.

232 "destroyed": quoted in Eyman, *Charlie Chaplin vs. America*, 335.

233 "Father was quite…": Michael Chaplin, *I Couldn't Smoke the Grass on My Father's Lawn* (New York: G.P. Putnam's Sons, 1966), 66.

233-234 "This is my…": quoted in Lynn, *Charlie Chaplin*, 527.

234 "Even when his remarks…": ibid., 528.

234 "I cannot cope…": quoted in ibid., 529.

235 "Whenever Charlie finished…": Scovell, *Oona*, 193.

235 "loving devotion and…": Bloom, *Limelight and After*, 108.

235 "I'll always think…": quoted in Scovell, *Oona*, 265.

235 "the most bafflingly…": quoted in Lynn, *Charlie Chaplin*, 303.

235 "Charlie is a…": quoted in Robinson, *Charlie Chaplin*, 574.

236 "like reading one's…": quoted in Vance, *Chaplin*, 357.

Alfred Hitchcock

240 "During the first…": Bill Krohn, *Hitchcock at Work* (London: Phaidon Press Limited, 2000), 114.

240 "About this time…": quoted in Donald Spoto, *The Dark Side of Genius: The Life of Alfred Hitchcock* (Boston: Little, Brown & Company, 1983), 347.

241 "the first version…": quoted in Peter Ackroyd, *Alfred Hitchcock: A Brief Life* (New York: Doubleday, 2015), 169.

242 "a sudden shift…": Spoto, *The Dark Side of Genius*, 368.

242 "a Hitchcock picture to…": quoted in Edward White, *The Twelve Lives of Alfred Hitchcock* (New York: W.W. Norton & Company, 2021), 68.

242 "cool adroitness…": Spoto, *The Dark Side of Genius*, 426-427.

242 "Style in directing…": quoted in David W. Galenson, *Old Masters and Young Geniuses: The Two Life Cycles of Artistic Creativity* (Princeton: Princeton University Press, 2006), 157.

242 "it's a natural tendency…": quoted in Robin Wood, *Hitchcock's Films Revisited: Revised Edition* (New York: Columbia Press, 2002), 61.

243 "had reached a point…": quoted in Spoto, *The Dark Side of Genius*, 421.

244 "was in a sense…": Peter Ackroyd, *Alfred Hitchcock*, 208.

244 "self-designed universe": quoted in Charlotte Chandler, *It's Only a Movie—Alfred Hitchcock: A Personal Biography* (New York: Simon & Schuster, 2005), 300.

245 "Hitchcock privately had…": Spoto, *The Dark Side of Genius*, 372.

245 "he was entering…": quoted in Patrick McGilligan, *Alfred Hitchcock: A Life in Darkness and Light* (New York: Regan Books, 2003), 625.

246 "Evan… there will be…": quoted in Ackroyd, *Alfred Hitchcock,* 213.

246 "apocalyptic poem": quoted in Donald Spoto, *The Art of Alfred Hitchcock: Fifty Years of His Motion Pictures* (New York: Hopkinson and Blake, 1976), 330.

247 "Hitchcock and his wife…": Bill Krohn, "*The Alfred Hitchcock Story* by Ken Mogg," *Senses of Cinema,* no. 5 (April 2000), https://www.sensesofcinema.com/2000/book-reviews/alfred/.

247 "the influence and importance…": Joe McElhaney, *The Death of Classical Cinema: Hitchcock, Lang, Minnelli* (Albany: State University of New York Press, 2006), 86.

247 "self-indulgent": quoted in Sidney Gottlieb, editor, *Alfred Hitchcock: Interviews* (Jackson: University Press of Mississippi, 2003), 140.

247 "did develop an…": Jack Sullivan, *Hitchcock's Music* (New Haven: Yale University Press, 2006), 265.

249 "While all of…": Robert Kapsis, *Hitchcock: The Making of a Reputation* (Chicago: University of Chicago Press, 1992), 74.

250 "we discussed *Marnie*…": quoted in Ackroyd, *Alfred Hitchcock,* 226.

250 "His collaborators gave…": Spoto, *The Dark Side of Genius,* 401.

251 "the camera was…": ibid., 472.

252 "dramatic and emotional…": quoted in White, *The Twelve Lives,* 140.

252 "to recreate the…": John Russell Taylor, *Hitch: The Life and Work of Alfred Hitchcock* (London: Faber and Faber Limited, 1978), 272.

252-253 "Hitchcock's ironic detachment…": Maurice Yacowar, *Hitchcock's British Films* (Hamden: Archon Books, 1977), 264-265.

253 "technical mixup": quoted in Gottlieb, *Interviews,* 137.

253 "pure cinema… like notes…": quoted in Ackroyd, *Alfred Hitchcock,* 25.

253 "denaturalized purism of…": quoted in Bruce Isaacs, *The Art of Pure Cinema: Hitchcock and His Imitators* (New York: Oxford University Press, 2020), 40.

254 "After all… the object…": quoted in Andrew Meyer, "The 'Plot' Thickens," *Film Comment,* vol. 11, no. 5 (September-October 1975), pp. 21-23. 22.

254 "cheat like they…": quoted in McElhaney, *The Death of Classical Cinema*, 233.

255 "*Marnie* was *The Taming of the Shrew*…": quoted in Chandler, *It's Only a Movie*, 273.

256 "great sick film": quoted in Bernard Benoliel, Gilles Esposito, Murielle Joudet, and Jean-François Rauger, *Alfred Hitchcock: All the Films—The Story Behind Every Movie, Episode, and Short* (New York: Black Dog & Leventhal Publishers, 2024), 364.

256 "you might have to…": quoted in Ackroyd, *Alfred Hitchcock*, 229.

257 "Hitchcock was never…": quoted in Sullivan, *Hitchcock's Music*, 275.

257 "made him a bird…": McGilligan, *Alfred Hitchcock*, 654.

258 "poring over short stories…": Spoto, *The Dark Side of Genius*, 483.

260 "realistic Bond": quoted in McGilligan, *Alfred Hitchcock*, 657.

260 "not a spy film…": Murray Pomerance, *An Eye for Hitchcock* (New Brunswick: Rutgers University Press, 2004), 93.

261 "favorite living novelist": quoted in McGilligan, *Alfred Hitchcock*, 662.

261 "I told him…": quoted in Spoto, *The Dark Side of Genius*, 489.

264 "suffer-in-silence…": Ken Mogg, "December 28 2000," *The MacGuffin*, https://hitchinfo.net/2000.html.

264 "Relationships matter…": Spoto, *The Art of Alfred Hitchcock*, 357.

265 "It speaks to…": quoted in Chandler, *It's Only a Movie*, 285.

265-266 "What *is* natural light?…": quoted in Herb A. Lightman, "Hitchcock Talks About Lights, Camera, Action," *American Cinematographer*, 12 June 2017, https://theasc.com/articles/flashback-hitchcock-talks-about-lights-camera-action.

266 "drastic change…": quoted in François Truffaut, *Hitchcock: Revised Edition* (New York: Simon & Schuster, 1984), 313.

266 "color films were…": quoted in Lightman, "Hitchcock Talks."

267 "would inspire rapturous…": Andrew Sarris, "The Company Man," *Cahiers du Cinéma in English*, no. 10 (May 1967), 58.

268 "What is my motivation…": quoted in Benoliel et al., *Alfred Hitchcock: All the Films*, 203.

268 "a notable expressive effect…": Wood, *Hitchcock's Films Revisited*, 203.

268 "young, vigorous and demanding…": quoted in Ackroyd, *Alfred Hitchcock*, 236.

268 "What do you want…": ibid.

270 "White on white!…": quoted in McGilligan, *Alfred Hitchcock*, 677.

270 "My God, Howard!…": quoted in Spoto, *The Dark Side of Genius*, 495-496.

270 "remained fascinated by…": White, *The Twelve Lives*, 247.

270 "compare different film stocks…": quoted in McGilligan, *Alfred Hitchcock*, 681.

271 "an intended turning point…": quoted in White, *The Twelve Lives*, 246.

271 "That's a privilege…": quoted in Sidney Gottlieb, "Unknown Hitchcock: the unrealized projects," *Hitchcock: Past and Future* (London: Routledge, 2004), edited by Richard Allen and Sam Ishii-Gonzáles, pp. 85-106. 101.

271 "… and they never…": quoted in Spoto, *The Dark Side of Genius*, 491.

272 "never get[s] beyond…": quoted in Gottlieb, *Interviews*, 154-155.

272 "too-late style": quoted in White, *The Twelve Lives*, 248.

272 "would certainly be different…": quoted in Gottlieb, *Interviews*, 119.

272 "was eager to direct…": McGilligan, *Alfred Hitchcock*, 524.

272-273 "We have to avoid…": quoted in ibid., 697.

273 "what were once suggestions…": Dan Auiler, contribution to Ken Mogg, *The Alfred Hitchcock Story* (London: Titan Books, 2008), originally published in 1999, 168.

273 "full of compromises…": quoted in Peter Bart, "Hitchcock Embroidery on a 'Torn Curtain,'" *The New York Times*, 21 November 1965, Section X, p. 11, https://www.nytimes.com/1965/11/21/archives/hitch-cock-embroidery-on-a-torn- curtain.html.

273 "to make my…": quoted in Krohn, *Hitchcock at Work*, 11.

274 "a few days…": Spoto, *The Dark Side of Genius*, 500.

275 "how an entire…": Éric Rohmer and Claude Chabrol, *Hitchcock: The First Forty-Four Films* (New York: Frederick Ungar Publishing Co., 1979), translated by Stanley Hochman, originally published in 1957, 152.

275 "The older he got…": White, *The Twelve Lives*, 235.

275 "lying around, knowing…": Joel Gunz, "Alfred Hitchcock and the Case of The Invisible Director: How Hitch's Light Touch Resulted

in Some of Cinema's Most Powerful Screen Moments," *Alfred Hitchcock Geek*, 26 September 2013, http://www.alfredhitchcockgeek.com/2013/09/alfred-hitchcock-and-case-of-the.html.

276 "Tristana's false leg…": quoted in Dan Callahan, *The Camera Lies: Acting for Hitchcock* (New York: Oxford University Press, 2020), 232.

277 "the tortured intensity…": Michael Walker, "The Old Age of Alfred Hitchcock," *Movie*, no. 18 (Winter 1970), pp. 10-13. 13.

277 "bereftness": Ken Mogg, , "May 1 – 2010," *The MacGuffin*, https://hitchinfo.net/2010.html.

278 "It's all look…": Nefastis, "On Her Majesty's Secret Service," *Letterboxd*, 24 June 2025, https://letterboxd.com/nefastis/film/on-her-majestys-secret-service/3/.

278 "Hitchcock wanted counterpoint…": quoted in Sullivan, *Hitchcock's Music*, 294.

278 "older, tired and…": Vincent Canby, "'Topaz': Alfred Hitchcock at His Best," *The New York Times*, 20 December 1969, https://archive.nytimes.com/www.nytimes.com/library/film/122069hitch-topaz-review.html.

279 "it is also possible…": Paula Marantz Cohen, *Alfred Hitchcock: The Legacy of Victorianism* (Lexington: The University Press of Kentucky, 1995), 157.

279 "if we re-perceive…": Slavoj Žižek, *Film Comment*, vol. 42, no. 1 (January-February 2006), p. 12.

280 "you might equally…": quoted in Joe McElhaney, "Touching the Surface: *Marnie*, Melodrama, Modernism," *Alfred Hitchcock: Centenary Essays* (London: British Film Institute, 1999), edited by Richard Allen and S. Ishii-Gonzalès, pp. 87-105. 89.

280 "until he could…": McGilligan, *Alfred Hitchcock*, 691.

280 "that a member…": White, *The Twelve Lives*, 198-199.

280 "profound ignorance of…": quoted in Spoto, *The Dark Side of Genius*, 488.

280-281 "*Topaz* isn't 'about'…": Richard T. Jameson, "Dinosaurs in the Age of the Cinemobile," *The Last Great American Picture Show* (Amsterdam: Amsterdam University Press, 2004), edited by Thomas Elsaesser, Alexander Horwath, and Noel King, pp. 155-164. 158-159.

281 "Spying and espionage…": David Freeman, *The Last Days of Alfred Hitchcock* (Woodstock: The Overlook Press, 1984), 174.

281 "*Topaz* is the first…": Walker, "The Old Age of Alfred Hitchcock," 11.

281 "to write the intelligence…": McGilligan, *Alfred Hitchcock*, 686.

282 "Hitch, in the late…": Freeman, *The Last Days*, 250.

283 "four-month standoff": Krohn, *Hitchcock at Work*, 270.

283 "I could have fought…": quoted in Ackroyd, *Alfred Hitchcock*, 240.

283 "horrible compromise": quoted in Gottlieb, *Interviews*, 124.

284 "which the director…": Bill Krohn, "A Venomous Flower: Alfred Hitchcock's *Topaz*," *Video Watchdog*, no. 74 (August 2001), pp.28-35. 32.

284 "Hitchcock, his composer…": Sullivan, *Hitchcock's Music*, 294.

284 "Be cold, do your job": Bill Krohn, *a_film_by*, 9 May 2004, https://www.fredcamper.com/afilmby/0009701.html.

285 "had worked his way…": Raymond Foery, *Alfred Hitchcock's Frenzy: The Last Masterpiece* (Lanham: Scarecrow Press, Inc., 2012), 7.

285 "third- or fourth-largest…": Dan Auiler, *Hitchcock's Notebooks* (New York: HarperCollins, 1999), 549.

286 "telling the world…": White, *The Twelve Lives*, 251.

286 "innocent man" & "itinerary of a killer…": François Truffaut, "Slow fade: The declining years of Alfred Hitchcock," *American Film*, vol. 10, no. 2 (November 1984), p. 40. https://hitchcockwiki.com/wiki/American_Film_(1984)_-_Slow_fade:_The_declining_years_of_Alfred_Hitchcock.

287 "important part of…": Peter Hutchings, "*Frenzy:* A Return to Britain," *All Our Yesterdays: 90 Years of British Cinema* (London: British Film Institute, 1986), edited by Charles Barr, pp. 368-374. 372.

287 "himself made *Frenzy*…": ibid., 373.

288 "The London here…": White, *The Twelve Lives*, 274.

288 "a Victorian relic…": ibid., xiii.

289 "a curious amalgam…": quoted in Taylor, *Hitch*, 283.

289 "was intractable about…": quoted in Spoto, *The Dark Side of Genius*, 510.

289 "an outdated language…": quoted in Foery, *Alfred Hitchcock's Frenzy*, 29.

289 "perhaps the Hitchcock…": Joseph Sgammato, "The Discreet Qualms of the Bourgeoisie: Hitchcock's 'Frenzy'," *Sight and Sound*, vol. 39, no. 3 (Summer 1970), pp. 134-137. 136.

290 "If Hitchcock hadn't…": quoted in Spoto, *The Dark Side of Genius*, 516.

290 "Hitchcock carefully calculates…": John Belton, *Cinema Stylists* (Metuchen: The Scarecrow Press, Inc., 1983), 70.

291 "see[ing] the killer…": quoted in Spoto, *The Dark Side of Genius*, 519.

291 "always to revert…": quoted in Mark Allison, "Frenzy at 50: The most violent film Hitchcock ever made," *BBC*, 4 July 2022, https://www.bbc.com/culture/article/20220704-frenzy-at-   50-the-most-violent-film-hitchcock-ever-made.

293 "realistic nightmare": McGilligan, *Alfred Hitchcock*, 703.

293 "despite the gruesome…": ibid.

293 "*Frenzy* is a naturalistic…": John Orr, *Hitchcock and Twentieth Century Cinema* (London: Wallflower Press, 2005), 67.

294 "loser… nonhero": quoted in Peter Bogdanovich, *Who the Devil Made It* (New York: Alfred A. Knopf, 1997), 549.

294 "Hitchcock's turn from…": Thomas M. Leitch, *Find the Director and Other Hitchcock Games* (Athens: University of Georgia Press, 1991), 244.

294 "[Hitchcock] said, late…": Ackroyd, *Alfred Hitchcock*, 120.

294 "When passers-by at…": quoted in ibid., 247.

295 "Life has been…": quoted in Allison, "Frenzy at 50."

296 "the idea of two…": quoted in Spoto, *The Dark Side of Genius*, 527.

297 "an experimental technique…": "Family Plot (1976), *The Alfred Hitchcock Wiki*, https://the.hitchcock.zone/wiki/Family_Plot_(1976).

297 "We've passed the point…": Carlos Valladares, "Family Plot," *Letterboxd*, 6 September 2015, https://letterboxd.com/cvall96/film/family-plot/.

297 "so flattered…": White, *The Twelve Lives*, 216.

297 "has the geometric…": quoted in John William Law, *Alfred Hitchcock: The Icon Years* (San Francisco: Aplomb Publishing, 2010), 182.

298 "obsession with structure…": quoted in Bill Krohn, "A Hitchcock mystery," *The MacGuffin*, no. 27 (December 2000), pp. 2-4. 4.

298 "I don't give…": quoted in White, *The Twelve Lives*, 152.

298 "was a real…": quoted in Yvonne Villarreal, "With 'Palm Royale,' Bruce and Laura Dern are (finally) father and daughter on screen," *Los*

Angeles Times, 27 March 2024, https://www.latimes.com/entertainment-arts/tv/story/2024-03-27/bruce-dern-laura-dern- palm-royale.

298 "of all the actors…": Taylor, *Hitch,* 295.

299 "He's as flexible…": quoted in Meyer, "The 'Plot' Thickens," 23.

299 "parts that would…": Cohen, *The Legacy of Victorianism,* 163.

299 "I never know…": quoted in Ackroyd, *Alfred Hitchcock,* 252.

299 "may be the only…": Krohn, *Hitchcock at Work,* 274.

300 "I never saw…": Taylor, *Hitch,* 293.

300 "the determinism of…": Krohn, "A Hitchcock mystery," 2.

300 "I think if…": quoted in Taylor, *Hitch,* 289.

300 "I want it…": quoted in Ackroyd, *Alfred Hitchcock,* 252.

300 "living Mondrian": quoted in Krohn, "A Hitchcock mystery," 2.

301 "the voice of…": quoted in Jacob Stolworthy, "Steven Spielberg tried to meet Alfred Hitchcock numerous times, but he refused," *The Independent,* 29 July 2020, https://www.the-independent.com/arts-entertainment/films/news/steven-spielberg-alfred-hitchcock-jaws-psycho-vertigo-bruce-dern-hollywood-a9644131.html.

301 "In the films of…": Cohen, *The Legacy of Victorianism,* 155.

302 "couldn't be bothered…": Chandler, *It's Only a Movie,* 302.

304 "my most interesting…": quoted in White, *The Twelve Lives,* 61.

304 "apply[ing] glue": quoted in Ackroyd, *Alfred Hitchcock,* 224.

304 "regarded more as…": Taylor, *Hitch,* 281.

304 "Retire?…": quoted in McGilligan, *Alfred Hitchcock,* 715.

204 "I have lots…": quoted in White, *The Twelve Lives,* 295.

304 "I retire when…": quoted in Spoto, *The Dark Side of Genius,* 554.

305 "I beg permission…": quoted in Ackroyd, *Alfred Hitchcock,* 259-260.

305 "Do you think…": Bogdanovich, *Who the Devil Made It,* 555.

Concluding Note: Late Style as a Way of Life

308 "twenty and eighty…": Pedro Costa, "A Closed Door That Leaves Us Guessing," *Rouge,* no. 10 (2007), originally published in 2005, translated by Downing Roberts, https://www.rouge.com.au/10/costa_seminar.html.

308 "you must keep…": ibid.

Index

Sticking Place Books (stickingplacebooks.com) is a New York-based publisher specializing in cinema, offering interview books, memoirs, critical and historical studies, screenplays, and essay collections. Our titles include:

Lessons with Kiarostami. Edited by Paul Cronin

In the Shadow of Trees: The Collected Poetry of Abbas Kiarostami

Still Film Crazy (After All These Years) by Patrick McGilligan

It's Only a Movie by Bruce Joel Rubin

Three Visionary Screenplays by Bruce Joel Rubin

Playing Among the Stars: Conversations with Damien Chazelle by Nathan Réra

The Magic Eye: The Cinema of Stanley Kubrick by Neil Hornick

A Shared Cinema: Conversations with Michael Ciment by N. T. Bihn

The Naughty Bits: What the Censors Wouldn't Let You See in Hollywood's Most Famous Movies by Nat Segaloff

Mexico: The Aztec Account of the Conquest by Werner Herzog

Werner Herzog/Rogue Filmmaker by David LaRocca

De Palma on De Palma: Conversations with Samuel Blumenfeld and Laurent Vachaud

Publication as Autobiography: Occasional and Forsaken Texts—and Endangered Cinema Species by Scott MacDonald

Filmmakers Thinking by Adrian Martin

Secret Cinema: The Rise and Fall of the Blue Movie by John Baxter

Casualties of War: An Investigation by Nathan Réra

Hollywood on the Tiber by Hank Kaufman and Gene Lerner

I Loved Movies… But: Conversations with Joseph McBride
by Danny Peary

A Reluctant Film Critic by Gerald Peary

The Zen of the Director by Peter Markham

Adventures in Auteurism: A Crusade for the Criminally Neglected
by Daniel Kremer

Persistence of Vision: A Collection of Film Criticism
Edited by Joseph McBride

Writings and Relics 1990–95 by Michael Almereyda

The Autobiography of Jane Brakhage by Jane Wodening
With P. Adams Sitney and David E. James

The Curse of Queen Kelly by Pamela Hutchinson

Lost Screenplays of the 1970s by Jim McBride

My Lunches with Henry Jaglom by Daniel Kremer

Bender's L.A. by Michael Elias

My Strange Love: Selected Film Reviews and Essays, 2001–2021
by Stuart Klawans

Dentists with Guns by David Mamet

Late Style in Film by Collin Brinkmann

Dressing the Story by Debra McGuire

Metafiction by David LaRocca

The Most Important Art by Ian Christie

Two Screenplays by Eve Babitz and Michael Elias

All That Black by Cristiana Astori

Night Moves: Twenty-four letters
by Dominic Lash and David R J Stent

Body Parts & Zero Tolerance by Alex Cox and Rudy Wurlitzer

www.ingramcontent.com/pod-product-compliance
Lightning Source LLC
Chambersburg PA
CBHW071447140726
47997CB00005B/1617